How to Do
Everything
with
Yahoo!

Alan Neibauer

Osborne **McGraw-Hill**

Berkeley   New York   St. Louis   San Francisco
Auckland   Bogotá   Hamburg   London
Madrid   Mexico City   Milan   Montreal   New Delhi
Panama City   Paris   São Paulo
Singapore   Sydney   Tokyo   Toronto

Osborne/**McGraw-Hill**
2600 Tenth Street
Berkeley, California 94710
U.S.A.

For information on translations or book distributors outside the U.S.A., or to arrange
bulk purchase discounts for sales promotions, premiums, or fund-raisers, please contact
Osborne/**McGraw-Hill** at the above address.

How to Do Everything with Yahoo!

1234567890 VFM VFM 019876543210

ISBN 0-07-212561-6

Publisher	Brandon A. Nordin
Vice President and	
Associate Publisher	Scott Rogers
Acquisitions Editor	Jane Brownlow
Project Editor	Betsy Manini
Acquisitions Coordinator	Cindy Wathen
Technical Editor	Bill Bruns
Copy Editor	Peter Weverka
Proofreader	Linda Medoff
Indexer	James Minkin
Computer Designers	Jani Beckwith
	Gary Corrigan
Illustrators	Kevin Curry
	Robert Hansen
	Michael Mueller
	Beth Young
Series Design	Michelle Galicia
Cover Design	Dodie Shoemaker
Cover Photo	Stockbyte®

This book was composed with Corel VENTURA™ Publisher.

Dedication

To Joanne Cuthbertson
Thanks for a great ride, and our best wishes for everything in the future.

About the Author

Alan Neibauer is a best-selling author and corporate trainer. He has
written over 30 popular computer books, including the well-known
The Official Guide to Corel WordPerfect Suite 7 for Windows 95,
The Official Guide to Corel WordPerfect Suite 8, Word for Windows
Made Easy, and two editions of *Access for Busy People.* A graduate
of the Wharton School, University of Pennsylvania, Neibauer has
worked as a high school and college teacher, and has helped many
in New Jersey and Pennsylvania achieve their presence on the Internet.

Contents at a Glance

Contents

Acknowledgments

Yahoo!!! That about sums up my feeling when Joanne Cuthbertson at Osborne/McGraw-Hill asked me to write this book. I mean, I love writing and I love surfing the Internet, so here was a perfect assignment.

So I'd like to thank Joanne for asking me to write this book, and everyone else at Osborne for their wonderful support. (By the way, I'll miss you Joanne!) My thanks to Betsy Manini for the wonderful job she did as project editor, and to copy editor Peter Weverka for his attention to detail. I also want to thank technical editor Bill Bruns for diligently checking everything out, and acquisitions coordinator Stephane Thomas. My appreciation also goes to proofreader Linda Medoff, indexer James Minkin, and the production team of Jani Beckwith and Gary Corrigan on layout, and Robert Hansen, Michael Mueller, and Beth Young on graphics.

And then there's Barbara. Like Yahoo!, my wife Barbara should have an exclamation point after her name to show how special, exciting, and dynamic she is. I could not have done this without her, and certainly wouldn't want to.

Introduction

A whole book on Yahoo!?

That's the question I was asked over and over as I worked on this book. In fact, I asked myself the same thing when I started to write it. A whole book just on Yahoo!?

Well, if I wasn't a Yahoo! believer before I started this book, I certainly am now. I totally understand why they put the exclamation point at the end of the name. Yahoo! is one terrific place to visit on the Internet.

If you think Yahoo! is just a search engine, then you have a lot of surprises coming to you. It is true that Yahoo! is a powerful place to search for information of all types. But Yahoo! is so much more, it is difficult to classify it. Let's see . . .

Yahoo! is a search engine, an online calendar and address book, an e-mail service, a place to store files and share photographs, and a place to share the Internet with your family. It is a place to have a Web site, a source of information when you're away from home, a place to find people and track down your roots. You can get maps and driving directions, learn about stocks and investing, and even maintain your portfolio online. Yahoo! is a place to learn about and get loans, auto insurance, automobiles, and real estate. You can rent an apartment, compute and pay your taxes, and buy and sell at auctions. Yahoo! lets you plan vacations, make reservations, play games, get television and film listings, and keep up with news, sports, and weather. It lets you send and receive instant-messages, chat with friends, speak to and hear other Yahoo! members, post messages, and join and create clubs. And you can create and run an online store and have your own domain hosted on the Internet.

Yahoo!

Almost anything you want from the Internet can be found at Yahoo!, and except for some commercial applications such as running an online store and hosting your domain, it's all free. Nada. Not a dime.

In this book, you will learn how to do everything with Yahoo!, which is why this book is called *How to Do Everything with Yahoo!*. You will master all of the powerful, time-saving, money-saving, and entertaining things to do on Yahoo!

This book is both a tutorial and a reference guide to Yahoo!. You can read this book from cover to cover to learn about all of Yahoo!'s features, or you can go directly to a specific chapter if you're ready to use the Yahoo! features discussed there.

This book is divided into six parts. In **Part I,** "Making Yahoo! Your Web Portal," you'll learn how to take advantage of the free Yahoo! membership to make Yahoo! your Internet home.

You will learn, for example, how to get a free Yahoo! membership and an e-mail address, how to personalize your Web browser and home page, and how to maintain your calendar online. You will also learn how to exercise parental controls for young Web surfers, create your own Web site, store and share files online, and use Yahoo! when you're away from home.

Part II of the book is all about finding things on the Internet. You'll learn how to search for information, people, and businesses, get maps and driving directions, and track down your family history.

Taking care of business is the focus of **Part III.** You will learn how to find the best investments and maintain an online portfolio. You'll also learn how to borrow money, how to buy, rent, or sell real estate and automobiles, and how to get insurance and save money on income taxes.

In **Part IV** of the book, you will learn how to buy and sell at Yahoo! auctions, shop a virtual mall without leaving your house, and find the best prices on just about everything.

Part V is all about travel, entertainment, and current events. You will learn how to plan a vacation or business trip, and how to make airline, hotel, and car-rental reservations. You will learn how to play games online, even against other Yahoo! members in real time, and where children can find games suitable for them. You will also learn how to get information about television programs and schedules, movies, news, sports, and weather.

Becoming part of the Yahoo! community is the focus of **Part VI.** Here you will learn how to send and receive instant-messages, even with voice-chat software. You will learn how to take part in chats, join or create special-interest clubs, and take part in message boards on thousands of subjects.

Throughout this book are special features to help you learn and get the most from Yahoo!. You'll find notes, tips, shortcuts, and warnings, and every chapter has special "How To . . ." sections that focus on a special feature or technique.

Yahoo! is such a dynamite place to explore the Internet, that we've included six more chapters about Yahoo! on Osborne/McGraw-Hill's Web site for this book. To access them, you should go to www.osborne.com and click on the *How to Do Everything with Yahoo!* link to the bonus chapters about Yahoo! On our Web site you will find chapters that cover:

- Borrowing money online
- All about insurance
- The take on taxes
- Finding out about TV, radio, and movies
- Running an online store
- Hosting a Web site

Yahoo!, like the Internet itself, is dynamic and constantly changing. In an effort to keep at the top of the Internet heap, Yahoo! adds new features and modifies others. From one day to the next, you'll find new things to do on Yahoo! and changes to familiar features that you've already used. So in some cases, what you see on your screen may be a little different from what you see in this book, and you might find some features that Yahoo! added after this book was published.

You'll find Yahoo! a great place to enjoy the Internet experience. If you want to share your experiences with me, or just chat, contact me at aneibauer@yahoo.com. You see, I not only write about Yahoo!, I use it as well.

Part I

Making Yahoo! Your Web Portal

Chapter 1

Welcome to Yahoo!

How to . . .

- Use Yahoo! even if you do not have your own Internet account
- Get free Internet service
- Get free e-mail
- Keep your calendar online and share it with others
- Personalize your browser and Yahoo! start page
- Create family accounts for safe surfing
- Store files online
- Get a free home page
- Search the entire Internet for information and people
- Get news, weather, and sports information
- Send and receive instant messages
- Join chats and clubs
- Run a business
- Plan a vacation
- Play games
- . . . and lots more!

Yahoo! is your portal into the best of everything that the Internet has to offer. What is a portal? A *portal* is an entry point, a starting place, and a way to get into something. You want an Internet portal to give you access to a wide range of locations and features. A good Internet portal will provide everything you need for most of your Internet work—e-mail, your own personal Web site, news, weather, stock information, and other services that make the Internet experience fun and efficient.

Chances are, your Internet Service Provider (ISP) has given you a portal through its home page. But chances are, the features and services of Yahoo! are better. Once you connect to the Internet, just sign up as a Yahoo! member for a free lifetime account.

In this chapter, I'll introduce all of the features that make Yahoo! such a great place to enter the world of the Internet. In later chapters, I'll cover all of these features in detail and show you exactly how to use them.

No ISP Required

One thing to keep in mind as you read this book is that you don't need an ISP to take advantage of the Internet and most of Yahoo!'s features. You only need access to the Internet because Yahoo! provides all of the features of an ISP except the actual dial-up connection. Figure 1-1 shows the initial Yahoo! screen with just some of its features.

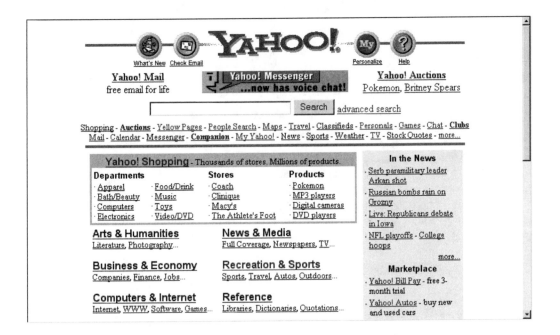

Yahoo!

Fortunately, places such as local libraries and cyber cafés that stir up a little Internet with the lattes are popping up all over to offer free or inexpensive Internet access. You can use the connection provided by one of those locations, and then access Yahoo!, where you can get your own e-mail address and Web site.

Most libraries, for example, have one or more computers dedicated to public Internet access. Using the free Internet connection, you sign up for a free Yahoo! account, and then you can take advantage of most of Yahoo!'s features. Your Internet experience can be totally free.

Note

Some Yahoo! features record small files, called cookies, on your computer that must be present to later access the feature. You probably will not be able to take advantage of these features on public-access computers.

A cookie is a block of data stored on your computer by the Web server of the site you visit. When you revisit the site, the cookie sends information about you back to the server of the site you are visiting. It may contain information to identify you, including your account information and other details. A cookie can instruct the server to send you a customized version of the Web site based on what part of the Web site you used the last time you visited.

 **Get Totally Free Internet**

You can also get totally free Internet services without even leaving your house. Yahoo! has joined with K-Mart and Bluelight.com to offer totally free Internet access through the Spinway.Com access service. There's no sign-up charge, no software to buy, and no monthly bill to pay. The service offers hundreds of local telephone numbers throughout the United States, but you'll need to check these access numbers to make sure they are local and toll free.

You use your Yahoo! member ID and password (you'll learn how to get them for free in Chapter 2) as your ISP logon name and password. You'll have to download a free program and install it on your computer; but after that, you get unlimited free Internet access.

Advertising supports the program, but as long as you are in Yahoo!, no special advertisements appear on your screen. If you leave Yahoo! to visit elsewhere on the Internet, however, you'll see a window like the one shown here in your browser:

Clicking the Links button in the window provides access to many Yahoo! features, so you can quickly return to Yahoo! (and remove the box from the screen):

To sign up for the service, go to www.bluelight.com or look for the link shown here on the Yahoo! home page, although the link does not appear all of the time.

Free ISP Today

After you click the link, follow the onscreen directions to download the software and sign up for your free Internet account.

A number of companies besides Yahoo! provide free Internet access. (A few companies do charge a nominal, one-time fee for software, but most are totally free.) Most of these companies display a small window on the screen that contains links to popular sites as well as advertising messages. As long as you leave the window on the screen, you can browse to your heart's content. Some of the companies disconnect you if you don't click an ad in their window every 30 minutes or so, but some don't care whether you click ads. One company (www.ifreedom.com) removes its banner for 20 minutes after each visit to an advertised site, and one (www.freewwweb.com) shows no banner at all. Almost all of the companies place no restrictions on the sites you can visit, although one (www.freensafe.com) filters out "objectionable" sites.

For your free access, you usually have to complete a form with some demographic information, and you also have to agree to let the company track the sites you browse. The company sells that information to online marketers.

Some of the companies offer free access throughout the United States, and some cover specific geographic areas. Some of the nationwide providers are

- www.freewwweb.com
- www.altavista.com
- www.freei.net
- www.netzero.com
- www.ifreedom.com
- www.freensafe.com

These free ISPs can be useful as your only Internet provider. They are also mighty nice as a second provider when your primary one is busy or being used by another member of the family.

Feeling Right at Home

Everyone feels more at home in a friendly, familiar environment. This is just as true for your Internet home, so Yahoo! gives you several ways to customize the screen to your own tastes and interests.

First, you get up to six customizable pages called *My Yahoo!*. You decide what types of information are displayed on these pages. For example, you can customize a page for your location—to get your hometown news, weather, sports, and even traffic reports from any computer. Then, using your free account, you sign on to My Yahoo! (actually your Yahoo!) and get a kind of warm, fuzzy feeling when you see your name on the screen and the news that interests you.

There are a lot of ways to personalize Yahoo!, however, in addition to customizing your My Yahoo! home page:

- Create your own free Web site to share information with friends, family, and the world.
- Add a personalized toolbar, called the Yahoo! Companion, to your browser.
- Create family accounts for safer Web surfing and parental controls.
- Store your calendar online to keep track of appointments and events.
- Store your address list online.
- Store documents and other files online with a personal briefcase.

All of these features are designed to make you feel at home at Yahoo! and give you the true power of the Internet.

Your free Web site, for example, is part of Yahoo! Geocities. With handy online tools, you can create and manage a Web site similar to the one in Figure 1-2. Create animated logos and images, include games that viewers can play, and even add links to online stores that will pay you for referring surfers. You can use the site for almost anything you want, and build a Web site without any additional software other than your Web browser.

The free Web sites are grouped into *neighborhoods*, which are collections of sites that share a common theme. You can place your site in a neighborhood to increase its exposure and share information with others who have similar interests.

Yahoo! Companion is a special toolbar that fits on your browser's screen. The toolbar gives you instant access to Yahoo! and your customized My Yahoo! pages, along with your Yahoo! e-mail account and stock portfolio. Companion is also a great place to start searching for information of all sorts.

Family accounts control the type of access your children are given in Yahoo!. You create a Yahoo! account for each child and provide his or her name and age. Children under the age of 18

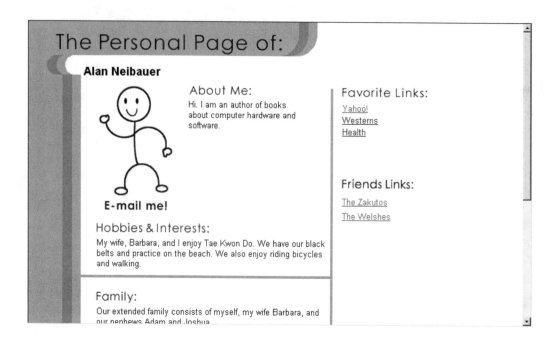

FIGURE 1-2   A sample Yahoo! Web site

cannot participate in auctions or access a Yahoo! adult chat, club, or shopping area. Children under 13 can't sign up for special offers, sweepstakes, or promotions, or run a personal ad.

 *Family accounts will not keep sites from being displayed in the results of a Yahoo! search.*

Yahoo! Calendar lets you maintain your schedule online and share it with others. A typical Yahoo! Calendar is shown in Figure 1-3.

With Calendar, you can be reminded about meetings, appointments, birthdays, and other events. You can schedule a meeting or party and automatically send e-mail invitations to other users. The group calendar feature lets you create a special calendar for a club or association to keep track of meetings and social events.

Keeping an address list online lets you access e-mail addresses, mailing addresses, and phone numbers from any location. If you use more than one computer, perhaps one at work and one at home, you can maintain one address list without worrying about adding new names or updating records in two locations.

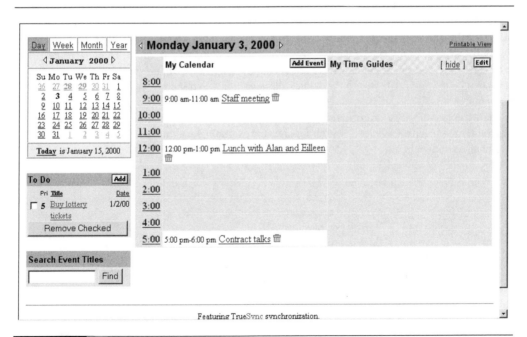

FIGURE 1-3   Yahoo! online calendar

The personal briefcase is an area on the Yahoo! computer where you can securely store your own files. For example, suppose you're writing a letter at home and don't have time to finish it. Rather than save the letter just to your hard disk, you can store a copy of it in your Yahoo! briefcase. Then, during the lunch hour at work, or at your local library or cyber café, you can retrieve the letter and complete it.

The Little Engine That Could

Yahoo! started as an Internet search engine. A *search engine* is a site that lets you find information on the Internet. You enter a word or phrase that you are interested in and the search engine displays a list of sites where that word or phase is found. The list includes hyperlinks to each site. A *hyperlink* is something you click to go to the site being referenced. So whatever you need information on, just tell the engine and it does the work for you.

Now searching the Internet is more of an art than a science. Entering a single search word might locate thousands of sites that have nothing to do with what you're looking for. That's fine if you have the time to scan the list and find information by trial and error, but learning how to search is well worth the effort.

Yahoo! was one of the very first search engines on the Internet and it is still one of the best. It is a perfect place to look for, and more importantly to find, information. It makes locating information easy by offering two ways to search—by keywords or by category.

When you search by keywords, you're looking for Web sites that contain the words that you specify. A basic search looks for the words in any order. For example, with some search engines, looking for the words *swing dancing* will locate thousands of sites containing either the word *swing* or the word *dancing,* but not necessarily both words, and you end up with a list of Web sites that have nothing to do with the dance craze. A Yahoo! search for *swing dancing*, however, will yield mostly sites that relate just to that topic, although a few extraneous sites may creep in from time to time.

There are lots of ways to refine searches to get just what you are looking for, and Yahoo! gives them to you. The Advanced Search feature, for example, lets you specify how the words are related, as shown here:

Select a search method: Select a search area:
     ⦿ Intelligent default   ⦿ Yahoo Categories
     ○ An exact phrase match   ○ Web Sites
     ○ Matches on all words (AND)
     ○ Matches on any word (OR)

Find only new listings added during the past 4 years ▾

So you can look for sites that contain both words, either word, or just the phase in the exact order and case you enter. You can also use special operators along with the search words to narrow down the sites that are located. You'll learn all about searching in Chapter 8.

Yahoo! also lets you search for information by using categories. You can find sites by subject and work through a list of subtopics that further define what you are looking for. All of the sites listed actually relate to the subject you're looking for, so you avoid having to scan lists of inappropriate locations.

The list of major topic headings is shown here:

Arts & Humanities
Literature, Photography...

Business & Economy
Companies, Finance, Jobs...

Computers & Internet
Internet, WWW, Software, Games...

Education
College and University, K-12...

Entertainment
Cool Links, Movies, Humor, Music...

Government
Elections, Military, Law, Taxes...

Health
Medicine, Diseases, Drugs, Fitness...

News & Media
Full Coverage, Newspapers, TV...

Recreation & Sports
Sports, Travel, Autos, Outdoors...

Reference
Libraries, Dictionaries, Quotations...

Regional
Countries, Regions, US States...

Science
Animals, Astronomy, Engineering...

Social Science
Archaeology, Economics, Languages...

Society & Culture
People, Environment, Religion...

Click the major category in which your information fits, and then the appropriate subtopic.

As an example, suppose you're into the new craze of swing dancing. Start your search by clicking Recreation & Sports to see these options:

- Amusement and Theme Parks@
- Automotive *(4599)* NEW!
- Aviation *(1155)* NEW!
- Booksellers@
- Chats and Forums *(5)*
- Cooking@
- Dance@
- Employment *(7)*
- Events *(10)*
- Fitness@
- Gambling *(275)*

- Games *(18435)* NEW!
- Hobbies *(2647)* NEW!
- Home and Garden *(615)* NEW!
- Magazines *(63)*
- Motorcycles@
- Outdoors *(7740)* NEW!
- Pets@
- Sports *(33747)* NEW!
- Television@
- Toys *(752)* NEW!
- Travel *(54617)* NEW!

Items with the "at" sign (@) are listed under more than one category. The number indicates the number of items that will be listed.

Next, click Dance to see the types of dances:

- Apparel@
- Ballet *(266)*
- Ballroom *(121)*
- Books@
- Break Dance@
- Butoh *(16)*
- Capoeira@
- Ceroc@
- Commercial@
- Contemporary *(79)*
- Contra Dancing@
- Country Western *(48)*
- Dance Therapy@
- Dancers *(29)*
- Disabilities@
- Education *(137)*
- Events *(20)*
- Exotic Dancing@
- Festivals *(17)*
- Flamenco *(24)*
- Folk and Traditional *(514)* NEW!

- Jazz *(13)*
- Libraries *(5)*
- Merengue *(4)*
- Middle Eastern@
- Modern *(163)*
- Museums *(2)*
- News and Media *(24)*
- Notation and Documentation *(19)*
- Organizations *(51)*
- Performing Groups *(19)*
- Regional Information *(22)*
- Renaissance *(9)*
- Salsa *(19)*
- Samba *(8)*
- Scottish Country Dancing@
- Square Dance *(84)*
- Swing *(114)*
- Tango *(32)*
- Tap *(14)*
- Tour Operators@
- Web Directories *(13)*

Finally, click Swing to display the choices, as shown in Figure 1-4. From that location, you can start a club, select from additional subtopics, or go to sites such as the Cat's Corner, Educated Feet, or JiveNet. Searching may be one of the first reasons why folks use Yahoo!, but there are plenty more.

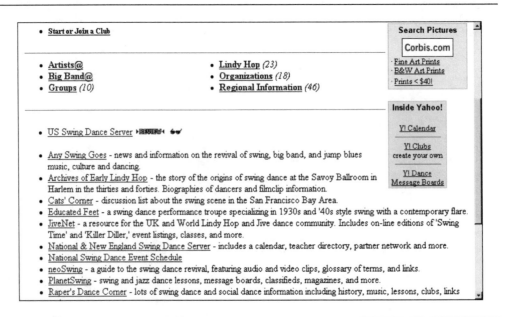

FIGURE 1-4   Results of a Yahoo! search

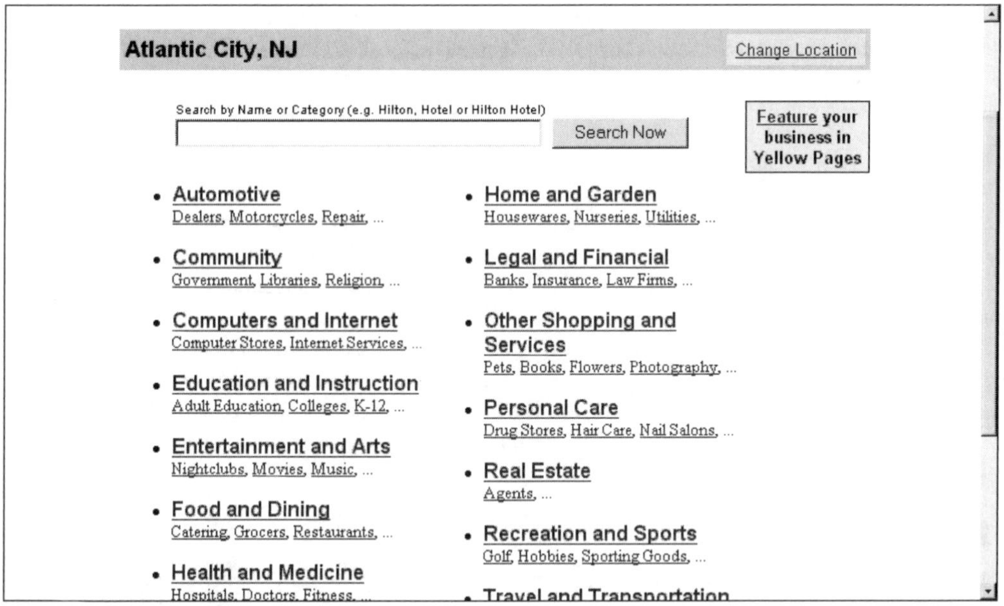

Atlantic City, NJ   Change Location

Search by Name or Category (e.g. Hilton, Hotel or Hilton Hotel)

[   ]   Search Now   Feature your business in Yellow Pages

- **Automotive**
  Dealers, Motorcycles, Repair, ...
- **Community**
  Government, Libraries, Religion, ...
- **Computers and Internet**
  Computer Stores, Internet Services, ...
- **Education and Instruction**
  Adult Education, Colleges, K-12, ...
- **Entertainment and Arts**
  Nightclubs, Movies, Music, ...
- **Food and Dining**
  Catering, Grocers, Restaurants, ...
- **Health and Medicine**
  Hospitals, Doctors, Fitness, ...

- **Home and Garden**
  Housewares, Nurseries, Utilities, ...
- **Legal and Financial**
  Banks, Insurance, Law Firms, ...
- **Other Shopping and Services**
  Pets, Books, Flowers, Photography, ...
- **Personal Care**
  Drug Stores, Hair Care, Nail Salons, ...
- **Real Estate**
  Agents, ...
- **Recreation and Sports**
  Golf, Hobbies, Sporting Goods, ...
- **Travel and Transportation**

FIGURE 1-5   Looking for a business in Yahoo!

Find People and Business

Information is just one thing you can locate on Yahoo!. You can also use Yahoo! to find people and businesses. Trying to locate an old college friend or an associate that you need to contact? Looking for a certain type of store or business in your area or elsewhere?

Use Yahoo! People Search to find a telephone number, address, or e-mail address. You can enter as little as a person's last name to get a nationwide listing, or the name, town and state to narrow your search. The information is drawn from the nation's telephone directories, so it is relatively up to date and complete. Use the People Search when researching your genealogy, for example, to track down persons with your last name.

Yahoo! Yellow Pages lets you find businesses. You can enter the business name or type, or use the categories shown in Figure 1-5. You can search for businesses in a specific city or zip code, or nearest to an address that you specify.

Free E-Mail

Even if you already have an e-mail address from your ISP, getting a free e-mail account from Yahoo! is a great idea. You can use your free address, which will be something like alan@yahoo.com, to both send and receive mail.

Getting free e-mail is perfect when your e-mail account is maintained at the office or you share a single ISP e-mail address with other members of the family and you want to send or receive mail without it being seen by prying eyes. Because your Yahoo! address is Web based, you can check your e-mail from any computer that has access to the Internet. So you can send and receive mail from work, a friend's house, the library, or the neighborhood cyber café—and only you will have access to it.

Tip *You can also use your Yahoo! address to sign up for free offers on the Web so the multitude of resulting junk mail and spam does not clog up your other inbox.*

The Yahoo! e-mail address is universal and free for life. No matter how many times you change ISPs, your Yahoo! address is always the same. You won't have to notify correspondents of a change of e-mail address if you have to switch ISPs. People can continue to send mail to your Yahoo! address without a change.

You can also use your Yahoo! e-mail address to send and receive files. Did you ever wait a long time for a file to download from your ISP's mail system only to discover it was junk? With Yahoo!, you can log on to the Internet and see the size and sender of e-mail attachments. You can then choose to download the file to your computer or delete it from your Yahoo! mailbox.

Shopping

Shopping on the Web is great way to compare prices, look for sales, and locate hard-to-find products. Yahoo! makes it easy to shop through its secure online shopping service. Imagine getting an instant price comparison from major companies and then being able to order a product from the comfort of your home. You can even add your billing and shipping information to a special secure Yahoo! location to make purchasing even easier.

Through Yahoo!, you have access to thousands of stores and millions of products starting from these options.

You can start with one of the suggested departments, stores, or products, or just click Yahoo! Shopping to see the main shopping screen shown in Figure 1-6.

Yahoo! Shopping - Thousands of stores. Millions of products.			
Departments		**Stores**	**Products**
· Apparel	· Food/Drink	· Toys R Us	· Pokemon
· Bath/Beauty	· Music	· Eddie Bauer	· MP3 players
· Computers	· Toys	· Gap	· Digital cameras
· Electronics	· Video/DVD	· Victoria's Secret	· DVD players

You can search by entering a keyword, find a product by its category, or look through the featured stores. The window also includes links to hot products and featured items that are changing regularly. The results of your search will show one or more merchants that offer the item, and compare merchants' prices, shipping fees, and other information. You can then purchase the item by selecting the merchant of your choice.

If you're looking for a gift for someone else and are not sure of what to get, Yahoo! shopping is a great place to start. It's easier to browse through items from the comfort of your home than walk through a mall, and you don't have to walk between distant stores to compare prices.

If you're expecting, or hoping, for a gift from someone else, you can even create a gift registry. Stroll through the Yahoo! shopping mall looking for items you'd like to own, and add them to a wish list. Friends and relatives can view the list online when they are ready to buy a gift for you.

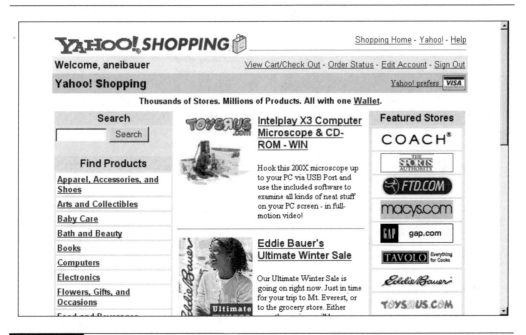

FIGURE 1-6   Yahoo! shopping mall

If you like haggling, there's even Yahoo! auctions. Bid on products of all types or sell those old things that have been lying around the house. You can get some real bargains in the auctions as well as turn unwanted items into cash.

As an alternative to the auctions, you can buy and sell through the Yahoo! classifieds. Run an ad just like you can in the newspaper, only do it for free.

Tip   *A feature called Yahoo! Points lets you earn points to redeem for free merchandise by using various Yahoo! services.*

News, Weather, and Sports

Yahoo! is like having your own radio or television news show online. Late-breaking stories and weather reports are available 24 hours a day. The top news stories are right on the screen as soon as you go to Yahoo!.

Click on a headline to read the details or click the More link to display other top stories. Getting your hometown weather is just as easy with the Weather link.

If you want news, weather, and sports to appear automatically on the screen, you can install the Yahoo! ticker. The ticker scrolls

In the News

· Few Y2K delays on first work day
· Israel and Syria open round of talks
· Weekend's top movies
· NCAA football, NFL

more...

the latest sports scores, news headlines, weather, and stock information across the screen as you work:

Russia Routs Chechens · US 1 Person in EgyptAir Cock

You can customize the contents of the ticker and decide how it appears. All you need is a free Yahoo! account and free ticker software that you can download from Yahoo!. If you have a Yahoo! mail account, the ticker will even notify you when mail is being received.

Keeping in Touch

E-mail is only one way to keep in touch electronically. With Yahoo!, you have a number of ways to communicate with friends, relatives, and even strangers if you wish.

Yahoo! Messaging is one fun way. When you log on to Yahoo! Messaging, you can see if any of your friends are also logged on. You can then send and receive instant messages—notes that pop up right on the screen while you're surfing the net. You can send and receive files as well. Yahoo! messaging, by the way, can also inform you about stock prices, tell you when Yahoo! mail is arriving, and even remind you about appointments on your Yahoo! calendar.

Tip *If you do not want to be disturbed by instant messages from other users, there is an invisible mode that prevents other Yahoo! users from knowing you are online.*

To communicate with any number of persons at once, you can start or join a chat. Online chats are written or spoken conversations with any number of persons. Depending on your hardware, you can type messages back and forth or speak into your microphone and hear messages from other users. Chats are a great way to meet new people and to arrange conversations with friends and relatives in faraway places. In fact, you can designate the names of friends you want to chat with. Yahoo! will search the chat rooms for those people so you can engage them in a conversation. Special chats are even set up so you can speak with celebrities of all types.

Yahoo! clubs are another way to share information. A *club* is a private chat for persons who share a common interest. The person who creates the club—and you can create your own—can control who has access to the chat and what messages appear. There are Yahoo! clubs on a number of subjects, ranging from topics in business and finance to sex and romance, and you can create a new club for a special interest of your own. Using the Yahoo! Member Directory, you can look for persons who share your interests and invite them to join.

Messages boards offer another approach to communications. Unlike a chat, which occurs in real time, a message board is like a global e-mail system. You can read messages left by other persons, post your own messages, or respond to others. The messages remain on the system for several months, so you can take part in rather extensive conversations called *threads*.

Yahoo! Greetings also let you stay in touch by sending decorative, and even animated and musical, electronic greeting cards through e-mail. Anyone with an e-mail address can receive a greeting card, whether or not they are a Yahoo! member.

If you're looking for something more than a distant cyber relationship, you can use the Yahoo! Personals. As shown in Figure 1-7, you can post and respond to ads for any type of relationship. What's more, for the sake of privacy, you can keep responses in a personals mailbox that is separate from your regular e-mail account.

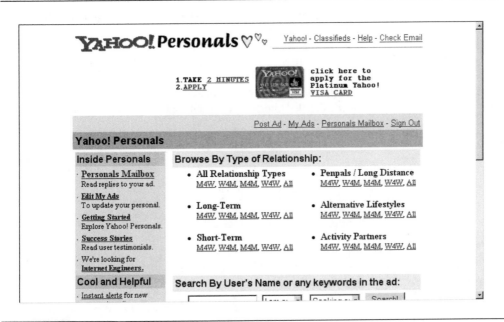

FIGURE 1-7   Get close with Yahoo! personals

Traveling

Yahoo! offers a variety of services for exploring the wonders of the world, whether you're going on a business trip, planning a vacation, or just crossing town.

For planning business trips and vacations, there's Yahoo! Travel, shown in Figure 1-8. You can make airline, car, hotel, and cruise reservations, as well as research the best fares. Along the way, you can search out interesting places to visit. Yahoo! can store your itinerary and keep track of your reservations and account information.

If your trip requires driving a car, get detailed directions before even turning the ignition key. Yahoo! maps can show the exact location of almost any address or site in the United States. The maps can also show you detailed, turn-by-turn driving directions.

To find a location, for example, just enter the address and click Get Map to see a detailed map like the one in Figure 1-9. Use the tools on the map to zoom in and out. Zoom out when you want to see a wider geographic area but less detail; zoom in when you need more detail and individual street names. Click the compass points to make the map move north, south, east, or west and see the area surrounding your destination.

As an extra bonus, you can use the onscreen tools to locate nearby hotels, restaurants, and other businesses. If you're planning a business trip, for example, you can find the hotels and business services closest to your destination.

The driving directions option lets you specify two addresses—your starting address and your destination. Yahoo! will then give you detailed directions between the two, as shown in Figure 1-10.

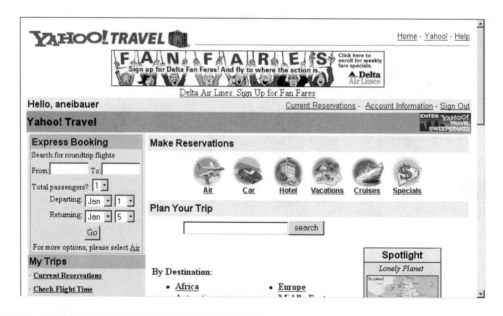

FIGURE 1-8 Yahoo! Travel for business and vacation travel plans

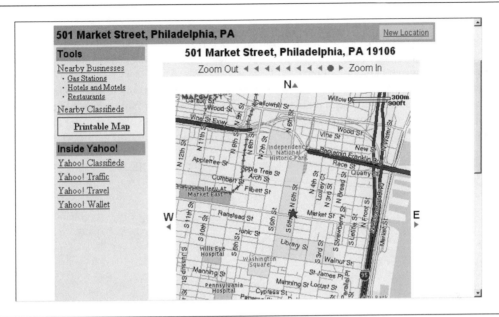

FIGURE 1-9 Finding locations with Yahoo! maps

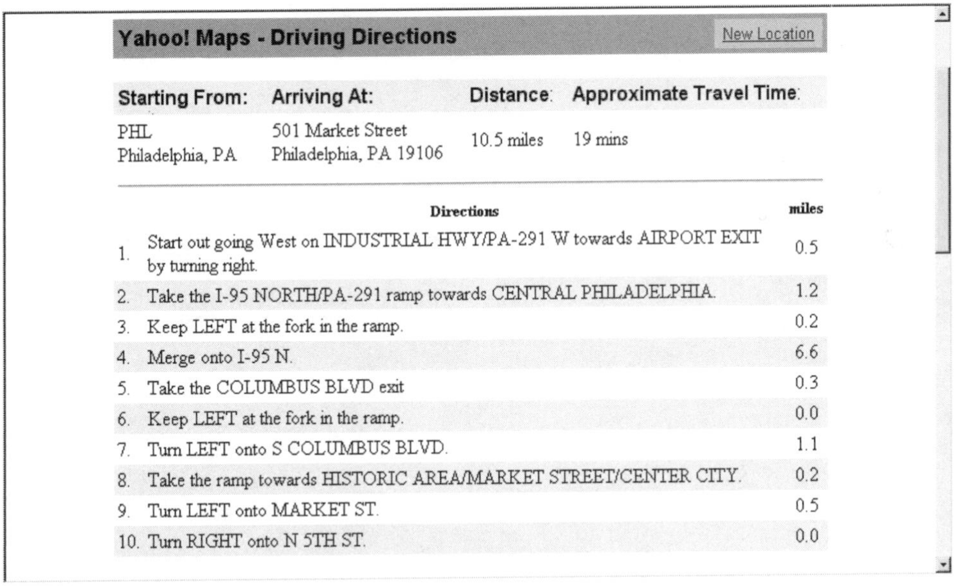

Yahoo! Maps - Driving Directions New Location

Starting From:	Arriving At:	Distance:	Approximate Travel Time:
PHL Philadelphia, PA	501 Market Street Philadelphia, PA 19106	10.5 miles	19 mins

Directions	miles
1. Start out going West on INDUSTRIAL HWY/PA-291 W towards AIRPORT EXIT by turning right.	0.5
2. Take the I-95 NORTH/PA-291 ramp towards CENTRAL PHILADELPHIA.	1.2
3. Keep LEFT at the fork in the ramp.	0.2
4. Merge onto I-95 N.	6.6
5. Take the COLUMBUS BLVD exit	0.3
6. Keep LEFT at the fork in the ramp.	0.0
7. Turn LEFT onto S COLUMBUS BLVD.	1.1
8. Take the ramp towards HISTORIC AREA/MARKET STREET/CENTER CITY.	0.2
9. Turn LEFT onto MARKET ST.	0.5
10. Turn RIGHT onto N 5TH ST.	0.0

FIGURE 1-10 Detailed driving directions from Yahoo!

Just for Fun

To take your mind off of business, school, or family pressures, log on to Yahoo! to play games. There are single-player games that you play by yourself, as well as board games and card games of all types that you can play with others.

Compete against other Yahoo! members in games such as backgammon, chess, checkers, mahjong, bridge, and poker. You can also play fantasy sports such as fantasy basketball, football, and hockey. All of the games are free and require no special software other than your Internet browser.

Note *You may not be able to play games if you are behind a corporate firewall or using Web TV.*

Chapter 2

Sign On to a Free E-Mail Account and Address Book

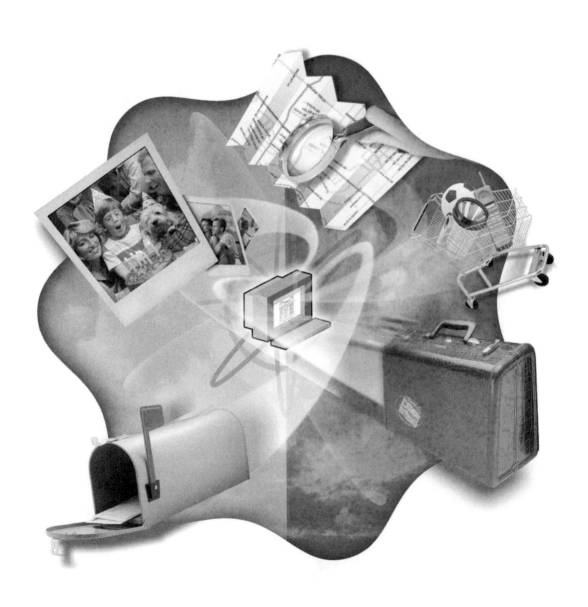

How to . . .

- Get free Yahoo! membership
- Get a free Internet mail account
- Send and receive e-mail from Yahoo!
- Send and read file attachments with Yahoo! e-mail
- Maintain your address book online
- Create distribution lists for broadcasting e-mail
- Customize the Yahoo! e-mail and address book features

One of the first things you'll want to do with Yahoo! is to sign up for a free e-mail account. The e-mail account gives you the capability to send and receive e-mail, and use Yahoo! from any computer connected to the Internet. Each Yahoo! member gets 3MB of mail space on the Yahoo! server to store messages. If your storage area fills up, new e-mail sent to you is rejected and returned to the sender.

Signing Up

Signing up for an e-mail account also makes you a member of Yahoo! so you can take advantage of other features that are reserved for members, including

- Creating your custom My Yahoo! pages
- Participating in Yahoo! auctions
- Saving files in the Yahoo! Briefcase
- Using Yahoo! messenger
- Maintaining your investment portfolio online
- Creating a Yahoo! calendar
- Using the Yahoo! companion toolbar

To sign up for a Yahoo! account, you'll need to enter some basic information about yourself, and you'll need to select a user name and password. For security, use a different name and password than you have for your ISP. You will not be asked for a charge card number, your address, your social security number, or any other information that should be kept private.

2

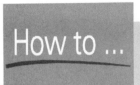

Register from Other Locations

You can also sign up for Yahoo! by accessing any service that requires Yahoo! membership, such as My Yahoo!, clubs, or auctions. The enrollment process is the same; only the options you get when you finish signing up vary. When you sign up from the My Yahoo! option from the Mail feature, for example, you see a screen where you can send and receive e-mail. Sign up from the Auctions page, however, and you see a screen where you can bid on auction items.

Note *If you see a link labeled What Does This Mean?, you can click it to get help information about the feature or function being displayed.*

When you're ready to join Yahoo!, follow these steps:

1. Log on to the Internet and navigate to *www.yahoo.com*. The easiest way is just to enter **www.yahoo.com** in the browser's address box and press the ENTER key.

2. Look for the Mail option near the top of the screen in the row of options:

Shopping - **Auctions** - Yellow Pages - People Search - Maps - Travel - Classifieds - Personals - Games - Chat - **Clubs**
Mail - Calendar - Messenger - **Companion** - My Yahoo! - News - Sports - Weather - TV - Stock Quotes - more...

3. Click Mail to display the screen shown in Figure 2-1. After you have a Yahoo! account, you will use this page to sign into Yahoo! and identify yourself so you can check your e-mail or send new e-mail messages.

4. Since you're signing on for the first time, click Sign Me Up! to open the Sign Me Up form shown in Figure 2-2.

5. Enter the name you want for your Yahoo! mail address and ID.

6. Enter and retype the password you want to use to log on to Yahoo!

7. If you forget your password, you can get it from Yahoo!, but to do so you'll need to answer a question that verifies your identity. Select the item that you want Yahoo! to ask for:

   ■ City of Birth

   ■ Pet's Name

   ■ Anniversary Date

8. Enter the answer to the item you selected.

9. Enter your current e-mail address.

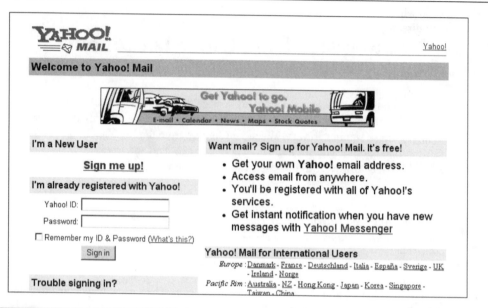

FIGURE 2-1   Signing into Yahoo! mail

FIGURE 2-2   Signing up for Yahoo! membership

10. Choose whether you want to include your Yahoo! e-mail address in an online e-mail directory.

11. Enter your name and zip code.

12. Select your gender.

13. Choose an occupation and industry from the two lists.

14. Choose whether you want to be notified about Yahoo! events and products.

15. Optionally, select check boxes that indicate your hobbies and interests.

16. Click Submit This Form.

> **Tip** *You will be notified if the user ID you picked has already been reserved by someone else or you forgot to complete any required information. Make your correction and submit the form again.*

17. A confirmation appears and recaps your Yahoo! ID and current e-mail address. Click Continue To My Yahoo!. The Welcome To Yahoo! Mail screen appears so you can verify your Yahoo! e-mail address and your first and last name.

18. Click Sign Me Up! You are now a Yahoo! member.

The e-mail window appears, as shown in Figure 2-3. The e-mail window shows that you have one unread message (a welcome note from Yahoo!) and that you have used 0 percent of your 3MB of disk space. Navigation buttons appear on the left side of the window so you can work with e-mail and other Yahoo! features.

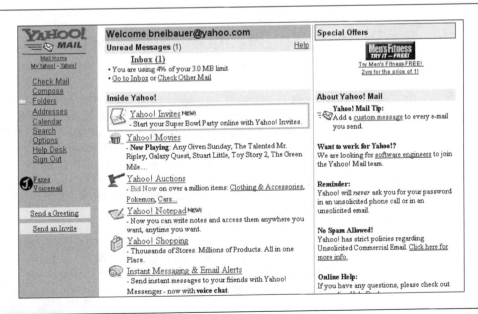

FIGURE 2-3   Yahoo! mail window

The numbers in parentheses after Unread Messages and Inbox indicate the number of messages that you have not yet read. If you've read every message, the word "Inbox" is replaced with the words "No Unread Messages."

There is a lot on this screen to explore. You can access Yahoo! shopping, learn about movies and instant messaging, sign up for special offers and features, and get help information on the mail feature.

Signing In

Each time you go on the Internet and access a Yahoo! service that requires membership, you see the Yahoo! ID and Password text boxes, shown at right.

After you enter your ID and password and click Sign In, Yahoo! temporarily saves a copy of your ID and password. You can then use other member services without signing in again—until you close your browser, leave Yahoo!, or click a link that says Sign Out.

I'm a New User
Sign me up!
I'm already registered with Yahoo!
Yahoo! ID:
Password:
☐ Remember my ID & Password (What's this?)
Sign in

 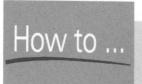 *If another person's name appears when you enter Yahoo!, look for a link labeled Change User. Click that link to sign in under your own name. If Change User does not appear, click Sign Out.*

How to ... Protect Your Yahoo! Password

The Sign In form also contains a check box labeled Remember My ID & Password. If you select this check box, Yahoo! stores your user ID and password on your computer as a *cookie*. A cookie is a small file that an Internet site saved on your computer. When you access the same site again, it reads the information in the cookie to determine your ID name, password, or other information about your previous visits to the site. Choosing Remember My ID & Password means you won't have to sign on to Yahoo! each time you access it. Yahoo! will automatically retrieve your ID and password and sign you in automatically— as long as you do not delete the cookie from your computer.

If you share your computer or you are accessing Yahoo! from a public site such as a library, however, you do not want anyone else to access Yahoo! services under your member ID. Someone could access your e-mail to send messages under your name or bid on items in an auction as if they were you. So do not enable the Remember My ID & Password check box and always click Sign Out when you have finished using Yahoo!.

Reading E-Mail

To read a message that you have received, click the Check Mail, Go To Inbox, or Inbox links. The Check Other Mail link lets you look for e-mail on other e-mail servers, such as your ISP, so you can use Yahoo! as a comprehensive e-mail program. You'll learn about that later.

A typical Inbox is shown in Figure 2-4. The Inbox lists each message by its sender, date, size, and subject. The Inbox is just one of several folders that Yahoo! provides to organize e-mail.

By default, messages are listed in date order, from the newest to the oldest. Click the arrow next to the Date heading to sort the dates from oldest to newest. To sort by Sender, Size, or Subject, just click the heading, and then use the arrow next to it to change the order from descending to ascending.

To delete a message, select the check box next to it and click either Delete button. Deleting a message places it in the Trash folder, which you'll learn about later in the last section of this chapter, "Working with Folders."

To read a message, click its subject. Figure 2-5 shows how a message appears. The heading shows you the message's date, sender, subject, and the e-mail addresses of the persons receiving the message.

Above and below the messages are buttons for managing e-mail.

Shortcut   *On many Yahoo! screens you'll see identical rows of options, one above and one below whatever items are displayed. Yahoo! does this to make it easy to access the features from either the top or bottom of the window.*

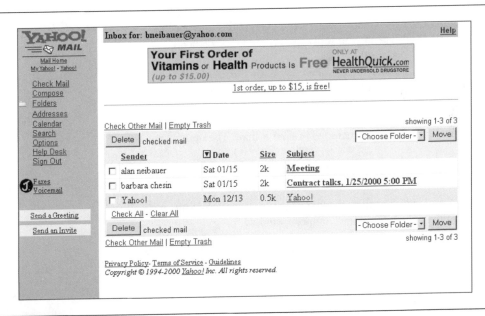

FIGURE 2-4   Yahoo! mail Inbox

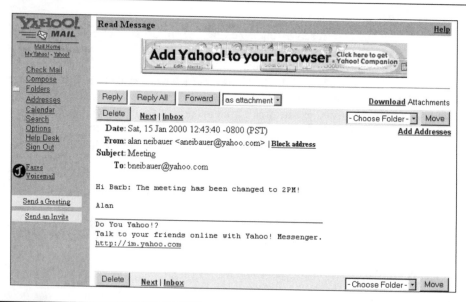

FIGURE 2-5   A message in the Yahoo! Inbox

Click the Reply button to send a reply to the sender of the message. The Compose window, where you enter and send your reply, appears. To also send your reply to everyone who received the message, click Reply All.

Click the Forward button to send a copy of this message to another person. The Compose window will appear so you can enter the e-mail address of the recipient and a message of your own. Before clicking Forward, however, choose how you want the text of the original message to be included in your e-mail. The options are

- **As Attachment**   Includes the original message as a file that the reader can choose to download.

- **Inline Text**   Displays the text of the message following any text that you enter in the Compose window.

Click the Delete button to move the messages into the Trash folder. Use the Move button to move the message to another folder.

2

Click the Inbox link to return to the Inbox, click Prev to see the   **Prev | Next | Inbox**
previous message in the Inbox, or click Next to see the next message.

If you no longer want to receive e-mail from the sender of the message, click the Block
Address link in the Mail window to see these options, and then click Yes:

- Block the email address "alann@worldnet.att.net" from sending mail to this account?

  Yes | I wish to block all mail from "alann@worldnet.att.net".

  No | I do not wish to block this address.

Mail from this sender will be deleted rather than added to your Inbox.

Shortcut   *Use the Add Addresses link to add the address of the sender to your address book. See the sidebar "Add a Sender's Address," later in this chapter.*

Sending a Message

When you want to send a message using Yahoo!, click Compose on the left side of the screen.
Yahoo! lets you create plain-text and formatted messages. The Compose window for writing
plain-text messages is shown in Figure 2-6.

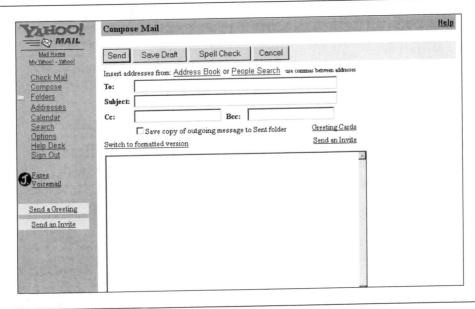

FIGURE 2-6   Creating an e-mail message

Enter the e-mail address of the recipient, the subject, and the addresses of anyone to whom you want to send a carbon copy or blind copy. Both types of copies send the e-mail to the individual you specify. With a blind copy, however, other recipients do not know that the blind copy recipient was sent a copy. If you want a record of the message, select the check box labeled Save Copy Of Outgoing Message To Sent Folder. You can use the Sent folder to review your messages or copy text from a message and send it to other recipients. Enter the text of the message in the last text box.

Yahoo! provides a spell-check program to check your spelling. As with spell checkers in programs such as Microsoft Word, Yahoo!'s spell-checker compares each word in your e-mail message against its dictionary. When it finds a possible misspelled word, you see a box like the one shown at top right.

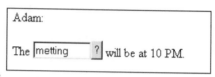

Click the question mark next to the word for options such as these shown next.

You can manually retype the word and click Change, or select a word from the Suggestions drop-down menu and then click Change. Click Leave Unchanged if the word is spelled correctly.

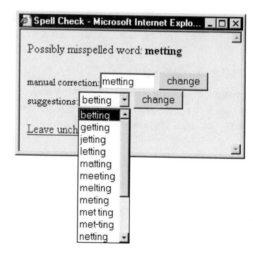

If you are ready to send the message, click the Send button. If you're not ready to send it but want to work on it later, click Save Draft. You'll be able to reopen the message in the Draft folder, complete it, and send it at a later time.

Sending Attachments

Sometimes you'll want to send a recipient a file that you have on your computer. It may be a photograph that you scanned, a document that you wrote, an interesting item, or a program that you downloaded from the Internet.

You send a file along with an e-mail by including it as an attachment. Yahoo! lets you attach as many as three files with a message, but their total size cannot exceed 1.5 megabytes.

To send an attachment, click Edit Attachments under the message box to open the dialog box shown in Figure 2-7. Under Step 1, enter the path and name of the file you want to attach, or click the Browse button to locate the file using Windows Explorer.

Click the Attach File button and repeat Step 1 to attach up to two additional files. Click Done to return to the Compose window. The names of the files will be listed in the Attachments text box.

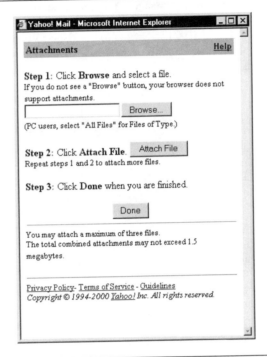

FIGURE 2-7   Sending an attachment with an e-mail

Formatted Messages

Almost anyone on the Internet can receive plain-text messages, but they are just text without any formatting. A formatted message with different fonts and special effects to highlight text can have greater impact and is more likely to be read. Many e-mail systems can accept and display formatted messages.

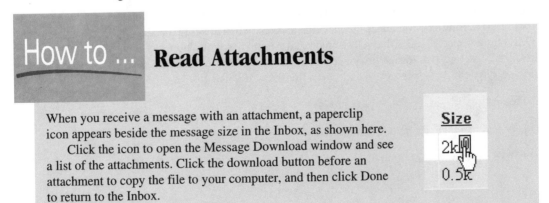

How to ...   Read Attachments

When you receive a message with an attachment, a paperclip icon appears beside the message size in the Inbox, as shown here.

Click the icon to open the Message Download window and see a list of the attachments. Click the download button before an attachment to copy the file to your computer, and then click Done to return to the Inbox.

There are two ways to format Yahoo! messages. You can select formats from a special toolbar or manually insert HTML tags.

To add some pizzazz to your e-mail, select Switch to Formatted Version in the compose window to see the toolbars shown here:

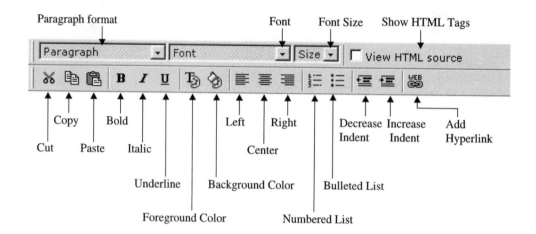

Use the toolbars to format and arrange text just as you would in a word-processing program. To underline text, for example, click the Underline button, type the text you want underlined, and then click the button again. To underline text you've already typed, drag over the text with the mouse and then click the Underline button.

Use the Font list to change the font, and the Size list to change the font size, just as you would in a word-processing program such as Microsoft Word.

Note *Select the check box labeled View HTML source if you want to see the HTML tags that create the formats.*

If you want to manually insert HTML tags into a plain-text message to format it, select the HTML Tags Allowed option under the message text box when creating a plain-text message. HTML tags are special codes that tell the recipient's e-mail program how to format and display messages. Most tags that format text have a start and end code. For example, to display a word in boldface, type <b> before the word and </b> after the word, like so:

Please reply <b>immediately</b> or else!

In the e-mail message, the sentence looks like this:

Please reply **immediately** or else!

2

Other start and end codes, as shown in Figure 2-8, format text in italics and underline, increase or decrease the size, or create headlines. Use the code <p> to end a paragraph and <br> to enter a line break.

Including Signatures

A *signature* is a standard closing that you can automatically add to the end of a message. It may be your name and title; a witty or inspirational message; or an advertisement for Web site, product, or company. You have to create a signature before you can add it to a message.

If you chose to use the signature on all messages, the Use Signature check box will be selected whenever you compose a message. But you can deselect the check box if you decide not to include a signature with a specific message. You can select the check box to include a signature when it is not on by default.

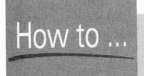

Create or Edit a Signature

To create or edit a signature, follow these steps:

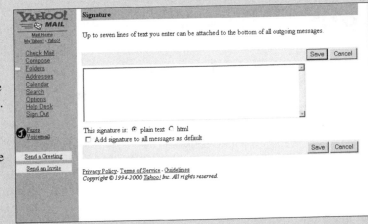

1. Click Options on the left side of the window.

2. In the screen that appears, click Signature to see the options in the screen shown here.

3. Type up to seven lines of text that you want to appear at the bottom of messages, or edit the text of the current signature.

4. Select HTML if you want to format the signature with html tags.

5. Select Add Signature to All Messages as Default if you want to use the signature on all new messages.

6. Click the Save button.

`<b></b>`	**Bold**
`<i></i>`	*Italic*
`<u></u>`	<u>Underline</u>
`<h1></h1>`	# Heading 1
`<h2></h2>`	## Heading 2
`<h3></h3>`	### Heading 3
`<h4></h4>`	Heading 4
`<h5></h5>`	Heading 5
`<h5></h5>`	Heading 6
`<Font Size=+1></Font Size>`	Increase Font 1 size
`<Font Size=+2></Font Size>`	Increase Font 2 sizes
`<Font Size=+3></Font Size>`	Increase Font 3 sizes
`<Font Size=+4></Font Size>`	Increase Font 4 sizes
`<Center></Center>`	Center

FIGURE 2-8   Sample HTML tags for formatting e-mail

Maintaining Your Address Book

Rather than type recipients' e-mail addresses each time you compose a message, you can store recipients' information in an online address book. You can then select one or more recipients for each message without having to type their e-mail addresses. In addition to e-mail addresses, you can store postal addresses and company and personal information in the Yahoo! address book.

The address book is available from many locations in Yahoo!, so you can access it whenever you need to insert or check an address. For example, you'll be able to invite persons in the address book to meetings with Yahoo! Calendar or call them from Yahoo! Phone Booth.

When you are composing a message, you can access the address book by clicking the Address Book link shown here:

Insert addresses from: <u>Address Book</u> or <u>People Search</u>   use commas between addresses

The book is empty until you enter your first address. An address book with contacts, however, appears as in Figure 2-9. An underlined letter in the alphabet indicates that a last name has been filed under the letter. Click a letter to display just the names that start with the letter, or click All to display everyone in the address book.

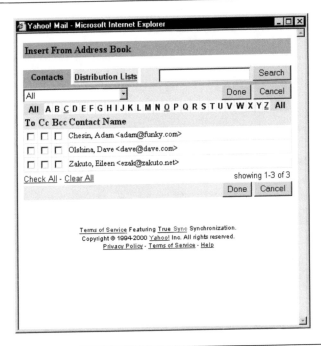

FIGURE 2-9   Selecting names from the address book

To send an e-mail to a person in the address book, select the To, CC, or BCC check box in front of his or her name, depending on how you want to send the e-mail message. Selecting CC sends a copy of the message to the addressee in such a way that other recipients know he or she is receiving it. Selecting BCC sends a copy but does not let other recipients know that the copy was sent. To send an e-mail to everyone in the book, click Check All. When you've finished selecting recipients, click the Done button. You'll learn about the Distribution Lists tab later in the section "Working with Distribution Lists."

To enter and edit entries in the book, click Addresses in the Yahoo! mail window. If you have not entered any items into the address book, you see helpful hints in the address book. Click Add Contact to open the New Address Book Entry window shown in Figure 2-10 and add a person to the book.

The screen contains the basic address book information, as well as the option to assign the contact to a category. Categories help you organize contacts into common groups. To add a contact to a category, pull down the Category list (you'll find it in the lower-right corner) and choose one of these options:

- Unfiled
- Commercial
- Personal
- Professional

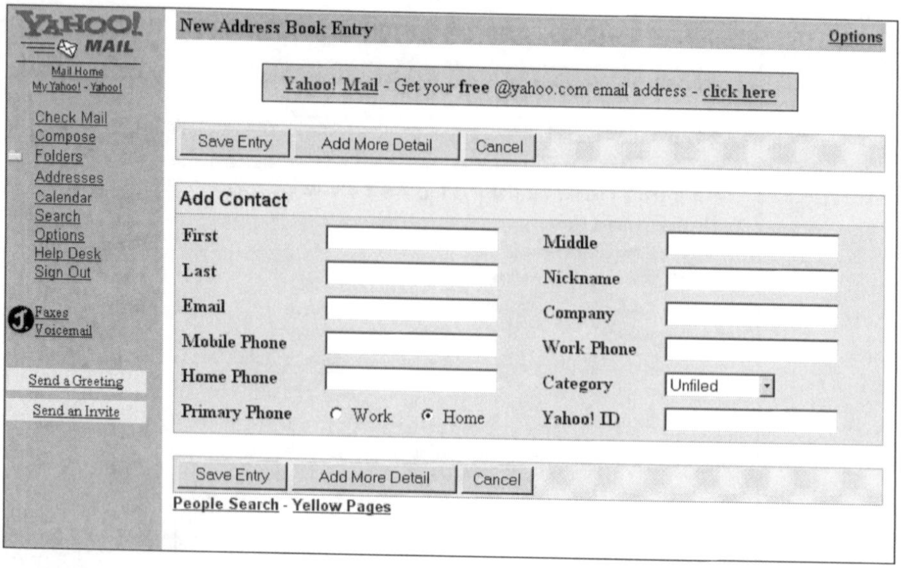

FIGURE 2-10   Enter a new address book listing

If you want to enter more details, click the Add More Detail button. The New Address Book Entry window expands so you can enter more phone numbers, home and work addresses, e-mail addresses, Web site addresses, and personal information such as birth dates and anniversaries.

Click Save when you've finished entering or editing the address. All of your contacts appear in the address book, as shown in Figure 2-11. You can send mail to one or more persons in the address book by selecting names, as you've already learned, and then clicking the E-mail button.

To edit a person's information, click the Edit icon on the right side of the address book to display the Add/Edit Contact Details form. You can also click the contact's name to open the Contact Detail form and then click the Edit Contact button. Make your changes and then click Save.

If you just want to change the category to which a contact is assigned, you can do so from the address book. Select the contact and then click Move to see these options:

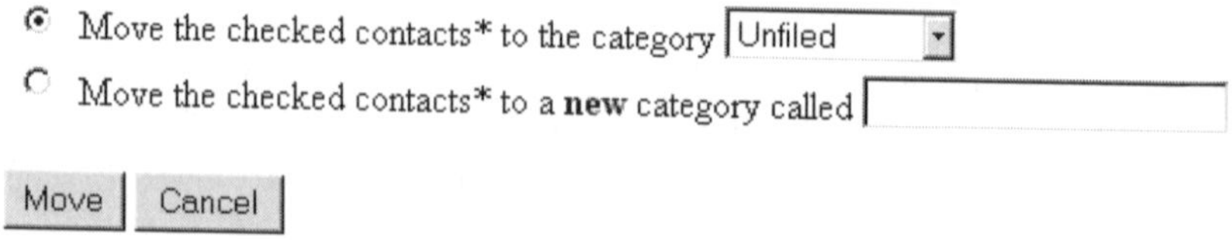

To move the contact to an existing group, select the first option, pull down the list, and select the group. To assign a contact to a new group, select the second option, enter the group name, and then click the Move button.

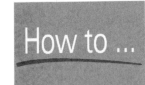

Add a Sender's Address

If you receive an e-mail from a person not in your address book, you can quickly add his or her e-mail address to your list of contacts. When you are reading the message, click the Add Addresses link to see the sender's address, as shown here:

Add Checked	Cancel

Check All - Clear All

	Email Address	First Name	Last Name	Nickname	
☐	alann@worldnet.att.net	Alan	Neibauer		Add More

Check All - Clear All

Add Checked	Cancel

Select the check box to the left of the sender's e-mail address and then click the Add Checked button. Yahoo! will insert the sender's name and e-mail address into your address book.

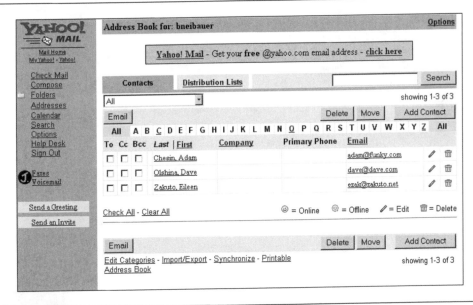

FIGURE 2-11   Maintaining the Yahoo! address book

Working with Distribution Lists

A *distribution list* is a collection of addresses. You can send e-mail to everyone in the list, or move everyone in the list to a new category, by entering the name of the list rather than the names of individual members in the To box.

Yahoo! includes a built-in list called Everyone that contains all of the contacts in your address book. To send an e-mail to everyone in your address book, for example, just type **Everyone** in the To box of the message. When you send the message, it will go to everyone in your address book.

 *You can also address mail to everybody by clicking Select All in the address book and then clicking the E-mail button.*

If you want to create a custom distribution list with only selected contacts, open the address book and click the Distribution Lists tab to see the options shown in Figure 2-12.

Notice that there are also buttons to delete a list or move it to a category. You cannot edit or delete the Everyone group.

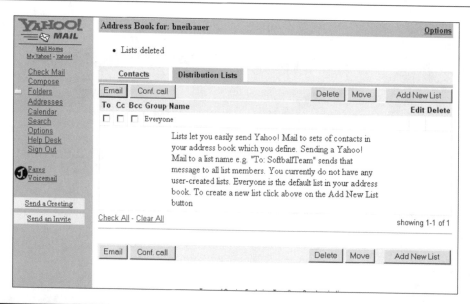

FIGURE 2-12 Distribution list options

To create a new list, click the Add New List button to see the window in Figure 2-13. You can add individual contacts to a list or all the names that are assigned to a category. To assign an entire category of users to a list, pull down the list just above the View button, choose the category, and click View to display only those contacts. Choose All from the list to display all of the address book entries.

In the Add Members list, select the contacts that you want to add to the group, and then click Add. Yahoo! moves the selected names to the Members of List group on the right side of the window. To remove a person from the list, select the name on the right and click Remove. Finally, enter the name for the new group in the Members of List text box, and then click Done to return to the address book.

To add or remove names from an existing list, by the way, select it in the Distribution List tab of the address book and click Edit.

The Conf. Call button in the Distribution Lists tab lets you make a conference telephone call to all the members of the selected group. There is a charge for this service. The Move button lets you move all members of a selected list to a new category.

To access a distribution list while you are composing a message, click the Address Book link and then click the Distribution List tab. You can then select the To check box next to the list and click Done to send an e-mail message to all list members.

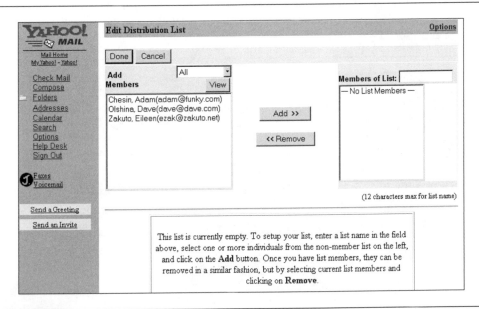

FIGURE 2-13   Creating a new distribution list

Setting Yahoo! Options and Preferences

Yahoo! offers quite a few ways to customize the mail and address book features to your tasks. The two main categories of options are Mail and Address Book.

For general options, click Options on the left side of any mail window to see the choices in Figure 2-14. The options are divided into three categories: Personalization, Mail Management, and Delivery Services.

Personalization Options

Use the Personalization options to make changes to your Yahoo! account information and mail. The options let you customize how mail is displayed on your screen, and the name and e-mail address that recipients see with your mail. You can also add an automatic signature to messages and create a vacation response that Yahoo! returns to senders when you are not available to read and respond to mail.

Changing Your Account Information

Select Account Information to display the Review My Account Information screen, where you can change your Yahoo! name and password, member information, and address.

Information about you is stored in a profile that is made available to other Yahoo! members. Your default profile is stored under your Yahoo! ID name, and you can create other profiles as well. Your profile includes information about you that you want others to see, as well as a photograph and a sound file.

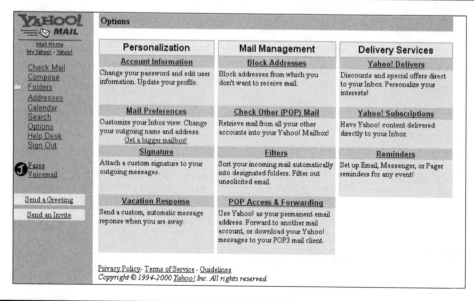

FIGURE 2-14   Yahoo! options

To create a profile, click Edit/Create Profile in the Review My Account Information screen to see the options shown in Figure 2-15. Since you start out with only one profile, it is used as the default.

Tip   *Click Create New Public Profile if you have not yet created a profile.*

Select Edit next to your profile name to change your default profile, or click the Create New Public Profile button to start a new one. If you sign up from Yahoo! Messenger, a subject discussed in Chapter 19, you can alert other Yahoo! members when you are online. If you do not want other members to know when you are online, select the check box called Check The Box To Hide My Online Status From Other Users.

If you choose to create a new profile, you'll have the following options:

- Enter a name for the profile
- Name
- Location
- Age
- Sex
- Marital status

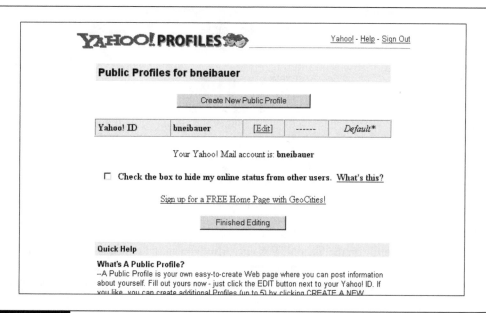

FIGURE 2-15   Setting your user profile

- Occupation
- E-mail address
- Display/hide the e-mail address in the profile
- Hobbies
- News about you
- Favorite quote
- Place the profile in the member directory
- Your home page
- Up to three links

When you've finished, click the Click Here When Done button.

If you decide to edit your profile, you'll see the options shown in Figure 2-16. Choose Edit Profile Information to change the basic information about you and your account. By clicking Edit Pictures and Voice on the Yahoo! Profile screen, you can choose a stock graphic to display in your profile or give the address of a custom photograph on the Internet:

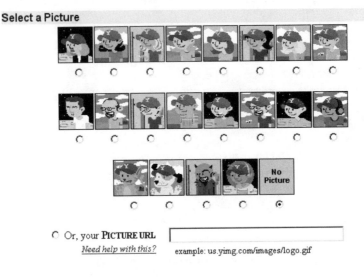

You can also specify the address of a voice file to add to your profile. If you don't have a voice file, there is a link that gives instructions for recording one for free over your telephone. You will get a phone number to call (which is not toll free) and an access code that lets you record and save a voice file on the Yahoo! Web site. After you hang up, you'll get an e-mail that explains how to link the voice file to your profile.

The Change Page Colors option in the Yahoo! Profile screen allows you to change the colors displayed in your profile.

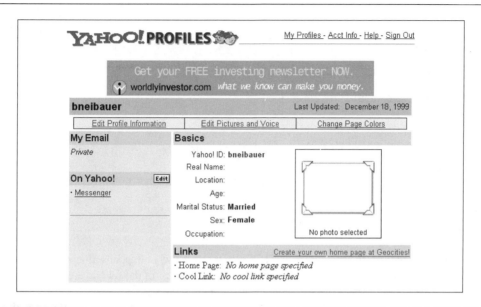

FIGURE 2-16   Editing a profile

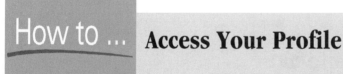 **Access Your Profile**

You can quickly edit your profile at any time by following these steps:

1. Click More on the initial Yahoo! screen.
2. Click Profiles.
3. Click Edit My Profile.
4. Enter your Yahoo! ID and password if you are not yet signed in.
5. Click Edit.

If you want your friends to quickly see your profile, give them this link:

http://profiles.yahoo.com/*User-ID*

as in

http://profiles.yahoo.com/aneibauer

Changing Your Mail Preferences

The Mail Preference option determines how your messages and Inbox appear. For example, you can change the return name and return e-mail address that is sent along with your e-mail, choose to save messages in the Sent folder, and remove the bulk mail folder where Yahoo! places unsolicited bulk mail.

Options for viewing mail in the Inbox include:

- Sort messages in ascending or descending order.
- Choose the number of messages to show at one time.
- Show brief headers or all message headers.
- Change the font size.
- Change the screen width for viewing messages.
- Change the screen width for composing messages.

There are also options for handling e-mail. You can choose what happens after you move or delete a message. The default action is to display the next message in the folder; but you can choose to go to a folder, such as the Inbox, rather than display the next message.

You can also choose the default action for forwarding mail, as an attachment or inline, and choose the number of lines in the original message to include when you reply to a message.

How to ... Set an Automatic Vacation Response

When you'll be out of touch for a while, you may want to send an automatic response to people who send you e-mail. This way, they know that you received their messages but are unable to personally respond to it at this time. With Yahoo!, you can create a response message that is sent automatically to everyone who sends mail to your Yahoo! address.

Start by choosing Vacation Response on the Options menu. In the screen that appears, specify the dates that you'll be away, and enter up to ten lines of text. You can also specify an additional ten lines that you want to send to one or two specific domains. Use these additional lines, for example, to send a special message to persons within your company or school domain.

Click Turn It On to activate the message.

Mail Management Options

Mail Management options generally let you control which messages are received and displayed in your Inbox. They also let you manage mail from other e-mail services.

Blocking Addresses

Junk mail is an unfortunate side-effect of the e-mail revolution. To reduce the amount of junk mail you receive, you can have Yahoo! automatically delete messages that were sent by specific senders. Deleting these messages automatically is called *blocking an address*. After you specify the e-mail address of a sender you want to block, Yahoo! deletes messages from the sender from your Inbox before you even have a chance to read them. You can specify up to a hundred addresses to be blocked.

Tip *See "Managing E-Mail with "Filters" and "Bulk Mail," later in this chapter, for more information about Yahoo!'s effort to reduce junk mail*

To add or remove blocked addresses, click Block Addresses on the Options menu to see the options shown in Figure 2-17. To block an address, enter it in the text box on the right and click the Block Address button. To remove a blocked address so you can receive mail from the sender again, select an address in the list on the left and click the Delete button. You will find it under the Blocked Addresses list box.

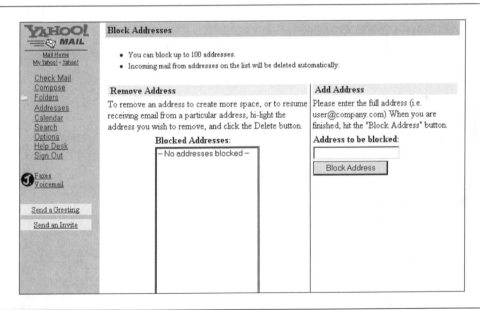

FIGURE 2-17   Blocking an address

Check Other (POP) Mail

If you have more than one e-mail account, you have to remember to check each account for new mail. Skipping an account and missing an important piece of mail would be easy.

To help you keep up with your mail, Yahoo! lets you use your Inbox form for more than just Yahoo! mail. You can designate other e-mail accounts to check from within Yahoo!, and in so doing, check all of your mail from one central location.

Now for the small print: You can only use Yahoo! to check mail from POP providers. *POP providers* are ISPs and Internet-based e-mail services that give you a mail server name that can be accessed with generic e-mail software such as Outlook Express and Eudora. AOL, for example, has its own e-mail system that is not POP, so you cannot check AOL mail from Yahoo!

To add up to three other POP accounts to your Yahoo! Inbox, you need to get some information from your ISP:

- The POP server name, such as postoffice.worldnet.att.net

- Your user name, which is usually the part of your e-mail address before the @ sign

- Your mail password, which may be different than your ISP logon password

To add the server to your Yahoo! account, select Check Other (POP) Mail on the Options menu. You can also choose Check Other from your Yahoo! Inbox or from the main mail screen. In the screen that appears, which shows mail servers you've already set up, click Add Mail Server to see the options shown in Figure 2-18.

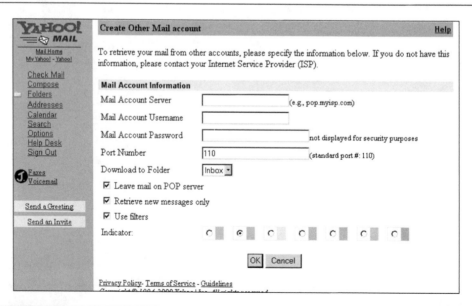

FIGURE 2-18   Adding a mail server

Enter the information requested, including the folder in which you want the messages to appear. Notice that options at the bottom of the form let you choose these settings:

- **Leave Mail On POP Server** does not delete the message from your ISP mail server when it is downloaded to Yahoo!. Choosing this option lets you later download the message from another mail program, such as Outlook Express. By choosing this option, you can check your e-mail from any computer connected to the Internet and retrieve it later into your e-mail program at home.

- **Retrieve New Messages Only** downloads just new messages to your Yahoo! Inbox.

- **Use Filters** applies filters (explained shortly) to the server's mail.

Each message in your Inbox will be color-coded to indicate the server that it was received on. The indicator option lets you choose which color to mark this server.

Click OK to return to the list of servers:

Add Mail Server						
Server Name	**User Name**	**To Folder**	**Use Filters**	**New Messages Only**	**Edit**	**Delete**
postoffice.worldnet.att.net	alann	Inbox	Yes	Yes	🖉	🗑	Check Mail

When you want to check your e-mail, just click the Check Mail link for the POP server.

Managing E-Mail with Filters

Another way to manage e-mail is to use filters. *Filters* allow you to channel mail to specific folders automatically. You can use a filter, for example, to move mail from your work domain to a special folder, or to automatically delete mail from a specific sender.

To add a filter, select Filters on the Options menu or from any other Yahoo! mail screen—you'll see it in several places. In the screen that appears, which will show any filters you already created, click Create to see the options in Figure 2-19.

Now, using the pull-down lists and check boxes, define the filter. That is, define how you want a message to be handled.

1. Select the field that you want to use for the filter: From, To/Cc, Subject, or Body.

2. Select the criterion: Contains, Does Not Contain, Begins With, Ends With.

3. Enter the text you want to compare with the field, such as a sender's e-mail address or subject.

4. Select the folder in which you want the message to be placed.

5. If you have more than one filter, you'll see up- and down-pointing buttons. Use these buttons to change the position of a filter. The filters are applied in the order listed.

Note *The check box labeled Forward to my Wireless Device lets you send e-mail to a page or cell phone, as described in Chapter 7.*

6. Click Save.

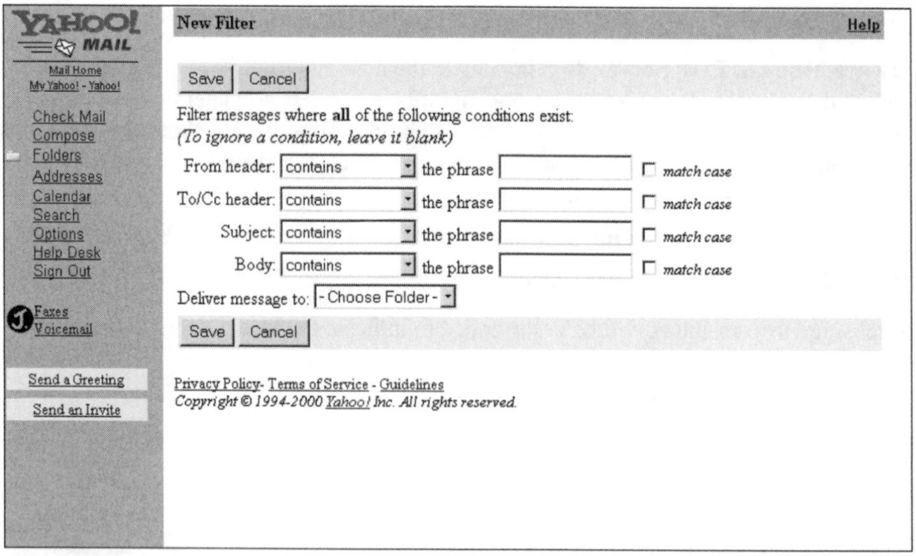

FIGURE 2-19   Creating a filter

Downloading to Another E-Mail Program with POP Access & Forwarding

Internet access to your Yahoo! e-mail is convenient because you can get mail from any computer on the Internet. However, you may find it easier to access your Yahoo! mail from home with a program such as Outlook Express or Eudora.

The POP Access & Forwarding option lets you download your Yahoo! mail to another e-mail program that offers POP service. You can also automatically forward your Yahoo! mail to another e-mail address. Forwarding is a good choice if your mail server does not support POP mail, which is the case with AOL.

Select POP Access & Forwarding from the Options menu to see the choices in Figure 2-20. Click Web and POP Access if you want POP access to your Yahoo! mail, or enter the address for forwarding your Yahoo! mail.

Finally, choose either HTML Messages or Text Messages Only under Step 2 and click the Submit button. Choose Text Messages Only if you are forwarding mail to an AOL account.

Delivery Services

Use these options to take advantage of special Yahoo! features:

■ **Yahoo! Delivers** lets you receive e-mail about special offers and discounts from Yahoo! and other merchants. You select categories of interest, enter your e-mail address, and select the frequency of notices—either once a week or one to three times a week. You also specify the format your e-mail system can read, either HTML or Plain Text.

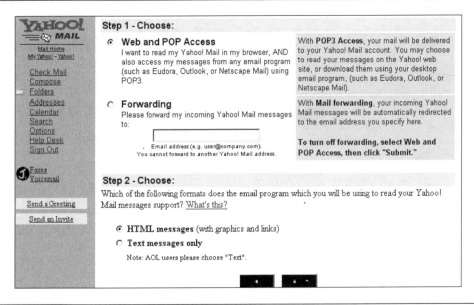

FIGURE 2-20   Forwarding mail to other servers

■ **Yahoo! Subscriptions** lets you sign up for online newsletters, including the Yahoo! Daily Wire, which offers noteworthy Web sites and news; Yahoo! Weekly Picks, which appears on Monday; and Yahoo! Weekly Live Wire, which comes out on Fridays.

■ **Reminders** lets Yahoo! send e-mail that reminds you of important events, such as holidays, birthdays, and anniversaries.

Address Book Options

In addition to the general mail options just described, you can customize Yahoo! by setting address book options. Clicking Options from the address book lets you make the following settings.

General Preferences

General Preferences settings let you specify the number of addresses to display in the address book at one time, as well as the default category to display. You can also choose not to use JavaScript to display your mailbox. JavaScript is a programming language used over the Internet to create interactive forms. You should only use JavaScript if you have a newer Web browser (version 3.0 or later) and are not accessing the Internet through a company firewall.

The General Preferences settings also let you specify the address to use as a default when your create driving maps that direct you to or from address book locations. You can specify a default phone number for conference calling as well.

Edit Categories

Which information is displayed in the address book depends on the category of contacts you choose to display. You can decide which information to display by choosing Edit Categories to open the screen shown in Figure 2-21. For example, the figure shows that when you choose to display Commercial contacts, the address book contains the company name, contact name, work phone, e-mail address, and tools that you select to display.

To change the information displayed or to select tools for certain categories, click the Edit icon for that category. You will then be able to specify which fields to display for that category. You'll also be able to select the Yahoo! tools that will be available from the address book. The options are shown here:

Tools (checked tools will appear in Tools column when applicable)

☐ Find Business	☐ Default Email*	☑ Other Email*	☐ Profile	☑ Maps
☐ Drive	☑ Y! Greetings			

Selecting Maps, for example, allows you to display a map and driving directions to a contact's address.

The Edit Categories option also lets you create new categories and choose which fields and tools to display.

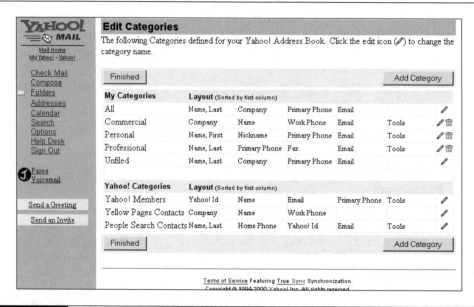

FIGURE 2-21   Options for address book categories

2

Import/Export

Yahoo! may be just one of the places where you store e-mail addresses and contact information. You can combine addresses from various sources by using the Import/Export option.

Importing means to add addresses from other locations, such as an Outlook Express address book, to the Yahoo! address book. *Exporting* means the opposite—adding contacts from your Yahoo! address book to the address book in some other program.

After you click the Import/Export option, you select whether you want to import or export addresses. To import addresses, you select the format and name of the file containing the addresses you want to add to Yahoo! To export addresses, you choose to add Yahoo! addresses to Microsoft Outlook, the Palm Desktop, or the Netscape address book. There is also an option to save the addresses in the CSV format. Choose that option when you want to export addresses to programs such as Outlook Express.

Printable Address Book

Suppose you just want to take a printed copy of your Yahoo! address book with you? The Printable Address Book option lets you display a special version of the address book that is suitable for printing.

You can either choose one of the standard formats or create a custom format for printing the address book. Standard formats include the summary layout and the detailed layout format. In the summary layout format, only the fields that appear when you choose to display all categories are printed. In the detailed layout format, all of the address book fields are printed.

You can also choose to create a custom layout by selecting from these fields:

Customize Layout Options

General Information

☑ First Name	☑ Middle Name
☑ Last Name	☐ Nickname
☐ Company	☐ Title
☑ Email	☐ Yahoo! ID
☐ Comments	

Phone Numbers

☑ Home	☑ Work
☐ Pager	☐ Fax
☐ Mobile	☐ Other

Mailing Addresses

| ☑ Work Address | ☑ Home Address |

Internet Information

| ☐ Alternate Email 1 | ☐ Alternate Email 2 |
| ☐ Personal Website | ☐ Business Website |

Select the check boxes next to the names of fields that you want to print.

When you have finished selecting a standard or custom layout, click Display for Printing. The address book opens in the layout you chose in a browser window. Click Print in your browser's toolbar to print the address book.

Edit Custom Fields

The Edit Custom Fields option lets you name up to four additional fields to display in the address book. Use these fields to track contact information that you can't track in the other fields.

Advanced Options

Choosing Advanced Options lets you delete all of the information from your Yahoo! address book. The page that appears warns you that the action cannot be undone. So once you proceed, all of the names and addresses in the address book are deleted and cannot be restored unless you enter them again.

If you decide not to erase your address book, click Cancel. To delete all of the addresses, click the link Delete All Contacts From Your Address Book. In the page that now appears, click Delete to confirm the action, or click Cancel if you change your mind.

Synchronize

You might already be recording contact and calendar information on your computer with programs such as Microsoft Outlook and ACT!, or using a handheld device such as the Palm Pilot, Palm III, or other device using the Windows CE operating system.

You can synchronize your computer or handheld device with your Yahoo! address book, calendar, and To Do lists, so all of your information is up to date in all locations. Choosing the Synchronize option shows you how to download a free program that will synchronize the information for you, even resolving conflicts in schedules and avoiding duplicate entries.

Working with Folders

The Inbox is only one location that Yahoo! provides for storing messages. In addition to the Inbox, your mail account includes these folders:

- Drafts
- Sent
- Trash
- Bulk Mail

Messages that are not quite ready to be sent are kept in the Drafts folder. If you start to compose a message but do not complete it, for example, click Save Draft to move the message to the Drafts folder. You can later open the message in the Drafts folder to complete and send it.

The Sent folder contains copies of messages that you have sent. The Sent folder is useful when you want to confirm that indeed you sent a message or you want to copy a message or parts of a message into another e-mail. By default, however, messages are not automatically placed in the Sent folder. By default, messages are deleted after being sent. To save sent messages in the Sent folder, open the Mail Preferences menu and choose Yes next to the Save Sent Messages option.

The Trash folder stores messages that you have deleted. Yahoo! places messages in this folder in case you change your mind later and want to retrieve them. After you delete messages from the Trash folder, they cannot be restored. You can delete the mail in this folder by selecting Empty Trash from the Inbox.

The Bulk Mail folder stores messages that Yahoo! automatically places there. Looking for certain words in the title or text of a message, Yahoo! determines if the mail is unsolicited junk mail. If an e-mail message is junk, it is sent to the Bulk Mail folder. Because Yahoo! stores messages in the folder for just 30 days and then deletes them, you should review the folder periodically.

To display your folders, click Folders in any mail window. As shown in Figure 2-22, you'll see a list of folders with the number of messages and unread messages in each one. Click the name of a folder to open it. Open folders look just like the Inbox.

You can create additional folders called *personal folders*. Personal folders are ideal for storing certain types of mail, such as mail from specific senders or mail that relates to certain topics. You can create a Business folder, for example, to store mail that pertains to your company, or a Team folder for messages from members of your bowling team.

To create a folder, enter the new folder name and click the Create New Folder button. Use the Rename and Remove buttons to change the name of or delete a personal folder.

To move mail from one folder to another, select it in its current folder, pull down the list next to the Move button, choose the folder in which you want to place the message, and click Move.

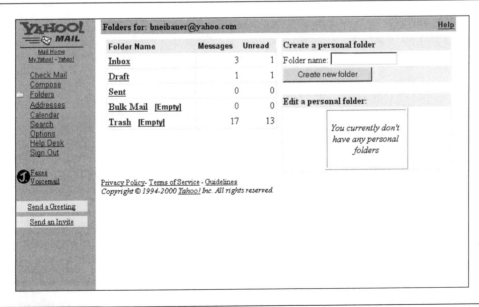

FIGURE 2-22   Click a folder's name to open it

Bulk Mail

Yahoo!'s bulk mail feature is a giant step toward reducing the amount of junk e-mail you receive, but it is not perfect. Messages can be placed mistakenly in the folder. A message you send to your spouse with the subject "Who loves you baby?" may accidentally be treated as bulk mail.

If you discover a message that Yahoo! mistakenly deemed a bulk-mail message, open the message and click the Send To Yahoo! For Review button. Yahoo! will reconsider the rules that classified the message as bulk mail. If you want to make sure you receive such mail even if Yahoo! does not change its rules, create a filter that channels such messages to your Inbox. The filter will override the bulk-mail classification, but only for your own mailbox. The overall rule will still be applied to other Yahoo! users.

If you do not want Yahoo! to apply bulk-mail rules to incoming messages, open the Mail Preferences menu and select Inbox in the Bulk Mail Delivery section.

Chapter 3

Personalize Your Browser with Yahoo! Companion

How to . . .

- How to add the Yahoo! Companion toolbar to your Web browser
- How to store your Internet bookmarks online
- How to get instant access to e-mail, news, and financial information
- How to create a custom My Yahoo! page

Now that you have a Yahoo! account, it's time to go beyond e-mail and start taking advantage of all the other features that Yahoo! has to offer. In this chapter, you'll learn two ways to customize Yahoo! and make your Internet experience more pleasant and efficient.

Yahoo! Companion

When you want instant access to the best features of Yahoo! and the Internet, customize your Web browser with Yahoo! Companion.

Yahoo! Companion is a special toolbar added to your Web browser window. While you can use Companion if you're not a member of Yahoo!, members get special features that make Companion even more fun to use. Use Companion to get

- Instant access to the Yahoo! home page and searches
- Bookmarks to popular Internet locations
- A place to store your bookmarks on the Internet for easy access no matter which computer you are on
- Stock quotes and an online portfolio
- Alerts when you get e-mail
- Personalized buttons and shortcuts
- The Stock Market toolbar for detailed financial information

Getting Yahoo! Companion

Most programs that you download are placed on your hard disk. You then run the program to install it on your computer. To install the same program on another computer, you can copy it to a floppy disk or a removable disk such as a Zip drive, or even send it to another person as an e-mail attachment.

When you download Yahoo! Companion, however, you actually install it as part of your Web browser. An installation program isn't placed on your disk. This means you have to download the Companion on each computer on which you want to use it. Downloading and installing Yahoo! Companion, however, takes only a few minutes.

CHAPTER 3:   Personalize Your Browser with Yahoo! Companion   **57**

3

To download and install Yahoo! Companion, follow these steps:

1. Connect to the Internet and go to Yahoo! at www.yahoo.com.

2. Click Companion in the list of items above the Yahoo! categories:

<u>Shopping</u> - **<u>Auctions</u>** - <u>Yellow Pages</u> - <u>People Search</u> - <u>Maps</u> - <u>Travel</u> - <u>Classifieds</u> - <u>Personals</u> - <u>Games</u> - <u>Chat</u> - **<u>Clubs</u>**
<u>Mail</u> - <u>Calendar</u> - <u>Messenger</u> - **<u>Companion</u>** - <u>My Yahoo!</u> - <u>News</u> - <u>Sports</u> - <u>Weather</u> - <u>TV</u> - <u>Stock Quotes</u> - <u>more...</u>

A screen shows you some of the benefits of Yahoo! Companion.

3. If you want to read additional details on this feature, click Learn More About Companion Here! Click Get Back To Yahoo! Companion when you have finished reading.

4. Click Get Yahoo! Companion Now. The Companion will start to download, and you'll see this dialog box.

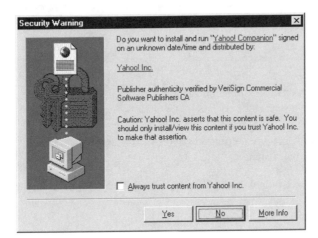

5. Click Yes.

6. If you have not already signed into Yahoo! with your ID and password, you'll see the instructions shown in Figure 3-1 along with the Companion guest toolbar, which is designed for persons who are not Yahoo! members. Another browser window will open in the background to tell you that you have successfully loaded the toolbar. You can close that window. Click Sign In, enter your Yahoo! ID and password, and then click Sign In again.

7. The Edit Yahoo! Companion window appears, shown in Figure 3-2. You can choose any of the standard toolbars or just click Finished to accept the default buttons. You can also click Make My Own to customize the toolbar. If you decide to customize, you'll get the same choices you get with the Add/Edit Buttons option, which are described in the next section.

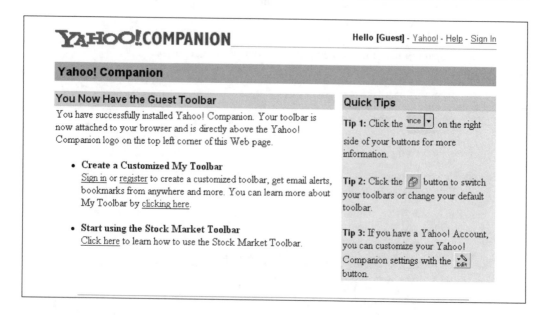

Instructions for using Companion

8. Click Finished. A message reports that you've successfully updated Companion. Now navigate the Web as usual.

After you sign in, the Companion toolbar appears and offers special features for Yahoo! members:

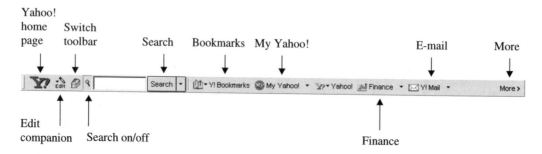

Note *You must be connected to the Internet for most of the buttons to appear.*

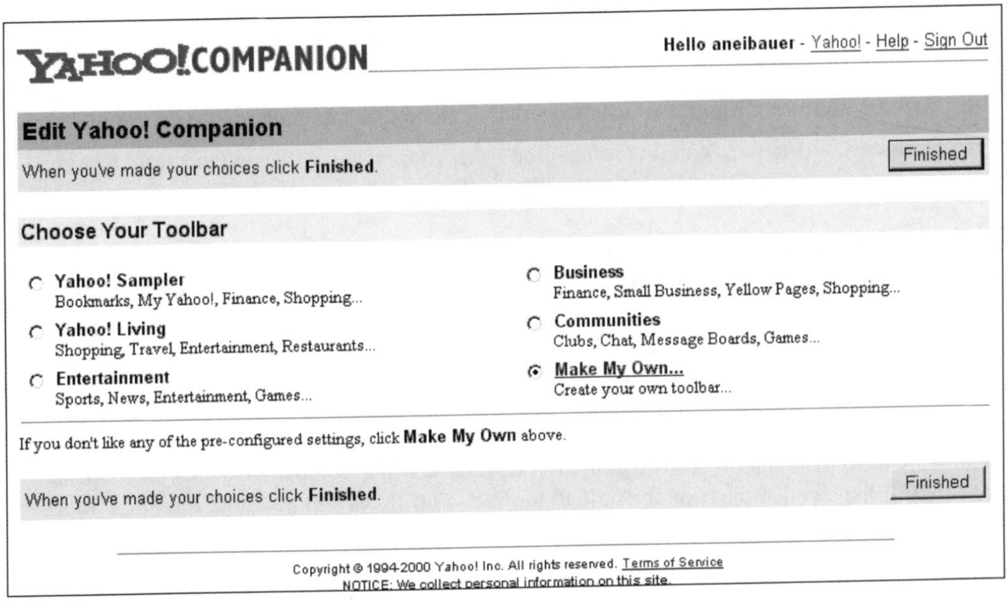

YAHOO! COMPANION
Hello aneibauer - Yahoo! - Help - Sign Out
Edit Yahoo! Companion
When you've made your choices click Finished.
Finished
Choose Your Toolbar
Yahoo! Sampler
Bookmarks, My Yahoo!, Finance, Shopping...
Yahoo! Living
Shopping, Travel, Entertainment, Restaurants...
Entertainment
Sports, News, Entertainment, Games...
Business
Finance, Small Business, Yellow Pages, Shopping...
Communities
Clubs, Chat, Message Boards, Games...
Make My Own...
Create your own toolbar...
If you don't like any of the pre-configured settings, click Make My Own above.
When you've made your choices click Finished.
Finished
Copyright © 1994-2000 Yahoo! Inc. All rights reserved. Terms of Service
NOTICE: We collect personal information on this site.

FIGURE 3-2 The Edit Yahoo! Companion window and the member's Companion

Each time you connect to the Internet, you'll have to sign in to Yahoo! to get your member Companion. Click the Sign In button on the Guest Companion. Enter your ID and password and then click Sign In. Your My Yahoo! page will appear. Now you're ready to navigate the Web.

Using Yahoo! Companion

The first button on Companion takes you to the Yahoo! home page. Click this button for quick access to all of Yahoo!'s features. Now let's take a look at the other default buttons in the Companion member toolbar.

Customizing Companion

Use the Edit button to customize Companion, get information about it, and remove it from your browser. Click the button to display these options:

- **Add/Edit Buttons** Lets you add and remove modules from your Companion toolbar. Of the 40 possible Yahoo! features for Companion, only 11 are shown by default.
- **Icons and Colors** Lets you choose between showing both icons and names for each button, or just icons. You can also choose between standard icons and color icons.
- **Refresh Toolbar** Redisplays the toolbar to reflect any changes made by you or Yahoo!

- ■ **Help**   Displays information about using the Companion.
- ■ **What's New in Yahoo! Companion**   Connects to a Yahoo! site that describes new Companion features.
- ■ **About Yahoo! Companion**   Displays the version of Companion on your computer.
- ■ **Uninstall**   Removes Yahoo! Companion from your browser. If you later want to again use Companion, you have to reinstall it from the Yahoo! Web site.

Switching Companion Toolbars

Companion actually includes two toolbars: the default customizable toolbar called My Toolbar and the Stock Market toolbar, which offers buttons for investment and financial services.

Click the third Companion button on the left to choose which toolbar to display or to make the one that is displayed at the time the default toolbar. You'll learn more about the Stock Market toolbar in Chapter 11.

How to ... Add Companion Buttons

To add new buttons to Companion or to remove buttons for features you are not interested in, follow these steps:

1. Click the Edit button on Companion.
2. Choose Add/Edit Buttons. You see a list of Yahoo! features, including Sports, Weather, Clubs, Message Boards, Maps, and Restaurants.
3. Select the check boxes next to the names of features you want on the toolbar; Deselect the boxes next to features you want to remove.
4. Click Update.

Getting E-Mail Alerts

If you are signed in and Yahoo! receives e-mail addressed to you, an Alerts button automatically appears in the Companion toolbar, as shown at right. Click the button to see the number of messages that you have received, and then click to open your Inbox.

Searching

Because the search engine is such an integral part of Yahoo!, it shouldn't be a surprise that Companion provides a convenient and powerful search function with a search box and menu.

By default, the search text box is displayed on Companion. If you do not want to use it for searches, you can click the Search On/Off button to remove the box. In so doing, you can make room on Companion for more Yahoo! features.

With the box onscreen, however, you can easily perform a search of the entire Internet or select a specific type of search. To perform a general search, enter a keyword or phrase in the text box and click the Search button.

If you are looking for specific type of information, enter the keyword or phrase, pull down the list next to the Search button, and choose from these options shown on the right.

Selecting News Photos, for example, will search the Internet for a photograph relating to your search text. Choose Address Book from the list to search your Yahoo! address book for a specific person. Choose Shopping from the list to locate a product you are interested in purchasing.

If you choose an option from the menu without entering a keyword or phrase, you see a form that you can fill out to continue searching. Selecting Address Book, however, opens your Yahoo! address book so you can see its contacts.

Using Bookmarks

Each Web browser has a bookmark list on its main menu or on a toolbar. Microsoft Internet Explorer, for example, calls bookmarks *favorites* and places bookmarks on the Favorites menu. When you find a Web site on the Internet that you'll want to return to, you add a bookmark. The bookmark notes the location of the Web site and adds it to the bookmarks or favorites list. The bookmarks are stored in a special file or folder on your hard disk. To instantly return to a Web site without surfing, you just pull down the browser's Bookmarks or Favorites menu and click the name of the bookmark.

If you access the Internet from a computer other than your own, your bookmarks will not be listed. For example, suppose you have several computers in your home or office. On the computer that you use most of the time, you add several of your favorite Web sites to the bookmark list. If you log on to the Internet on another computer, however, your bookmarks will not appear when you pull down the Bookmarks or Favorites menu. Instead, you'll see the bookmarks that belong to the person who usually uses the computer.

In addition, if you use more than one Web browser, you won't automatically be able to access the same bookmarks from each browser. A site you add to the Bookmarks list in Netscape Navigator, for example, does not automatically appear when you start Microsoft Internet Explorer.

Yahoo! makes bookmarks more accessible by letting you store them online. When you log on to the Internet using any browser on which Yahoo! Companion is installed, you can access your own custom bookmarks by signing onto Yahoo! with your Yahoo! ID and password. It doesn't matter which computer you are using.

If you have several computers in the house, for example, you can install Yahoo! Companion on each one. Then, in whichever computer you are using, just log on to Yahoo! using your ID and password for your bookmarks to be available.

The default bookmark list contains sites that Yahoo! thinks you'll be interested in seeing. An example is shown here.

Most of the bookmarked locations are interesting, so take a minute to look at them. Just click Bookmarks in Companion and then choose the topic you are interested in seeing.

The real benefit of Yahoo! bookmarks, however, is that you can add your own bookmarks. When you are viewing a site that you'd like to add to the bookmark list, choose Add Bookmark from the list. Yahoo! adds the name of the site to the bottom of the bookmarks list. Now all you have to do is choose the name to display the Web site.

Editing Bookmarks The bookmark list is totally customizable. You can delete bookmarks, change their names and the Web sites they represent, import your favorites list from Microsoft Internet Explorer, and export your Yahoo! bookmarks to Internet Explorer. You can add bookmarks that let you quickly send an e-mail, go to an Internet newsgroup, or open a file on your disk. You can also organize your bookmarks into folders, grouping sites by category or some other classification.

To edit your bookmark list, select Edit/Import Bookmarks from the drop-down menu to see the options in Figure 3-3. The list shows each of the default bookmarks. To remove one from the list, click its check box and then click Delete.

To add a new bookmark, even an e-mail link or newsgroup name, click Add Bookmark to see the options in Figure 3-4.

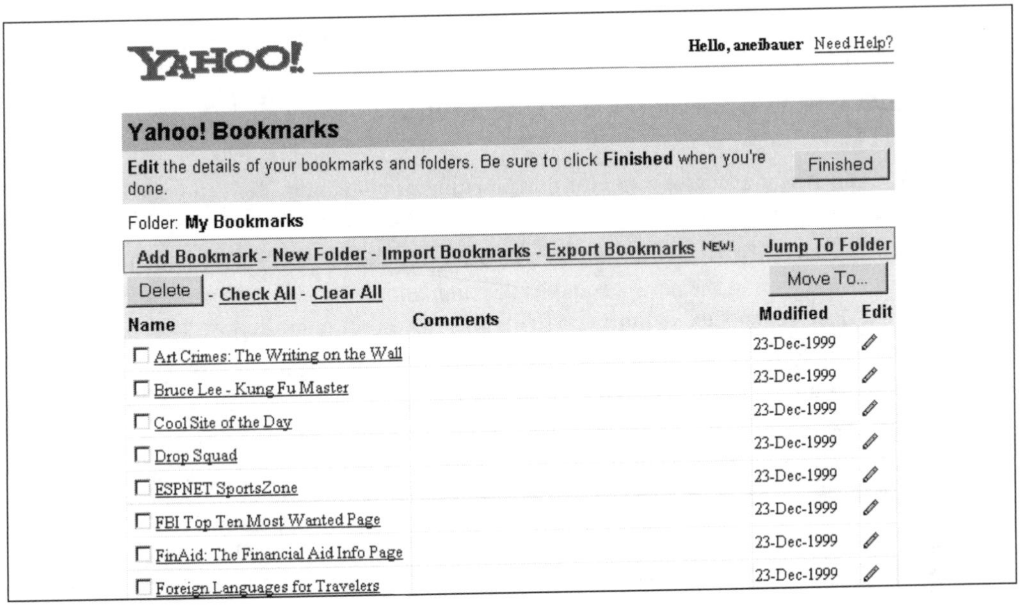

YAHOO!   Hello, aneibauer Need Help?

Yahoo! Bookmarks

Edit the details of your bookmarks and folders. Be sure to click **Finished** when you're done.   [Finished]

Folder: **My Bookmarks**

Add Bookmark - New Folder - Import Bookmarks - Export Bookmarks NEW!   **Jump To Folder**

Delete - Check All - Clear All   [Move To...]

Name	Comments	Modified	Edit
☐ Art Crimes: The Writing on the Wall		23-Dec-1999	✎
☐ Bruce Lee - Kung Fu Master		23-Dec-1999	✎
☐ Cool Site of the Day		23-Dec-1999	✎
☐ Drop Squad		23-Dec-1999	✎
☐ ESPNET SportsZone		23-Dec-1999	✎
☐ FBI Top Ten Most Wanted Page		23-Dec-1999	✎
☐ FinAid: The Financial Aid Info Page		23-Dec-1999	✎
☐ Foreign Languages for Travelers		23-Dec-1999	✎

FIGURE 3-3   Customizing Yahoo! bookmarks

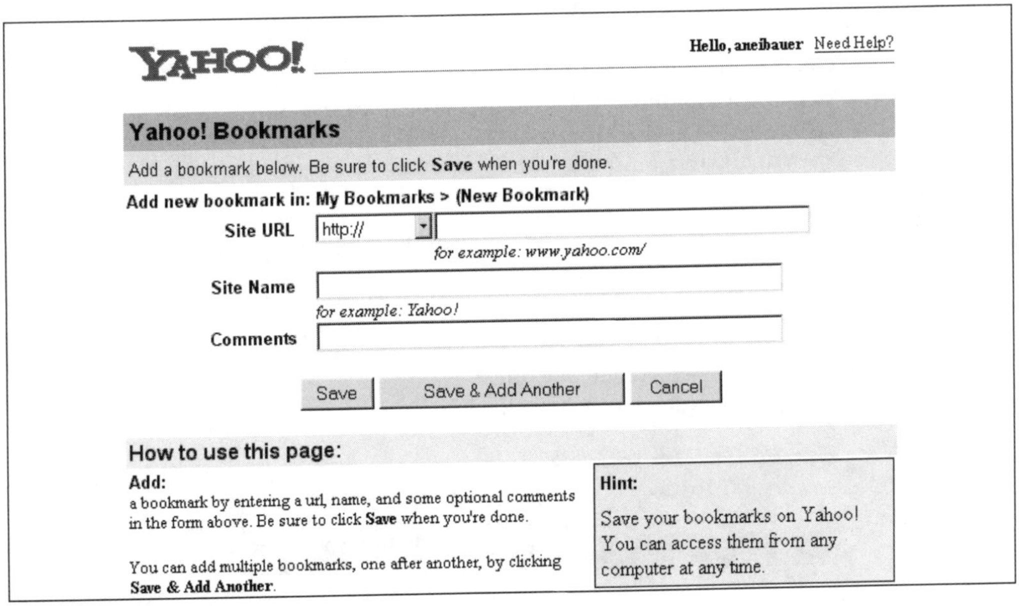

YAHOO!   Hello, aneibauer Need Help?

Yahoo! Bookmarks

Add a bookmark below. Be sure to click **Save** when you're done.

Add new bookmark in: **My Bookmarks > (New Bookmark)**

Site URL   [http:// ▾][   ]
            for example: www.yahoo.com/

Site Name   [   ]
            for example: Yahoo!

Comments   [   ]

        [Save]   [Save & Add Another]   [Cancel]

How to use this page:

Add:
a bookmark by entering a url, name, and some optional comments in the form above. Be sure to click **Save** when you're done.

You can add multiple bookmarks, one after another, by clicking **Save & Add Another**.

Hint:

Save your bookmarks on Yahoo! You can access them from any computer at any time.

FIGURE 3-4   Adding a new bookmark

Choose the type of bookmark from the Site URL list. The options are

- **http://** This is the prefix for the standard type of Internet Web site. The letters stand for Hypertext Transfer Protocol.

- **https://** Use this choice to connect to a secure Web site. Also known as Secure HTTP or S-HTTP.

- **ftp://** This prefix accesses a site for downloading or uploading files using the File Transfer Protocol, the protocol for sending files over the Internet.

- **telnet://** This prefix accesses a site in which you emulate a computer terminal to connect to a server on the network and issue commands as if you were at the server's console. Most Telnet sites require you to log on with a user name and password.

- **Mailto:** Use this type to enter an e-mail address. Clicking the bookmark opens your e-mail program with a message already addressed.

- **Newsgroup** Use this type to enter the name of a newsgroup that you can access to send and receive newsgroup messages. Selecting this type of bookmark opens your default newsgroup reader, such as Outlook Express.

- **Local file** Use this type to specify the name of a file on your disk that you want to access from the bookmark list.

In the box next to the pull-down list, enter the URL of the site, the e-mail address, the newsgroup name, or the path and name of the local file, depending on the type you selected.

In the Site Name box, enter the name that you want to appear in the bookmark list, and enter an optional description of the bookmark in the Comments box.

Click Save to add the bookmark and return to the Edit/Import Bookmarks page, or click Save & Add Another to remain in the Add Bookmark function.

Even after you've added a bookmark or a folder to the list, you can still edit it. Select the item that you want to modify and click the Edit icon on the far right of its listing to see a window similar to the one shown in Figure 3-5. Change the URL, name, or comment as desired, and then click Save.

Bookmark Folders As your bookmark list grows, you will find yourself scrolling up and down to display all of your favorite Web sites. To save time scrolling, you can organize bookmarks into groups called folders, as shown here.

To go to a bookmark in a folder, point to the folder name in the bookmarks list and then click the bookmark:

CHAPTER 3: Personalize Your Browser with Yahoo! Companion   **65**

3

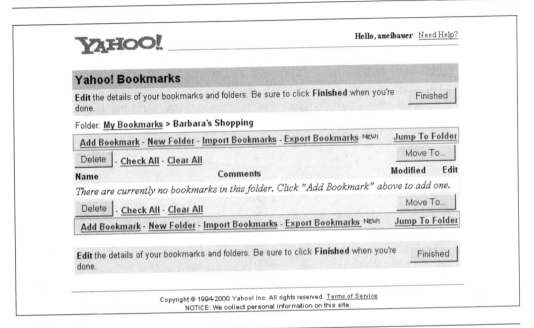

FIGURE 3-5   Opening a custom bookmark folder

How to ... **Send E-Mail from Companion**

Suppose you frequently send e-mails to a friend to let her know about interesting sites on the Internet. Rather than start your e-mail program and select her address manually, use the Yahoo! companion bookmark feature:

1. Click Edit/Import Bookmarks from the Companion Bookmark menu.

2. Click Add Bookmark.

3. Choose Mailto: as the bookmark type.

4. Enter the recipient's e-mail address.

5. Click Save.

When you want to send the person mail, just select the bookmark from the list. Yahoo! opens a mail window that is already addressed to the recipient who is named in the bookmark.

Start by creating a new folder to store a group of bookmarks. To do so, click New Folder, and, in the screen that appears, enter a folder name and optional description. Click Save or Save & Add Another to add the folder to your list.

Next, add bookmarks to the folder. You can add new bookmarks directly to the folder or move existing bookmarks into it.

To add bookmarks, you first have to open the folder. Either click the folder name in the bookmark list, or click Jump To Folder and then select the folder name in the list that appears. The folder opens with its own set of buttons and lists, as shown in Figure 3-5. Now add a bookmark just as you learned how to do for the main bookmark list.

Note *To return to the main list, click Jump To Folder and click My Bookmarks.*

If you already entered bookmarks to the main list and want to move a bookmark to a folder, you can move it to a folder. Select one or more bookmarks to place in the folder and then click Move To to see a list of folders. In the screen that appears, choose the folder in which you want to place the bookmarks and then click Move.

The Import Bookmarks feature lets you copy the items in your Internet Explorer Favorites folders to your Yahoo! bookmarks. By importing bookmarks this way, all of your favorites will be available whenever you are online and using Yahoo! Companion. Select Import Bookmarks to get step-by-step directions for importing bookmarks. You perform all of the steps online, directly from the screen. As the directions explain, you click a link that lets you run the Favtool.exe program over the Internet. This program converts the Favorites into a format that Yahoo! can import into the bookmarks list. You then choose another option on the screen to add the favorites to your bookmarks list.

The Export Bookmarks feature lets you save your Yahoo! bookmarks in a file on your computer in such a way that you can add your bookmarks to your browser's favorites list. Select Export Bookmarks to get step-by-step directions for the process.

My Yahoo!

Use the My Yahoo! Companion button to open and edit your custom My Yahoo! page. You'll learn more about My Yahoo! later in this chapter.

3

Yahoo

The Yahoo menu gives you access to the Yahoo! home page, My Yahoo!, your Yahoo! mail, and the Yahoo! features shown here:

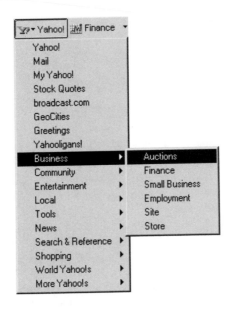

Selecting an item with an arrow at its right will display another menu of options.

Finance

The Finance button and menu give you access to a range of financial information, as well as your own private stock portfolio. Clicking Finance takes you to Yahoo!'s main finance information page, where you'll find information and links of all types. Pull down the list next to the button to see the options shown at lower right.

By creating your own portfolio, you can store a list of your investments and stocks you may be tracking and access them immediately. You can then display the total value of your entire portfolio by clicking Quotes Portfolio.

You'll learn more about this Companion feature, and investing with Yahoo!, in Chapter 11.

Y! Mail

Use the Y! Mail button to go your Yahoo! Inbox. Pull down the list next to the button for these options:

- Compose
- Send a Greeting
- Help

More

The More list shows additional features and links, such as those shown at right.

Use the list to navigate to various Yahoo! sites, as well as to other Internet sites.

My Yahoo!

As a Yahoo! member, you get up to six personal pages, each full of information that you will find useful. You can customize the pages, called My Yahoo!, to display just the information you want.

Use My Yahoo! to check your e-mail and stock portfolio, see how your favorite sports teams are doing, check the weather, and even see the day's television listings in your area. In fact, the page automatically shows information that is local to your community, such as weather, sports, news, and television listings. A typical My Yahoo! page is shown in Figure 3-6. Notice that you can include your own personal greeting, such as "Welcome Barbara!"

To access My Yahoo!, click My Yahoo! on the Yahoo! home page or click My Yahoo! on the Companion toolbar and then sign in with your ID and password if you haven't done so already. You can also click Sign In on the Guest Companion toolbar and then complete the sign-in process.

 *Go directly to My Yahoo! by going to this address: http://my.yahoo.com/.*

The My Yahoo! page is divided into two sides, a narrow left-hand side, and a wider right-hand side. The different sides of the page contain sections called *modules*. You can determine which modules appear and the contents of each module. You are restricted as to which side a module can appear on, however. For example, you can only place the TV listing module on the right side because it is too wide to fit on the left. The narrow weather module, on the other hand, can only be placed on the left side.

On the default page shown in Figure 3-6, the right modules are Headlines and TV, while the left column contains these modules:

- **Message Center** Shows the number of unread messages and offers quick access to your Inbox and Calendar

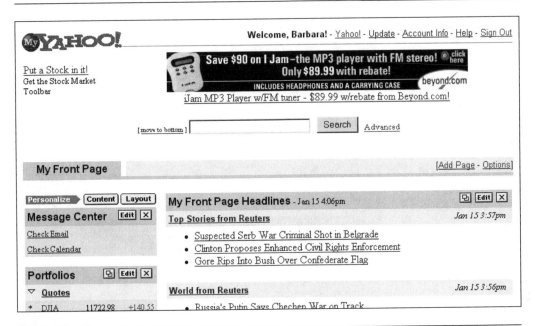

FIGURE 3-6   A typical My Yahoo! page

- ■ **Portfolios**   Lets you track the value of stocks and get stock quotes
- ■ **Weather**   Shows the temperature in your area and gives access to extended weather forecasts
- ■ **Scoreboard**   Shows the results of recent games played by your area's sports teams

There are quite a few ways to customize your My Yahoo! page. Let's take a look at them now.

Personalizing the Content

One of the first things you might do to My Yahoo! is to customize the content by adding and deleting modules (you can have as many as 20), and changing the title from My Front Page to something a little more personal.

There are two ways to add contents to the page, from drop-down lists and from a menu of modules. The drop-down lists provide a minimum of options, so let's look at them first.

At the bottom of the My Yahoo! page you'll find two lists: Add Left Side Content and Add Right Side Content. Pull down a list to choose the modules that you'd like to insert in the corresponding column and then click Add, as shown in Figure 3-7.

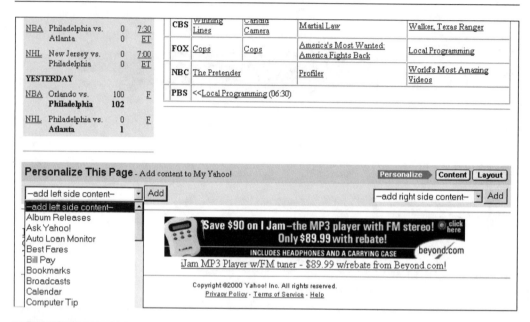

NBA	Philadelphia vs.	0	7:30
	Atlanta	0	ET
NHL	New Jersey vs.	0	7:00
	Philadelphia	0	ET
YESTERDAY			
NBA	Orlando vs.	100	F
	Philadelphia	**102**	
NHL	Philadelphia vs.	0	F
	Atlanta	**1**	

CBS	Winning Lines	Candid Camera	Martial Law	Walker, Texas Ranger
FOX	Cops	Cops	America's Most Wanted: America Fights Back	Local Programming
NBC	The Pretender		Profiler	World's Most Amazing Videos
PBS	<<Local Programming (06:30)			

Personalize This Page - Add content to My Yahoo!   Personalize [Content] [Layout]

—add left side content— [Add]   —add right side content— [Add]

—add left side content—
Album Releases
Ask Yahoo!
Auto Loan Monitor
Best Fares
Bill Pay
Bookmarks
Broadcasts
Calendar
Computer Tip

FIGURE 3-7 Adding content from My Yahoo!

On the other hand, to add and remove modules or change the name of the page, click Content (next to the Personalize icon) to open the window shown in Figure 3-8.

In the Page Name box, enter the name that you want to be your page title. Names can be up to 20 characters long.

Next, select the check boxes next to the names of the modules that you want to appear and deselect the boxes next to the names of modules that you no longer want on the page. The modules are grouped into 13 categories:

- My Yahoo! Essentials
- Business and Finance
- Health
- News & Weather
- Personal Finance & Shopping
- Personal Information Management
- Technology & Computing
- Community

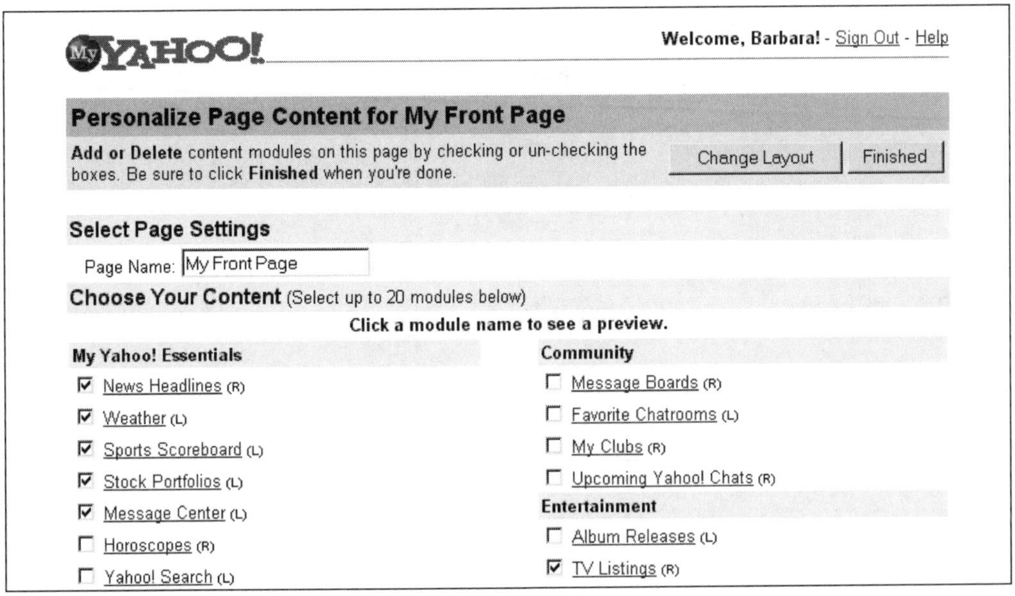

3

Welcome, Barbara! - Sign Out - Help

Personalize Page Content for My Front Page

Add or Delete content modules on this page by checking or un-checking the boxes. Be sure to click **Finished** when you're done.

Change Layout | Finished

Select Page Settings

Page Name: My Front Page

Choose Your Content (Select up to 20 modules below)

Click a module name to see a preview.

My Yahoo! Essentials	Community
☑ News Headlines (R)	☐ Message Boards (R)
☑ Weather (L)	☐ Favorite Chatrooms (L)
☑ Sports Scoreboard (L)	☐ My Clubs (R)
☑ Stock Portfolios (L)	☐ Upcoming Yahoo! Chats (R)
☑ Message Center (L)	**Entertainment**
☐ Horoscopes (R)	☐ Album Releases (L)
☐ Yahoo! Search (L)	☑ TV Listings (R)

FIGURE 3-8	Changing My Yahoo! content

- Entertainment
- Reference & Tools
- Sports
- Travel
- Web & Internet

A letter, L or R, indicates whether a module appears on the left or right side of the My Yahoo! page. Click Finished when you have finished making your changes. The modules for the categories are listed in Table 3-1.

Changing the Layout

You can also change the order of items in each column as well as the color scheme of your page. Click Change Layout when personalizing your content, or click the Layout button on your My Yahoo! page to display the options in Figure 3-9.

To change the order of a module in one of the columns, select it in the appropriate list and then click the up arrow to move the module up the column, or the down arrow to move the module down. To delete a module, select it and click the Remove button (the X).

Category	Modules
My Yahoo! Essentials	News Headlines (R)
	Weather (L)
	Sports Scoreboard (L)
	Stock Portfolios (L)
	Message Center (L)
	Horoscopes (R)
	Yahoo! Search (L)
Business & Finance	Company News (R)
	Upgrades/Downgrades (L)
	Zacks Earnings Surprises (L)
	Currency Converter (R)
	Small Business Tip (R)
	Small Business Features (R)
Health	Health Tips (L)
	Healthy Meal (L)
	Mayo Clinic Health Oasis (R)
	Nutrition Physician (L)
	Today´s Fitness Feature (R)
	Vitamins & Herbs (L)
News & Weather	Lead Photo (R)
	News Clipper (R)
	Broadcasts (L)
	Lottery Results (L)
	Traffic Reports (R)
Personal Finance & Shopping	My Auctions (R)
	Auto Loan Monitor (L)
	Mortgage Monitor (L)
	Bill Pay (L)
Personal Information Management	Address Book (R)
	Calendar (L)
Technology & Computing	Computer Tip (L)
	Downloads (L)
	Shareware (R)

TABLE 3-1   My Yahoo! Modules

Category	Modules
Technology & Computing	ZDNet Rumors & Content (L)
Community	Message Boards (R)
	Favorite Chatrooms (L)
	My Clubs (R)
	Upcoming Yahoo! Chats (R)
Entertainment	Album Releases (L)
	TV Listings (R)
	Movie Showtimes (R)
	Top Box Office Movies (L)
	New Movie Releases (L)
	Upcoming Movie Releases (L)
	Top Ten (L)
Reference & Tools	Yellow Pages (R)
	Maps (L)
	Phone Search (R)
	E-Mail Search (R)
	Saved Searches (L)
	Bookmarks (L)
	Package Tracker (L)
Sports	Ski Report (L)
	Team Calendars (R)
	Team News (R)
Travel	Best Fares (L)
	Destination Spotlight (R)
Web & Internet	Inside Yahoo! (R)
	My Yahoo! Announcements (L)
	Net Events (R)
	Web Site Tracker (R)
	Yahoo! Categories (R)
	My Local (L)
	Domain Registration (L)
	Ask Yahoo! (L)
	Daily Picks (R)

TABLE 3-1   My Yahoo! Modules *(continued)*

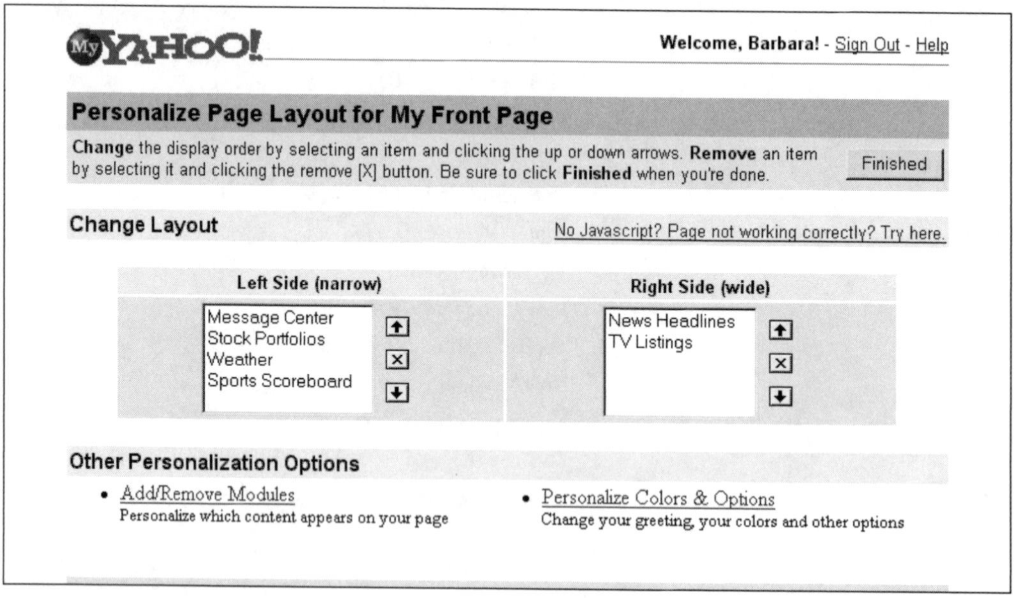

FIGURE 3-9 Changing the layout of My Yahoo!

Choosing Add/Remove Modules in the Other Personalization Options section lets you change the content of the page. Choosing Personalize Colors & Options lets you change the personal greeting from "Welcome, Barbara!" (or whatever your name is) to another greeting. You can also change the colors used for headlines, subheadings, and the background. You can choose from eight standard color schemes or select individual colors for a custom appearance. You can also choose how often your browser refreshes the My Yahoo! page so you can get the most current information.

Editing Modules

After you select which modules you want to display, you can do even more to personalize your My Yahoo! page by customizing each module's content.

Look at the three icons on the right side of each module header, shown at right.

The first button is called Detach. Clicking Detach places a copy of the module in a separate window in the foreground. With the module there, you can navigate the Internet and leave this window open for quick reference or links to other sites.

The Edit button displays options for customizing the module itself. Which options are displayed depends on the module. The options are in the following list.

- ■ **Message Center**   You can choose to display links to messenger, address book, personal mail alerts, and your online briefcase.
- ■ **Portfolios**   You can specify which stocks to display and create one or more portfolios, or groups of stocks.
- ■ **Weather**   You can select either Fahrenheit or Celsius, and choose additional cities to display.
- ■ **Headlines**   You can choose the categories and sources of stories to display, as shown in Figure 3-10. You can also choose the number of headlines in each category (from 1 to 9) and change the order in which the categories are displayed.
- ■ **TV Listings**   You can select your channel provider—the cable company, the metropolitan area nearest you for local listings, or a satellite company.
- ■ **Scoreboard**   You can select which results and schedules to display for professional sports, NCAA Football, NCAA Men's Basketball, NCAA Women's Basketball, and NCAA Hockey.

Use the Delete button next to a module name to remove the module from your My Yahoo! page.

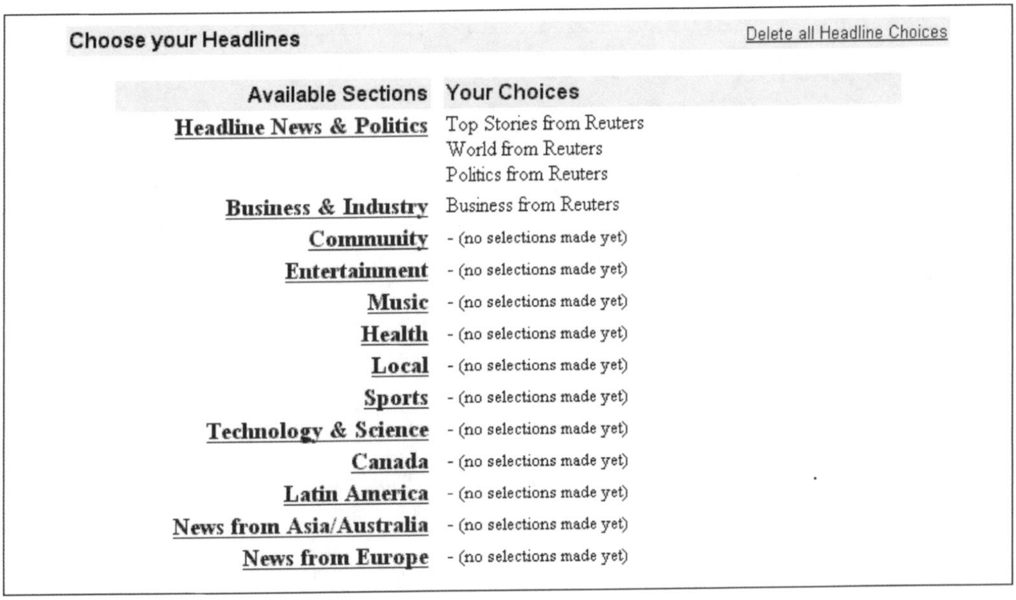

Choose your Headlines   Delete all Headline Choices

Available Sections	Your Choices
Headline News & Politics	Top Stories from Reuters
	World from Reuters
	Politics from Reuters
Business & Industry	Business from Reuters
Community	- (no selections made yet)
Entertainment	- (no selections made yet)
Music	- (no selections made yet)
Health	- (no selections made yet)
Local	- (no selections made yet)
Sports	- (no selections made yet)
Technology & Science	- (no selections made yet)
Canada	- (no selections made yet)
Latin America	- (no selections made yet)
News from Asia/Australia	- (no selections made yet)
News from Europe	- (no selections made yet)

FIGURE 3-10   Customizing your headline module

Adding My Yahoo! Pages

To add another page to My Yahoo!, click Add Page. You see the Create a New Page option, as shown in Figure 3-11. You can select a theme for the page or click Make My Own to display the Personalize Page Content options for the page. Here you can change the name of the page, choose which modules appear, or click Change Layout for the layout options. Your page appears on a tab on My Yahoo!, where you can click the page name to display it:

My Front Page	**Business**		[Add Page - Options]

After you create more pages, the Add A Page screen lists them, as shown here. You can click the links to delete, rename, or change the content of a page.

Your Pages (2 of 6)		
My Front Page	Delete Page	Rename/Change Content
Business	Delete Page	Rename/Change Content

If you have more than one page, you see extra options on the Personalize Page Content screen. Select the Set As Default check box to make the current page the one that is shown when you first enter My Yahoo!. Choose the Delete Page option to remove the page from My Yahoo!.

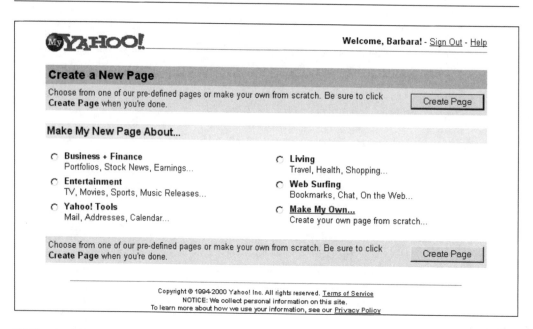

FIGURE 3-11   Adding another My Yahoo! page

Chapter 4

Manage Your Calendar Online

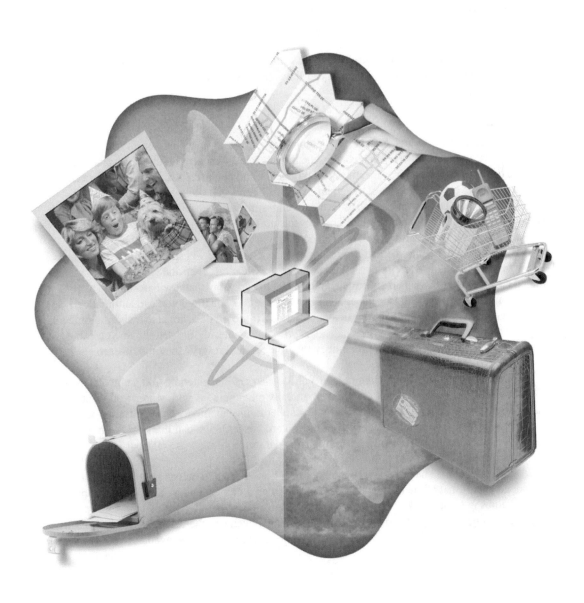

How to . . .

- How to store your calendar on Yahoo!
- Keep track of appointments, birthdays, and anniversaries.
- Send invitations to meetings
- Share your calendar with other users
- Add holidays and other events to your calendar
- Maintain a To Do list of things you have to do, and even your favorite television shows

Now that you're feeling at home with Yahoo!, it's time to take one more step toward making Yahoo! your Internet portal. With Yahoo!, you'll never miss an important date again.

Calendar Features

Before looking at the calendar in detail, let's look take a quick look at some of its features.

A calendar is a place where you record a schedule of events—an activity that takes place on a certain day. Some events, such as meetings, appointments, and phone calls, take place at a specific time, and some events have both a start and an end time. Events that occur at a specific time are called *timed events*. Other events, such as birthdays and anniversaries, mark a date on your calendar but do not reserve a specific time period. These events are called *all-day events*.

An event can be a one-time activity or can occur at intervals such as daily, weekly, monthly, or yearly. You could use the calendar, for example, to schedule a weekly staff meeting, a monthly review session, or a daily exercise class. You describe the event just once and tell the calendar how often it occurs. Yahoo! will automatically add the event to every day that it will occur.

When you use the calendar to schedule an appointment or meeting, you can automatically send e-mail invitations to the other participants. In fact, if the invitees are also Yahoo! members, they can quickly add the event to their calendars without re-entering the details. So you can use the calendar to schedule a meeting, notify the invitees, and reserve the time on each participant's calendar.

You can set up two types of calendars in Yahoo!—a personal calendar and a club calendar.

A *personal calendar* is meant for yourself and any other persons with whom you want to share your calendar. By sharing a calendar, you can let family members or business associates see selected calendar items so they know when you are busy. Others can mark an event that is on your calendar on their own calendars. Making calendar items public lets you easily publish a list of events for your company or circle of friends.

A club calendar is shared by every member of a Yahoo! club. You can post meeting notices and social events that all members should be aware of on a club calendar. You'll learn about Yahoo! clubs in Chapter 21.

In addition to adding your own activities and special events to the calendar, you can use a feature called Time Guides to track items such as sports team schedules, events from a friend's calendar, holidays, and stock splits. Because the calendar is integrated with other Yahoo! features, you can instantly add to your calendar Yahoo! chats or local activities that appear onscreen. If you see a TV program you want to watch on the Television listing module of My Yahoo!, for example, you can easily add it to your calendar so you don't miss the program.

You can have Yahoo! remind you of a scheduled event by sending you an e-mail or an instant message when you log on. Have Yahoo! remind you of an anniversary, for example, a few days beforehand so you can buy a card or gift. Reminders can be set from five minutes to 14 days before an event.

The calendar also lets you maintain a record of your To Do list. A To Do list stores tasks that you have to complete. You can specify a due date and have Yahoo! remind you as the deadline approaches. You can prioritize tasks to help organize your time, and make tasks appear on your calendar so they can be shared with others.

Yahoo! calendar and To Do list items, as well as address book entries, can be synchronized with Microsoft Outlook, Palm Pilot, Palm III, and other popular organizers and devices so your calendar is always up to date.

Understanding the Calendar

You have to be a Yahoo! member to take advantage of the calendar. If you are a member, access the calendar by clicking Calendar on the top of the Yahoo! window. If you have not yet signed on, enter your ID and password and then click Sign In to see a calendar similar to the one shown in Figure 4-1. If you are not yet a member when you go to the calendar, click the Get Your Own Yahoo! Calendar link to sign up for Yahoo! membership.

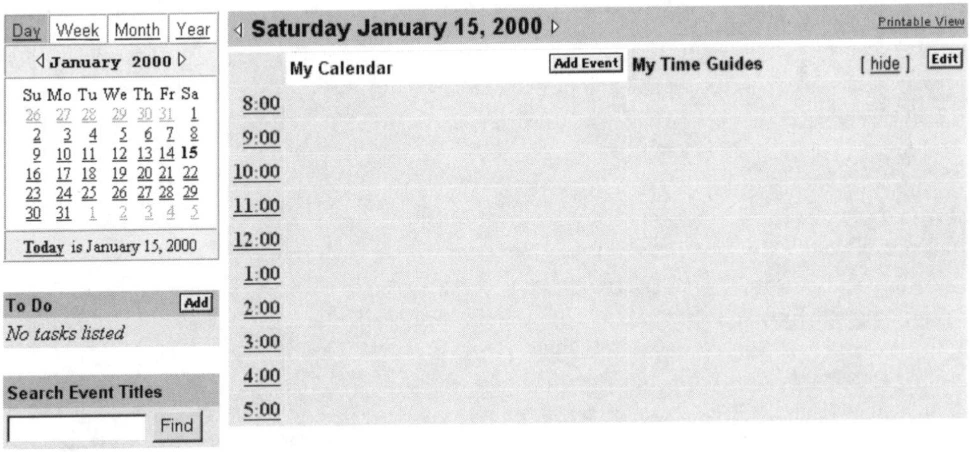

FIGURE 4-1   A Yahoo! calendar

The calendar shows the current date with the hours from 8 A.M. to 5 P.M. You can extend the times shown to track earlier and later events. The calendar has two columns—My Calendar for displaying your own activities, and My Time Guides for tracking other events. The miniature monthly calendar on the left is for displaying other dates. Notice the To Do list below the calendar. Below the To Do list is a Search Event Titles box that lets you search your calendar for activities.

To display the schedule for a certain day, click the day in the miniature monthly calendar. To quickly return to the current day, click the Today link at the bottom of the miniature calendar. Use the arrow icons on the left and right side of the month and year name to view different months. Click the left arrow to go back or the right arrow to go forward a month.

Tip *You can customize many aspects of the calendar's appearance, as well as its functions, by using Calendar options. See "Customizing Your Yahoo! Calendar," later in this chapter.*

The default calendar shows a single day, from 8 A.M. to 5 P.M., in one-hour increments. You can also display an entire week, month, or year by clicking Week, Month, or Year on top of the miniature calendar. In Week view, for example, the calendar displays seven days, starting with the current day of the week. Click any day to see an hour-by-hour list of events. A monthly calendar is shown in Figure 4-2. Notice that, in Month view, the miniature calendar displays the months. In Month view, clicking an arrow next to the year in the miniature calendar changes the month being displayed.

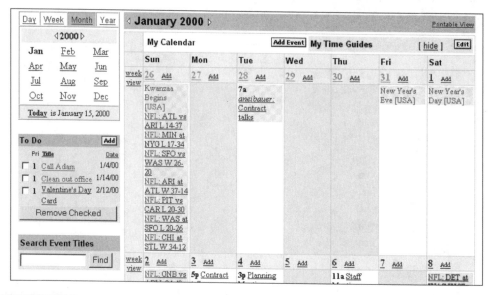

FIGURE 4-2   Yahoo! calendar in Month view

In Year view, you see 12 small monthly calendars, and the miniature calendar looks like this so that you click an arrow to change the year.

Scheduling an Event

When you are ready to add an item to the calendar, there are two ways to go about it:

- Display the date of the item and click the time.
- Click Add Event in the Calendar window.

In either case, the New Event window opens, as shown in Figure 4-3, so you can schedule the event. Follow these steps to schedule an event:

1. Enter a name for the event. The name you enter will appear on your calendar.

2. Set the date of the event. Either use the text boxes and pull-down lists, or click the calendar icon to select the date from a pop-up calendar, shown at right.

3. Specify either an all-day event or a timed event. An all-day event does not have a starting or ending time and is useful for entering events such as anniversaries, birthdays, and all-day meetings.

> **Tip** *Adding an event that occurs before 8 A.M. or after 5 P.M. automatically extends the times shown in the calendar window. You can also extend the time by choosing Calendar Preferences on the Options menu.*

4. If you selected a timed event, use the pull-down lists to specify the starting time and the duration of the event.

5. Pull down the Type list and choose the type of event.

6. Choose an option from the Sharing section:

   - Private prevents other persons from seeing that the event is scheduled at that time.
   - Public allows others to see the details of the event.
   - Show As Busy allows others to see that you have an appointment at that time. However, the details of the event are not shown.

7. Enter optional notes about the event. You can enter up to 120 characters.

8. Click Save to add the event and return to the calendar screen, or click Save and Add Another to save the event and remain in the New Event window.

Save	Save and Add Another	Cancel

New Event

Title   80 characters max.

Type
[Appointment ▾]

Date and Time
[January ▾] [15 ▾] [2000 ▾] [▦]

  ◯ All day event
  ◉ Timed event: [1 pm ▾] [:00 ▾]

    Duration: [1 ▾] hours [:00 ▾] minutes

Sharing   What's this?
  ◉ Private   ◯ Show as Busy   ◯ Public

Notes   120 characters max.

☐ **Repeating**   This event does not repeat.
☐ **Reminders**   There are no reminders for this event.
☐ **Invitations**   There are no invitations for this event.

Save	Save and Add Another	Cancel

FIGURE 4-3   Adding an event to the calendar

The event appears in the calendar like this:

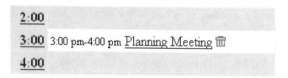

2:00

3:00   3:00 pm-4:00 pm Planning Meeting 🗑

4:00

If you want to remove an event from your calendar, click the trashcan icon to its right. The Delete Event window appears with a summary of the event so you can confirm that you actually want to remove it. Click Delete in the Delete Event window to remove the event or click Cancel if you change your mind.

To print a copy of your schedule, click the Printable View link to display a version of the calendar without the other Yahoo! links and buttons, and then click the Print button in your browser or select Print from the File menu.

Click the event—it appears as an underlined link—to see additional details about it or make changes to it. When you open an event, you'll see a new section at the end of the window, as shown next.

Want to tell others about this event?

Cut and paste the URL below and mail it to your friends. When they click on it, it will add the event to their own personal Yahoo! Calendars! Be sure to send your email in HTML format.

```
<A HREF="http://calendar.yahoo.com/yc/us/?
v=60&ST=20000104T150000&TITLE=Planning+Meeting&DUR=0100&VIEW
=d" target=_calendar>
```

If you want to notify persons about the event without sending them an invitation, copy the HTML text in the box and send it as part of an e-mail message.

4

To print the details of an event, click Printable View and then click your browser's Print button.

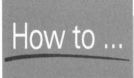

How to ... **Find Events in Your Calendar**

Dates for which events have been scheduled appear in a darker color than other dates in the miniature calendar. One way to check future events is to scan the miniature calendar and click the dark-colored dates.

As your calendar grows, however, you'll find it time-consuming to scan days for a particular event. To locate a specific event quicker, follow these steps to use the Search Event Titles text box:

1. Enter a word or phrase that appears in the title of the event you are looking for.

2. Click Find.

You will see a list of items that contain the text, as shown here:

Search Results for "meeting"

Date	Time	Event	Delete
1/4/2000	3:00 pm - 4:00 pm	Planning Meeting	🗑
1/6/2000	11:00 am - 12:00 pm	Staff Meeting	🗑

showing 1 - 2 of 2

Click a date to open the calendar or click an event title to see additional details.

Customizing Events in the Calendar

There are three additional sections in the New Event form:

- ■ **Repeating** Lets you schedule multiple occurrences of an event
- ■ **Reminders** Lets you have Yahoo! send you a reminder about an event
- ■ **Invitations** Lets you send e-mail notices about the event to other persons

To complete one of these sections of the form, click the plus sign (+) next to its name to expand the form. The plus sign changes to a minus sign (–) that you can use to collapse, or hide, a section of the form that you expanded.

Repeating Events

A repeating event occurs at a regular interval such as daily, weekly, or monthly. The repeating options are shown here:

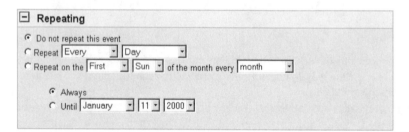

To schedule an event that occurs every day or at some other interval, select the Repeat option button. Then pull down the first list and choose Every, Every Other, Every Third, or Every Fourth. Next, pull down the second list and choose from the options shown here.

Use the Repeat On The option to schedule events on the first, second, third, or last occurrence of a particular day. For example, you could schedule an event for the first Monday of every month or the last Friday of every quarter (every three months).

By default, events are repeated indefinitely until you remove them from the calendar. To schedule an ending date for a recurring event, click Until and choose the ending month, date, or year.

 This icon indicates repeating events in the calendar. When you edit a repeating event, you'll be given the chance to apply your changes to all of the scheduled dates, just the future dates, or just the current event being edited, as shown here:

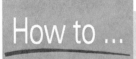

Create Reminders

4

Yahoo! calendar is a great feature, but you could easily miss an important event if you forget to sign into Yahoo! and check your schedule. To avoid missing activities, use the Reminders section to have Yahoo! send one or two reminders of the event.

The reminder can come as an e-mail or an instant message that pops up on your screen if you're running Yahoo! Messenger, or it can be sent to a mobile device such as a pager, cell phone, or portable information manager.

The options in the Reminders section of the New Event form are shown here:

> **Reminders**
>
> ○ Do not send a reminder
> ○ Send a reminder |—— ▼| before and |—— ▼| before the event via:
>
> ☑ Email: alan@hispager.com
> ☐ Yahoo! Messenger Get Yahoo! Messenger Have questions?
> ☐ Mobile device: [   ]
>   Enter email address for pager, cellphone, etc.
>
> **Note:** Your reminder(s) will be sent in **GMT -00:00 Greenwich Mean Time**. If this is not your time zone, change it in Calendar Preferences before saving this event.
>
> **Invitations** There are no invitations for this event.

Select the Send a Reminder option button and choose up to two times when the message will be sent. The options range from five minutes to 14 days before the event. Next, choose the check boxes for each of the ways you want Yahoo! to remind you (you can select any number of the three choices) and enter the e-mail address or mobile device number.

See "Calendar Preferences," later in this chapter, for information about setting your time zone.

Sending Invitations

The Invitations section of the New Event form lets you enter the e-mail addresses of persons you want to be notified about the event. Enter multiple addresses separated by commas. You can also click the Address Book link to add addresses from your address book.

When you save the event, the Send Invitations screen opens, as shown in Figure 4-4. Check the details of the invitations, adding or deleting recipients and making any changes needed, and

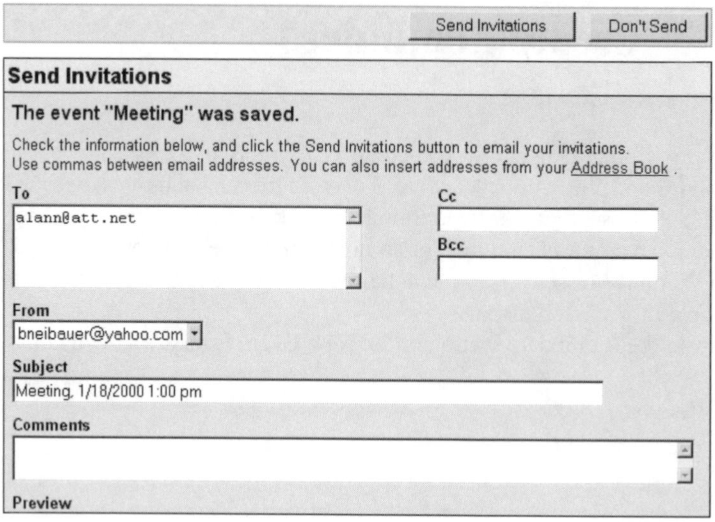

FIGURE 4-4 Sending invitations to an event

then click Send Invitations. Click Don't Send if you change your mind about inviting participants.

Invitation recipients will get an e-mail like this one:

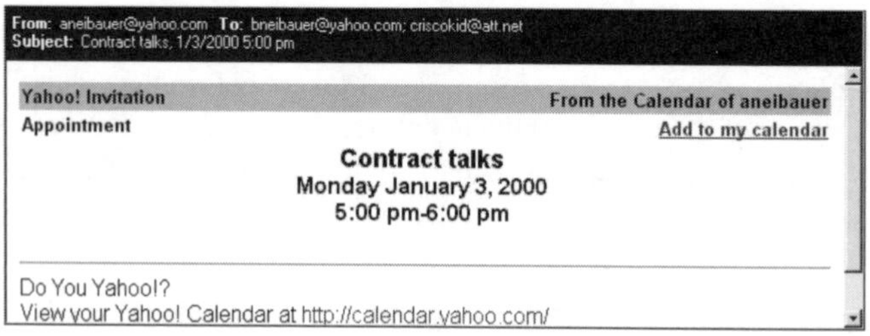

If an invitee is a Yahoo! member, he or she can click the Add to My Calendar link to connect, sign into Yahoo!, and automatically add the event to his or her calendar.

Setting Times Guides

Time guides are events other than your own that you want to track on your calendar. Use time guides, for example, to see when your favorite sports team is playing, when that big stock is set to split, or even when friends have meetings on their calendars that they set as public.

To add a time guide to your calendar, click Edit on the right side of the calendar to display the My Time Guides options shown in Figure 4-5. The category of items you can add to your calendar are shown on the left. Click the link under a category to select an event or item to add to your calendar. Select the Day, Week, or Month check boxes to determine the view in which the events will appear.

Note   *You cannot display individual calendar items in Year view.*

The categories of items you can add are

- **Clubs**   Click Join Clubs to select a Yahoo! club whose events you want to add to your calendar. Yahoo! Clubs are discussed in Chapter 21.

- **Financial Events**   Click Edit Portfolios to add stocks to a portfolio that Yahoo! tracks for you. You'll learn about portfolios in Chapter 11.

- **Friends**   Click Add/Remove Friends to enter the Yahoo! ID of persons whose calendars you want to track.

- **Holidays**   Click Add/Remove Holidays to designate the country whose holidays you want to add to the calendar.

- **Sports**   Click Add/Remove Teams to choose one or more teams whose schedules you want to add to the calendar.

My Time Guides   Back

Time Guides allow you to track your favorite events directly from your Yahoo! Calendar. View your friends' calendars, clubs' calendars, sports teams schedules and more from one place. Edit your Time Guides display options below and press the Save button to return to your Yahoo! Calendar. Learn more about Time Guides   Save   Cancel

Category	Time Guide	Show on Calendar Day	Week	Month
Clubs Join Clubs	No clubs selected			
Financial Events NEW! Edit Portfolios	Quotes	☐	☐	☐
Friends Add/Remove Friends	No friends selected			
Holidays Add/Remove Holidays	No holidays selected			
Sports Add/Remove Teams	No sports selected			

Layout
Choose how to show Time Guides on your Calendar.

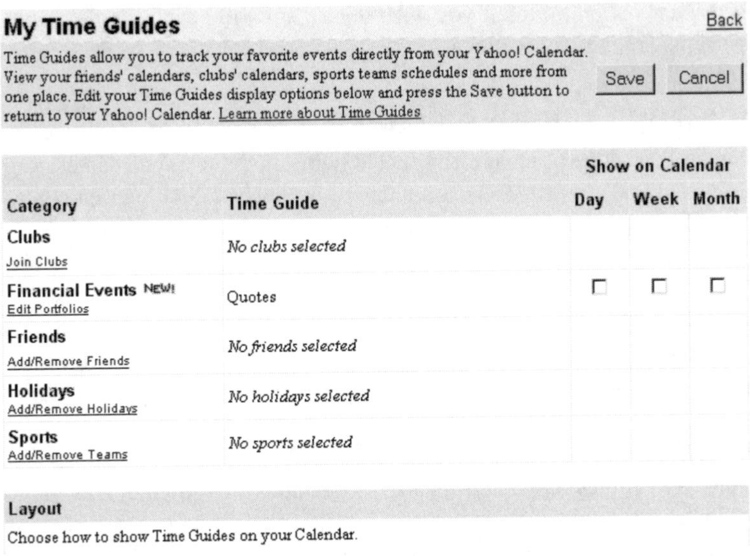

FIGURE 4-5   Adding a time guide to your calendar

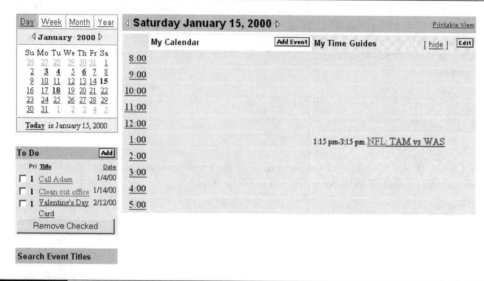

FIGURE 4-6   Calendar with time guides

Figure 4-6 shows a calendar with some time guides added.

The Layout options in the My Time Guides window determine where the time guide events appear. By default, time guide events appear in a separate column on the right side of the calendar. Select the Merged View option button if you want the calendar to have a single column in which your time guide events are merged with Yahoo's!.

Customizing Your Yahoo! Calendar

Because the calendar is designed to make you feel at home at Yahoo!, you can customize the way the calendar works and appears. Access a menu of options by clicking Options on the upper-right corner of the calendar window. Click the option you want to change.

Let's review the 12 categories of options that are available.

Calendar Preferences

Before adding too many events to your Yahoo! calendar, check out these options first. Choose Calendar Preferences on the Options menu to change these settings:

- **Default View**   Select Day, Week, Month, or Year.
- **Day View Grid Interval**   Determines the time intervals shown in Day view. Options are 15 minutes, 30 minutes, and 1 hour.

- **Week View Start Day**   By default, Week view shows seven days starting with the current day. Use this option to start each week with a specific day, such as Sunday or Monday.

- **Time Zone**   By default, Yahoo! assumes all calendar times are Greenwich Mean Time (GMT), the time of day in Greenwich, England. This standard convention is used to synchronize schedules all over the world. If you coordinate your schedule with other persons in different time zones, however, you can choose your time zone so that all events are shown in local time.

- **Daylight Savings Time**   Select this option if you want to set daylight savings time on or off, or you want Yahoo! to automatically adjust your calendar for daylight savings time.

- **Working Hours**   Set the default starting and ending times displayed in Day view on the calendar.

Click Save after setting your preferences.

Holiday Selections

You'll probably want to display holidays on your calendar so you know when you're having days off, or to be reminded to send a Valentine's Day or other holiday card. You can add

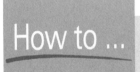

How to ... Share Your Calendar

By sharing your calendar, you let other Yahoo! members see your public events.

To share your calendar, click Calendar Sharing on the Options menu, and then, in the screen that appears, select the check box labeled Allows Others To View This Calendar. Your schedule will be stored in a location on the Internet such as this:

```
http://calendar.yahoo.com/public/aneibauer
```

Other Yahoo! members can then add your Yahoo! ID to the Friends section of the Time Guides. Any events that you designated as public will then appear on their calendars.

This option also lets you set the default permission assigned to all new events—Public, Private, or Show As Busy.

holidays from your own country as well as other countries to make it easier to work with international friends and clients.

Click Holiday Selections to see these main options:

- North American
- Latin American
- European
- Asian
- Oceania
- Religious

Choose the category for the holidays you want to add and then make your selections from the options that appear. Repeat the process for each set of holidays you want on your calendar, and then click Finished. Holidays appear in the My Time Guides column of the calendar, as shown here:

Advanced Options

This option presents only one choice: Delete All Events and To Do Items From Your Calendar. Selecting this choice deletes all events, time guides, and To Do tasks from your calendar. This option cannot be undone, so use it carefully.

Import and Export

You can move information among your Yahoo! calendar, Microsoft Outlook, and a handheld device that accesses the Palm Desktop software. Palm Desktop is a program that lets you move information between your handheld device and your computer.

If you already created a calendar in Microsoft Outlook, for example, you can import the appointments, meetings, and events into your Yahoo! calendar. You can also export items from Yahoo! to your Outlook calendar or Palm Pilot.

Choosing Import/Export from the Options menu presents you with four choices:

- Import from Palm Desktop
- Export to Palm Desktop
- Import from Outlook
- Export to Outlook

The Import from Palm Desktop option lets you bring your Palm's date book information into your Yahoo! calendar. First, use the features of your Palm device to save the date book information to a file on your computer. Then click Import/Output from the Options menu, specify the name of the Date Book Archive (DBA) file, and click Import Now under the Import From Palm Desktop section.

> **Note** *The Import/Export menu includes links to topics that show you how to import and export from Palm Desktop and Microsoft Outlook.*

Export to Palm Desktop saves your Yahoo! calendar as a Date Book Archive file that you can load into your Palm device. Just click Export Now under the Export to Palm Desktop section, and then use your Palm device to import the file.

Import from Outlook lets you bring your Microsoft Outlook schedule into Outlook. First, use Outlook to save its calendar as a Comma Separated Value (CSV) file. Then, in the Import from Outlook section, enter the path and name of the CSV file and click Import Now.

Finally, Export to Outlook saves your Yahoo! calendar information as a CSV file that you can import into Outlook. Click Export Now in the Export to Outlook section, start Outlook, and import the file into its calendar.

Reminder Options

Use the reminder options, shown in Figure 4-7, to set how and when Yahoo! reminds you of calendar events.

You can have Yahoo! send reminders to you via e-mail, as a Yahoo! instant message, or to a mobile device such as a pager. You can also have reminders sent for all new calendar events. Choose the Always Send A Reminder check box and then set one or two lead times. You can choose, for instance, to be reminded one hour before and then five minutes before an event.

> **Note** *You must download and run Yahoo! Messenger to receive instant messages and reminders.*

Time Guides

Choosing Time Guides on the Options menu lets you set and change time guides as discussed in "Setting Time Guides" earlier in this chapter.

To Do List Options

Select To Do List on the Options menu when you want to change the way completed To Do tasks are displayed. When you mark a To Do task as completed, it is no longer displayed by default on the To Do list. With this option, however, you can choose to display the item in the calendar on the day the task was completed.

Synchronizing Calendars

In addition to using the Yahoo! calendar, you may be recording appointments and other events in programs such as Microsoft Outlook and or in handheld devices. Maintaining multiple schedules can be time-consuming because you have to enter events more than one time. If you're using both Outlook and Yahoo! for scheduling, for example, you have to enter an appointment in Microsoft Outlook and enter it again in your online Yahoo! calendar.

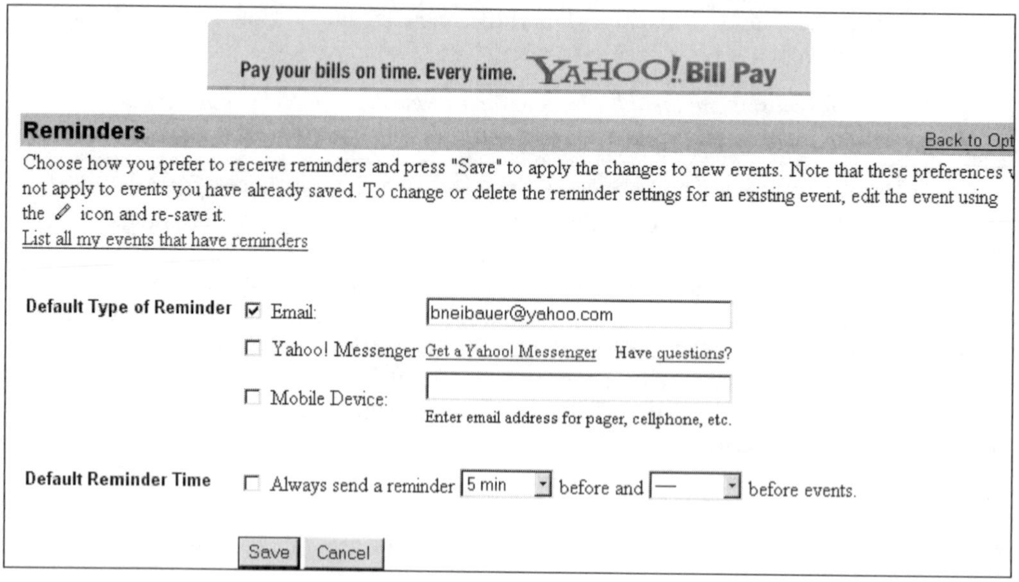

Pay your bills on time. Every time. YAHOO! Bill Pay

Reminders Back to Opt

Choose how you prefer to receive reminders and press "Save" to apply the changes to new events. Note that these preferences not apply to events you have already saved. To change or delete the reminder settings for an existing event, edit the event using the ✎ icon and re-save it.

List all my events that have reminders

Default Type of Reminder ☑ Email: bneibauer@yahoo.com

☐ Yahoo! Messenger Get a Yahoo! Messenger   Have questions?

☐ Mobile Device:
Enter email address for pager, cellphone, etc.

Default Reminder Time ☐ Always send a reminder [5 min ▼] before and [— ▼] before events.

[Save] [Cancel]

FIGURE 4-7   Setting reminders for calendar events

If you neglect to add an appointment to one of the calendars, your schedules do not match, and you have to check both locations to be sure not to miss an event. When you maintain more than one calendar, you should synchronize them so they all contain the same information.

Synchronization means that any additions, deletions, or changes to calendar items in one location are automatically made to the other. So you can add an appointment to Outlook on your desktop or laptop computer, and then update your Yahoo! calendar so it contains a complete record of your activities. All of your events will then be accessible from your own computer or handheld device, as well as from any computer with access to the Internet and your Yahoo! calendar.

Yahoo! lets you synchronize your calendar information, To Do items, and address book entries with these devices and systems:

- Outlook
- Palm devices (Pilot, III, V, VII)
- Palm Desktop
- WinCE devices
- ACT!
- REX Pro

To synchronize information, you have to download and install a free program called TrueSync. The TrueSync program synchronizes your calendars by automatically deleting duplicate events and resolving scheduling conflicts. Follow these steps to get started:

1. Choose Synchronize on the Options menu.

2. In the screen that appears, click Download and follow the instructions on the screen. An installation program will be downloaded to your computer. Note its name and the location where it is stored.

3. When the download is complete, and while you are still connected to the Internet, run the installation program that was downloaded by double-clicking it. A series of windows lets you select options and complete the process.

4. Click Next in the first window, which reports that you are installing the components from the Internet.

5. Read the program's license agreement and then click Next.

6. In the list of components that you can download, select the options for the devices and applications that you have. You have to select the TrueSync Plus and Yahoo! options, as well as options for the other programs or devices with which you want to synchronize. Click Next.

7. Click Next in the window that reports where the components will be stored on your disk.

8. Click Finish when the screen shows that all of the components of the program have been installed, as shown in Figure 4-8.

9. The TrueSync Plus for Yahoo! Setup Wizard will begin to configure the program for your system. Click Next.

The following components were successfully installed.

Component	Status
TrueSync Plus	Installed
Yahoo!	Installed
Outlook 2000	Installed

FIGURE 4-8   Report that your components have been installed

10. Choose the desktop application that you want to synchronize, such as Outlook 2000, and then click Next.

11. Enter your Yahoo! ID and password and then click Next.

12. You can now choose the type of permissions. You can assign all items the default Yahoo! permissions or the default permissions for your desktop application. Click Next.

13. Choose how you connect to the Internet, either through a dial-up account with a modem or by a local area network, and then click Next.

14. Click Next to have TrueSync get the information it needs from your application or connected devices.

15. TrueSync will connect to the Internet and get your calendar information from Yahoo! Click Next.

You will now be able to confirm or change the information that is found in the address book, calendar, and To Do list in Yahoo! and information in your other program or device. For example, you can select which category of contacts from the Yahoo! address book is synchronized with your Microsoft Outlook Contacts folder. Which screens appear next depends on the program or device with which you are synchronizing.

Let's look at what appears when synchronizing with Microsoft Outlook because all three elements—the address book, calendar, and To Do list—are synchronized when you are dealing with Outlook.

16. TrueSync lets you select which Yahoo! contacts are synchronized. As shown in Figure 4-9, TrueSync matches the Yahoo! contacts in the unfilled category with the contacts folder in Outlook 2000. You can use the pull-down lists to change the matching as needed, choosing another category of contacts that will be synchronized. Click Next when you have finished.

17. You can specify which fields are matched. Select from these options and then click Next:

- Names and numbers only
- Names, numbers, and addresses
- All matching fields

18. A screen appears so you can confirm or change the matching between the Yahoo! calendar with Outlook's calendar. Click Next.

19. A screen appears so you can confirm or change the matching between the Yahoo! To Do list with the Outlook Task folder. Click Next.

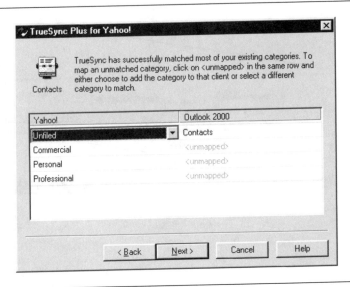

FIGURE 4-9   Confirming matching information

20. Click Finish to see these options:

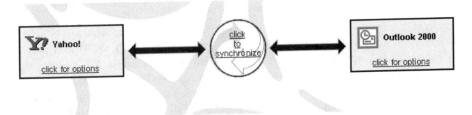

21. Use the Click To Synchronize button to start the process and synchronize your information. You can also choose the Click For Options link to customize the settings for your Yahoo! and desktop data or application.

22. TrueSync will complete the process and display a log, as shown in Figure 4-10. Click OK.

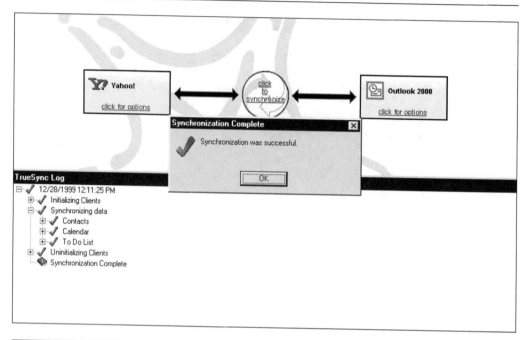

FIGURE 4-10   Synchronization log

You can later run TrueSync whenever you need to synchronize your information again. Choose TrueSync from the Start menu, or, depending on your system, click the TrueSync icon in the system tray on the taskbar. You can use the Client menu on the TrueSync toolbar to change your Yahoo! and application options and to add other applications, devices, and services to be synchronized. Use the Data menu option to change the mapping of contacts, calendar items, and To Do items. Icons for starting and stopping synchronization, as well as configuring contacts, calendars, and To Do lists, are on the TrueSync toolbar.

Group Calendar

The Group Calendar selection in the Options menu lets you join or create a club. You can then access the club's calendar. You'll learn more about clubs in Chapter 21.

Help

Choose Help on the Options menu to get answers to frequently asked questions about Yahoo! calendar. You'll also see links to Yahoo! mail, a link for reporting a calendar bug, a link for making suggestions, and a link to Yahoo!'s general online help area.

4

Account Information

Choose Account Information on the Options menu to access your Yahoo! account. You can change your password and edit the personal information stored as part of your Yahoo! profile.

Creating a To Do List

We all have tasks to perform, chores to do, and calls to make. To make it easier to remember the things you have to do, create a list of your tasks on your Yahoo! calendar. The To Do list is an area where you leave reminders to yourself about tasks you have to perform, as shown here.

To Do		Add
Pri	Title	Date
☐ 1	Call Adam	1/4/00
☐ 1	Clean out office	1/14/00
☐ 1	Valentine's Day Card	2/12/00
	Remove Checked	

To add an item to the To Do list, follow these steps:

1. Sign on to your Yahoo! calendar.
2. Click Add in the To Do list to open the window shown in Figure 4-11.
3. Enter a title, up to 35 characters.
4. Specify the date by which you'd like to complete the task, or click No Due Date.
5. Set the task's priority, from 1 to 5.

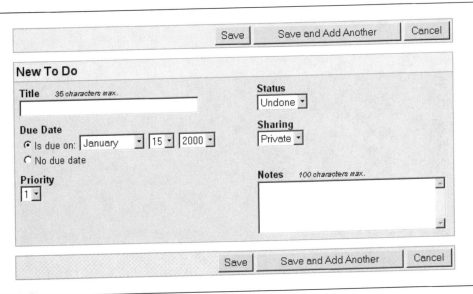

FIGURE 4-11   Adding a To Do task

6. Confirm the Status, either Undone or Done.

7. Select Public under Sharing if you want to publish the task to your public calendar.

8. Enter up to 100 characters of notes.

9. Click Save or Save And Add Another.

When you return to the calendar, a note appears showing that you have added, or updated, an item in your To Do list:

The To Do <u>Clean out office</u> was added to your To Do list.

When you complete a task, click it in the To Do list and choose Done from the Status list. By default, completed tasks are not shown in the To Do list. By choosing the To Do List feature on the Options menu, however, you can display the item in the calendar on the day the task was completed.

To sort the items in your To Do list, click Pri (Priority), Title, or Date. The column head that is not underlined shows how the list is currently sorted.

Chapter 5

Yahoo! for the Family

How to . . .

- Verify that you are qualified to create a family account
- Protect children from seeing adult-oriented material with a family account
- Set up a family account
- Add children to an account
- Access special features for seniors

Yahoo! has made accommodations for two very special parts of the family—children and seniors.

If you have children and you are concerned about their exposure to the Internet, Yahoo! is a great place to be. Yahoo! provides a feature called Family Accounts with which you can control what Yahoo! features your children access. You can also direct your children to Yahooligans, a Yahoo! feature that specializes in safe surfing for children.

Creating a family account is easy. You create a separate Yahoo! account for each child, and then add each child to your family account. Specifying the child's birthdate lets Yahoo! know which features should be available to the child. When your child logs on to Yahoo!, the permissions granted to his or her part of your family account are enforced.

Yahoo! also hasn't forgotten about the senior members of the family. The Yahoo! Seniors' Guide offers a great place for seniors to learn and have fun.

Verifying Adulthood

In order to create a family account, you have to prove to Yahoo! that you are an adult. Yahoo! gets its proof by examining your credit card number. Yahoo! verifies your credit card number and name with your bank, but don't worry about being charged. You will not be charged a thing, as all Yahoo! services are still free.

The card is just used to verify that you are an adult, and the credit card information is not retained after it has been verified. A record that you have been verified *is* maintained, however, so you can add children to your family account without going through the verification process again. Yahoo! uses a secure server when you submit the credit card number to prevent others on the Internet from seeing the information. When you arrive at the Web page where Yahoo! asks for a credit card number, look at your browser's address box. Instead of the notation *http://* before the address of the Web site, you see the *https://* notation. The letter *s* indicates a secure transmission. If *https://* does not appear, you may need to update your browser to a newer version.

 *Setting up a family account is the only time Yahoo! asks for a credit card number.*

5

What Is a Family Account

Before creating your family account, you should have a clear idea of exactly what a family account is and what it is not.

A child under 13 years old who is registered with a family account is not allowed to do the following:

- Create a public profile.
- Add their address and telephone number to their account.
- Start a Yahoo! club.
- Receive special offers from Yahoo!.
- Buy and sell at Yahoo! auctions.
- Take part in Yahoo! sweepstakes.
- Add their listing to People Search.
- Run personal ads in Yahoo!.
- Participate in any Yahoo! adult chat, club, or shopping area.

Children between the ages of 13 and 18 are not allowed to do the following:

- Buy and sell at Yahoo! auctions.
- Participate in a Yahoo! adult chat, club, or shopping area.

As a parent, you can edit the list of persons who can send your child instant messages, and you can block certain persons from sending your children e-mail. You can also change a child's password and account information, and you can sign in as your child to see exactly what features he or she can access.

If you see that your child is getting adult-oriented mail, for example, you can add the address of the sender to your child's blocked-addresses list. To do so, you simply sign in as your child by using his or her name and password, and then add the blocked address as you learned how to do in Chapter 2. You can also sign in as your child to confirm that he or she is not allowed to access adult Yahoo! sites.

Yahoo! does not allow children under the age of 13 to register by themselves—if they tell their correct birth date. When children submit their Yahoo! registration, they are told that only their parents can sign them up as part of a family account.

Protect Children through Safe Surfing

If you want to limit the types of information your child can see, check with your Internet Service Provider or look for programs that are designed for safe surfing.

Some ISPs provide parental control software free or at low cost. The software lets you lock out Web sites that have certain keywords in their titles and limit the amount of time your child can remain online. Here is a list of some of the available programs and their addresses, in case you want to learn about them:

- **CyberPatrol**   http://www.cyberpatrol.com/
- **CyberSentinal**   http://www.securitysoft.com/cybersentinel.html
- **CyberSitter**   http://www.cybersitter.com/
- **NetNanny**   http://www.netnanny.com/
- **SurfWatch**   http://www1.surfwatch.com/

Also consider two free ways to limit your child's surfing. The free ISP service at www.freensafe.com filters out objectionable sites when you log on through its service. If you want to use your current ISP but limit your child's access, you can download a free children's Web browser from http://www.chibrow.com/informat.htm.

You should discuss potential problem content on the Internet with your child, and direct him or her to Yahooligans!, a site designed for children between the ages of 7 and 12.

Children 13 years and older, however, can sign up for their own accounts without a parent's permission. You can add a child who has already registered for Yahoo! to a family account and thereby control the child's access to Yahoo! services; but to do so, you need to get the child's Yahoo! password.

With the benefits of having a family account in mind, you should also thoroughly understand what a family account cannot do:

- A family account does not prevent a child from surfing the Internet. There are no restrictions on the sites a child can see.

- A family account does not place any restrictions on the results of Yahoo! searches. A search of the Internet in Yahoo! can result in listings with adult-oriented information.

- Outside of Yahoo!, a child can still enter personal information in forms and sign up for offers or promotions.

■ A child can send and receive e-mail and instant messages.

■ There are no restrictions on the chats your child can join that are outside of Yahoo!.

Setting Up a Family Account

Before you set up a family account, have your credit card information handy. You can use MasterCard, Visa, or American Express. You can set up the account and verify your charge information the first time you add a child to the account, or you can verify your charge and add children later.

Follow these steps to create a family account and register a child:

1. Connect to the Internet and to Yahoo!.

2. Click More in the list of links at the top of the Yahoo! page.

Shopping - **Auctions** - Yellow Pages - People Search - Maps - Travel - Classifieds - Personals - Games - Chat - **Clubs**
Mail - Calendar - Messenger - **Companion** - My Yahoo! - News - Sports - Weather - TV - Stock Quotes - more...

3. Click Family Accounts to see the screen shown in Figure 5-1.

- Email - Free_Email@yahoo.com.
- Family Accounts - Tools for parents.
- Games - Poker, chess, hearts, backgammon...
- GeoCities - Build your own home page.

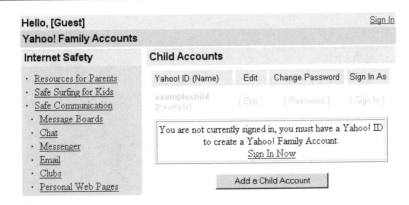

FIGURE 5-1   Family Accounts options

4. If you have not yet signed up for Yahoo!, click Sign In Now in the Family Accounts page, enter your ID and password, and click Sign In to return to the Family Accounts page.

5. Click Add a Child Account.

6. Enter your ID and password, and then click Submit to see the Instant Account verification screen. The screen explains why Yahoo! requires credit card information to start a family account.

Instant Account Verification

In order to create a Yahoo! Family Account, you must be 18 years of age or older and you must be the parent or legal guardian of the children whose accounts you add.

Yahoo! will verify your age with our **free**, instant Account Verification system. To proceed you'll need a valid credit card (Mastercard, Visa, or American Express).

Don't worry, this is just for verification, your credit card will not be billed.

Secure Account Verification	Go Back

Note: The account verification process is fast and free. All it takes is a few minutes and you'll be on your way. For more information about the adult verification process visit our Verification FAQ. Also, Yahoo! respects your privacy, to learn more about how Yahoo! uses this information, please read our Privacy Policy.

---

7. Click the Secure Account Verification button to enter your credit card number and expiration date on the screen.

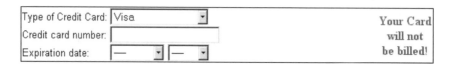

8. From the pull-down list, select which type of credit card you use.

9. Enter the card number and expiration date.

10. Scroll down the page and verify your personal information, including your age, name, e-mail address, and zip code.

11. Click Finished.

Yahoo! checks your card information with the bank and, if the information matches, reports that your account has been verified. It now offers two options:

- Finish adding a child account.
- Continue directly to family.yahoo.com.

If you are not ready to add a child's account, choose the Continue option. You can later add an account by choosing Add A Child Account on the Family Accounts screen. You will not have to enter your charge card information again when you add a child to the account.

Whether you decide to add your child's account now or afterward, you'll see the options in Figure 5-2.

Before adding a child to your family account, the child must be registered in Yahoo!. If your child is not yet registered, click Create a New Account for Your Child. If your child is registered, enter his or her name and password and click the Add Child button.

Yahoo! opens the Review Child's Account Information window, which contains information from the child's current account, if any, as shown in Figure 5-3. Complete the form by assigning

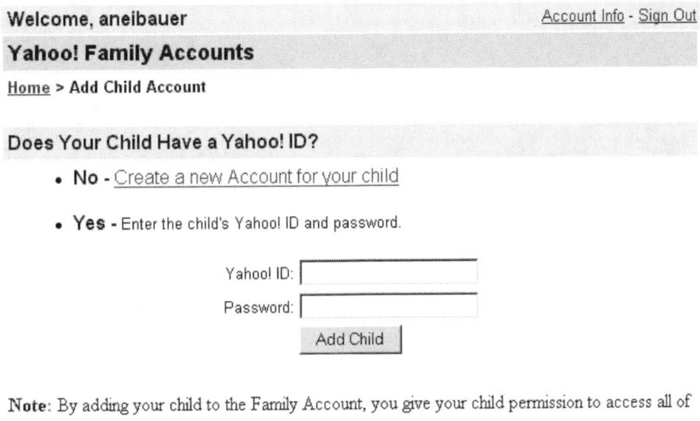

Welcome, aneibauer   Account Info - Sign Out

Yahoo! Family Accounts

Home > Add Child Account

Does Your Child Have a Yahoo! ID?

- **No -** Create a new Account for your child

- **Yes -** Enter the child's Yahoo! ID and password.

Yahoo! ID: [ ]
Password: [ ]
Add Child

Note: By adding your child to the Family Account, you give your child permission to access all of

FIGURE 5-2   Select whether to create a new account or use your child's existing account.

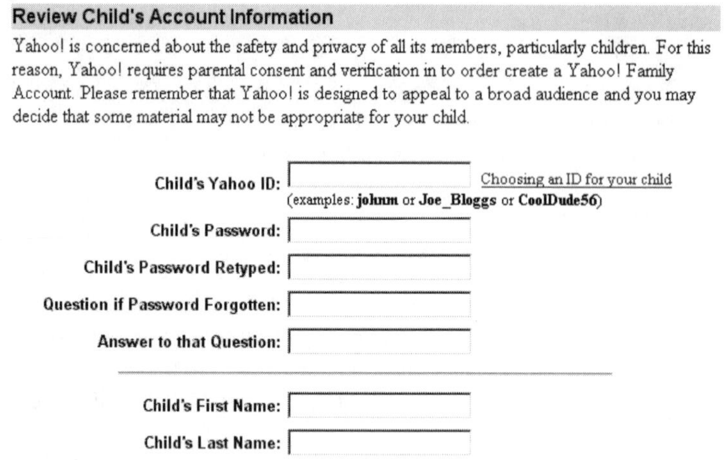

Review Child's Account Information

Yahoo! is concerned about the safety and privacy of all its members, particularly children. For this reason, Yahoo! requires parental consent and verification in to order create a Yahoo! Family Account. Please remember that Yahoo! is designed to appeal to a broad audience and you may decide that some material may not be appropriate for your child.

Child's Yahoo ID: [   ] Choosing an ID for your child
(examples: **johnm** or **Joe_Bloggs** or **CoolDude56**)

Child's Password: [   ]

Child's Password Retyped: [   ]

Question if Password Forgotten: [   ]

Answer to that Question: [   ]

Child's First Name: [   ]

Child's Last Name: [   ]

FIGURE 5-3 Complete your child's account information.

an ID and password if the child is not already registered. You'll also have to enter your ID and password to verify that you are granting the child permission to use Yahoo!.

Click Add Child Account to return to the Family Accounts page, which displays children's accounts, as in Figure 5-4. Your child now has a Yahoo! account and can use all Yahoo! services except those restricted by the family account.

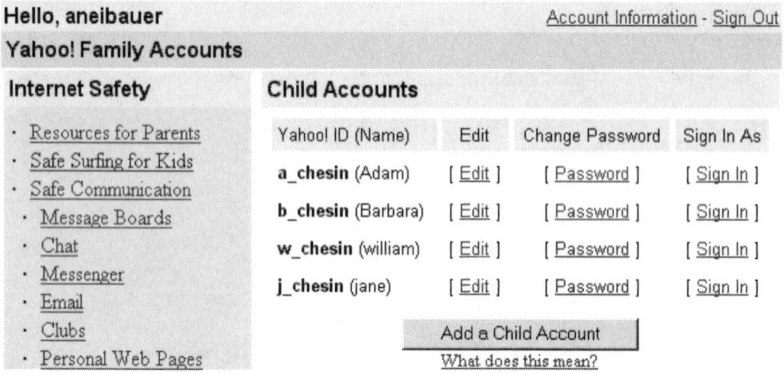

Hello, aneibauer Account Information - Sign Out
Yahoo! Family Accounts

Internet Safety

- Resources for Parents
- Safe Surfing for Kids
- Safe Communication
- Message Boards
- Chat
- Messenger
- Email
- Clubs
- Personal Web Pages

Child Accounts

Yahoo! ID (Name)	Edit	Change Password	Sign In As
a_chesin (Adam)	[Edit]	[Password]	[Sign In]
b_chesin (Barbara)	[Edit]	[Password]	[Sign In]
w_chesin (william)	[Edit]	[Password]	[Sign In]
j_chesin (jane)	[Edit]	[Password]	[Sign In]

Add a Child Account
What does this mean?

FIGURE 5-4 Children listed in a family account

Working with Child Accounts

From the Family Accounts page, you can edit the account information, change the password, or sign in as your child. Signing in as your child lets you experience the services that your child can access in case you want to modify your child's Yahoo! options, including his or her public profile.

Note *A child can only be added to one parent account.*

Click Edit next to the child's name to change his or her account information or the public profile of a child over 12 years old. Refer to Chapter 2 if you need help with editing and creating public profiles.

Click Password to change your child's password:

Yahoo! Password for b_chesin	
Choose a **New Password:**	
Now, **Confirm New Password:**	

Enter and retype a new password, and then click the Finish button. Yahoo! will send your child an e-mail reporting that his or her password has been changed. Tell your child the new password so he or she can log on to Yahoo!. Your child can always change passwords again after they sign in. However, once a child is added to your family account, you can change his or her password from the Family Accounts menu without knowing the new password that the child created.

Use the Sign In option to have Yahoo! treat you like your child. Clicking Sign In next to a child's name logs you on to Yahoo! as your child. Because you are already logged on under your own name, you will not have to enter your child's password. Clicking Sign In next to a child's name displays the options shown in Figure 5-5.

Use the options on the left to see what services your child can access. Use the options on the right to change your child's Yahoo! settings. To modify your child's profile, for example, click Edit Public Profiles. You can then change the profile as you learned to do in Chapter 2. You'll learn about the other settings in later chapters.

After you sign in as your child, Yahoo! treats you as if you were the child. To access your own e-mail or calendar, or to work with family accounts again, you have to sign off as your child and log on as yourself. When you have finished changing your child's settings, click Sign In as Yourself, enter your ID and password, and then click Sign In. You can also use the Sign Out or Change User links that appear on other pages.

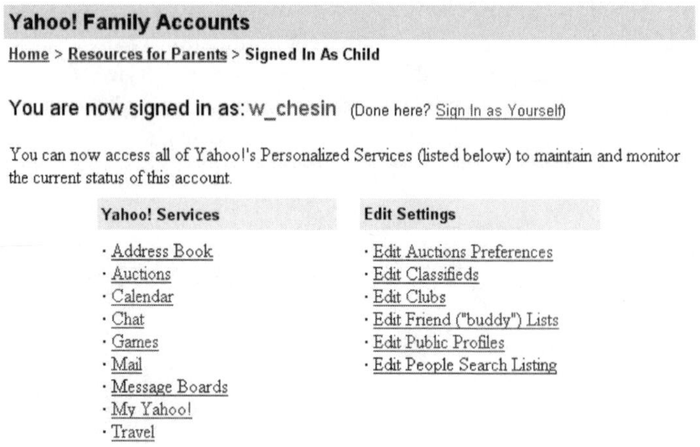

Yahoo! Family Accounts

Home > Resources for Parents > Signed In As Child

You are now signed in as: w_chesin (Done here? Sign In as Yourself)

You can now access all of Yahoo!'s Personalized Services (listed below) to maintain and monitor the current status of this account.

Yahoo! Services	Edit Settings
· Address Book	· Edit Auctions Preferences
· Auctions	· Edit Classifieds
· Calendar	· Edit Clubs
· Chat	· Edit Friend ("buddy") Lists
· Games	· Edit Public Profiles
· Mail	· Edit People Search Listing
· Message Boards	
· My Yahoo!	
· Travel	

FIGURE 5-5   Signing in to Yahoo! as your child

Using a Child Account

When a child signs in to Yahoo! using an ID and password, he or she has access to all Yahoo! features within the limits set by the age group he or she belongs to. For example, a child under 13 who tries to create a public profile sees this message:

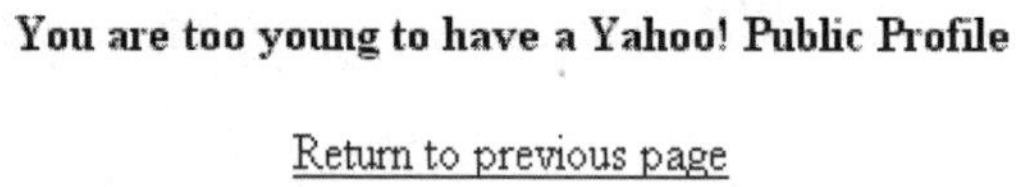

You are too young to have a Yahoo! Public Profile

Return to previous page

Children under 18 years old will see this warning if they try to buy or sell at a Yahoo! auction:

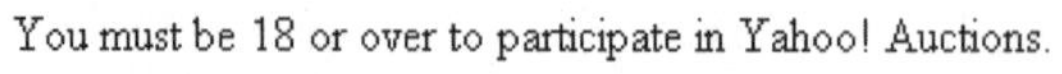

You must be 18 or over to participate in Yahoo! Auctions.

When a child goes to the Chat area, it automatically displays the Teen options, as shown in Figure 5-6. A child who attempts to enter an adult chat room sees the message shown at right.

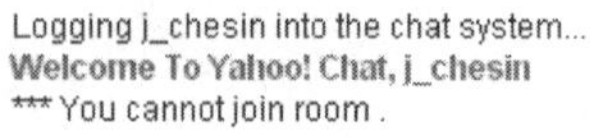

Logging j_chesin into the chat system...
Welcome To Yahoo! Chat, j_chesin
*** You cannot join room .

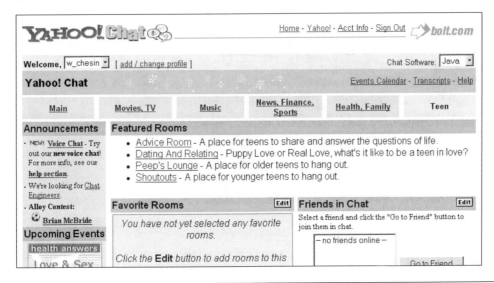

FIGURE 5-6   The chat screen automatically displays the teen interest area.

Yahooligans!

For children, one of the best places to enter the Internet is Yahooligans!, which is shown in Figure 5-7. The features and links are designed entirely with children in mind. They provide a balance of education and entertainment.

You can reach Yahooligans! in two ways:

■ Use your browser to go directly to the site at http://www.yahooligans.com/.

■ Click More on the main Yahoo! page and then click the link for Yahooligans!

Note   *Your child does not have to be a member of Yahoo! to access and use Yahooligans!*

At Yahooligans!, there are minimal links to advertisements and commercial sites, and each one is clearly marked with the letters AD, as shown here:

FIGURE 5-7   Yahooligans! for children

If you do not want your children following those links, just tell them not to click any picture that has the letters AD in front of it.

From the main Yahooligans! page, children can reach interesting sites of all types, play games, and learn in the process. Clicking Club, for example, offers your child access to features such as these (although the content varies periodically):

■ Games, including chess, checkers, fish, tic-tac-toe, word search, and reversi

■ Shout Out, a forum for posting ideas and opinions

■ Hyper Site, where children can access and vote on cool sites

■ This Day in History tells what happened on a specific day of their choosing, such as their birthday

■ Web-Celeb provides photographs and information on a celebrity of the month

■ Random Link jumps to randomly selected but child-safe Web sites

■ Jokes suitable for children

■ Daily Trivia, an updated trivia information and contest

■ News, stories, and photographs from around the world

■ Sports, the latest news, and statistics on teams and players

■ Downloader, a source for pictures, sounds, and video

■ Cam For Kids, which are live Web cams at interesting locations around the world

Additional links further down the Yahooligans! page offer links to Net Events, What's New, News, Almanac, Sports, and Web Celeb. The Almanac, for example, is a wonderful online children's encyclopedia with the categories shown in Figure 5-8. It is a great way for young children to discover information and learn the research skills that they need for school.

Tip *Teachers can learn how to use Yahooligans! in their classroom by clicking Teacher's Guide at the bottom of the Yahooligans! screen.*

All of the direct links from Yahooligans! are monitored by Yahoo! for their content. Yahoo! makes the following promises:

- They will not collect any information about your child.

- They will not provide any means for children to post information about themselves, although links that eventually lead to sites where children can post information may become available.

- Yahooligans! does not use cookies anywhere on its site, although Yahooligans! does collect IP address for administrative purposes. Cookies are small files that a Web site can place on your computer. They can later access your files to get information about you, such as the last time you logged on to the site and user preferences. Some cookies can be used to get personal information,which you may not want revealed.

5

FIGURE 5-8   The Yahooligans! Almanac

Guidelines for Safe Surfing

The Internet is a wonderful resource, full of useful and fun information. The freedom that allowed the Internet to grow so quickly, however, means that no restrictions have been placed on its content. Certainly, the Internet contains material more suitable for adults than children, and others might consider material that you find reasonable to be inappropriate.

While companies such as Yahoo! and your ISP can take some steps to control the content that youngsters can view, they really can't do much to police a child's viewing. And while there are programs you can purchase to reduce your child's exposure to inappropriate content, little can be done to combat an inquisitive mind.

Only your child can decide what he or she is exposed to on the Internet. However, you can take a proactive role in guiding your child to a healthy and safe Internet experience.

First, take the time to become familiar with Yahoo! and the Internet in general. Spend some time going through the various Yahoo! features. Experiment with searches, chats, and clubs. The more you know about the Internet, the better you can guide your child and share their online adventure.

> **Tip** *Patents can learn more about Yahooligans! and safe surfing from the Family Accounts screen and by clicking Parent's Guide at the bottom of the Yahooligans! screen.*

Learn about Yahoo! Family Accounts and any parental controls that your ISP provides. Visit a local computer store or shop online for software that filters Internet content so that you can control the content your child is exposed to.

If you want to monitor your child's exposure on the Internet, place the computer that you use to surf the Internet in the living room, den, or other area where you can keep an eye on your child. While you can trust your child to exercise good judgment, you can still provide some overall supervision by periodically scanning the material being displayed.

If your child has a computer in his or her room and you feel comfortable with that, periodically view the History folder in the browser to review recently visited sites. Discuss with your child any objectionable sites that you encounter.

The most effective way to protect your child, however, is through an open and ongoing dialog. Spend some time explaining the basic rules of safe surfing with your child:

- Never give any personal information about yourself or your family over the Internet. Never give your full name, phone number, address, age, sex, the name of the school you attend, or the names of neighborhood locations that you frequent.

- Never arrange a physical meeting with anyone you meet on the Internet.

- Do not read e-mail or instant messages from an unfamiliar or unsolicited address, and never respond to such mail or messages.

- Only participate in chat rooms that you have approved in advance.

Plan ahead for how your child should cope with inappropriate material. Explain that clicking the Home button quickly returns you to the ISP's initial Web site. Show your child how to use Yahoo! Companion and the Favorites or Bookmarks lists to access approved sites. Make your child feel comfortable reporting to you a site that claims to be child-friendly but contains offensive material.

Come to a consensus about the amount of time your child spends online and in chat rooms. You may want to place a limit on the amount of time that a child can remain online or restrict your child to certain hours. Consider a rule whereby children cannot go online until their homework is done. Tell your children to balance the time they spend online with exercise and other important activities.

Discuss with your child the fact that sometimes the people that go online are not who they claim to be. Children can never be sure whether they are really chatting with another youngster or an adult.

Resources for Seniors

Youngsters certainly aren't the only members of the family who have special interests and needs. An ever-increasing number of us are joining the ranks of seniors, and Yahoo! certainly hasn't overlooked our side of the family.

To access information for seniors, go to www.seniors.yahoo.com to see the options in Figure 5-9. The page contains links of special interest to seniors, including top news stories, message boards, and sites such as AARP and the Interactive Aging Network. There is a Daily Detour section with links to entertaining topics, such as crossword puzzles, horoscopes, lottery results, and the Bingo! Zone.

Sections
▶ Main Page
Books
Computers
Entertainment
Finance
Food and Dining
Gardening
Genealogy
Government
Health
News and Magazines
Organizations
Recreation and Sports
Travel

The Sections area shown on the right contains links to major Yahoo! pages devoted to seniors.

Click a section to access information and links of all types. Each section contains a Top Picks area with recommended resources, and a More Yahoo! Area with links to additional resources on Yahoo!.

More Yahoo!
· Alternative Medicine
· Alzheimer's Disease
· Diseases
· Drugs
· Health
· Long Term Care
· Managed Care
· Medicare
· Parkinson's Disease
· Pharmacies
· Senior Health
· Yahoo! Net Events: Health

The More Yahoo! Choices in the Health section, for example, contains the links shown in the illustration at left.

Choosing Computers and Internet, for example, provides access to Yahoo! Senior's Guide: Tech Tips and to SeniorNet, an online service dedicated to teaching seniors how to use computer technology.

FIGURE 5-9   Yahoo! Senior's Guide

The Finance and Investment area provides a variety of links to financial information of all types, including general guides to these areas:

- **American Association of Individual Investors**   Information on personal financial management
- **Crash Course in Wills and Trusts**   A practical guide to the law about wills and trusts
- **FinanCenter**   Calculators and advice about investments, mortgages, loans, and credit cards
- **HomePath**   A guide to home shopping and financing
- **IRS Digital Daily**   Official tax resources from the Internal Revenue Service
- **Insurance News Network**   Information about all types of insurance, as well as the Standard and Poor ratings of insurance companies
- **Quicken.Com Retirement**   Information on tax and estate planning
- **Social Security Online**   Official site of the Social Security Administration
- **What Investors Should Know**   Investment guides from the National Association of Securities Dealers

Chapter 6

Creating Your Home Page

How to . . .

- Choose a Yahoo! GeoCities neighborhood
- Create a Web site using wizards
- Design and maintain a Web site with Page Builder
- Insert add-ons to your Web site
- Maintain a Web site guestbook

It is now time to make your presence known on the Web and stake your claim on the Internet. Using Yahoo!, you can create your own Web site and present information about yourself, your family, your business, or any topic that you want to share with the millions of persons who surf the Web.

Yahoo! offers a free Web site as part of GeoCities, a community of Web sites with all of the tools needed to develop them that Yahoo! acquired in 1999. In fact, Yahoo! gives you a variety of ways to create a GeoCities Web site. You can follow easy-to-use wizards, upload a professionally designed Web site, or choose from different Web sites in between. You can, for example, start your Web site with the wizard and then refine it by using a variety of other tools and techniques.

Web Site Basics

Before looking at the exact steps for creating a Web site, you should understand some of the basic principles that are involved.

When you connect to a site on the Web, you see a Web page. A *Web page* is really just a special document on a computer hard disk that contains information, as well as hypertext links to other documents on the Web. A *hypertext link*, better known as a *hyperlink*, is a graphic or line of text that you can click to move to another Web location.

Each computer that is connected to the Internet is assigned an address called an *IP address*. The address is associated with the name you type to reach it. When you type **www.microsoft.com**, for example, your ISP locates the IP address associated with the name and connects to that site.

One specific file on a Web site acts as the *home page*, the first page displayed when someone accesses a site with his or her browser. The file may be called index.htm, index.html, default.htm, or another name that the Web site host specifies. When someone goes to your Web site, the home page is transferred to his or her computer. When the transfer is complete, the browser displays the home page on the computer screen.

Most Web sites consist of more than one file, however. A Web site can be any number of files linked together by hyperlinks. It may also include pictures and other graphics that are stored separately on the site but are displayed along with the home page or other pages.

Yahoo! gives you 15 megabytes of disk space in which to store your Web site files. You can also divide the space into subdirectories to better organize your site. If you need additional space, you can purchase it from Yahoo!.

For a document to be used as a Web page and displayed by a Web browser, it must be written using special formatting codes. These codes tell the Web browser how to display the document on the screen and what to do when a visitor clicks a hyperlink. These formats are known as *HTML (Hypertext Markup Language),* and the codes are called *HTML tags.* You can create a Web document using a word-processing program by typing the HTML tags. However, trying to visualize how a Web page will appear from just looking at HTML tags is difficult. Because the tags must be entered using specific formats, it is all too easy to make a mistake entering the HTML and get a terrible mess when you view your Web page on a browser screen. Luckily, Yahoo! lets you create Web pages without having to worry about HTML tags.

Note *Other formats can be used to create Web pages, but Yahoo! offers HTML tools.*

6

As with most Yahoo! features, your 15 megabytes of Web site space on GeoCities and all the tools you need to create your Web site are free. Yahoo! supports the free sites, however, by displaying a small window called the *Ad Square* on the screen. Wouldn't you know it, the Ad Square presents advertisements, as shown here:

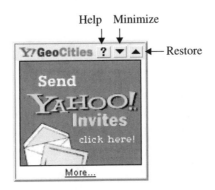

A visitor to a GeoCities Web site can minimize the Ad Square by clicking the Minimize button, but visitors cannot remove it entirely from the screen.

Note *You can substitute another Yahoo! feature, called GeoGuide, in place of Ad Square.*

Welcome to the Neighborhood

Yahoo! organizes its members' Web sites into 41 groups called *neighborhoods.* Individual sites are called *homesteads.* By putting your site (homestead) in a neighborhood, you increase its visibility among persons who share your interests. Users can browse Web sites by neighborhood, for example, and get exposed to Web sites they might never have seen otherwise.

When you create a Web site in Yahoo!, you are asked to select the neighborhood in which you want to place it. So take some time to review the neighborhoods shown in Table 6-1 to determine which is the most appropriate for your Web site. The 41 neighborhoods are organized into 13 general categories.

Category	Neighborhood	Focus
Arts and Literature	Paris	Romance and poetry
	SoHo	Art and artists
Business and Money	WallStreet	Investing, finance, and the stock markets
	Eureka	Small business
	MadisonAvenue	Advertising and public relations
Cars & Trucks	MotorCity	Cars, trucks, motorcycles
	Baja	Adventure travel and off-roading
Computers, Science & Tech	SiliconValley	Computers
	ResearchTriangle	New and emerging developments and the future of technology
	TimesSquare	Games and role-playing adventures
	CapeCanaveral	Science, aviation, and space exploration
Education	Athens	Education and philosophy
	CollegePark	University life
Entertainment	Hollywood	Television and movies
	SunsetStrip	The club scene, and rock and punk music
	Nashville	Country music
	TelevisionCity	Television
	Area51	Science fiction and fantasy
	Vienna	Classical music, opera, ballet
	Broadway	Theater and musicals
Family	Heartland	Hometown values
	EnchantedForest	Sites created by and about children
	Petsburgh	Pets
Government & Politics	CapitolHill	Government and politics
	Pentagon	The military and defense industry
	RainForest	The environment
Health & Beauty	FashionAvenue	Beauty and fashion
	HotSprings	Health and fitness
	RodeoDrive	Shopping

TABLE 6-1   Yahoo! GeoCities Neighborhoods

Category	Neighborhood	Focus
Home & Food	PicketFence	Home improvement
	NapaValley	Food and wine
Lifestyles	WestHollywood	Gay and lesbian lifestyles
	SouthBeach	Chatting
	Wellesley	Women
	Tokyo	Anime and Asian culture
	BourbonStreet	Jazz and Southern culture
Sports & Recreation	Augusta	Golf
	Colosseum	Sports
	Yosemite	Outdoor activities
	Pipeline	Extreme sports
Travel	TheTropics	Travel and vacation

TABLE 6-1   Yahoo! GeoCities Neighborhoods *(continued)*

Getting Started

Your first step in building a Web site is to access Yahoo! GeoCities. From there, you can create a Web site, edit pages that you've already created, and even upload a Web page from your computer to your Web site space.

To reach GeoCities, follow these steps:

1. Click More on the initial Yahoo! page.

2. Click GeoCities to see the Yahoo! GeoCities page shown in Figure 6-1.

3. If you have not yet signed in, click Sign In, enter your Yahoo! ID and password, and click Sign In.

4. If the GeoCities terms of agreement appears, read it and then click I Accept.

The GeoCities pages includes three Web site–building options, as well as these features:

■ **Search Home Pages**   Look for Yahoo! member Web sites by entering a keyword or member name.

■ **Explore Neighborhoods**   Browse through Web sites according to neighborhood.

■ **Cool Home Page Add-Ons**   Access elements that you can add to your Web site.

■ **New and Notable**   Learn about recently added or improved features.

FIGURE 6-1   Yahoo! GeoCities home page

■ **Member Tools**   View links to features just for Yahoo! GeoCities members. Features include managing your Web site files, signing up for extra space, and accessing your member account.

Using a Wizard

A *wizard* is a series of dialog boxes that take you step by step through a complex process. By responding to the questions in the boxes or filling in information, you complete the process without having to know the technical aspects of the task you are performing.

By using the wizard, you can create a rather sophisticated Web site without knowing anything about HTML tags. As you learn more about Web site building, however, you can later edit your Web site pages to add even more features.

Let's go through the steps of creating a Web site using the Yahoo! Wizard:

1. In the Yahoo! GeoCities home page, click Yahoo! Wizards.

2. If this is the first time you've used the wizards or created a Yahoo! GeoCities Web site, you will see the Pick A Neighborhood For Your Home Page screen.

3. Click the neighborhood in which you want to place your Web site. You see the About Your Home Page form.

4. Enter the information about your Web site:

   ■ Enter up to three phrases that describe your home page.

   ■ Enter a topic that best describes your home page.

   ■ State whether you would like to receive e-mail about making money with your home page (the Pages That Pay program).

5. Click Submit to see a summary of your page details.

Your Yahoo! ID and Home Page Information	
Your Yahoo! ID is:	**azakuto_2000**
Your Alternate Email Address is:	**alann@att.net**
Your home page URL is:	**http://www.geocities.com/Pentagon/Camp/4903** (Would you like a different address?)
Your home page URL shortcut is:	**http://www.geocities.com/azakuto_2000**

6. Print a copy of the screen or make a note of the two Web site addresses: your home page URL and your home page URL shortcut. You can access your Web site with either address. Your home page URL represents the exact location of your site within the Yahoo! system, including the neighborhood (Pentagon in the example), the street (Camp), and the address (4903).

Note *A* URL *is an abbreviation of Uniform Resource Locator, the Web address of a site or document on the Internet.*

7. Click Build Your Page Now! to see the Wizards page shown in Figure 6-2. The Wizards page shows thumbnail sketches of several completed Web pages. Underneath each page is a link.

8. Click the link for the page you want to create. The Start With A Yahoo! Wizard page appears. It offers information about the wizard and explains the type of information that you'll be asked to enter.

9. Click Launch Yahoo! Wizard.

Launch Yahoo! Wizard - **to begin building your**
Personal Home Page. HAVE FUN!

10. A series of boxes appears so you can select options and enter information that you want to appear on the Web site. Click Begin, fill in the boxes, and keep clicking Next to move from box to box. At one point, you will be asked if you want to make the page your home page.

11. If you want to use the page as your home page, choose Yes and then click Next. The page will be called index.html and will be displayed whenever a person accesses your

site with his or her browser. If you click No and then Next, enter the name you want for the page in the box that appears, and then click Next.

12. A congratulations message appears and shows the address of the page you created. Give this address to persons you want to access your page. Click Done. The Now That You Have Finished page appears with information about accessing the page. From here, you also choose another color scheme or template to use for the page.

13. Click Home to return to the Yahoo! GeoCities home page.

If you selected to make the page your home page, it is now located at this address:

http://www.geocities.com/*your_ID*/

So if your Yahoo! ID is Jdoe, your Web site is as follows:

http://www.geocities.com/Jdoe/

A very basic Web site created by the Yahoo! Wizard is shown in Figure 6-3.
If you gave the page another name, such as mysite, then it can be accessed by navigating to this address:

http://www.geocities.com/Jdoe/myside.html

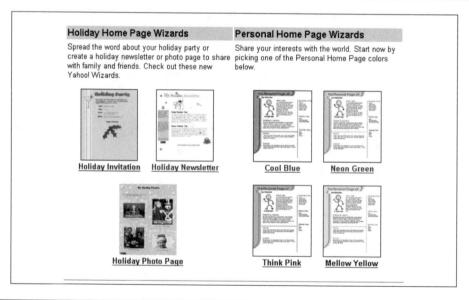

Holiday Home Page Wizards

Spread the word about your holiday party or create a holiday newsletter or photo page to share with family and friends. Check out these new Yahoo! Wizards.

Holiday Invitation   Holiday Newsletter

Holiday Photo Page

Personal Home Page Wizards

Share your interests with the world. Start now by picking one of the Personal Home Page colors below.

Cool Blue   Neon Green

Think Pink   Mellow Yellow

FIGURE 6-2   Selecting a starting design

FIGURE 6-3   Sample basic Web site

Editing Wizard Web Sites

After you view your Web site, you may want to add or delete elements, or change text or graphics.

If you want to make changes to the site you created with the wizard, just repeat the steps to start the wizard. Because you already have a wizard page on your site, however, the first wizard dialog box will ask if you want to create a new page or edit an existing one.

To edit an existing wizard page, select Edit Existing Page, as shown on the right. Pull down the list box under that option, choose the page you want to edit, and then click Next.

To create another Web site page, click Create A New Page and then click Next. Fill in the dialog boxes to create the page and then give it a name other than index.html—or give it the name index.html if you want it to replace your current home page.

You can use Page Builder to edit Web sites you created with a wizard, but then you will no longer be able to edit the page with the wizard

Using Page Builder to Create Web Sites

Rather than use a wizard to create your page, you can use Page Builder. Page Builder lets you select a template or a blank page as a starting point for your site and then customize it as you wish.

You create a Page Builder site graphically, by adding elements and then placing them where you want them to appear. You can add graphics and text and other special Web site features simply by clicking and dragging.

Follow these steps to create a Web page with Page Builder:

1. In the GeoCities home page, click Build a Page. If this is the first time you've created a Yahoo! GeoCities home page, you'll see the Pick A Neighborhood For Your Home Page screen.

2. Click the neighborhood in which you want to place your site. You see the About Your Home Page form.

3. Enter the information about your Web site:

   ■ Enter up to three phrases that describe your home page.

   ■ Enter a topic that best describes your home page.

   ■ State whether you would like to receive e-mail about making money with your home page (the Pages That Pay program).

4. Click Submit to see a summary of your page details.

5. Print a copy of the screen or make a note of the two Web site addresses, your home page URL and your home page URL shortcut. You can use either address to access your Web site.

6. Click Build Your Page Now! to see your page under construction.

7. Click Page Builder to see the Start with a PageBuilder Template page, which is shown in Figure 6-4.

8. Click one of the templates you'd like to use. The Start With A Template page appears.

9. Click Launch Page Builder. Yahoo! will take from three to five minutes to set up Page Builder so it can do its work. You'll see a small window with an animated graphic that shows a house being built, along with a message warning you not to close the window. After Page Builder has set up, you'll see the Page Builder window with the template, as shown in Figure 6-5.

Note *Click OK if a message appears reporting new features.*

10. Create your Web site as explained in the next section.

FIGURE 6-4   Choosing a starting template for Page Builder

11. When you've finished, click Save to see the Save and Publish Page box. It will list the names of any existing pages on your Web site.

12. Type a new page name. If you want to replace an existing page with a new one, select its name from the list.

13. Click OK. Yahoo! will save the page, show you its URL address, and ask if you want to view the page at this time.

14. If you select not to view the page, close Page Builder by choosing Exit from its File menu. If you select to view the page, it will appear in a new window on your screen. Close the window when you have finished previewing the page to return to Page Builder. You can then either modify the page and save it again or exit Page Builder.

Working with Page Builder

Page Builder is an easy way to create powerful Web sites because you do so visually. You see your page as you're working on it and can preview it to make sure it looks and works the way you want.

In Page Builder, each item on the page—a section of text or a graphic, for example—is an object. You can move and change the size of an object, delete it, or change its contents without

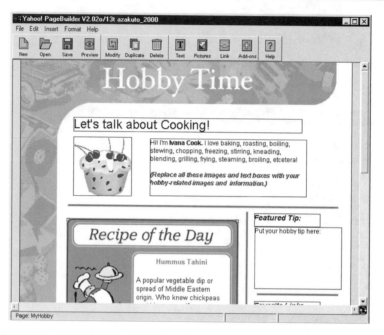

FIGURE 6-5   Page Builder with template

disturbing the other objects. When you click an object, it is surrounded by a border and square handles, as shown on the right. Click an object to select it.

To move an object, point inside the border, hold down the left mouse button, and then drag the mouse where you want the object to appear. Objects cannot overlap each other. If you position an object so it overlaps another object, Yahoo! displays a red crosshatch pattern where the objects overlap. Move the object so the pattern disappears:

To change the size of an object, drag one of the handles. You can make an object smaller or larger:

- Drag a handle on the corner to change the height and width of the graphic but keep its proportions.

- Drag the left or right center handle to change the width.

- Drag the top or bottom center handle to change the height. For example, dragging the right side of this text box to the left made it smaller so the graphic was able to fit beside it without overlapping:

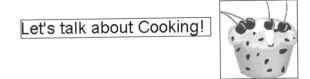

- To delete an object, select it and then press DELETE.

- To modify an existing object, click it so handles appears around it and then click the Modify button in the Page Builder toolbar.

Working with Text

If you want to change any of the default text that came with the Page Builder template, double-click the text, or click it once and then click the Modify button. The text is surrounded by a double border with handles, and the text toolbar appears, as shown here:

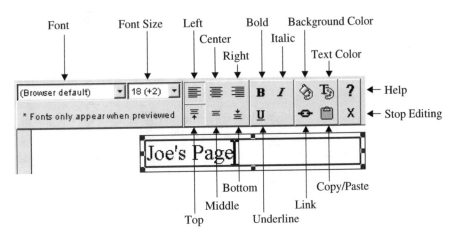

 **Align Objects**

If you want to align two or more objects in relation to each other, use the Align command rather than attempting to drag each object into position separately. Here's how:

1. Select the first object in the group that you want to align.

2. Hold down the SHIFT key and select the other objects.

3. Choose Align from the Page Builder Edit menu to open the Align Items dialog box shown here:

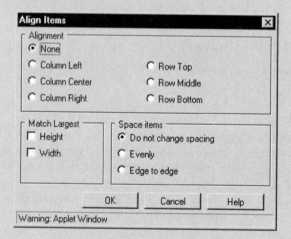

4. In the Alignment section, select how you want the items aligned in relation to each other.

5. In the Match Largest section, choose whether you want all of the items to be the same size as either the largest or smallest of the objects.

6. In the Space Items section, choose how you want the items spaced from each other.

7. Click OK.

You can now move the insertion point within the text to edit it or to add more text. Use the buttons and lists on the toolbar to format text as you would in a word-processing program. The Left, Center, Right, Top, Middle, and Bottom buttons affect where the text appears in the box surrounding it. Click outside of the box when you have finished editing.

The Link button lets you use the text as a hyperlink. See "Working with Hyperlinks," later in this chapter.

To insert new text on your page, click the Text button on the toolbar, shown at left. You can also choose Basics and then Text from the Insert menu. A text box appears with handles along with the text toolbar. Click in the box and type and format your text. When you have finished entering the text, drag the box where you want it to appear.

Working With Graphics

Most of the templates come with at least one graphic. You can change the default graphic or add additional pictures to the page. Yahoo! has a collection of graphics that you can choose from, and you can also use graphics you have on your computer or graphics from other Web sites.

To modify an existing graphic object, double-click it or select it and then click the Modify button. You see the Select Picture dialog box shown in Figure 6-6.

Use the options in the box to change the graphic that is displayed and how it appears.

To select another of Yahoo!'s graphics, follow these steps:

1. In the Collection list, choose one of the graphic groups. The options are shown here:

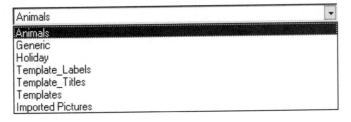

2. In the Picture List, click the name of the picture that you want to use. A preview of the graphic appears.

3. To view thumbnails of all of the graphics in a collection, click the View Thumbnails button to open another window with views of all of the pictures in the group. Then point to a thumbnail to see its name and size and click a picture to select it.

4. Click OK when you're ready to insert the graphic into the document.

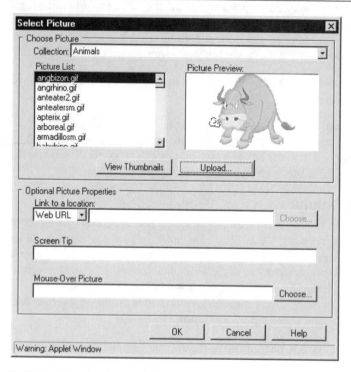

FIGURE 6-6   Adding or changing a graphic object

To insert a graphic that you have on your computer, click Upload to see the Upload Image dialog box:

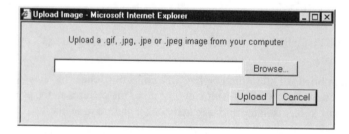

Enter the path and name of the graphic on your computer, or click the Browse button to locate the graphic in the traditional Choose File dialog box. Click Upload to transfer the image to your Web site.

You can use a graphic as a hyperlink through the Link To A Location option. See "Working with Hyperlinks," the next section in this chapter.

Use the Screen Tip box to specify the text you want to appear when someone points to the picture with his or her mouse.

The Mouse-Over Picture option is a terrific feature. It lets you choose a second graphic that appears when the user points to the picture on your site. You could use this feature, for example, to display "before" and "after" pictures of the same item, or as a way to include two graphics in the same space. Click the Choose button next to the Move-Over Picture text box and select or upload the graphic you want to use.

Working with Hyperlinks

It is easy to add your own hyperlinks to a Web page. Remember, a hyperlink is an object that you click to go to another location on your Web site or another location on the Internet. You can also click hyperlinks to quickly create an e-mail to a specific recipient. When the user points to a hyperlink, the mouse pointer appears as a little hand, indicating that the object is a hyperlink.

You can create a hyperlink from any object on a Web page. To create a hyperlink, follow these steps:

1. Select the object that you want to use as the hyperlink. Create the object first if it does not yet exist on your Web site.

2. Click the Link button in the Page Builder toolbar to display the Hot Link dialog box. To create a link from a graphic object, you can also double-click it to open the Select a Picture dialog box, and use the Link To A Location options.

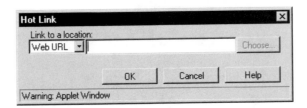

3. Choose the type of object that the link points to. The options are shown here on the right.

4. Enter the address of the location:

■ If you chose Web URL in step 3, type the Web site address of the page you want to display when the link is clicked.

■ If you chose My Page, click Choose to see a list of pages on your Web site. Select the page you want the link to display and then click OK.

■ If you chose My File, click Choose to see the Select File dialog box. Locate the file you want the link to open and then click OK.

■ If you chose E-Mail, the e-mail address that you have on record appears. You can leave the address as is to have mail sent to you, or enter the address of someone else.

■ If you chose Other, enter the address or name of the other server type, such as an FTP address for uploading or downloading files.

5. Click OK.

If you later need to change the link, select the object and click the Link button again.

Add-Ons

Yahoo! provides a number of special features you can add in addition to the ones on the toolbar. These features are called *add-ons*, and you access them by clicking the Add Ons button on the toolbar. Clicking the button opens the dialog box shown in Figure 6-7. In general, select an add-on by following these steps:

1. Choose a category to display icons for the add-ons within a category.

2. Click the add-on you want to insert.

Table 6-2 lists the add-ons that are available in each category. Select add-ons from the Animation category to insert animated graphics or text, or from the Instant Info category for

FIGURE 6-7   Add-ons for Web sites

dates, countdowns, and links to other information. The Interactive category provides the means for users to interact with you or Yahoo!, and the Forms and Scripts category lets you build custom forms for advanced Web sites.

After making changes to your Web site in Page Builder, click the Save button on the PageBuilder toolbar. You have to save the site before you can thoroughly test how everything within it works.

> **Tip** *You can also insert add-ons by using the Insert menu on the Page Builder menu bar.*

Basics   The Basics category contains common Web site elements. The Text add-on provides the same feature as the Text button on the Page Maker toolbar, while the Picture and Upload add-ons perform the same as using the Pictures button. This section explains adding lines, counting hits, adding buttons and bullets, and adding background music and graphics from the Basics category.

Horizontal and vertical lines help create a pleasant effect and separate elements on a Web page. Inserting a line is similar to inserting a graphic. To insert a line, follow these steps:

1. Click the Add-Ons button on the Page Builder toolbar.

2. Choose Basics from the Category list.

3. Click Vertical Lines or Horizontal Lines.

4. Select a group to display a list of the lines in a collection. Click the Upload option to use a line graphic you have on your disk.

Category	Add-Ons
Basics	Text, Picture, Upload Picture, Background, Background Music, Buttons, Bullets, Horizontal Lines, Vertical Lines, Counter
Fun and Games	Game Cheats, Indulgence Advisor, Recipe of the Day, Slot Machine, Tic-Tac-Toe, Love Test, Baby Countdown, Birthday Countdown, Countdown to the Big Day, Baseball 99, Video Poker, Beanie Babies Trivia, Computer Games Trivia, Entertainment Trivia, Current Events Trivia
Animation	Animated Logo, Fading Images, Gliding Image, Rotating Image, Random Image
Instant Info	Baby Countdown, Birthday Countdown, Big Day Countdown, Wedding Countdown, Time and Date Stamp, Yahoo! Search Box, GeoCities Search Box, Stock Charter, Counter, Yahoo! Maps, Yahoo! Directions, Mortgage Calculator
Interactive	Yahoo! Presence, Message Board, GeoGuide
Forms and Scripts	Check boxes, radio buttons, buttons, text fields, text areas, list boxes, and HTML code editor

TABLE 6-2   Add-Ons for Yahoo! Web Sites

5. Click the line you want to insert. Use the View Thumbnails option to display the lines in the group.

6. Click OK.

7. Adjust the size and position of the line by dragging.

If you want to know how many people access your Web site, insert a *hit counter*. The counter increments each time a person opens your site or clicks the Refresh button while viewing it. Inserting a counter in a Yahoo! Web site is easy because Yahoo! takes care of maintaining the counter for you. To insert a counter, follow these steps:

1. Click the Add-Ons button.

2. Choose Basics from the Category list.

3. Click Counter.

4. Move the counter where you want it to appear on the page.

5. Add any desired text, such as "you are viewer number," as a separate text object above the counter.

You are visitor number

0 0 0 0

Buttons and *bullets* are small graphics that add some design element to a page. You typically use a button as a hyperlink and a bullet to call attention to a text object. You add a button or bullet in much the same way as you do a line by following these steps:

1. Click the Add-Ons button.

2. Choose Basics from the Category list.

3. Click Button or Bullet.

4. Select a group to display a list of the buttons or bullets in a collection. Click the Upload option to use a graphic you have on your disk.

5. Click the specific object you want to insert. Use the View Thumbnails option to display the object in the group.

6. Click OK.

To use an inserted button as a hyperlink, click to select it and then define a hyperlink as you learned to do in "Working with Hyperlinks," earlier in this chapter. If you inserted a bullet, drag it to a position near a text object.

A *background* is a graphic that appears behind the text, graphics, and other objects on the page, much like the background of your Windows desktop. *Background music* is a music file that plays while a Web site is being viewed. In order to add background music, you must have the music file on your disk. Background graphics can also be from your disk, but you can get them as well from a collection of graphics or colors provided by Yahoo!.

To insert a background on your site, use these steps:

1. Click the Add-Ons button.

2. Choose Basics from the Category list.

3. Click Background.

4. Select a group to display a list of the background graphics in a collection. To add a solid color rather than a graphic, click Set Background Color, choose a color from the pallet that appears, and then click OK. You can also click the Upload option to use a graphic that you have on your disk.

5. Click OK.

Fun and Games   The add-ons in the Fun and Games category offer games and trivia contests in which users can participate. As shown here, the viewer can use the mouse to play the Slot Machine add-on.

To insert an add-on from the Fun and Games category, choose Fun and Games from the Category list and then click the item you want to insert. In some cases, a box for the add-on appears in Page Builder. Drag the box to the position where you want it to appear.

In other cases, a dialog box appears with options that must be set. If you choose Birthday Countdown, for example, you'll be asked to select the month and day of your birth date. A Countdown add-on is shown here:

As its name applies, a Countdown add-on counts down to the date in question. It shows the number of days, hours, minutes, and seconds until the event.

Animations   The options in the Animations category use two or more images to create a visual effect, such as one image fading into another or one graphic rotating over a second. You can choose images from the Yahoo! clip art collection or upload graphics that you have on your computer.

The process is generally the same as other add-ons. Follow these steps:

1. Click the Add-Ons button.

2. Choose Animations from the Category list.

3. Click the add-on that you want to insert.

In the dialog box that appears, select the graphics to use for the animation, and other options that affect its appearance. For example, the options for the Animated Logo add-on are shown here:

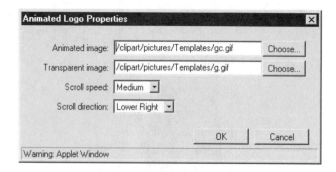

The add-on uses two graphics, a transparent image that appears in the background and an animated image that moves across it. You can accept the default images or click Choose to open the Choose Picture dialog box shown in Figure 6-8.

Use the Choose Picture dialog box to select the graphic from the Yahoo! clip art collection, or click the Upload button to use a graphic from your disk or a Web site.

How many images you can select and the other options in the Choose Picture dialog box depend on the animation you are dealing with.

■ The Animated Logo add-on lets you choose two graphics, select a scroll speed, and select a direction for the animated graphic.

■ The Fading Images add-on lets you choose five graphics, the number of seconds for the fade out and pause between pictures, and a background color.

■ The Gliding Images add-on lets you choose three graphics, the length of the glide and the pause between images, and either a background image or a solid color.

■ The Rotating Image add-on lets you choose a rotating and background graphic, the rotation and pause time, the rotation axis (either vertical or horizontal) and the background color.

■ The Random Images add-on lets you select up to three graphics and a background color.

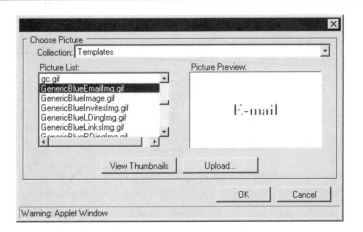

FIGURE 6-8   Selecting a graphic for an animation

Instant Info   The Instant Info category offers add-ons that present information of some sort. As you can see in Table 6-2, earlier in this section, some of the add-ons are duplicates of those found in other categories, but others are unique to Instant Info. Depending on the object, selecting an option from the Instant Info category either places the object on the page immediately or displays a dialog box of options for the object.

- ■ **Wedding Countdown**   Shows the amount of time until a wedding date that you specify.
- ■ **Time and Date Stamp**   Shows the date and time in the format of your choice. You can choose the background and foreground colors, and the font, font style, and font size; specify the date format; and choose to include the time in 12-hour format or 24-hour military format.

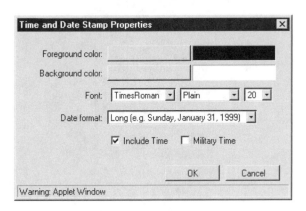

- **Yahoo! Search Box**   Displays a box, like the one shown at right, in which you can enter a keyword for a Yahoo! search.

- **GeoCities Search Box**   Displays a box to enter a keyword to search GeoCities Web sites. You can choose the box color.

- **Stock Charter**   Charts the prices of up to four stocks of your choosing, as shown in Figure 6-9. You'll need to enter the ticker symbol for each of the stocks you want to chart.

- **Yahoo! Maps**   Inserts a link to a map of the location of your choosing. Click the link to display a detailed map. You'll learn more about Yahoo! maps in Chapter 10.

- **Yahoo! Directions**   Displays a form for entering a starting address to see a map to a location of your choosing.

- **Mortgage Calculator**   Calculates either the monthly payments or principle amount of a mortgage based on user input. You can choose a color scheme for the calculator; the mortgage information is entered from your Web site.

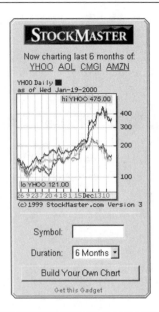

FIGURE 6-9   Charting stocks on your Web site

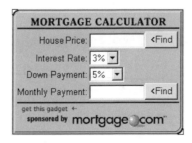

Interactive   The options in the Interactive category let you interact with other people. The options are

- Yahoo! Presence
- Message Board
- GeoGuide

The Yahoo! Presence add-on displays a graphic indicating whether you are logged on to Yahoo! Messenger or not. You can choose either a large or small icon.

If a person accessing your Web site sees that you are currently logged on, they can send you an instant message using the Yahoo! Messenger program or look for you in a chat room.

The Message Board lets people post and read public messages. *Posting* means to add a message to the board so everyone who accesses the message board can read it. The messages are organized into *threads*. A thread contains a message on a given topic and all replies to the message. People can either respond to a message by adding their response to the thread, or they can post a message on a new topic and in so doing start a new thread.

When others access your site, the box shown here will invite them to add a message to your board.

Clicking the box opens your message board, as shown in Figure 6-10. At the top of the screen are navigation buttons for displaying messages and the text of the first message on the board. Notice that the number of the message and the total number of messages is also shown, along with links to post a reply. If there are any replies to the displayed message, you'll also see a link to view replies to the message.

The viewer can use the Previous, Next, First, and Last links to move between messages, or enter the number of a message in the Go to Message # box and click Go to display a specific message.

At the bottom of the screen are the messages listed along with their subject, the ID of the person who posted the message, and the date and time the message was posted. To read a message, click it in the list. You see the text of the message in the upper section of the screen. The message displayed is indicated in the list by the arrow, as shown at right.

My Message Board My Home Page - Sign Out - Help

Administrative tools - Delete Msg - Edit board settings

We've made some changes, learn more about guestbooks and message boards.

< Previous | Next> [First | Last | **Msg List**] Post

My Message Board 1/20/00 3:48 pm

Welcome to my Yahoo! GeoCities Message Board.

Message: 1 of 2
View Replies to this Message

< Previous | Next> [First | Last | **Msg List**] Post

Go to Message # Go

| 2 | Let's do dinner | Barbara Neibauer | 1/20/00 3:50 pm |
| 1 => | My Message Board | azakuto_2000 | 1/20/00 3:48 pm |

FIGURE 6-10   Yahoo! message board for your Web site

To post a reply to a message, click the message so it appears in the upper part of the screen, and then click the Post link. Yahoo! opens the form shown in Figure 6-11. Fill out the form and then click either Post or Preview Before Posting at the bottom of the form.

To post a new message and start a new thread, click Msg List. This illustration shows a list of messages:

Go to: Start | Most Recent | Previous 40 | Next 40 | Msg # Go   **Post**

#	Subject	Author	Date (ET)
2	=> Let's do dinner	Barbara Neibauer	1/20/00 3:50 pm
1	My Message Board	azakuto_2000	1/20/00 3:48 pm

Click Post to open the message form and complete your message, and then click Post.

From the message list, you can also click Start to display the text of the first message or Most Recent to see the last message posted.

When a message has been replied to, you'll see this link below the text of the message:

View Replies to this Message

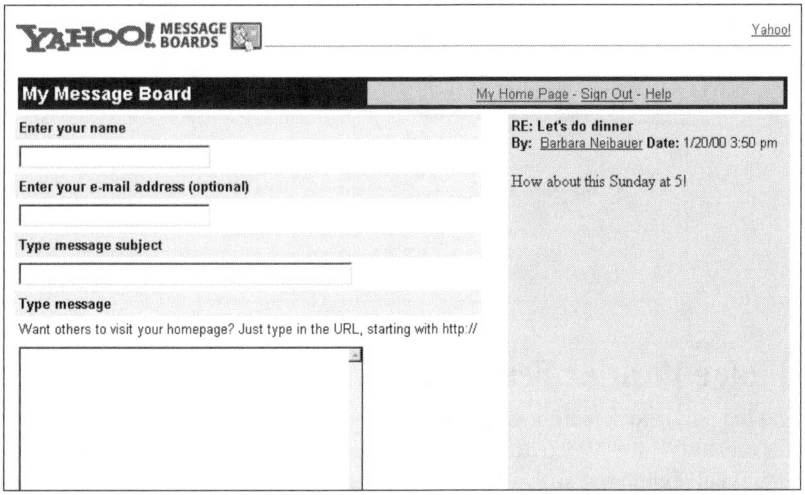

FIGURE 6-11   Posting a reply on the message board

Click the link to display a message list containing only replies to the current message.

The GeoGuide option offers an alternative to the Ad Square. GeoGuide is a horizontal banner that appears on your Web site with a message or advertisement from Yahoo!. If you use GeoGuide, you are a member of Yahoo! Banner Exchange. As a member, you allow banners from other Yahoo! sites to appear on your page and others allow your banner to appear on their pages. Exchanging banners this way increases the visibility of your Web site.

YAHOO! GeoCities Banner Exchange   Info

> **Note** *You'll learn more about exchanging banners in the section "Banner Exchange," later in this chapter.*

Forms and Scripts   If you are an advanced Web site builder and know HTML programming, you can use the Forms and Scripts add-ons to create your own online interactive forms. The choices in this category include check boxes, radio buttons, buttons, text fields, text areas, list boxes, and a simple HTML code editor.

You can easily insert any of the add-ons into a Web page, but using the responses to the form requires knowing how to program HTML. A sample form, for example, is shown next.

ORDER FORM

E-Mail Address [_____]

Comments

[text area]

Shipping [UPS ▾]

○ PC

○ Mac

○ Other

☑ Send more information

☑ Add me to your mailing list

[Submit]

Advanced Page Builder Features

More than a graphic editor for creating single Web site pages, Page Builder is a development environment for creating entire Web sites. From within Page Builder, you can add additional pages and even upload completed Web sites that you've developed and stored on your computer.

Working with Multiple Pages

To add another page to your site so you can create a link between pages, click the New button or choose New Page From Template on the File menu.

■ Clicking New opens a blank page in which you can insert text and graphic elements.

■ Choosing New Page From Template lets you select a Page Builder template as the basis for the new page. In the Load Pre-Made Page box that appears, choose the template you want to use and then click the Load button.

Click Open in the Page Builder toolbar to open another existing page in your Web site.

To add pages or graphic files that you have on your computer to your Web site, choose Import Images And Files from the File menu. You'll see the options in Figure 6-12. Enter the path and names of up to five files, or click the Browse buttons to locate the files, and then click the Upload button. If you upload a file named index.html, it will become your new home page. Remember to also upload any supporting files, such as graphics, that you want for the page. You can then open and edit the pages in Page Builder or use the graphic files as objects. After the pages have been uploaded, click OK in the message box that appears to continue working in Page Builder.

The File Manager option on the File menu opens another interface for working with your Web site files. Refer to the discussion of File Manager in the section "Advanced Editing," later in this chapter, for more information.

There are also a variety of properties to customize a page and Web site. Keep reading to find out what they are.

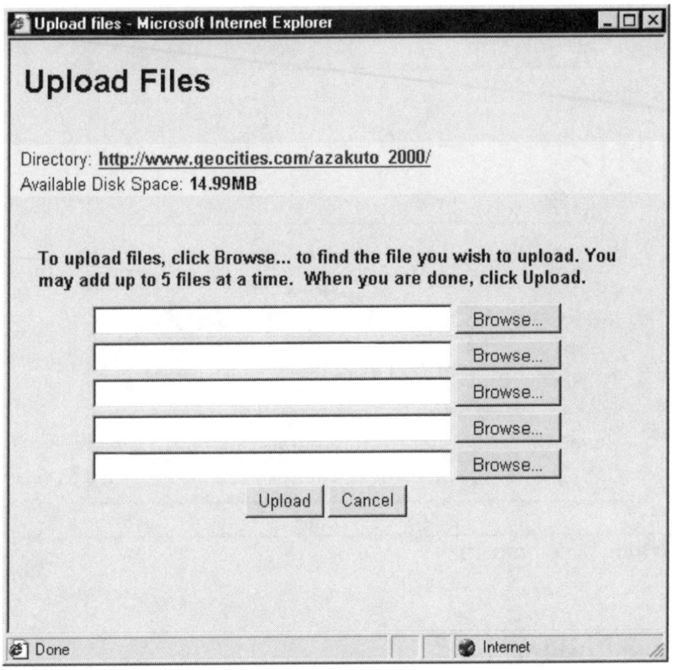

FIGURE 6-12   Uploading pages

Setting Page Properties

The page properties define the page's title, size, and colors. Page properties also help search engines index your page so that others can locate it on the Internet. To set the properties, choose Page Properties from the Page Builder Format menu. You'll see the Page Properties dialog box shown in Figure 6-13.

1. In the Title box, enter the text that you want visitors to your Web site to see in the title bar of their browsers.

2. In the Keywords box, enter any keywords that identify your page to search engines.

3. Enter your name in the Author box.

4. Select the Center check box if you want your page to be centered on the screen.

5. Change the width and height of the page, if desired. Enter the size in pixels.

6. Choose the default colors for text, links, and visited links. The Links color is used for hyperlinks that the viewer has not yet clicked.

7. Click OK.

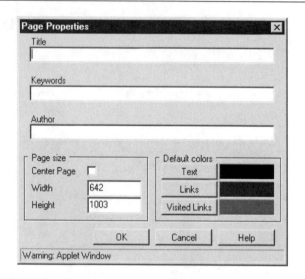

FIGURE 6-13
Setting page properties

Customizing Page Builder

There are also options you can set to customize the way Page Builder functions. Choose Preferences from the Page Builder Edit menu to open the Preferences dialog box shown in Figure 6-14. All of the options are selected, or turned on, by default. Deselect any of the options you want to turn off and then click OK. You can later select the option to turn it back on again.

The options are as follows:

- **Show Tooltips**   Displays the name or use of a toolbar when you point to it with the mouse
- **Show Tip Of The Day At Startup**   Displays a useful tip on using Page Builder each time the program starts
- **Show Overlapping Elements**   Displays the crosshatch pattern where objects overlap
- **Auto Properties**   Automatically assigns default properties to new objects based on the properties of similar existing ones
- **Show Outlines of Elements**   Places a border around each object to identify it as a separate page element
- **On Startup, Begin With The Last Page Edited**   Displays the last page you worked on when you start Page Builder
- **Cache Enabled**   Stores elements of Page Builder on your computer to help it start faster

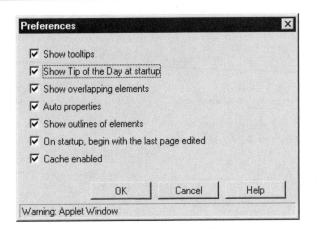

FIGURE 6-14	Customizing Page Builder

 You can also select Advanced Page Properties and Advanced Properties from the Format menu to add HTML code to either the page or a selected object.

Editing Pages

After you create and save a Web site or pages you created with Page Builder, it is easy to change the pages or add pages. From the GeoCities home page, click Edit, and then sign in if necessary to see the options in Figure 6-15.

Unless you are an advanced Web site builder, click Launch Page Builder. Page Builder starts and displays the last page that you worked on. You can now make changes to the page, open a page, or create a new one. To edit another page, for example, click Open to display a list of pages on your site. Click the page you want to edit and then click OK.

When you have finished editing the page, click Save to see the Save and Publish Page dialog box. Enter a new name for the page or select an existing name to replace it, and then click Save.

Advanced Editing

The Advanced section of the Edit Pages option lets you change files by editing their HTML tags. You can also create subdirectories, delete files, and change the organization of files.

First, choose whether you want to show the files on your site or enter the specific name of a file you'd like to edit. If you choose to show files, select the check boxes for the types of files you want to display—HTML, GIF, JPG, and others.

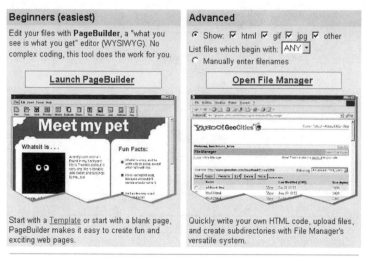

FIGURE 6-15   Editing options for GeoCities Web sites

  GIF and JPG (pronounced JPEG) are graphic files.

Then click Open File Manager to display a list of files and subdirectories, if you have any, as shown in Figure 6-16. The icons next to each item in the list indicate if the page is a subdirectory or was created with Page Builder or Yahoo! Wizard.

Caution *After you edit a Yahoo! Wizard Web page, you can no longer edit it using the wizards. However, you can edit it with Page Builder or by manually changing its HTML codes.*

The options at the top of the page let you perform these functions:

- **New**   Create a new Web site page by writing HTML codes.
- **Copy**   Make a copy of an existing Web page that you edit.
- **Rename**   Change the name of the selected page.
- **Edit**   Add, delete, or edit the HTML codes on the selected page.
- **Delete**   Remove the selected page from your Web site.
- **Move**   Move the selected page to a subdirectory.

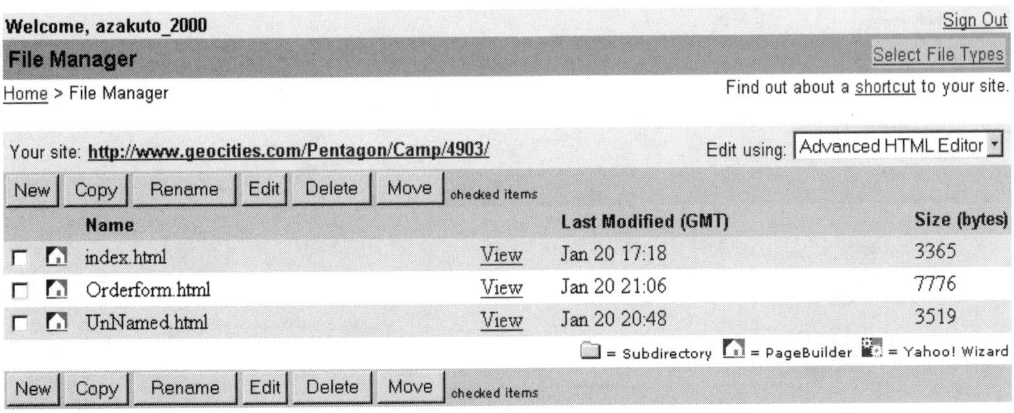

FIGURE 6-16   File Manager for GeoCities Web sites

To create a subdirectory, click New in the Subdirectories section, enter a name for the subdirectory in the box that appears, and then click Create Subdirectory.

Below the list of files and subdirectories in File Manager you'll find the EZ Upload options and several hyperlinks, as shown in Figure 6-17. *Uploading* means to transfer files from your hard disk to your Yahoo! site. You can upload HTML, graphics, and other files that make up a Web page. For that matter, you can simply upload files that you want to store online in your Yahoo! space.

You can use Microsoft Front Page, Microsoft Word, and any other program that lets you create Web sites and then transfer those Web sites to Yahoo!. Using the EZ Upload section, you can transfer up to five files at one time. Follow these steps to transfer files to your Yahoo! Web site:

1. Choose Automatically Convert Filenames To Lowercase to make your filenames compatible with the Yahoo! naming convention.

2. Choose Automatically Change ".HTM" Extensions To ".HTML" to match the Yahoo! naming convention. The default home page, for example, must be named in lowercase: index.html.

3. Enter the path and name of up to five files, or use the Browse buttons to locate the files on your computer.

4. Click Upload files.

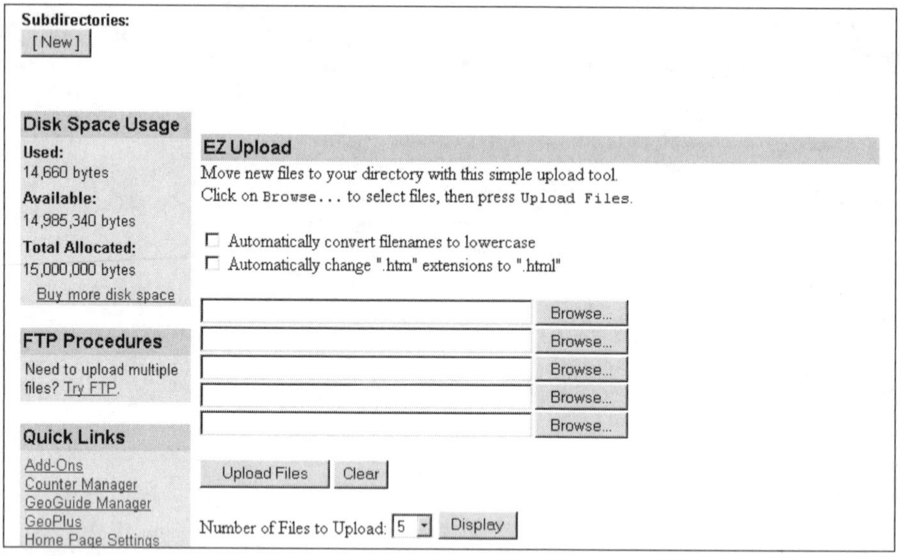

Subdirectories:
[New]

Disk Space Usage

Used:
14,660 bytes

Available:
14,985,340 bytes

Total Allocated:
15,000,000 bytes

Buy more disk space

FTP Procedures

Need to upload multiple files? Try FTP.

Quick Links

Add-Ons
Counter Manager
GeoGuide Manager
GeoPlus
Home Page Settings

EZ Upload

Move new files to your directory with this simple upload tool.
Click on Browse... to select files, then press Upload Files.

☐ Automatically convert filenames to lowercase
☐ Automatically change ".htm" extensions to ".html"

[   ] Browse...
[   ] Browse...
[   ] Browse...
[   ] Browse...
[   ] Browse...

[Upload Files] [Clear]

Number of Files to Upload: [5 ▼] [Display]

FIGURE 6-17   Uploading files

The Disk Space Usage section shows how much of your 15 megabytes of space is used and how much you have left. You can also click Buy More Disk Space to purchase additional space from Yahoo!

The FTP Procedures section explains how to upload files using an FTP program. FTP stands for *File Transfer Protocol*. There are several FTP programs that are designed just for uploading and downloading files.

The Quick Links section offers links to these features:

- **Add-Ons**   Lets you add features to your Web pages
- **Counter Manager**   Displays the number of hits on your Web pages and lets you change the number displayed by the hit counter
- **GeoGuide Manager**   Lets you exchange banners with other Yahoo! members
- **GeoPlus**   Offers additional Web site space and features for an additional cost

- ■ **Home Page Settings** Lets you change the theme, category, and other options concerning your Web site
- ■ **Move Me** Moves your Web site to another neighborhood
- ■ **Page Builder** Launches Page Builder
- ■ **Pages That Pay** Explains how to make money with your Web site

The Add-Ons option takes you to the list of add-ons that are also available from the GeoCities home page. Click a category of add-ons to see the features in a category. Figure 6-18, for example, shows the add-ons in the Interactive category.

The lists includes the same features that are available by clicking the Add-Ons button in Page Builder, but may also contain one or more additional features. The adds-ons available in Page Builder are indicated by the Try This In Page Builder link. Click that link to start Page Builder and insert the selected add-on.

Click Preview to see a sample of the add-on, or click Get It to access the HTML code required to insert the add-on in your Web site. Add-ons without the Try This In Page Builder link can only be inserted using HTML tags. For more information about the add-on, click its name.

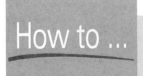 **Make Money with Pages That Pay**

The Pages That Pay feature lets you make money from your Yahoo! GeoCities Web site. You can insert links on your page to certain merchants who are affiliated with Yahoo! and earn money when someone makes a purchase from the merchant by going there from your page.

The commissions vary, but can be as high as 15 percent, and some merchants even pay commissions on your own purchases.

To start earning money, click the Join Today link on any Pages That Pay page and follow the instructions.

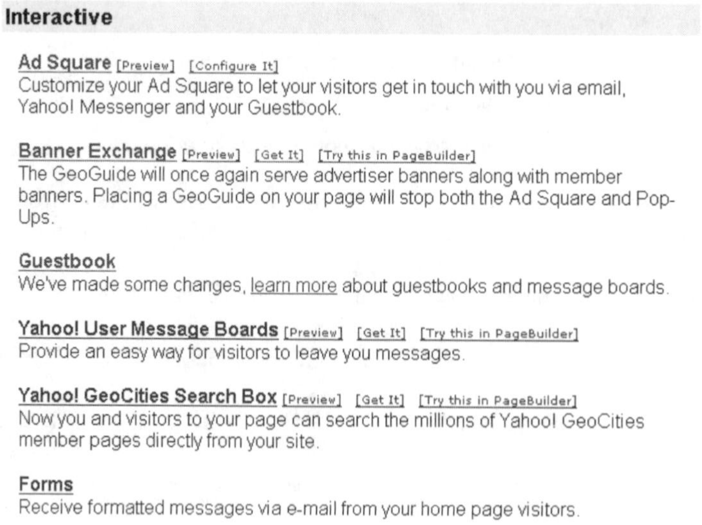

Interactive

Ad Square [Preview] [Configure It]
Customize your Ad Square to let your visitors get in touch with you via email,
Yahoo! Messenger and your Guestbook.

Banner Exchange [Preview] [Get It] [Try this in PageBuilder]
The GeoGuide will once again serve advertiser banners along with member
banners. Placing a GeoGuide on your page will stop both the Ad Square and Pop-
Ups.

Guestbook
We've made some changes, learn more about guestbooks and message boards.

Yahoo! User Message Boards [Preview] [Get It] [Try this in PageBuilder]
Provide an easy way for visitors to leave you messages.

Yahoo! GeoCities Search Box [Preview] [Get It] [Try this in PageBuilder]
Now you and visitors to your page can search the millions of Yahoo GeoCities
member pages directly from your site.

Forms
Receive formatted messages via e-mail from your home page visitors.

FIGURE 6-18   Interactive add-ons

Table 6-3 shows the additional add-ons that are available here but not in Page Builder.

Category	Add-On	Function
Interactive	Add Square	Lets you add links to the Ad Square. You can display your profile and allow others to send you mail and instant messages, sign your guestbook, send the displayed page as an e-mail, and go to the neighborhood in which your page is located.
	Instant Crime Watch	Displays a scrolling list of crime-related headlines.
	Web site headlines	Displays a scrolling list of news headlines.
	Guestbook	Lets you add a guestbook that viewers can sign and leave a short message in.
Fun and Games	Basketball 99	Displays basketball scores, schedules, and other information.
	Star Trek Trivia	Offers a trivia game for Star Trek fans.
	Star Wars Trivia	Offers a trivia game for Star Wars fans.

TABLE 6-3   Some Additional Add-Ons Not Available in Page Builder

Category	Add-On	Function
Animation & Multimedia	Drop–down menu	Lets you create a menu bar with drop-down menus on your page.
	Horizontal site menu	Lets you add a menu bar across the top of your page.
	Image Highlight menu	Lets you add visual effects to graphic objects.
	Scrolling text and images	Lets you add a box of scrolling text or graphics.
	Things	Lets you insert interesting multimedia objects.
	Streaming media	Lets you insert streaming video, such as wedding or family movies, in your site. However, the feature requires paying an extra charge.
	Vertical menu	Lets you add a menu bar down the side of your page.

TABLE 6-3   Some Additional Add-Ons Not Available in Page Builder *(continued)*

6

GuestBook

The Guestbook is a good example of using HTML code to add a feature to your Web site. The guestbook has two parts: the sign-in page where persons leave information about themselves, and the view entries page where persons can display sign-in information about other persons.

When you select Guestbook from the Interactive add-ons, the Guestbook Set-Up form appears. The form has four parts:

- **Guestbook Sign-In Page section**   Here, you specify the greeting that appears on the sign-in page, the colors of the page, and the overall layout. You can also specify up to nine fields of information to obtain. By default, for example, the sign-in form prompts for a name, URL (Web site address), and e-mail address. You can change these or add prompts, such as for a favorite site, hobby, or any other information you'd want the person signing in to enter.

- **Guestbook View Entries Page section**   Here, you determine how the entries appear. You can set the background and text color, the color of hyperlinks, and the page title. You can also place a separator line between the heading and lists, as well as between entries.

- **Set Aside Your Cut & Paste Code section**   Here, you see the HTML code you'll need to insert in your Web page to let users access the guestbook. You can either copy the text from that page or click the Pop-Up My Code button to display the code in a separate window that you can leave onscreen as you edit your page.

■ **Save Your Guestbook To Your Homestead Directory section**   You click Save My Guestbook to add two pages to your site: addbook.html and geobook.html. These are the actual guestbook files:

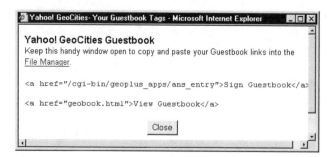

You then have to copy the HTML code for your guestbook into your Web page. Follow these steps:

1. Select Guestbook from the Interactive add-ons.

2. Choose options from the page to customize your guestbook.

3. Click Pop-Up My Code to display the code for the guestbook.

4. Click Save My Guestbook.

5. Go back to the Edit Pages screen.

6. Click Open File Manager.

7. Select the page on which you want to place the guestbook links and click Edit to see the HTML code for the page.

8. Find a location where you want to place the links. This might require some trial and error, but the safest place to put the code is at the bottom of the HTML code, just above the </BODY> instruction. Insert a blank line before the line to make room for the code, as shown at right.

```
</center>

</body>
</html>
```

9. Drag over the code in the pop-up box, right-click, and choose Copy from the shortcut menu.

10. Right-click where you want to place the code and select Paste.

```
</center>
<a href="/cgi-bin/geoplus_apps/ans_entry">Sign Guestbook</a>

<a href="geobook.html">View Guestbook</a>

</body>
</html>
```

11. Click Save.

12. Close the pop-up code window.

When you view your Web site, the guestbook links look like this: <u>Sign Guestbook</u> <u>View Guestbook</u>
When visitors click the Sign Guestbook link, they open the
sign-in form, as shown in Figure 6-19. Visitors can enter the information they wish to leave and
click the I'm Done! button. A Thank You message appears. Visitors can click Return To My
Homestead to return to your Web site.

Click the View Guestbook link to see the book's entries, as shown in Figure 6-20. If a person
entered his or her e-mail address, it appears as a link. You can click the link to send an e-mail
message to someone who made an entry in your guestbook.

Banner Exchange

The banner exchange is a great way to expose your site. A Yahoo! member can create a graphic
called a *banner*. Member banners will be inserted at random on Yahoo! GeoCities Web site pages
that have a GeoGuide add-on. The banners are hyperlinks to the members' Web sites; so if a person
sees a banner that looks interesting, he or she can click it to go quickly to a Web site.

You have to create the banner yourself using a graphics program. The banner must be 468
pixels wide and 60 pixels high, and no larger than 8KB.

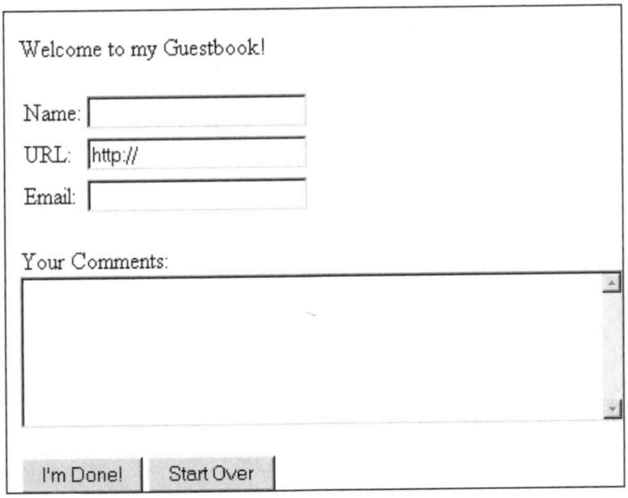

6

Welcome to my Guestbook!

Name:
URL: http://
Email:

Your Comments:

I'm Done!   Start Over

FIGURE 6-19   Signing a guestbook

```
┌─────────────────────────────────────────────────────────────┐
│  ┌───────────────────────────────────────────────────────┐  │
│  │  YAHOO! GeoCities Banner Exchange              Info   │  │
│  │            Welcome to my Guestbook!                    │  │
│  │  ═══════════════════════════════════════════════════  │  │
│                                                             │
│     Eileen Zakuto - 01/20/00 21:21:56                       │
│                                                             │
│     Comments:                                               │
│     I like your website.                                    │
│                                                             │
│     Alan Neibauer - 01/20/00 21:18:15                       │
│     My URL:http://www.neibauer.net                          │
│     My Email:alan@neibauer.net                              │
│                                                             │
│     Comments:                                               │
│     Hi...welcome to Yahoo!                                  │
│                                                             │
│  ═══════════════════════════════════════════════════════   │
│     My Home Page | Visit Pentagon/Camp | Explore Yahoo!     │
│     GeoCities | Get your own free homepage                  │
│                                                             │
└─────────────────────────────────────────────────────────────┘
```

FIGURE 6-20   Viewing a guestbook

1. Create the banner and then upload it to your Web site. Make sure you insert the GeoGuide add-on into your index.html page.

2. Choose the Interactive add-on group from the GeoCities page.

3. Click Banner Exchange to open the Yahoo! GeoCities Banner Exchange page. It will provide information about the Banners feature.

4. Click the Submit It link.

5. In the page that appears, enter the URL where the banner is located. You must enter the specific URL, not just the Web site shortcut, like so:

   http://www.geocities.com/Pentagon/Camp/4903/banner.gif

6. Click Submit. The banner is sent to Yahoo!. Yahoo! will review the banner to determine if it is appropriate for the program.

7. Click the GeoGuide Banner Exchange link on the Yahoo!   GeoGuide's Banner Exchange.
   GeoCities Banner Exchange page, shown at right.

8. Select a background color for your GeoGuide box, and choose the types of banner that you will permit on your site. Level 1 banners have been determined to be suitable for viewers of all ages; Level II banners are of general interest. Choose All Banners if you do not want to place any restrictions on the banners that will be displayed.

Chapter 7

Your Yahoo! Home Away from Home

How to . . .

- Store files online with Yahoo! Briefcase
- Use Yahoo! with pagers, cell phones, Web phones, and personal digital assistants (PDAs)
- Get stock, weather, and other information on your mobile device
- Create a Yahoo! menu on your PDA
- Download software for your PDA

You now have your e-mail and calendar on Yahoo!, and you've personalized them for your preferences and tastes. The next step is to make Yahoo! an extension of your home computer.

With Yahoo! Briefcase and Yahoo! Mobile, you can access your files and Yahoo! services no matter where you are. Using Briefcase, you can store your files online and access them from any computer that is connected to the Internet. With Yahoo! Mobile, you can get your e-mail, view your calendar, and even be alerted about news, financial information, and weather conditions from a pager or other mobile device.

Yahoo! Briefcase

In addition to your e-mail space, Yahoo! gives each member 10 MB of free disk space for storing files of almost any type. You can use this space, called the *Briefcase*, to store backup copies of important files or store files that you'd like to access from any location.

For example, suppose you start a document at home but don't have time to complete it, so you plan to continue working on the document at the office. One alternative is to copy the document to a floppy disk, carry the disk to your office, and copy the document from the floppy to the hard disk in the office. When you complete the document, you copy the file to the floppy disk, carry the disk home, and copy it to the hard disk. Copying files this way assumes that the file isn't larger than 1.4 MB and can fit on a regular floppy.

A better alternative is to store the document online in your Yahoo! Briefcase. To do so, you upload the document from home to your Yahoo! disk space. *Upload* means to copy a document from a computer to a computer on the Internet. When you get to the office, you download the same document from Yahoo! *Download* means to retrieve a document from a computer on the Internet. With the document downloaded, you can then complete it at the office. When you have finished working on it, you can upload it to Yahoo! so that you can download it again from home.

Documents that you upload and download to the Briefcase can be as large as 5 MB, so you can use your Briefcase to store documents, graphics, and sounds. The Briefcase accepts most types of files, including graphic files, sound files, Web pages, Microsoft Word documents, Microsoft Excel spreadsheets, Microsoft Access databases, and other popular file formats.

Note *Graphic file types include JPEG (Joint Photographic Experts Group), GIF (Graphics Interchange Format), and BMP (bitmap). Sound file formats include MP3 (Moving Picture Experts Group) and AIFF (Audio Interchange File Format).*

In storing files online, Yahoo! asks that you abide by its guidelines and standards, as set forth in this statement:

> Yahoo! considers the contents of your Briefcase to be the private communications between you and the people you have designated to have access to your Briefcase. Yahoo! will not monitor, edit, or disclose the contents of a User's private communications, except that User agrees Yahoo! may do so: (a) as required by law; (b) to comply with legal process; (c) if necessary to enforce Yahoo!'s Universal Terms of Service and these Community Guidelines; (d) to respond to claims that such contents violate the rights of third parties; (e) to protect the rights or property of Yahoo! or others; and (f) to identify or resolve technical problems or respond to complaints about the Service.

You can share Briefcase files with others. Rather than send a large file to a person as an e-mail attachment, for example, you can upload it to your Briefcase and grant permission for others to access the file. Persons to whom you grant access can download the file to their computers when it is convenient for them. This is a perfect way to distribute a file to a number of persons without sending a copy to each individual.

Accessing Your Briefcase

You don't have to do anything special to create a Briefcase—it is yours automatically as long as you are a registered Yahoo! member. To get to your Briefcase, follow either of these steps:

- Point your browser to http://briefcase.yahoo.com/.
- From the Yahoo! More screen, click Briefcase.

If you are not already logged on to Yahoo!, enter your Yahoo! ID and password and then click Sign In. You'll see your Briefcase, as shown in Figure 7-1. The default Briefcase contains two folders: My Folder and My Photo Album.

You can store any types of files in My Folder, but only graphic files in My Photo Album. The Briefcase window shows you how much of the 10 MB of space you are using, the number of files in the Briefcase, the total size of the files in each folder, the type access, and the date the folder was created. You also see the familiar Yahoo! edit and delete icons for editing and deleting folders.

To display the contents of a folder, just click its name.

Adding Files to Your Briefcase

When you are ready to add a file to your Briefcase, connect to the Internet and go to your Briefcase. Next, decide in which folder you want to place the file:

- To add a file to My Folder, click Add File.
- To add a graphic to My Photo Album, click Add Photo.

Hello, **aneibauer**! Welcome to your briefcase.   Options
Folder List

Showing 1 - 2 of 2 folders (0 KB used of 10000 KB total)   Create: ☐Folder | ☑Album

Name	Files/Photos	Access	Created	Add	Edit	Delete
☐My Folder	0 (0 KB)	Private	9-Jan-2000	Add File	✎	🗑
☑My Photo Album	0 (0 KB)	Private	9-Jan-2000	Add Photo	✎	🗑

Showing 1 - 2 of 2 folders (0 KB used of 10000 KB total)   Create: ☐Folder | ☑Album

For quick access, bookmark http://briefcase.yahoo.com/aneibauer Tell your friends!

Welcome	Getting Started
The holidays may be over but the sharing goes on! Use Yahoo! Briefcase to share with friends and family the	**Add briefcase to My Yahoo! now!** To add a shortcut to your briefcase from My Yahoo!, simply click here! Don't forget you can get easy access to briefcase from Yahoo! Companion! More help. **How do I share photos and files with friends?** Click on "Edit" next to either folder above.

FIGURE 7-1   An empty Yahoo! Briefcase

You'll see the options shown in Figure 7-2.

If you know the path and name of the file, enter it in the topmost text box. To locate the file, click Browse to open the Choose File dialog box. Then, use standard Windows techniques to locate and select the file. Make certain, for example, that the Files Of Type box is set at All Files (*.*) so you'll see a list of all files and folders in the current location.

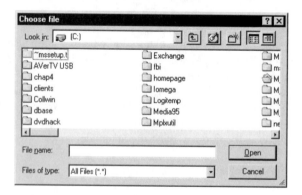

The Look In list shows the name of the current folder that contains documents to open. Documents and other folders in that location are displayed in the large box below it. To choose another disk or folder, click the down arrow to the right of the list and choose from the items that appear. To open a subfolder whose name is listed in the large window, double-click it. When you find the file you want to upload, double-click it, or click it once and then click the Open button.

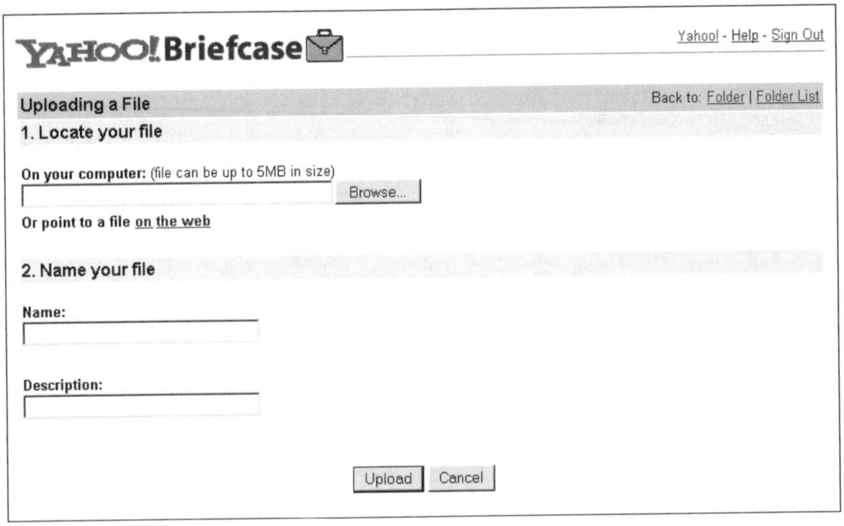

7

YAHOO! Briefcase

Yahoo! - Help - Sign Out

Uploading a File

Back to: Folder | Folder List

1. Locate your file

On your computer: (file can be up to 5MB in size)

[ ] Browse...

Or point to a file on the web

2. Name your file

Name:

[ ]

Description:

[ ]

Upload   Cancel

FIGURE 7-2   Placing a file in a Briefcase folder

Enter an optional name for the file that clearly identifies it, give the file an optional brief description, and then click Upload to begin the transfer process. Yahoo! reads the file from your disk and records it on its disk in your Briefcase folder.

You can also add a link to a Web page to the Briefcase. You can then click the link to open the page, just as you would a favorite Web site or bookmark. Placing a link in the Briefcase is particularly useful when you are sharing a folder with friends because they have access to Web sites that you want to make available to them. To add a Web site link to a Briefcase, click the underlined On The Web link. Then enter the address of the site and click Add Link.

From the Adding A File Link page, click Upload From Your Computer if you change your mind and want to add a file or photo instead of a link.

When the file is uploaded, Yahoo! opens the folder in which you placed it. Figure 7-3, for example, shows a user's My Folder section of the Briefcase. To return to the list of folders, click the Folder List link next to the Back To prompt shown at right.

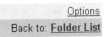

Working with Briefcase Files

Each file in the folder is shown with its name underlined, along with its type and size. Files less than 1,000 bytes large will be shown as having 0 KB, although they do take up space in the Briefcase. You'll also see the date that the file was posted, or uploaded, to the Briefcase.

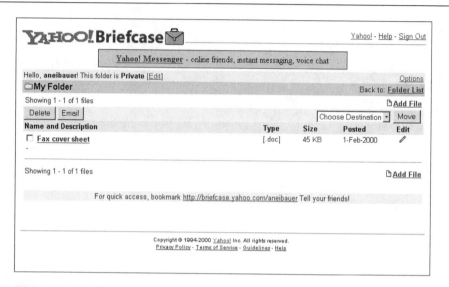

FIGURE 7-3   Open folder

Downloading Files   To download a file to your computer, click its name to open the File
Download dialog box, which offers two options for downloading files:

- Open This File From Its Current Location
- Save This File To Disk

Click Save This File To Disk and then click OK to open the Save As dialog box:

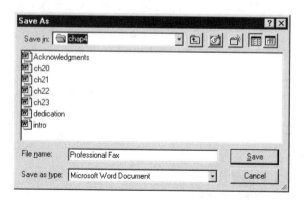

If you click a Web link in a folder, the Web site will be displayed in your browser.

Tip

Use the Save In list, and the large box below it, to locate the folder where you want to place the downloaded file. You can change the name in the File Name box if you want to store the file under a different name than the one in the Briefcase. Click Save to download the file.

You can use the Open option in the File Download dialog box when the file is a type that your system recognizes. For example, you can select to open a text file—one with the TXT extension—because Windows knows how to display a text file on your system. Generally, however, it is recommended that you never open a file directly from the Briefcase, but download it to your computer first.

Changing and Deleting Files   Your Yahoo! Briefcase stores files differently than a traditional folder on a disk. With a traditional folder, you cannot have two files under the same name. If you copy a file whose name matches that of an existing file, you'll be asked if you want to replace the current file.

Your Yahoo! Briefcase stores files in a *virtual folder*. The files are stored on Yahoo!'s computers wherever Yahoo! can find space for them, but their names are displayed in a single folder onscreen. If you upload a file whose name matches an existing one in the folder, the new file will be placed in the virtual folder without any trouble. In fact, any number of identically named files can be kept in the same folder. Each is stored separately without replacing another.

This can be a benefit if you need to store more than one version of a file. Each will have the same name but a different date—the date that you uploaded it to your Briefcase. You can use the date to differentiate the versions of the file. If you want to replace a current file with a newer version, however, you'll need to delete the original before uploading its replacement.

To delete a file from a folder, select the check box to the left of its name and then click Delete.

To change the optional name and description that you gave to a file when you uploaded it, click the Edit icon to the right of the file's name. Change the names in the box that appears, and then click Modify Document to return to the folder.

Sending Files to Others

You will soon learn how to share your folders with other persons so that they can access the folder to download any files that it contains. If you only want to make one file available to a specific user, however, you can e-mail him or her a link to the file.

E-mailing a link is different than e-mailing an actual file. When you e-mail a file as an attachment, the entire file is downloaded to the person's Inbox. The file has to be uploaded from your computer as part of the e-mail process.

E-mailing a link sends the recipient a hyperlink that points to the location of the file in your Briefcase. The recipient then clicks the link to display the File Download box and get access to the file.

To e-mail a link to one or more files, select the check box next to the file names and then click the e-mail button. You see the options shown in Figure 7-4. Type the e-mail address of the recipient. To send links to more than one person, separate the e-mail addresses—you can send links to as many as five recipients—with spaces or commas. You can also type a brief message that will be included with the e-mail. Click Send E-mail. A message appears reporting that the e-mail was sent successfully. Send the e-mail to others or click Folder or Folder List (next to the Back To prompt) to return to another Briefcase location.

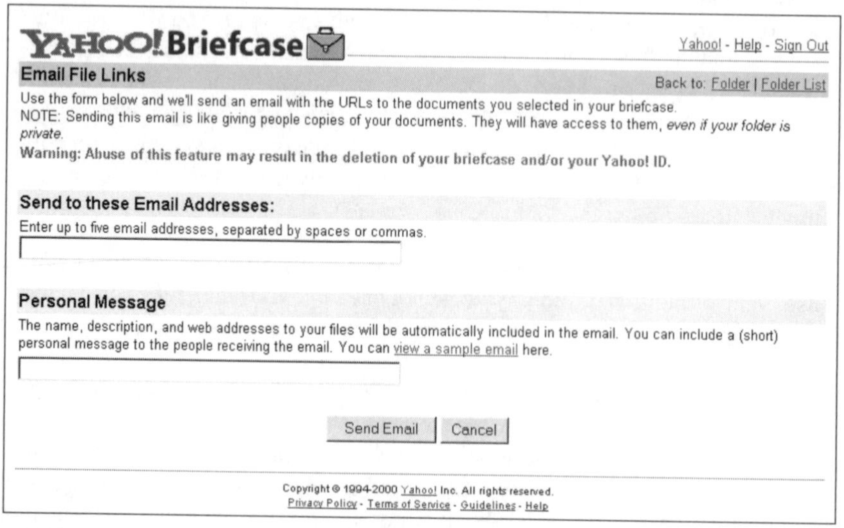

YAHOO!Briefcase 🖅   Yahoo! - Help - Sign Out

Email File Links   Back to: Folder | Folder List

Use the form below and we'll send an email with the URLs to the documents you selected in your briefcase.
NOTE: Sending this email is like giving people copies of your documents. They will have access to them, *even if your folder is private.*

Warning: Abuse of this feature may result in the deletion of your briefcase and/or your Yahoo! ID.

Send to these Email Addresses:
Enter up to five email addresses, separated by spaces or commas.

[   ]

Personal Message
The name, description, and web addresses to your files will be automatically included in the email. You can include a (short) personal message to the people receiving the email. You can view a sample email here.

[   ]

                    [Send Email]   [Cancel]

                    Copyright © 1994-2000 Yahoo! Inc. All rights reserved.
                    Privacy Policy · Terms of Service · Guidelines · Help

FIGURE 7-4   E-mailing a link to a Briefcase file

 *You cannot use the Move option until you create your own custom folders.*

The e-mail is sent directly from Yahoo!; it is not placed in your e-mail system's Outbox. The e-mail will include links to the files and your e-mail address, as well as the filename, a description of the file, and the file size of each of the files, shown at right.

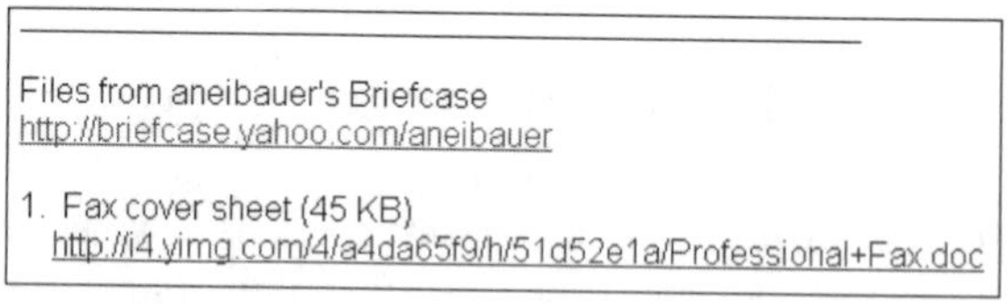

Files from aneibauer's Briefcase
http://briefcase.yahoo.com/aneibauer

1. Fax cover sheet (45 KB)
   http://i4.yimg.com/4/a4da65f9/h/51d52e1a/Professional+Fax.doc

Sharing Folders

Sending an e-mail link lets you share one or more specific files with others. If you want to share multiple files without the overhead of sending e-mails, you can share an entire folder.

You can share a folder with everyone and make it available to anyone who accesses the Briefcase over the Internet. And you can also share a folder with specific Yahoo! members by providing the Yahoo! ID of those persons who will have access to the folder.

The current sharing status of a folder is shown in the Access column in the folder list and next to your name in the open folder. Private status means that no one can access the folder without signing in with your ID and password. The other possible status options are Everyone and Friends.

To share a folder, use either of these techniques:

- From the Folder List, click the Edit icon to the right of the folder name.
- From the open folder, click Edit.

Yahoo! opens the window shown in Figure 7-5. In addition to renaming the folder, you can choose the type of access you want to allow. If you select Friend, enter the ID of all Yahoo! members that you want to access the folder. Only those persons will be able to download the files in the folder by giving their Yahoo! membership IDs. Separate the IDs with a space or comma. Click Modify Folder when you've finished.

To make it easy for persons to access your folder, give them this address:

http://briefcase.yahoo.com/*your_ID*

or

http://briefcase.yahoo.com/bc/*your_ID*

Going to that address takes persons directly to your Briefcase as a guest. When they go to that site, they will see the folder list showing folders designated for sharing with Everyone. To see folders designated for friends, they have to click the Sign In link shown at right.

> Don't see your friend's shared folders? **Sign In**

You can change the access type at any time by choosing Edit the Folder.

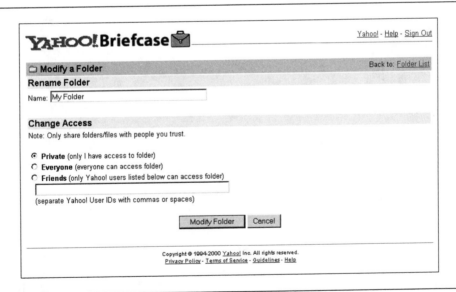

FIGURE 7-5   Sharing a folder

 *You can access someone's Briefcase by looking at her public profile. If that person has chosen to list her Briefcase on her profile, all you need to do is click the link to access the public files in her Briefcase.*

Adding Briefcase to Your Profile

You can also make it easy for others to access your Briefcase by adding it to your public profile. To quickly access your profile, select More from the initial Yahoo! screen, click Profiles, and then click Edit My Profile. Enter your Yahoo! ID and password and click Sign In if you are not yet signed in, and then click Edit. Look for the On Yahoo! section shown at right.

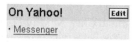

Click Edit in that section to see a list of the Yahoo! features that you can add to that section, as shown in Figure 7-6 . Select the check box for Briefcase and then click Finish.

Tell your friends to access your profile at the following site, and then click the Briefcase link in the On Yahoo! section:

http://profiles.yahoo.com/*Your_User-ID*

Creating Folders

You can create your own custom folders to supplement the two folders that Yahoo! supplies in your Briefcase. Create a new folder, for instance, to share some but not all files with the public

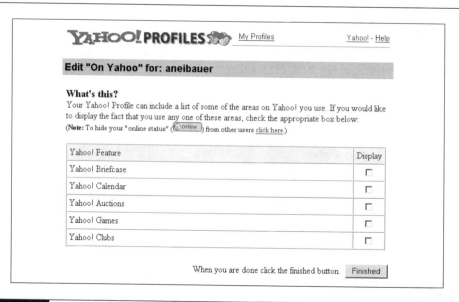

FIGURE 7-6   Adding features to your profile

or friends. You can leave My Folder set at the default private access where you store files that you do not want to share, and use your custom folder for shared files.

You should also create folders to help organize your online files. Create one folder to store work documents and another for personal files, for example. Create a new album for each type of graphic file you want to store. Organize your pictures by subject in albums.

To create a new folder, click the Folder or Album links next to the Create prompt at the top of your Briefcase Folder List. Choose Album only if you want to create a folder for graphic files. Yahoo! displays the options shown in Figure 7-7.

Enter a name for the folder and select the level of sharing (Private, Everyone, or Friends) and click Finished. Your new folder appears in the folder list, and you can add files to it just as you've already learned to do with default folders.

Moving Files to Folders

If you already have files in a Briefcase folder, you can move them to a custom folder that you created. Open the folder containing the file you want to move. Select the check box next to each file you want to move, pull down the Choose Destination list, select the folder, and then click Move.

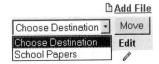

You can only select a custom folder from the list, not one of the default Yahoo! folders.

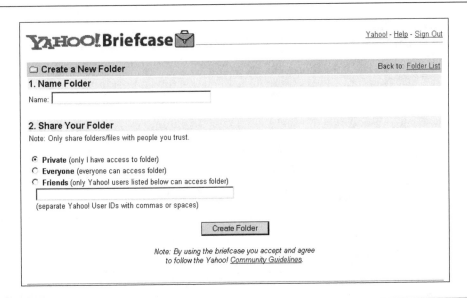

FIGURE 7-7   Creating a new folder

Yahoo! Mobile

Storing your files online is just one way you can take advantage of Yahoo! when you're on the road. Yahoo! offers a whole range of services for the road warrior. Yahoo! Mobile lets you get many Yahoo! services on mobile devices, including these:

- Pagers
- Cell phones
- Web phones
- Personal digital assistants (PDAs)

At Yahoo! Mobile, you'll get step-by-step directions and even the software you need to use Yahoo! mail, messenger, and other services on your mobile device called Yahoo! To Go. You'll be able to check your mail and calendar. You can also be notified about meetings, stock quotes, sports scores, the weather, and even auctions.

Caution *To be notified about events, you'll need a pager or mobile phone with text-messaging capability, an e-mail address, and a Yahoo! ID. To check your e-mail and calendar, you'll need a PDA that uses Palm OS Windows CE, a modem, and a Web browser.*

You access all the Yahoo! mobile features from Yahoo! Mobile. Click More in the main Yahoo! page and then click Mobile to see the options shown in Figure 7-8.

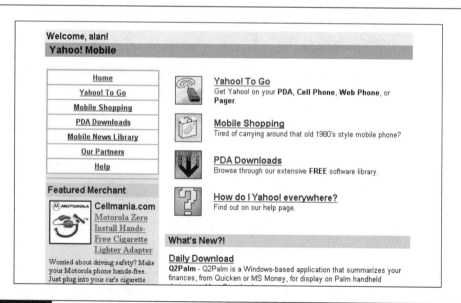

FIGURE 7-8   Yahoo! Mobile

Shortcut *Go directly to Yahoo! Mobile at http://mobile.yahoo.com/wireless/home.*

The choices are as follows:

- Yahoo! To Go lets you receive Yahoo! information on your mobile device.
- Mobile Shopping features hardware and software for mobile users.
- PDA Downloads offers free software for mobile computing.
- How Do I Yahoo! Everywhere? provides detailed help information.
- Mobile News Library provides top news stories of interest to mobile users.
- Our Partners offers links to mobile service providers.
- What's New highlights top news stories.
- From The Mobile News Library presents selected stories from the Mobile News Library.

Yahoo! To Go

The Yahoo! To Go option lets you set up your mobile device and Yahoo! so that they work together, as well as specify the content that will be sent to your device. Clicking Yahoo! To Go from the Yahoo! Mobile page displays three options: Mobile Alerts, Yahoo! On Your PDA, and Yahoo! On Your Phone.

Mobile Alerts

Mobile Alerts lets you specify the information that Yahoo! automatically sends to your mobile device. Click My Alerts from the Yahoo! To Go page to display the types of alerts that you can select, as shown in Figure 7-9. The options are as follows:

- **My Stock Alert**   Sends you market price information concerning stocks in your portfolio.
- **My Weather Alert**   Sends you weather reports for areas of your choosing.
- **My Horoscope Alert**   Sends you a daily horoscope.
- **My Other Alerts**   Lets you forward your Yahoo! e-mail and auction information.

Click the link for the type of alert you want to create. If you haven't yet told Yahoo! the type of device you are using, however, you'll be taken through the steps of registering your device so Yahoo! knows how to communicate with it.

Tip *Follow these steps and enter your regular e-mail address to have alerts sent to you via e-mail.*

1. Click Add Alert. Read the information that appears and then click Continue. You now select the type of device.

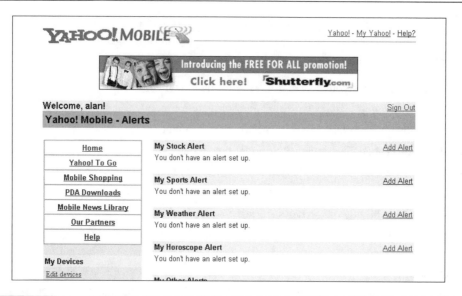

FIGURE 7-9   Yahoo! Alerts

2. On the Device Type pull-down list, select Cell Phone or Alphanumeric Pager.

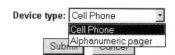

3. Click Submit to see the options shown in Figure 7-10.

4. Enter a name for the device.

5. Select the message length, either summaries (up to 90 characters) or the full message (up to 300 characters).

6. Choose the maximum number of messages to receive in the Message Limit list.

7. Choose your time zone.

8. Click Submit.

9. Enter your device's e-mail address and click Send. If you do not know the e-mail address of your pager or cell phone, ask your communications provider.

10. Yahoo! displays the Verify Wireless Device screen that shows your e-mail address and a box in which you have to enter a confirmation code. It also sends your device a message with the code. Enter the code in the Verify Wireless Device box and click Verify My Account to display your device list, as shown in Figure 7-11. Here, you can add a new device or edit or delete a listed device.

11. Click Finished. You are now ready to set up alerts.

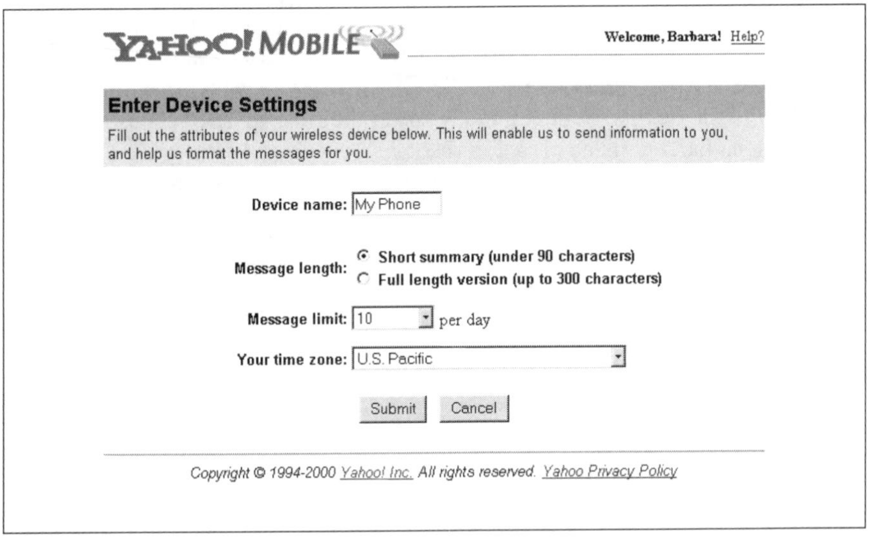

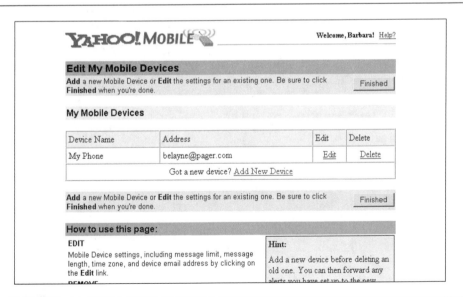

FIGURE 7-10   Selecting device options

FIGURE 7-11   Registered mobile devices

Setting Up Alerts You can now click Add Alert in the My Alerts page to set up a stock, weather, or horoscope alert, or click links that help you forward your e-mail and auction information.

Selecting Add Alert in the My Stock Alerts section, for example, displays the list of stocks in your Yahoo! portfolio, as shown in Figure 7-12. Select whether you want price information midday, at the close of the market, or both midday and at the closing. Then choose the mobile device to which to send the report and click Finished.

The options for your horoscope, shown here, let you choose your sign, the time and frequency of delivery, and the device.

Step 1: Choose a sign
Aquarius (January 21 - February 19)

Step 2: Select time of delivery
Time: 1 :00 pm
Frequency: Daily

Step 3: Select delivery method
Mobile Device: My Phone (bneibauer@yahoo.com)

Weather options let you select one or more cities, and the time and frequency of delivery. You'll learn more about getting weather information from Yahoo! in Chapter 18.

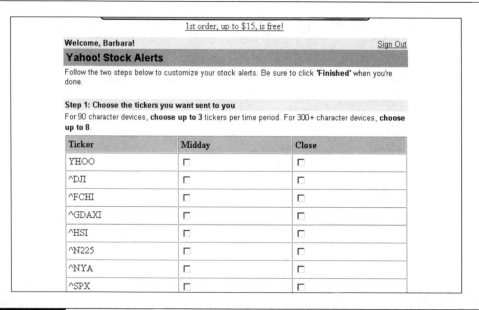

1st order, up to $15, is free!

Welcome, Barbara!   Sign Out
Yahoo! Stock Alerts

Follow the two steps below to customize your stock alerts. Be sure to click **'Finished'** when you're done.

Step 1: Choose the tickers you want sent to you
For 90 character devices, **choose up to 3** tickers per time period. For 300+ character devices, **choose up to 8**.

Ticker	Midday	Close
YHOO	☐	☐
^DJI	☐	☐
^FCHI	☐	☐
^GDAXI	☐	☐
^HSI	☐	☐
^N225	☐	☐
^NYA	☐	☐
^SPX	☐	☐

FIGURE 7-12 Setting up stock alerts

When you return to the My Alerts page, the alerts you set up will be listed, as shown in Figure 7-13. Next to each alert is a description, a time, and the delivery device. The bell icon means that the alert is turned on and notifications will be sent to you. To temporarily turn off the alert, click the icon. Yahoo! will remove the color from the icon to show that the alert is turned off. Click the icon again when you want to reinstate it.

The options under My Other Alerts are Yahoo! Mail and Yahoo! Auctions. Clicking Yahoo! Mail shows a summary of how to set up an e-mail filter, which selects the messages that you will accept into your Yahoo! inbox and those that you will forward to your device. See Chapter 2 for more information.

Clicking Yahoo! Auctions lets you have the status of auctions for which you are either a buyer or seller sent to your pager. See Chapter 19 for more information on Yahoo! Auctions.

My PDA

The Yahoo! On Your PDA option on Yahoo! To Go lets you set up to browse Yahoo! using a custom menu from the Web browser on your PDA. Clicking My PDA lets you configure Yahoo! for your PDA and see some sample PDA pages so you can get an idea how you can use Yahoo! to your best advantage, as shown here.

7

 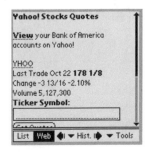 

Note
To set up Yahoo! on your PDA, you'll need a PDA with Palm Organizer, a modem, and a browser.

To set up Yahoo! for your PDA, follow these steps:

1. Click My PDA and then click Continue to display the options shown in Figure 7-14.

2. Enter a device name.

3. Select the device type: Palm III, Palm IV, Palm VII, Visor, pdQ Smartphone, Windows CE, Apple Newton, or Other.

4. Select the browser type: HandWeb, ProxiWeb, pdQ Browser, Avantgo, Qbrowser, or Other.

5. Select the modem type: Minstrel, Palm (clip-on), GSM Phone, or Other.

6. Select either Monochrome or Color.

7. Click Submit.

My Stock Alert				Add Alert
Description		Time	Delivery	Edit|Del
📢 YHOO		**Midday**	**My Phone**	✏️ 🗑️
My Sports Alert				Add Alert
Description		Time	Delivery	Edit|Del
📢 Boston Bruins		**Gametime**	**My Phone**	✏️ 🗑️
My Weather Alert				Add Alert
Description		Time	Delivery	Edit|Del
📢 Atlantic City, NJ		**1 pm**	**My Phone**	✏️ 🗑️
My Horoscope Alert				
Description		Time	Delivery	Edit|Del
📢 Scorpio		**1 pm**	**My Phone**	✏️ 🗑️

Welcome, Barbara!   Sign Out
Yahoo! Mobile - Alerts

Home
Yahoo! To Go
Mobile Shopping
PDA Downloads
Mobile News Library
Our Partners
Help

My Devices
Edit devices
Add new device

Welcome to Alerts
Get stocks, weather, email, and more sent to your mobile device. Add any alert to get started, and change your settings any time.

My Other Alerts
Yahoo! Mail: Filter and forward mail to your device.
Yahoo! Auctions: Get notified of your auction status.

FIGURE 7-13   Listing of your alerts

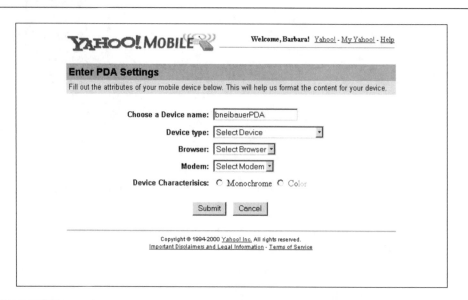

FIGURE 7-14   Setting up a PDA

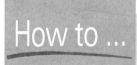

Change Your PDA Layout

The items that you select in the Personalize Content for Your PDA page will appear as a menu on your PDA. You can change the order in which options appear by clicking Change Layout from the Personalize Content for Your PDA page.

A list box appears showing each of the items that you added to your PDA menu.

Organize Your Selections

| Address Book |
| Calendar |
| Email |
| Stock Quotes |
| Movie Showtimes |
| Sports |
| Ski Reports |
| Weather |

To change the position of an item, click it in the list box and then click the up or down arrow. Clicking the up arrow moves the item up on the menu; clicking the down arrow moves the item down.

You can also click the X button to delete the selected item.

When you're through adjusting the order of items, click Finished.

The Personalize Content for Your PDA screen appears, as shown in Figure 7-15. In the Choose Your Content section of the page, select the check boxes for the items that you want displayed on your PDA. Click Finished or click Change Layout to set the order in which the items appear and then click Finished.

You'll now see a list of your devices with the items that will be on your PDA's Yahoo! menu:

Device Name	My PDA Start Page	Edit	Delete
bneibauerPDA	Address Book, Calendar, Email, Stock Quotes, Movie Showtimes, Sports, Ski Reports, Weather, Lodging, People Search	Edit	Delete

You can edit or delete the device, or set up additional devices.

Accessing Your PDA Page

When you want to get Yahoo! information on your PDA, start the PDA's browser to connect to the Internet, and then go to this site:

http://mobile.yahoo.com/home

Sign in to Yahoo! with your ID and password, and then click Sign In to display your custom Yahoo! menu on your PDA. Click the link for the item you want to display.

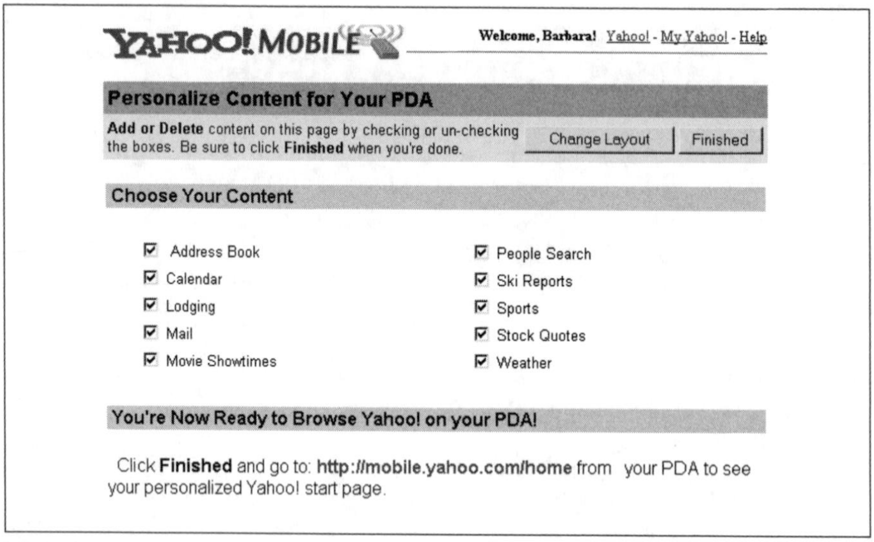

FIGURE 7-15 Adding content to your PDA Yahoo! menu

Yahoo! Mobile Shopping

The Yahoo! Mobile Shopping option in Yahoo! Mobile connects you to a virtual wireless communications shopping mall similar to the one in Figure 7-16. You'll find devices of all types, as well as accessories and service plans.

You can search for pagers, PDAs, wireless phones, and other products, and in so doing compare prices from hundred of companies. When you find the product you want, and at the price you want to pay, you can purchase the item online through Yahoo!'s secure shopping service. You'll learn all about Yahoo! shopping in Chapter 15.

PDA Downloads

The PDA Downloads section of Yahoo! Mobile provides thousands of free or inexpensive programs designed for Palm Organizer or Windows CE devices. As shown in Figure 7-17, you can search for a product by a keyword such as *calculator* or *e-mail*, or you can browse by category. Start by clicking either Palm or Windows CE to choose the system your device uses, and then search for the program.

When you find a program, you'll see a summary of it, its size, and the number of times it has already been downloaded from Yahoo! Click Download Now on the summary page to see additional details about the program, including user reviews and a table of information, as shown in Figure 7-18.

FIGURE 7-16   Yahoo! Mobile Shopping

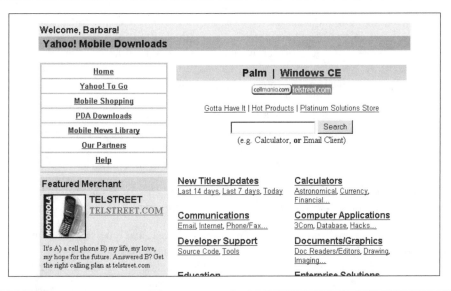

FIGURE 7-17   Searching for PDA downloads

Palm OS: Software | Hardware | Bundles | Most Popular | Must Haves | Hot Products | Resources
Windows CE: Software | Hardware | Most Popular | Must Haves | Hot Products
Home > Calculators >   Help | My Basket

Auto Lease Calculator

download a demo

Auto Lease calculates monthly lease payments. Auto Lease provides the ability to select a
negotiated price or base the lease payment off the dealer invoice price + profit P dealer hold
back % (you set the profit $). This program is a Freeware Alpha version and will not expire.
Please provide bug reports to josh@wainer.org. ENJOY!

Average user Rating:	★★★☆☆ Add your review	Screen Shot
Downloads:	2213	
File Size:	17k	
Requirements:	None	
Date Submitted:	4/3/99	Screen Shot
License Type:	Freeware($0.00)	Not Available
Author:	Josh Wainer	
Author's Email:		
More like this:		handango

More Products by Josh Wainer

User Reviews

★★★★☆

FIGURE 7-18   Details on PDA programs

The Average User Rating indicates the opinion of users who have downloaded the program.
The ratings range from one star (the lowest) to five stars (the highest).

The Date Submitted gives you an idea how new the program is, although it may have been
created at any time.

The License Type indicates how the program is distributed:

■ Freeware means that the program is totally free.

■ Shareware Registration means that you are free to download and test the program,
but you are expected to pay the stated license fee if you continue to use it. Read the
documentation that comes with the program to learn how to register it.

Note *Some program descriptions include a link called Add This To My Basket. Click this link
to download and pay the registration fee in one secure step.*

The table also includes the author's name and e-mail address, and links to similar products.
Click the e-mail address to send the author a question or comment about the program. There may
also be links with which to see additional products by the same author, download manuals, and
obtain other supporting information.

When you're ready to download the program, click Download a Demo (which is the option
even when the program is a full copy and not a demo, by the way). The File Download dialog
box appears with the following choices.

■ Open this file from its current location.

■ Save this file to disk.

Select Save This File To Disk, and then click OK to display the Save As dialog box. Select the location where you want to save the file, make a note of where you will save it so you can get to it later on, and click Save. The file will be downloaded to your computer.

What you do with the file after you download it depends on its type. Many files are in the ZIP format. To save downloading time, the files that make up the program are zipped, or compressed, so they take up less room and can be sent faster. To unzip files sent this way, you need an unzipping program such as PKZIP or WINZIP, which you can also download over the Internet for free. After you install the unzipping program on your computer, you just double-click on the compressed file to expand it so it is usable.

Other programs are downloaded as executable programs with the EXE extension. Some of these are self-extracting ZIP files. You can double-click a self-extracting file to automatically unzip it without the need of an unzipping program. Other EXE files may install or run the program immediately.

Program Reviews

Below the table are any reviews that other Yahoo! members submitted about the software. It pays to read the reviews to get an insight into a program's features and value. Read all of the reviews before making a decision to download. A few negative comments may be followed by a number of positive reviews, or vice versa. While the Average Rating is a good general indication, you may find specific information in the reviews that is more meaningful.

To add your own review of the program, click Add Your Review to display a review form, as shown in Figure 7-19. Complete the form and click Submit Review to add your critique to the program.

Installing Software on PDAs

After you download a program from Yahoo! Mobile, you may have to install it on your PDA. The exact steps for installing the program depend on your specific device and its operating system.

If you are using a Palm device, for example, you'll need to run the Palm Desktop on your PC and use the Install Tool. If you are using a Windows CE device, you run the program on your PC and then synchronize your PDA.

Downloading Yahoo! Software

The PDA Downloads page also lets you download two Yahoo! programs: Messenger for PalmOS and Messenger for WinCE. These are mobile-device versions of Yahoo! Messenger for sending instant messages to and receiving instant messages from other Yahoo! members who are online. To use either version of the program, download it to your PC and then follow the instructions for installing it on your mobile device.

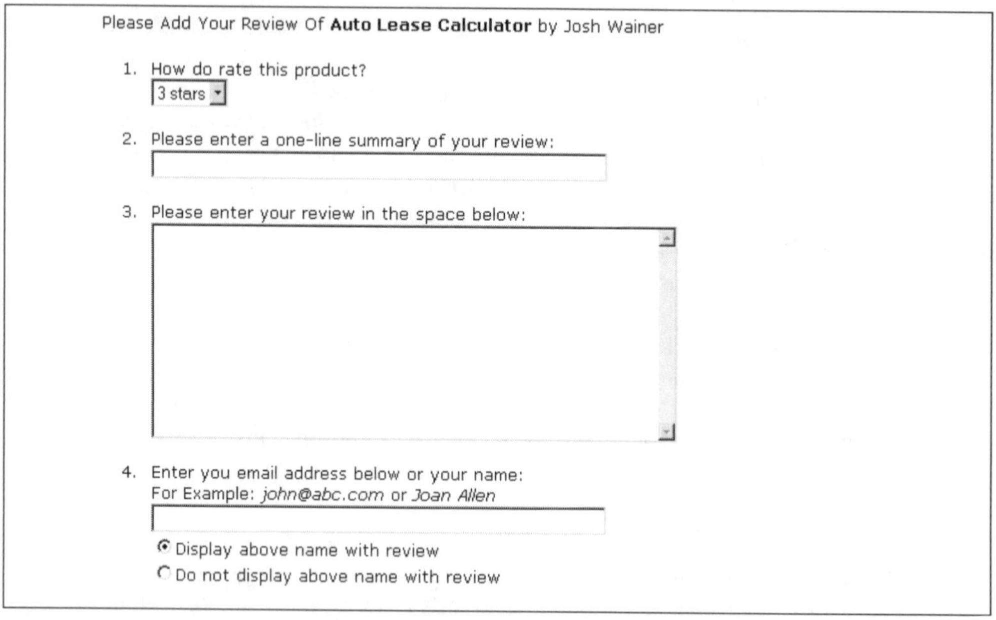

Please Add Your Review Of **Auto Lease Calculator** by Josh Wainer

1. How do rate this product?
   `[3 stars ▾]`

2. Please enter a one-line summary of your review:

3. Please enter your review in the space below:

4. Enter you email address below or your name:
   For Example: *john@abc.com* or *Joan Allen*

   ⦿ Display above name with review
   ○ Do not display above name with review

FIGURE 7-19   Adding your review to a PDA program

How Do I Yahoo! Everywhere

When you need additional help using Yahoo! Mobile features, choose How Do I Yahoo!
Everywhere from the Yahoo! Mobile page. Doing so opens the main Help page for Yahoo!
Mobile. It is divided into six sections:

- Top 5 Questions includes links to the most asked questions about Yahoo! Mobile.
- Yahoo! Mobile Basics covers the fundamental features of using Yahoo! on a mobile device.
- Yahoo! To Go includes frequently asked questions about Yahoo! Alerts and PDA features.
- Yahoo! Mobile Shopping provides answers about using the Yahoo! shopping service.
- PDA Downloads presents information about downloading and using software.
- Related Links lists additional topics of interest to mobile device users.

Getting News for Mobile Users

The Yahoo! Mobile page provides several ways for mobile device users to keep up with the
latest developments in mobile communications.

The What's New? section offers late-breaking news and top developments, as well as new downloads and product announcements. The From The Mobile News Library section contains a sample of stories from the Yahoo! Mobile News Library, a collection of stories of interest to mobile users. After each headline is the name of the publication in which the story appeared, as well as its date. Click a story to read about it in detail.

You can also choose Mobile News Library for a more comprehensive listing of news stories and product announcements, as shown in Figure 7-20. The page is generally divided into two categories: Wireless Communications Devices, and Handheld and Palmtop Computers.

Getting Alerts by E-Mail

Whether or not you have a pager or PDA, alerts can be sent to you by e-mail or through Yahoo! Messenger. Follow these steps:

1. Click More on the Yahoo! home page.

2. Click Yahoo! Alerts to open the Yahoo! Alerts page. This page will list the alerts that you create.

Tip *If the Yahoo! Alerts option is not displayed, go to http://alerts.yahoo.com/.*

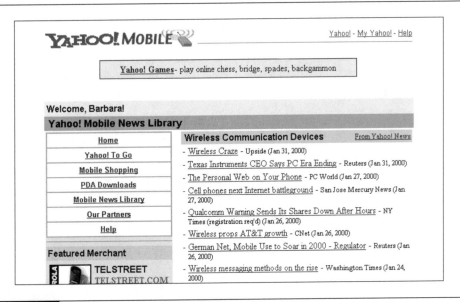

FIGURE 7-20   Stories of interest for mobile users

3. Select the type of alert you want to create from the list on the left side of the screen.

4. Click Create Alert. The options that appear depend on the type of alert you selected.

5. Enter a name for the alert.

6. Enter one or more words that the news story must contain to be sent to you. Separate the words with spaces.

7. Enter one or more words that the story should *not* contain.

8. Scroll the screen to see a list of news sources.

9. Select the check boxes for the sources that you want to be searched for stories.

10. Select how you want to be notified from these options. For instance, enter the e-mail address to which you want the alert sent or choose to be notified in Yahoo! Messenger when you are logged on to that feature.

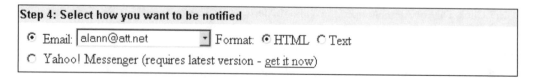

11. Select the time of delivery. You can choose up to two times daily, or immediately when stories are found.

12. Click Finished.

The Yahoo! News Alerts page appears and lists your news alerts. From this page, you can edit or delete alerts, or click Create Alert to add another alert of the same type. To return to the Yahoo! Alerts page, see a list of your alerts, and perhaps create other types, click Y! Alerts.

Part II

Navigating the World

Chapter 8

Finding Information and People on the Internet

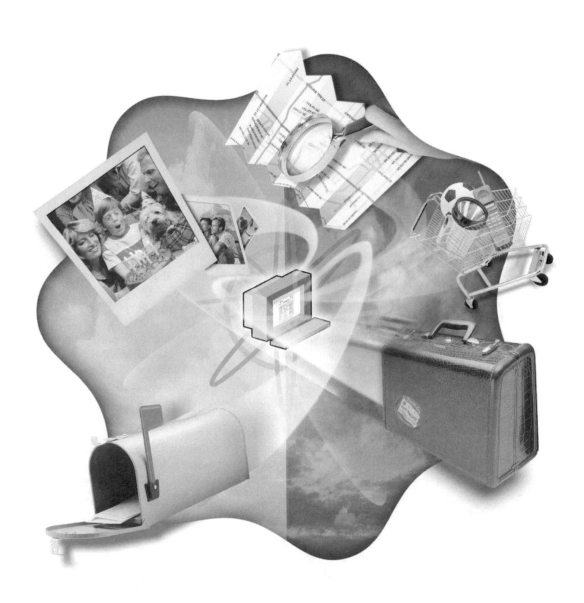

How to . . .

- ■ Search by category
- ■ Perform keyword searches
- ■ Fine-tune your searches
- ■ Search through newsgroups
- ■ Find phone numbers and addresses
- ■ Telephone people over the Internet
- ■ Find e-mail addresses
- ■ Locate businesses
- ■ Perform reverse searches

Yahoo!'s roots are as a search company, a place to locate information on the Internet. Just because Yahoo! has become a full-service Internet portal doesn't mean that the company has abandoned its roots. Helping you locate information is still a big part of Yahoo! and one of the main reasons why millions of Yahoo! users keep coming back.

Using Yahoo!, you can track down phone numbers and addresses, get a person's e-mail address, or get a map to a house or business. Not only is searching this way easy, it can also be quite enlightening.

How Searching Works

Before learning how to search with Yahoo!, you should know something about the way that searching works on the Internet.

In general, a search company operates in one of two different ways—as a directory service or a search engine.

A *directory service* collects information about Web sites and organizes it into categories and subcategories. When you want to locate information, you start with the topmost category and work your way through subcategories that pertain to the information you are looking for. This process of searching narrower and narrower subcategories to locate specific information is called *drilling down*. Someone who works for the directory service has to examine each site to determine where to place it in the directory, and a site may be placed in more than one location. The review process ensures that a site is placed in a category that accurately describes its contents.

A *search engine,* on the other hand, creates an index of words found on Web sites. Using special software called a *robot, crawler,* or *spider,* the search engine seeks out Web sites, retrieves their contents, and builds an index of the words on the site. When you enter a keyword as part of a search, the engine checks its index and lists all of the sites where the word is found.

Search engines get words from several locations on a Web site:

- ■ **Title**   A single line of text specified by the site developer, the title appears in the browser's title bar when the site is displayed in a browser.
- ■ **Description**   A brief summary of the site, again specified by the developer, the description does not appear onscreen but is part of the HTML from which the site is constructed.

- ■ **Keywords**   A list of words that the developer has entered to identify the site, the keywords also do not appear onscreen but are part of the HTML.
- ■ **Body**   The actual full contents of the site.

Unfortunately, some Web site developers include words in the description and keyword list that do not truly describe what is on the site. To attract more visitors to their sites, they load the description and keyword list with popular words that are frequently used in searches, even if the words are not found in the site itself. A site about safe swimming, for example, may contain the words "Pamela Anderson" or "Baywatch" just to increase the number of times it is accessed.

The full-text indexing of all the words on a Web site doesn't guarantee that the search results will be any more relevant. Words in a site can be indexed out of context. Just because a site contains a word does not mean that it contains any useful or relevant information pertaining to it. For example, a search for references to Outlook, a Microsoft program, can get sites that refer to the weather's outlook or Outlook Point.

Fortunately, many search engines rank the results of searches by relevance. They use an algorithm based on the position of words, the number of times a word is used, and other criteria to determine which sites are more likely to pertain to the subject of a search. The results are listed in order of relevance, with the most promising sites at the beginning of the list.

Yahoo! uses a combination of both systems. With Yahoo!, you can search through the hierarchy of categories or search by keyword or phrase.

When you search by category, you drill down from one level to the next until you find the subcategory with the information you want. You can then display a list of the Web sites that have been collected in the subcategory.

When you search by entering a phrase or keywords, Yahoo! scans its categories, its database of Web sites, and the index of a search engine. Then Yahoo! displays the results of the search in the following order:

- ■ Matching categories come first because they are most likely to be relevant to the search.
- ■ Matching sites from the Yahoo! directory of sites comes next.
- ■ Matching Web pages from a search engine called Inktomi (pronounced "Ink To Me"), which performs a full-text index of millions of Web pages, comes last.

The results are also ranked to provide more useful information:

- ■ Categories of sites that match higher in the hierarchy are ranked higher than those in lower subcategories. Those from higher levels usually represent a more meaningful match than those from subcategories.
- ■ Sites that have matching terms in the title are listed before sites with matching terms in the body. Again, the makers of Yahoo! feel that the title more accurately reflects the contents of the site than words, since words may be taken out of context.
- ■ If you enter multiple keywords, sites that match more of the words are ranked higher than sites that match fewer words.

8

Browsing by Category

Let's first take a look at locating information by using Yahoo!'s extensive database of categories.

The categories are listed on the Yahoo! home page, from Arts & Humanities to Society & Culture, as shown in Figure 8-1. Below each category are the names of two or more popular subcategories. Notice that all of the categories and subcategories are links.

If you see a subcategory that relates to the information you are looking for, click it. Otherwise, click the category name to go to the next level of categories within it. At the top of the list will be a link to a Yahoo! page on the subject, if there is one.

Below the link to Yahoo! Health are individual links to some Yahoo! sites, followed by the list of subcategories. Numbers following an item indicate the total number of references you'll find in that subcategory, although you may have to drill down through additional levels to reach the sites themselves.

The at symbol (@) indicates that the same subcategory is actually part of another branch in the Yahoo! hierarchy under a different category or subcategory, but the subcategory is listed here because it relates to the topic. For example, the Disabilities subcategory is followed by the at symbol. It is actually part of the Society and Culture category and can be found there as well. Clicking Disabilities branches to that subcategory under Society and Culture so you can continue the search. Yahoo! uses this technique to help you locate subjects that do not clearly fit under a single category, or branch, of the hierarchy.

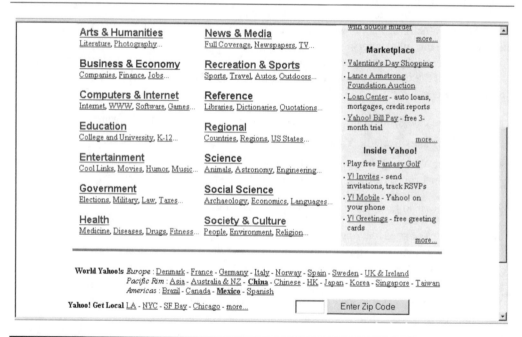

FIGURE 8-1   Yahoo! categories

When a category encompasses a large number of topics, you may see the alphabet on top of the page, with each letter as a link. Click the letter that starts the topic you are interested in to see a list of topics.

[A|B|C|D|E|F|G|H|I|J|K|L|M|N|O|P|R|S|T|U|V|W|Y]

To get you started, let's work through three examples of finding information from the categories.

Example 1: High Blood Pressure

Suppose your physician tells you that you have high blood pressure. When you get home from the doctor's office, you want to learn more about this condition. Follow these steps to do so:

1. Click the Health category in the Yahoo! home page to see the subcategories. Obviously, Health is the place to start.

2. Click Diseases and Conditions. There are a number of subcategories, but Diseases and Conditions seems the most appropriate.

3. In the alphabet links, click H to see the list of diseases and conditions starting with that letter, as shown in Figure 8-2.

4. High Blood Pressure is not listed, but Hypertension is, so click Hypertension. Among the choices, you'll find those that provide information on high blood pressure.

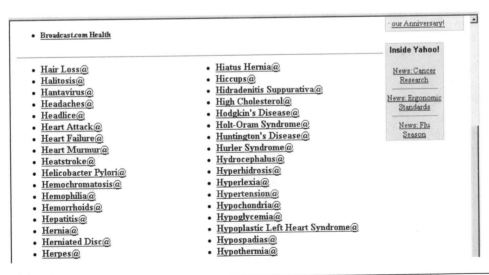

FIGURE 8-2   Diseases and conditions starting with H

The entire path is

Health > Diseases and Conditions > Hypertension

Example 2: Computer Reviews

You are considering buying a new desktop computer. You've narrowed the choices to one or two companies, but you want to read some unbiased reviews before making the final purchase. Follow these steps to learn more about a computer:

1. Click Computers and Internet in the Yahoo! home page. The Computers and Internet category is the best place to start.

2. Click Information and Documentation to see the types of information available.

3. Click Product Reviews, the obvious choice. You'll see a list of the types of products for which reviews are available.

- Accessories *(1)*
- Components *(352)* NEW!
- Desktop Computers *(749)*
- Modems@
- Networking *(29)*
- Notebook Computers *(441)*

- Peripherals *(1125)*
- Personal Digital Assistants (PDAs) *(89)*
- Printers@
- Scanners@
- Software@

4. Click Desktop Computers to see a list of computer vendors.

5. Click each vendor you are considering to read reviews of its products.

The entire path is

Computers and Internet > Information and Documentation > Product Reviews > Desktop Computers

Example 3: Some Vacation Fun

Vacation time is getting close, and you decide to visit the Hard Rock Hotel Casino in Las Vegas for some gambling and gamboling. You want to learn more about the hotel. There are several ways to find this information. You can start from the activity you will be performing or from the location you will be visiting.

If your idea is to search for recreation and travel information, you might locate the information by following these steps:

1. Click Recreation and Sports to see a list of activities.

2. Click Gambling, one of the main activities in the area you will be visiting.

3. Click Casinos, the type of location you are interested in, to see these options:

- Casino Management Software@
- Directories *(28)*
- Individual Casinos *(145)*

- Online Casinos *(300)* NEW!
- Organizations *(3)*
- Web Services *(5)*

4. Click Individual Casinos because you want information on a specific casino-hotel.

5. Click Hard Rock Hotel and Casino for the information you want.

The entire path is

Recreation and Sports > Gambling > Casinos > Individual Casinos > Hard Rock Hotel
and Casino

You could also approach the search from the location you will be visiting by following
these steps:

1. Click Regional to see the subcategories, since you're
trying to find information about a location.

- U.S. States
- Countries *(448075)* NEW!
- Regions *(6333)* NEW!

2. You are going to a specific state, so click U.S. States to
see a list of states.

3. Click Nevada, the state you will be visiting.

4. Click Cities to see the alphabet of links.

5. Click L, and then Las Vegas.

You now have two different directions where you can go from the subcategories under Las
Vegas—Recreation and Sports or Travel and Transportation. From the Las Vegas subcategory,
use either of these paths to get to the same place:

Recreation and Sports > Gambling > Casinos > Hotel Casinos > Hard Rock Hotel
and Casino

Travel and Transportation > Lodging > Hotels > Casinos > Hard Rock Hotel and Casino

To get to the Hard Rock Hotel and Casino Web page for lodging information, the entire path
is either:

Regional > U.S. States > Nevada > Cities > L > Las Vegas > Recreation and Sports >
Gambling > Casinos > Hotel Casinos > Hardrock Hotel and Casino

or

Regional > U.S. States > Nevada > Cities > L > Las Vegas > Travel and Transportation >
Lodging > Hotels > Casinos > Hardrock Hotel and Casino

Searching for Web Sites

By using Yahoo! categories to locate information, you can pinpoint information rather quickly; but sometimes quite a bit of trial and error is involved. Sometimes you follow a branch through a series of categories—even drilling down to the lowest level—and you still can't locate the information you want. The branch just doesn't cover what you imagined.

When you are looking for very specific information, you may find it more efficient to perform a search based on one or more keywords.

If you prefer searching in categories, remember that a keyword search locates matching subcategories first, so searching with keywords is also a fast way to find information within the category hierarchy. You can then use the categories to locate matching sites in the Yahoo! database. But, more important, a keyword search taps into the huge, frequently updated Inktomi index of Web sites.

The problem with keyword searches is that hundreds, even thousands of sites can be located, many of which are irrelevant to you. So the trick to using a keyword search is to formulate the search words carefully (or as carefully as possible) and thereby make sure useable sites appear in the search results.

 ... **Perform International Searches**

By default, Yahoo! searches its database for categories and Web sites around the world. If you are looking for resources in a specific country, click the country from these links at the bottom of the Yahoo! home page:

World Yahoo!s *Europe* : Denmark - France - Germany - Italy - Norway - Spain - Sweden - UK & Ireland
Pacific Rim : Asia - Australia & NZ - **China** - Chinese - HK - Japan - Korea - Singapore - Taiwan
Americas : Brazil - Canada - **Mexico** - Spanish

You will see options such as these under the Search text box:

> Search | advanced search
>
> **You are searching:** ⦿ All of Yahoo!   ◯ UK only ◯ Ireland only

Choose whether you want to search all of Yahoo! or in a specific country.

The restriction only applies to categories and sites in the Yahoo! databases. Inktomi still shows results from its entire index.

Search Basics

Performing a basic search is really easy. You start in the search text box at the Yahoo! home page.

> Search | advanced search

Enter a phrase or keywords that identify the information you are looking for. If you recently performed a search starting with the same characters, you can select from a list of recent searches.

> wizard   Search
> wizard
> wizards with pointed hats

Press ENTER or click Search. Yahoo! searches its categories, Web sites, and the Inktomi Web page index. Then it displays the results onscreen, as shown in Figure 8-3.

The Search Result note at the top of the screen tells you the number of Yahoo! categories that contain the word, and the number of sites within all its categories that contain the word. In the case of Figure 8-3, there are 16 categories and 607 Web sites in the Yahoo! database that contain the word *wizard* in one form or another. By default, a word is located even if it is part of a longer word that has the same root, so a search for *wizard* will find matches that contain *wizards* and *wizardry*.

Notice these links at the top and bottom of the page:

- ■ **Categories**   Displays matching Yahoo! categories
- ■ **Web Sites**   Displays matching sites from Yahoo! categories

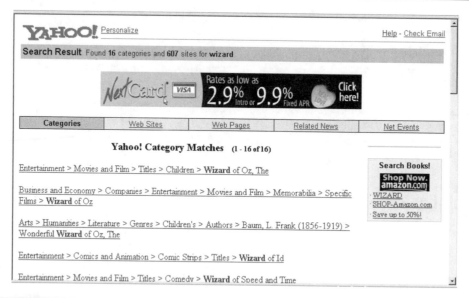

FIGURE 8-3   Results of a keyword search

- ■   **Web Pages**   Displays matching sites from the Inktomi index
- ■   **Related News**   Displays matching sites from a Yahoo! database of news headlines
- ■   **Net Events**   Displays matching sites from a Yahoo! database of Web events, including chats and other activities on the Internet

Yahoo! Categories and Web Sites

The list of matching categories is shown next. The heading Yahoo! Category Matches shows the total number of category matches and the number of those being displayed. The notation 1-16 of 16, for example, means that 16 categories match and that all of them are listed. The notation 1-16 of 32 means that 32 categories match but only 16 are displayed in the page. You see this notation at the bottom of the page to see additional results: **Next 20 Matches**

Note   *If no categories or Yahoo! Web sites match, you'll see the matching Inktomi Web pages.*

Each listing shows the complete branch Yahoo! follows to get to the match. This is helpful in eliminating categories that do not contain information that is useful to your search. For example, if you are looking for the word *wizard* as it relates to role playing games, you could ignore the links to the Wizard of Oz and to categories such as Soccer, Baseball, and Ice Hockey because they obviously relate to the names of sports teams.

To see the sites within one of the categories, just click it. For example, here's one of the categories that contain the word *wizard*:

Recreation > Games > Computer Games > Titles > Role Playing > **Wizard**ry

Each listing shows that it is located in the general category Recreation, below the subcategories Games, then Computer Games, then Titles, and then Role Playing. Click one of the links to drill down further or to open a specific site.

Below the matching categories is a list of Web sites in the Yahoo! directory that contain the search word, as shown in Figure 8-4.

Tip
Click the Web Sites link to go to the matching Web site list. Click Categories to return to the Category Matches.

The heading Yahoo! Site Matches shows the number of matching sites and the number displayed on the current page. Each shows the category in which the site is found, as well as the title and description of the site itself. Click the title to open the site, or click the category if you wish to see other sites within it.

At the bottom of the page, you'll find links to related searches, other search engines, and other interesting Yahoo! locations.

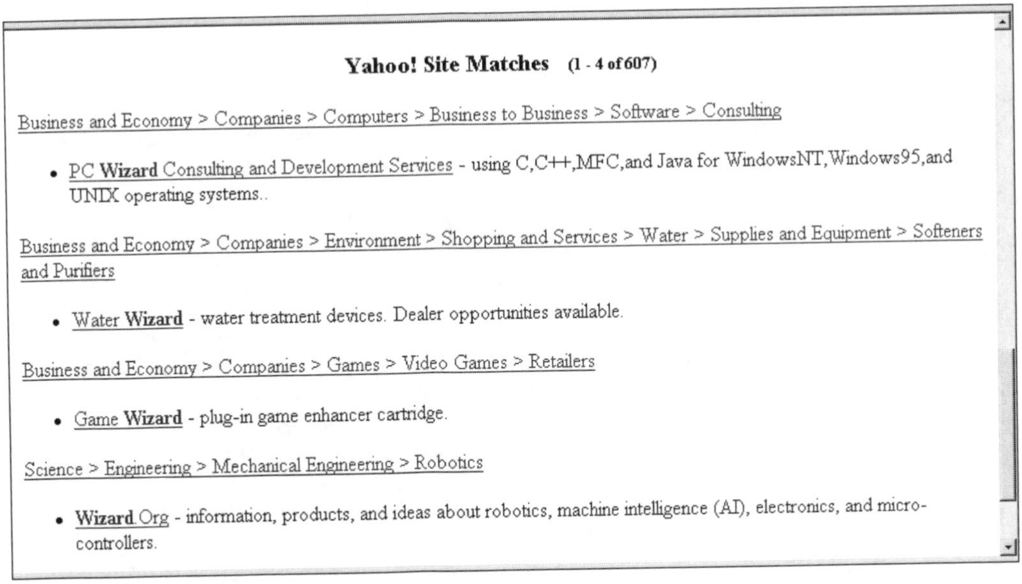

8

Yahoo! Site Matches   (1 - 4 of 607)

Business and Economy > Companies > Computers > Business to Business > Software > Consulting

- PC **Wizard** Consulting and Development Services - using C,C++,MFC,and Java for WindowsNT,Windows95,and UNIX operating systems..

Business and Economy > Companies > Environment > Shopping and Services > Water > Supplies and Equipment > Softeners and Purifiers

- Water **Wizard** - water treatment devices. Dealer opportunities available.

Business and Economy > Companies > Games > Video Games > Retailers

- Game **Wizard** - plug-in game enhancer cartridge.

Science > Engineering > Mechanical Engineering > Robotics

- **Wizard** Org - information, products, and ideas about robotics, machine intelligence (AI), electronics, and micro-controllers.

FIGURE 8-4   Matching Yahoo! Web sites

Yahoo! maintains a database of recently used search phrases. The Related Searches section lists recent searches that contain your own search word. Click one of the links to see the results of that search.

If you still can't locate your information on Yahoo!, click a link to one of the other search engines. Your search phrase will be transferred to the engine and its results displayed.

Use the Next Search box if you want to start another search.

Displaying Web Pages

If none of the categories and sites are appropriate, click the Web Pages link at the top or bottom of the listing. Doing so displays the results from the Inktomi index, as shown in Figure 8-5.

The heading on top of the page shows that there are 337,510 documents in the Inktomi database that contain the word *wizard*. The first 20 are shown on the page.

Each listing shows the site's title (as a link) and description, as well as the actual address of the site. Scan the list looking for sites you are interested in and click those sites you wish to visit. Click Next 20 Matches at the bottom of the page to display additional sites.

Tip *After viewing a site, click your browser's Back button to return to the list.*

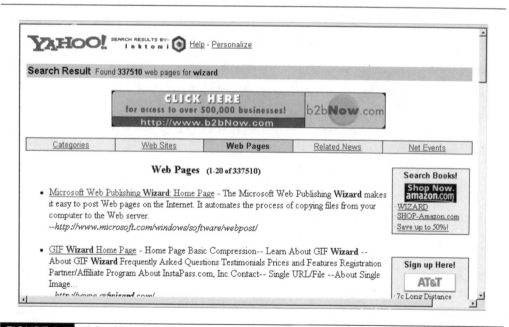

FIGURE 8-5 Matching documents in the Inktomi index

Improving Search Precision

Chances are that some, if not many, of the categories, sites, and Web pages located by your search will not contain the information that you are looking for. Even if some do, looking through hundreds, if not thousands, of Web sites to find information can be extremely time-consuming.

Internet searching is one case in which too much is not good. A search that locates ten sites that contain exactly what you want is better than a search that results in hundreds of sites that have nothing to do with your search. The goal of searching is to get results that fit your specifications, not simply a large number of sites.

A search that is too broad will return many sites that do not match your intent, even though the sites include the search text that you entered. For example, a search for information about the wizards of legend can turn up hundreds of sites about the Wizard of Oz. On the other hand, a search that is too narrow may overlook useful sites. For example, a search for *wizards with pointed hats* may find sites that include one or more words in the phrase, but no sites that really contain appropriate references.

There are several techniques that you can use to perform a more precise search.

Using multiple words, for example, usually locates relevant information. When you enter two or more words, Yahoo! looks for matches that contain all of the words. Here's an example:

Search Word(s)	Categories	Web sites	Web Pages
Soap	21	864	209,584
Opera	650	12,811	412,585
Soap Opera	9	176	32,942

Note *Because the content of the Internet is always changing, the number of results shown here are illustrative only because they reflect search results at one specific time.*

Using both words as the search phrase produces a narrower field of sites—sites that will more likely contain information on the subject. In a search for information about television soap operas, searching with the keyword *soap* or *opera* would produce broad results. The combination of words, however, more accurately reflects your intention.

Yahoo! uses a special intelligent search pattern, however. It will also locate Yahoo! categories and Web sites that contain one or more of the terms. Searching for *soap opera*, for example, will locate Yahoo! categories that contain the word *soaps* even if the word *opera* is not included because it matches the intent of the search.

You can also refine a search by simply adding an "s" to the end of nouns, as shown next.

Search Word(s)	Categories	Web sites	Web Pages
Soaps	19	792	36,901
Operas	156	1,437	32,603
Soap operas	9	175	10,920

8

In general, construct your search phrase using nouns, and leave out prepositions, conjunctions, and common words such as *and, the, of, a, in,* and *is.* Use modifiers, adjectives, and adverbs only when they clearly help to define the subject, as in *Gateway computer* or *rye bread.* This is particularly important with words than can be nouns or modifiers. For example, suppose your hobby is collecting antique tin containers. Here are the results of three searches:

Search Word(s)	Categories	Web sites	Web Pages
Tin	8	326	255,259
Tins	8	354	13,998
Collectible tins	0	74	13,859
Antique tins	0	54	1,627

The search for *tins* is obviously better than a search for *tin,* but *collectible tins* and *antique tins* are even better. In both cases, the word *tins* is used as a noun and further modified to narrow the results.

If you are looking for an exact phrase, enclose it in quotation marks, as in *"soap operas".* The quotation marks tell Yahoo! to look for the two words only in that exact order and combination. You have to be careful, however, not to enclose too many words and thereby make the search too narrow, as shown in these results:

Search Word(s)	Categories	Web sites	Web Pages
"soap operas"	9	27	10,349
"daytime soap operas"	0	2	238
"ABC soap operas"	0	1	56

If you are looking for information specifically on daytime soap operas, a better combination would be *"soap operas" daytime.* In this case, the search locates sites that contain the phrase *soap operas* as well as the word *daytime,* but not necessarily the entire phrase *daytime soap operas.* The search, by the way, returned no categories, 22 Yahoo! Web sites, and 1,148 Inktomi Web pages.

Tip *When you want to locate two words in a site using some search engines, you must either enclose the words in quotes to find an exact phrase or place a plus sign (+) in front of required words.*

You can also enter a minus sign (–) to specify words that should *not* appear. Searching for *soaps –opera* locates sites that contain the word *soaps* but do not refer to soap operas. Likewise, searching for *soap operas –daytime* might narrow the search somewhat. For example, while *soap operas* located 10,563 sites, *soap operas –daytime* found 9,907 sites.

You can also limit the search to text in a Web page's title or actual Internet URL address, rather than the entire body of the page. To do so, enter **t:** in front of the keyword to search in the title or **u:** in front of the keyword to search in the URL, like so:

- **t:soap opera**   Restricts the search to titles
- **u:soap opera**   Restricts the search to Internet addresses

By the way, the search for *t:soap opera* in my experiment located 909 matching Web pages, a vast majority of which probably have to do with television programs.

Because the URL restriction only searches Internet addresses, it does not return any matching pages from the Inktomi database. It does, however, locate sites in the Yahoo! database that contain the search words in the addresses. Searching for *u:soaps* located 54 matching Yahoo! Web sites.

When you search for a word, Yahoo! locates longer words with the same root. It will not, however, match words that contain just the letters. For example, searching for *cap* will locate sites with the word *caps* but not the word *cape*. To extend a search for a specific sequence of letters, such as all words that start with the letters *cap*, add the asterisk wildcard character (*), as in *cap**. The search for *cap** will find matches with *cape, capital, capricious,* and other words that begin with the letters *cap*.

8

Yahoo! Search Options

Because searching is such an important part of the Internet experience, Yahoo! provides some easy-to-use options. Click the Advanced Search link next to the search text box (at right) to see the options in Figure 8-6.

advanced search

There are four categories of options:

- The type of Internet documents searched
- How multiple search words are related
- The age of the sites searched
- The number of results displayed on each page

Your first choice is to select either Yahoo! or Usenet. Choose Yahoo! for the default search of all Yahoo! categories and Inktomi Web pages. *Usenet* is a collection of Internet discussion groups (called newsgroups) that cover thousands of topics. Select Usenet when you want to search these public discussions for your topic.

If you choose to search Yahoo!, you can select the search area—either Yahoo Categories or Web Sites. Selecting Yahoo Categories returns category, Web site, and Web page listings. Choosing Web Site will only display matching Yahoo! Web sites and Inktomi Web pages, not individual Yahoo! categories.

The Select A Search Method options determine how multiple search words are treated in a search:

- **Intelligent default**   Uses the default Yahoo! method in which a site must contain all of the words in the search box, and words with the same root are located.

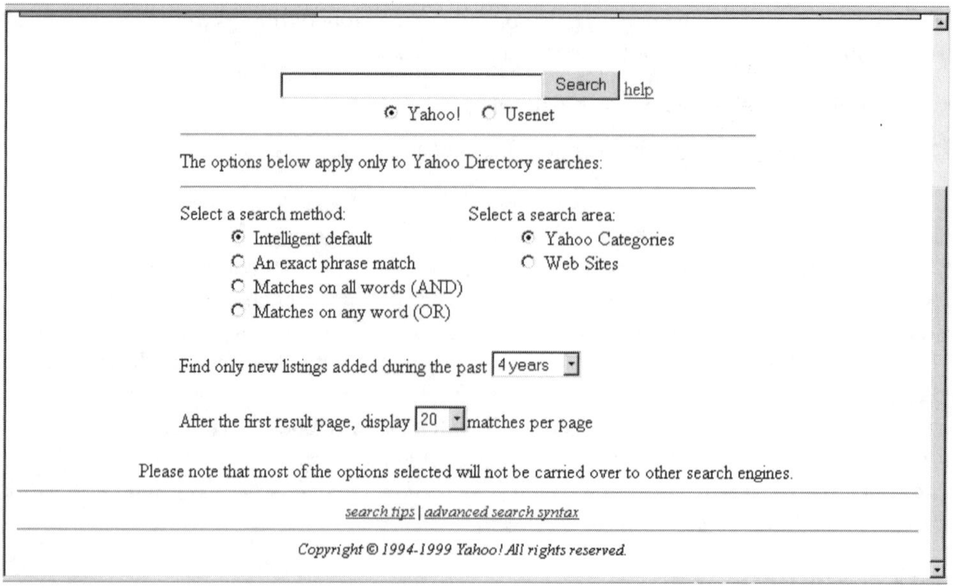

Search
help
Yahoo!
Usenet
The options below apply only to Yahoo Directory searches:
Select a search method:
Intelligent default
An exact phrase match
Matches on all words (AND)
Matches on any word (OR)
Select a search area:
Yahoo Categories
Web Sites
Find only new listings added during the past 4 years
After the first result page, display 20 matches per page
Please note that most of the options selected will not be carried over to other search engines.
search tips | advanced search syntax
Copyright © 1994-1999 Yahoo! All rights reserved.

FIGURE 8-6 Advanced search options

- **An exact phrase match** Operates as if you enclosed the words in quotation marks. To match, the entire phrase in the exact order in which you entered it must appear on a Web site.
- **Matches on all words (AND)** Locates only those references that contain all of the search words, although the words can be in any order.
- **Matches on any word (OR)** Locates only those references that contain any one or more of the search words.

4 years
1 day
3 days
1 week
1 month
3 months
6 months
4 years

If you want to limit the search to more recent citations, use the list box shown here: Choosing 1 week, for example, only lists sites that have been added to the Yahoo! or Inktomi database during the last week. This is a good way to locate recent news, or to repeat a search you performed in the past but get newer listings. If you performed a default search for a topic last month, for example, choose 1 month from the list to limit the results to items posted since your last search.

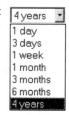

The final list lets you specify how many items appear on each page. Your choices are 10, 20, 50, and 100. With the default, you'll need to scroll the screen to display all 20 items, and then click Next Results to list additional sites. Choosing 10 requires less scrolling but means more of a delay as each page is displayed.

Choosing 50 or 100 is useful if you want to save or print a copy of the matching categories, sites, and Web pages. When a result page is displayed, for example, you can choose your browser's Save As or Print command on the File menu. Save As copies the page to your computer's disk, so you can later open the page in the browser and review the results or click a link to open a category or site. The Print command prints a copy of the page.

If a search resulted in 150 matches that you'd like to save or print out for future reference, and you only displayed 20 matches per page, you would need to use the Save As or Print command eight times to get a complete record of the results. After saving or printing one page, you'd need to click Next 20 Matches, and then save and print the next page, repeating the process until all of the matches are recorded. Choosing to display 100 requires you to use the Save As or Print command only once.

Tip *When you use the Save As command to save multiple pages, you need to enter a unique filename for each page.*

Searching Usenet

Usenet discussion groups offer a very public forum in which to discuss issues of all types. Most Internet Service Providers offer you a newsgroup server that lets you subscribe to newsgroups. As a subscriber to a newsgroup, you can read messages left by other members and contribute your own message to the group. When you log on to the newsgroup through your ISP, a list of new messages is automatically downloaded to your computer. You can then scan the message topics for one that interests you.

Newsgroup messages are organized in threads. A *thread* consists of a message and all of its replies. As a newsgroup member, you can reply to a message and list your reply with the others in the thread. You can also send, or post, a new message and thereby introduce a new topic that other members can reply to.

Through Yahoo!, you *cannot* subscribe to a newsgroup, scan its list of messages, or reply to messages. However, you can use Yahoo! to search newsgroups for specific topics, read the threads where the topics are discussed, and send an e-mail reply to a person who posted a message.

Select Usenet in the Advanced Search options page to perform a search and get a list of messages similar to the one in Figure 8-7. The list shows the date each message was posted, its subject, the forum (newsgroup) where it is located, and the name of the author.

Click a message that you would like to read to see it in its own window, as shown in Figure 8-8. You can click the Previous Article and Next Article buttons to move between messages in the thread, or click View Thread to see the complete list of messages in the thread by their author and date.

To send an e-mail to the person who posted a message, click the E-mail Reply button. Yahoo! opens your e-mail program and starts a new message that is addressed automatically to the person to whom you are replying.

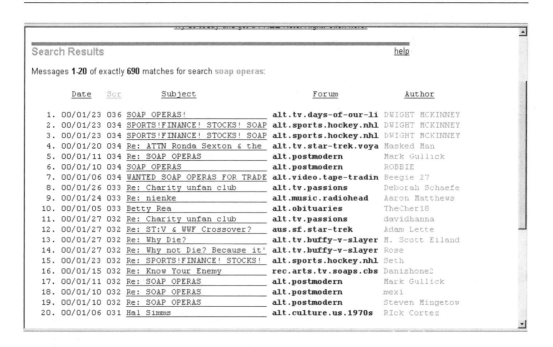

FIGURE 8-7 Matching messages from Usenet newsgroups

FIGURE 8-8 Message in a Usenet newsgroup

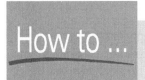 **Search Public Records**

In many Yahoo! search pages, you'll see an advertisement for 1800USSEARCH.com or Search Public Records. This service offers two kinds of reports, one for $19.95 and one for $39.95. The exact information you get depends on where the person for whom you are searching lives and the type of records that are available.

The Author Posting History option displays a list of all newsgroups to which the author has posted messages and the number of messages in each newsgroup. The Bookmark option redisplays the message in such a way that you can add its address to your browser's bookmarks or favorites list.

Finding Phone Numbers and Addresses

Most telephone companies offer a few calls to their directory service for free. But after the free calls, each request for information is billed to your account. With Yahoo!, you get unlimited telephone information about every place in the United States. And, through sites that you can access from Yahoo!, you can get information about most other countries as well.

Yahoo! is better than the phone company, in fact, because Yahoo! doesn't ask that question that all operator's ask: "What city please?" Using Yahoo!, you can find a telephone number even if you don't know where a person lives. Searching in Yahoo! is a great way to track down out-of-town friends or relatives when you're not exactly sure what city or town they live in.

Because the phone numbers are taken from real telephone books, you'll not only get a person's number, but the address that is kept on record. So even if you know someone's phone number, you can use Yahoo! to get his or her address.

To find a telephone number or address, follow these steps:

1. Click People Search in the Yahoo! home page. You can also find the People Search link on any Yahoo! feature that offers it, such as your address book or the form you see when composing an e-mail message. After you click People Search, you'll see the options in Figure 8-9.

2. Enter enough information to locate the person. You have to enter at least the person's last name, but the rest is optional. Of course, the more information you enter, the more likely you are to find the correct listing. If you know the state but not the city a person lives in, for example, just enter the state. If you are looking for an old friend who may have moved to parts unknown, just enter a name. Enter the first initial of the person's first name followed by an asterisks, as in **R***, if you're unsure how the person may be listed. Some persons list their name in the phone directory by their initial only or use an abbreviation such as Rob for Robert, for example.

3. Click Search. If any matching names are found, they appear in a list similar to the one shown in Figure 8-10.

If there is more than one listing, you'll need to scroll the list to locate the person you are looking for. You can also use the First, Prev, Next, and Last buttons to navigate the list of names.

If more persons are listed than you care to scroll through, click your Brower's Back button and enter some additional information to help narrow the search. For example, you could enter a complete first name, city, or state.

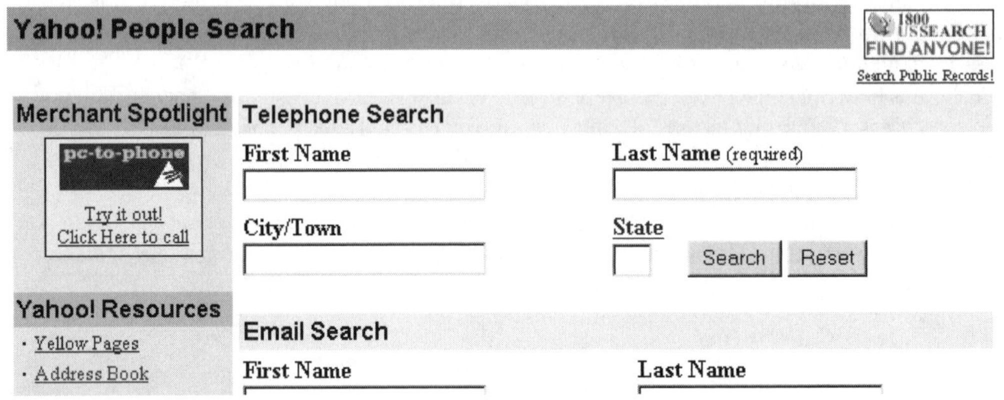

Yahoo! People Search

Merchant Spotlight

pc-to-phone

Try it out! Click Here to call

Yahoo! Resources
- Yellow Pages
- Address Book

Telephone Search

First Name

Last Name (required)

City/Town

State   Search   Reset

Email Search

First Name

Last Name

FIGURE 8-9   Searching for phone numbers and addresses

Phone Search Result

Showing 1 - 1 of 1

First | Prev | Next | Last   Search Again

Name	Phone (click to call)	Tools
A Neibauer 615 Byberry Rd Huntingdon Valley , PA	(215)938-0790	Try Email Search, vCard, Add to Address Book Search Public Records on 1800USSEARCH

First | Prev | Next | Last   Search Again

FREE CALLS
World-Wide!
Free long distance
PC phone calls.

1800
USSEARCH
FIND ANYONE!
Search
Public Records!

FIGURE 8-10   Results of a people search

If Yahoo! cannot find any matches, click the Back button and enter less criteria. If you entered the complete first name, for example, try just the first initial or no first name at all.

After you find a listing, then what? Notice that the name and phone number are underlined to indicate that they are hyperlinks, and that the Tools column contains additional links that let you do the following:

■ Find a business in the person's area

■ Make a phone call through the Internet

■ Add the person's name and address to your Yahoo! address book

■ Look for the person's e-mail addresses

Clicking a person's name displays what Yahoo! calls the *detailed listing*. Although the detailed listing contains no additional information about the person, it offers the same tools but with a link to see a map of the person's neighborhood.

Clicking the phone number accesses the Net2Phone service. This is a paid service that lets you make a phone call from your computer through the Internet to the person's telephone. You have to register for the service, download special software, and give credit card information to pay for calls, although Net2Phone usually has a free offer for an initial set of minutes.

The Net2Phone service is really quite interesting. Net2Phone places the call to the recipient's regular telephone, but you speak using your computer's microphone and hear the other party through your computer's speakers. You do not need a separate telephone to complete the call, just your Internet connection. The quality of the phone call depends on your hardware, the quality and speed of your Internet connection, and the amount of traffic currently on the Internet.

8

Tip   *Another source of free Internet telephone calls is http://www.dialpad.com.*

Clicking the Yellow Pages icon lets you locate a business in the person's area. We'll look at locating businesses in more detail later in the section "Finding Businesses." However, generally speaking, the icon takes you to a business search function that can find a business in a geographic area.

Note   *The Try E-Mail Search option looks for an e-mail address registered to the person.*

Clicking vCard saves the person's telephone and address information on your disk in a special format called a vCard. Some programs, such as Microsoft Outlook and Outlook Express, can import the information on a vCard into the address book.

- Add To Address Book inserts the name and address information into your Yahoo! address book.

- Create My Listing lets you create an address listing that will be stored in a Yahoo! database and be made available to other persons performing a people search.

Finding E-Mail Addresses

Because a growing number of people are communicating online, you may want to contact someone via e-mail rather than telephone. Using Yahoo! People Search, you can look for the e-mail address of a person just as easily as you can look for a telephone number.

Note   *Unfortunately, there is no universal source for e-mail addresses, such as the telephone directory, so the results of an e-mail address search may not be complete.*

To search for an e-mail address, start by filling in the E-Mail Search section of the People Search page, as shown here, or click Try E-Mail Search in the results of the search for a telephone number.

Email Search

First Name   Last Name

[   ]   [   ]

[Search] [Reset] Advanced

Enter the person's first name or initial, enter the last name, and then click the Search button. If any matches are found, they appear in a window similar to the one in Figure 8-11. Click the e-mail address to open your e-mail software and send the person a message, or click a person's name to go to a detail page.

If no address is found or you want to narrow a long list of addresses, click the Advanced hyperlink and search for an e-mail address using the options shown in Figure 8-12. The

Barbara Neibauer Atlantic City, NJ	bneibauer@yahoo.com	🔊 , Try Phone Search, vCard, Add to Address Book Search Public Records on 1800USSEARCH

FIGURE 8-11   Matching e-mail addresses

SmartNames, domain, organization name, and organization type might be the most useful fields in tracking down a person.

SmartNames substitutes common names in place of first names that you enter. As the screen shows, for example, entering **Bob** tells the software to search for **Robert** as well as Bob (Bob=Robert).

If you know or suspect that the person is a member of America Online, for example, enter aol.com as the domain.

If you happen to know which company the person works for, you can also try the company name as a domain, as in Microsoft.com or ibm.com. If you are not sure of the company's domain, just enter the company name and then choose a type of organization.

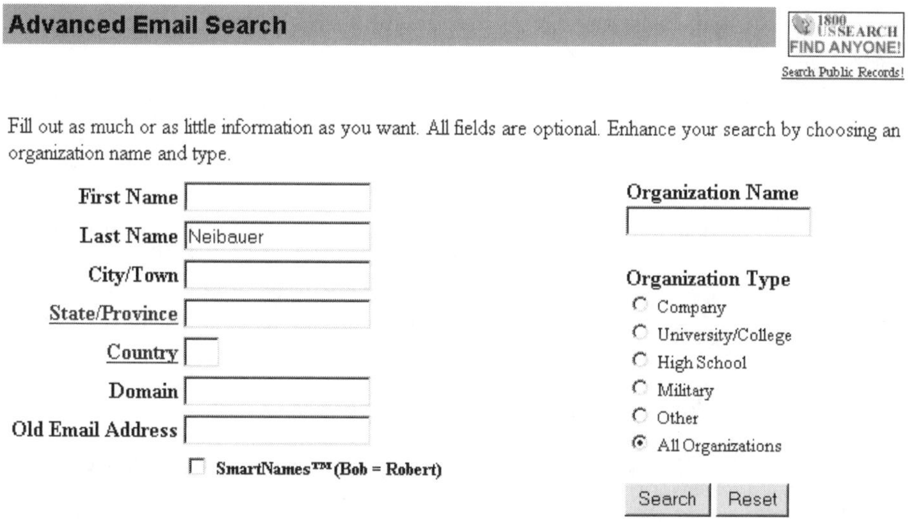

8

Advanced Email Search

1800 USSEARCH
FIND ANYONE!
Search Public Records!

Fill out as much or as little information as you want. All fields are optional. Enhance your search by choosing an organization name and type.

First Name	
Last Name	Neibauer
City/Town	
State/Province	
Country	
Domain	
Old Email Address	

☐ SmartNames™ (Bob = Robert)

Organization Name

Organization Type
- ○ Company
- ○ University/College
- ○ High School
- ○ Military
- ○ Other
- ● All Organizations

Search   Reset

FIGURE 8-12   Advanced search options for e-mail address

The type of organization often determines the full domain name. Educational institutions, for example, usually have the .edu extension; so if you enter **Temple** and select University/College as the type, the e-mail address is likely to be in the domain temple.edu.

Finding Businesses

Looking for something to buy, a place to go, or someone to hire? With Yahoo!, you can search for businesses as easily as people.

You start by specifying the geographic area of the business you're looking for. You can then browse through businesses in that area by type, or enter the name of the business you are looking for. If the business is not in the area that you searched, you can expand the search into nearby areas.

Here's how to start a search for a business:

■ From the Yahoo! home page, click Yellow Pages in the list of links at the top of the page.

Shopping - **Auctions** - Yellow Pages - People Search - Maps - Travel - Classifieds - Personals - Games - Chat - **Clubs**
Mail - Calendar - Messenger - **Companion** - My Yahoo! - News - Sports - Weather - TV - Stock Quotes - more...

■ If you are looking at a person's telephone and address listing from a people search, click the Yellow Pages icon to start at the person's address.

Tools
▲ Try
Add to

If this is not the first time you have used the Yellow Pages, the name of the last location you searched will appear. You'll need to change the location as described later to search another area. Likewise, if you clicked the Yellow Pages icon from a People Search screen, the neighborhood of the person displayed at the time will be used for the business search. We'll look at those contingencies later. For now, let's assume that this is the first time you have used the Yellow Pages.

Click the category of your search. You'll be asked to specify the geographic area to search, as shown in Figure 8-13. Use the Search In A City tab to locate a business in a specific city or zip-code area. Enter either the city and state or the zip code. Use the Search Near an Address tab to locate a business near a specific address. You can then enter a street address, city, and state or zip code.

Tip   *Both tabs offer a list of recently searched locations.*

If you have used the Yellow Pages before or you started from a People Search listing, the address will appear on the Yellow Pages home page. To search for a business in another location, click Change Location. You can then enter a new location or select a recently searched location from the recently searched locations list.

FIGURE 8-13   Specifying the area to search

The business type categories work much the same way as the categories for general searching. Clicking a major category displays a list of subcategories. You continue selecting subcategories to refine your search until you see specific listings such as those shown in Figure 8-14.

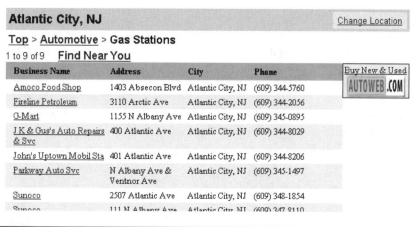

FIGURE 8-14   Results of a business search

If there are a large number of listings, you'll need to scroll the list or click Next Matches. You may also see the alphabet links, in which case you can click a letter to search for a business whose name starts with the letter you clicked.

Note   *A list of featured businesses may appear before the others. These are businesses that have a relationship with Yahoo!. You'll see links to their Web sites.*

Depending on how you initiated the search, you may see two other options:

- **Find Near You**   You may see this link if you started by looking for a business based on its city location. Click this link to enter a street address to use as the basis for a search.

- **Beyond (City Name)**   Click this link (for example, Beyond Atlantic City) to extend the search into the area surrounding the city being searched.

Click the business you are interested in to see detailed information about it. In addition to its name, address, and phone number, Yahoo! shows a map of its location.

To place an Internet to telephone call to the business, click the underlined phone number. You can also click Add To Address Book to insert the listing into your Yahoo! address book.

The Find Related section of the page, shown on the right, contains links to similar business categories. While looking at a listing for a service station, for example, you may see links to these types of establishments. Click a link to extend the search to a related business.

Find Related:
- Automobile Repairing & Service
- Service Stations - Gasoline & Oil - Mobil

The path to the business is shown at the top of the page. You can quickly go back to one of the previous levels to search for other business types.

Tip   *There may also be a link to Yahoo! Categories that relate to the business type.*

The map shows the location of the business and the roads surrounding it. There are three links under the map (you'll learn about them in Chapter 10):

- **Interactive Map**   Lets you navigate the geographic area and see locations adjacent to the one shown

- **Driving Directions**   Lets you get detailed step-by-step driving directions from a location you specify to the one shown in the map

- **Find Nearby**   Helps you locate other businesses in the geographic area

Chapter 9

Find Your Roots: Genealogy Online

How to . . .

- Search for relatives
- Use Yahoo!'s Genealogy Guide
- Search the Social Security Death Index
- Access the Genealogy How To Guide
- Follow genealogy links from Yahoo!

Yahoo! is a great place to start if you are researching your family history because it provides a way to share information with other genealogists around the world and to access thousands of sites that support family research.

Performing genealogical research online focuses on three areas:

- Making personal contacts
- Learning about resources
- Searching online databases

Because a great many people are online, you can use the Internet to locate near and distant relatives through a variety of channels. Through messages boards, chats, and genealogical organizations, for example, you might get lucky and find distant relatives who are researching a branch of a family tree that the two of you share. Sharing information with other family members is one of the best ways to get started in genealogy and to fill in the empty branches of a family tree. One bit of information leads to another, from one branch of the family to another, and sometimes the most useful bit of information comes serendipitously when you least expect it.

You can also use the people search techniques that you learned in Chapter 8 to locate relatives. In our highly mobile society, families can easily spread apart and lose touch with each other. Searching for extended family members who have moved and with whom you have lost contact is easy with Yahoo!'s directory resources and links.

The next level of genealogical research is learning which resources are available. Resources include organizations both private and public, as well as companies that perform genealogical research for a fee. Most of the information that is available to genealogical researchers is not available online. It is stored in hard copy form, on microfilm, and on other media. Through online research, however, you can find out where the records you need are stored and learn how to access them. In some cases, you can even arrange to have microfilm sent directly to you or to a local library or research center.

In this chapter, you'll also learn about online and offline services and software that you can purchase to help with researching and creating a family tree. If you need to research records in a foreign country, for example, you'll find companies and individuals who can do it for you. You can also purchase databases of information, such as census and immigration records, that will help your efforts.

Online databases are the third level of genealogical information. These are searchable databases from which you can retrieve information while you are online. A great many online databases are maintained by volunteer organizations that are interested in genealogy and want to share their information in the hopes of making contact with relatives. A few official governmental databases are available to the public, such as the Social Security Death Index. Unfortunately, most official records are not yet searchable online.

Searching for Relatives

The easiest place to begin researching your family genealogy is with the living. Contact as many relatives as possible, and get in touch with people who were close to your family and remember your relatives. You should also consider contacting physicians, attorneys, accountants, and other advisors who may have personal memories about family members and the events in their lives.

To locate relatives and other persons for your research, use the people and business search techniques covered in Chapter 8. Start by looking for relatives you know about. You can also use international directories to look for relatives who are living abroad.

Search for e-mail addresses, residential listings, and business listings. A relative may have opened a business under his or her name or founded a business in the past. If you know whom the person works for, check company and institution Web sites. Some company Web sites provide employee e-mail directories or links to the personnel department. As a last resort, look for the e-mail address of the company's Webmaster. E-mail the Webmaster and ask for the e-mail or mailing address of the personnel department.

9

Forward web-related questions, comments, etc. to: *webmaster@www.temple.edu*
For other University inquiries, see list of departmental e-mail addresses.

Buyer Beware

Most companies that offer genealogical research, services, and software over the Internet are reputable. They offer a valuable service, especially to those who cannot travel and collect information firsthand. But, as with all purchases both online and offline, you have to use discretion when you decide whether to buy.

Keep in mind that unless you are directly related to a famous, or infamous, family, no company can guarantee that it will be able to locate historical information about your family. Having the same surname as a famous family doesn't guarantee anything either. Imagine how many Kennedys would stake claims at the probate office if it were otherwise.

In some cases, you'll see advertisements for genealogical companies and software on Yahoo! pages. Family Tree Maker, it so happens, sponsors some of the Yahoo! genealogical resources. Brøderbund, the company that makes Family Tree Maker, and the other companies that appear on Yahoo! pages have been in business for some time and have earned good reputations. Just use the same caution with genealogical purchases that you use when you make other kinds of purchases.

To find members of the extended family, try searching the entire country for people who have a certain surname. Searching this way is most effective if you have an uncommon family name, where the chances are high that a person with the surname might be a relative. You should try a surname search even if your name is not that uncommon, however, on the chance that an interesting lead turns up.

Try searching for variations of the spelling of a name, especially if your family immigrated to the United States. The spelling of names was often changed when immigrants entered the country. I have relatives, for example, who spell the name Neibauer like so: Niebauer and Neubauer. You may have relatives who spell their names differently or who have anglicized their names.

Search also for other surnames in the family tree, not just your own surname. Married aunts and first cousins may have different last names, for example, even though they are closely related.

If your research locates a potential relative with an e-mail address, send him or her a brief e-mail to ask if they and you are related. If you only have a mailing address, send a brief letter. Explain that you may be related and provide the names of relatives that you may have in common. If you think a person is a cousin, for example, mention how you think the person is related to your side of the family.

Yahoo! Seniors' Guide—Genealogy Section

Because it is frequently a senior member of the family who is interested in the family history, Yahoo! has a section on genealogy within the Seniors' Guide. However, the information is useful to anyone searching his or her family roots.

To access the section, go to www.seniors.yahoo.com and click the Genealogy link on the left side of the page. You see the site shown in Figure 9-1. The page contains sections titled How To Articles, Top Picks, People Finder, Tree Talk, Daily Tip, and More Yahoo!.

People Finder provides a link to the People Search features. Tree Talk offers links to genealogy-related chats. Daily Tip offers a useful insight into family research.

'How To' Articles

The How To articles are a great place to start, especially if you are new to genealogical research.

Creating a Family History Book explains the basics of creating a family history book. The book will serve as a reference for all members of the family, and you can have copies of the book placed in the National Archives and other libraries for other genealogists to access. The articles cover planning, writing, and finishing the book, as well as using other documents and photographs.

Sharing Family Research at a Reunion explains how to learn about your family history from other family members. The article suggests holding a family reunion so you can share information, retell stories, and just get reacquainted with relatives. The article is divided into these subjects:

- Genealogy and history live
- Ways to share your genealogical research

- What was it like back then?
- Honoring the past
- Everyone grows on one
- Can anyone solve this mystery?
- Who are you?
- Making history
- Family history helps fund reunions
- Flavor yours ethnically
- There's lots more where these ideas came from

You can use the reunion to hold informal workshops on genealogy, as well as share pictures and label old pictures with the names of people whom you may not be able to identify. Make copies of pictures that are difficult to identify so that other family members can study them at length at home.

Tip *For more information about reunions, check out Reunions Magazine on the Web at http://www.reunionsmag.com/.*

9

Understanding Genealogical Acronyms is more than just a list of the acronyms that you'll find when conducting your research. The article explains how genealogists are certified. It also contains links to a variety of wonderful genealogical resources.

FIGURE 9-1   Yahoo! Seniors' Guide to genealogy

Using Photos in Your Research is a detailed article about how to use photographs for your research and incorporate them in your family history. The article is organized into these areas:

- Properly Labeling Your Photographs
- Using Photography to Document Your Research
- Getting Photographs from Microfiche And Microfilm
- How Photos Can Help You with Your Research

The importance of properly labeling photographs cannot be overstated. If you want to preserve your generation's family history, you should label your own snapshots so later generations will be able to identify the family members and places shown. The article recommends adding these notations to the back of all photographs:

- The date that the photograph was taken.
- The names and ages of the persons in the photograph, in the same order in which they appear.
- The location the photograph was taken, and any additional information about the circumstances.
- The name and relation of the person who took the photograph.
- The location of the original negative or slide.

Top Picks

The Top Picks section of the Seniors' Guide contains a number of links for useful information. You can search the records of the Social Security Administration for a relative's social security number, date, place of death, and other information. You can also access useful articles on genealogy and share information with other Yahoo! members on message boards.

Social Security Death Index

The Social Security Death Index is a searchable database of over 55 million persons that is maintained by the Social Security Administration. The online search tool is provided by Family Tree Maker, Yahoo!'s partner in the genealogy page of the Seniors' Guide. Follow these steps to use the index to get information about relatives who have passed away:

1. Click Social Security Death Index to see the form shown in Figure 9-2.
2. Enter enough information to identify the person you want to research. Enter the first and last name, and any other identifying information. Use just the last name to list all persons with that name in the index. The Soundex option will locate names that sound like the one you enter. Soundex codes are especially useful if you are not sure of the spelling of a name or if relatives have changed the spelling of a surname over the years.
3. Click Search Now.

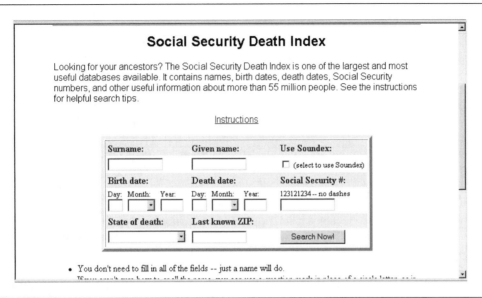

FIGURE 9-2   Social Security Death Index

A sample of the search results is shown in Figure 9-3. With this information, you may be able to learn more about the relative from other resources.

Social Security Death Index

The 6 name(s) below were found.

Name	SS#	Issue State	Birth	Death	Death State	Last Known Residence	Last Payment Location	AutoWrite Letter
NEIBAUER, JOSEPH	388-10-6196	WI	8 Apr 1898	Mar 1986	WI	Milwaukee, Wisconsin 53223		Write It
NEIBAUER, JOSEPH	502-09-1794	ND	1 Jan 1907	Nov 1965	ND	Bismarck, North Dakota 58501		Write It
NEIBAUER, JOSEPH	390-01-0611	WI	31 Dec 1911	Mar 1976	WI	Eau Claire, Wisconsin 54701		Write It
NEIBAUER, JOSEPH	394-01-5441	WI	25 Nov 1912	Oct 1977	WI	Mellen, Wisconsin 54546		Write It
NEIBAUER, JOSEPH	207-03-9465	PA	21 Jan 1913	Mar 1974	PA	Coal Township, Pennsylvania 17866		Write It
NEIBAUER, JOSEPH	164-12-7991	PA	27 Sep 1918	Jan 1973	PA	Jenkintown, Pennsylvania 19046		Write It

FIGURE 9-3   Results of a search in the Social Security Death Index

9

You can use the social security number, for example, to access military, financial, and employment information. The birth date and issue state information may help in getting birth records. The death date, last known residence, and last payment location may help in locating a death certificate or burial site.

To get more information from the Social Security Administration, click the Write It link. Doing so displays a form letter that is already addressed and written to the Social Security Administration. The letter requests information from the person's social security application. When the letter is displayed, use your browser's Print button to print out a copy. The letter will contain the person's name, social security number, birth date, and death date. Write in your own name, address, and phone number, and mail the letter with a check for $7.00 to the Social Security Administration. Its address is shown on the letter.

Genealogy 'How To' Guide

The Genealogy How To Guide choice from Top Picks accesses detailed articles and information about hundreds of archives and libraries that can be useful for your research, as shown in Figure 9-4.

There are also links to various reference tools, including lists of phones numbers and addresses that are of interest to genealogists, a dictionary of genealogy terms, information about the Family Tree Maker program, and form letters and other documents that you'll find useful in your research.

The directory page includes six links to resources, as shown here:

Clicking County Information, for example, displays a map of the United States. Click the state in which you are interested to find the location of record offices in each county, as shown in Figure 9-5.

The International, ethnic, and religious resources options display lists of links to ethnic and religious groups. Select a link to see a summary of genealogical tips for collecting records as well as addresses and links to various resources.

To make use of the form letters and other sample documents, follow these steps:

1. Click this link on the Genealogy How To Guide page.

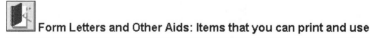

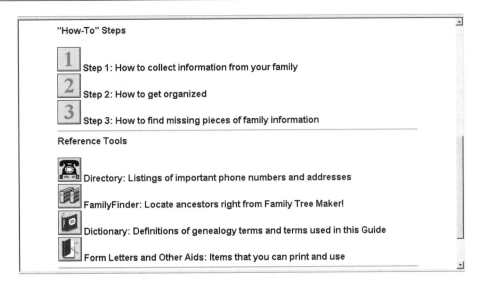

FIGURE 9-4   The Genealogy How To Guide

9

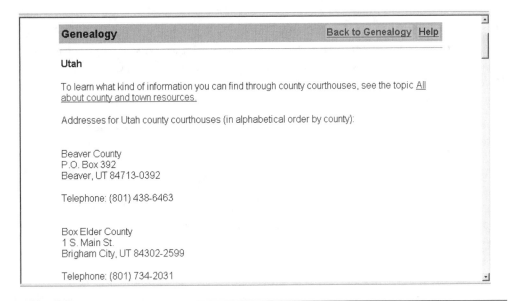

FIGURE 9-5   County information

2. Click the link for the type of letter or document you want to use, as shown here:

> Form letter for requesting genealogical information from an institution
>
> Form letter for requesting general information from an institution
>
> Form letter for requesting genealogical information from family members

The sample letter appears.

3. Start your word processing program.

4. Click the listing for your Web browser on the Windows taskbar to return to the sample document.

5. Click and drag the mouse to highlight the entire letter.

6. Choose Copy from your browser's Edit menu.

7. Click the button for your word processing program in the Windows taskbar.

8. Click the Paste button or choose Paste from your word processor's Edit menu.

9. Insert your own name and address in the letter, as well as the address of the organization to which you want to write. Include a description of the information you want. You may be able to copy the organization's name and address from another page on the Internet.

10. Print the letter.

Yahoo! Message Boards: Genealogy

The Yahoo! Message Boards: Genealogy link under Top Picks accesses Yahoo! message boards that are of interest to genealogists. You'll learn all about message boards in Chapter 21.

Through message boards, you can share information, find answers, and even locate relatives by reading and leaving messages.

Resource Links   The other items under Top Picks are genealogical links to organizations, research sites, and general resources.

More Yahoo!

The More Yahoo! section of the Seniors' Guide, shown at right, provides links to other Yahoo! features of interest to family researchers.

The Beginners' Guides, for example, represent a series of links to Yahoo! features and other Web sites.

More Yahoo!

- Beginners' Guides
- Genealogy
- Lineages and Surnames
- Organizations
- Reference
- Regional and Ethnic Resources
- Yahoo! Net Events: Genealogy

The other links lead to lists of Yahoo! categories and Web sites. For example, clicking Genealogy displays these subcategories:

- Beginners' Guides *(19)*
- Chats and Forums *(49)*
- Companies@
- GEDCOM *(7)*
- Lineages and Surnames *(2271)* NEW!
- Lookups *(1)*
- Magazines *(10)*

- Organizations *(95)*
- PAF *(3)*
- Reference *(50)*
- Regional and Ethnic Resources *(205)*
- Royal Genealogies *(9)*
- Web Directories *(37)*

Clicking Reference, on the other hand, leads to these sites:

- Cemeteries@
- Census Records *(18)*
- Church of Jesus Christ of the Latter-Day Saints: Family History Centers *(16)*
- U.S. Civil War Muster Rolls@

Chapter 10

Maps and Driving Directions

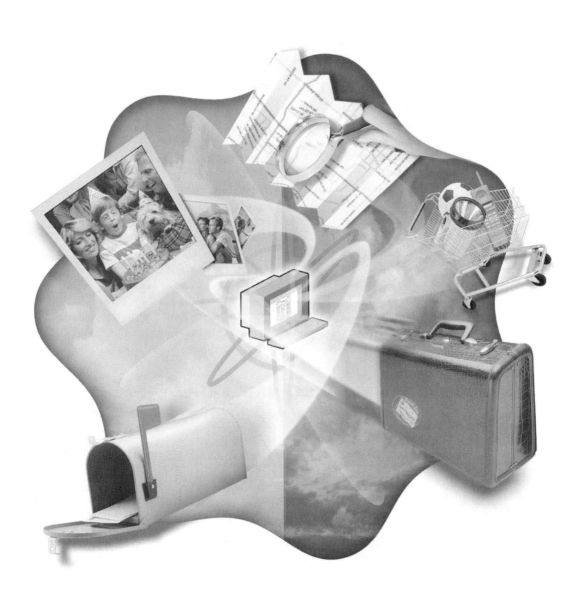

How to . . .

■ Get a map of a location

■ Use an interactive map

■ Print and e-mail maps

■ Get detailed driving directions

Locating people and businesses is one thing, but finding your way to them is another. To make sure you know how to get somewhere, or just to learn more about an area where a place of interest is located, you can use Yahoo! to map the location for you.

Mapping a Location

You might need a map to find your way somewhere—the airport, a business meeting, a social event, a relative's house. With Yahoo!, you can get a detailed street map that shows where something is located. What's more, you can get step-by-step driving directions that show every turn in the road between two different locations.

Next time you're planning a trip, you might use a map to select a hotel near a location you want to visit—a tourist attraction, convention center, or friend's house. Before making reservations at a hotel, for example, examine a Yahoo! map to see how close it is to your destination. If you're attending a convention, choose a hotel that's close to the convention site or easy to get to by public transportation.

You might also use Yahoo! maps just to learn more about an area. For example, you can learn how close an area is to an ocean or a river, whether it has any lakes or large parks, or what major roads are near it.

Yahoo! gets its maps from a company called MapQuest, which in turns gets its data from other vendors. Depending on the vendor, the information on a map may be several years old and may not show new streets and addresses.

Here's how to map with Yahoo!:

1. Click Maps in the Yahoo! home page to see the options shown in Figure 10-1.

Shopping - **Auctions** - Yellow Pages - People Search - Maps - Travel - Classifieds - Personals - Games - Chat - **Clubs**
Mail - Calendar - Messenger - **Companion** - My Yahoo! - News - Sports - Weather - TV - Stock Quotes - more...

2. If you need a map to an airport, click Airport Code. The Map and Driving Directions page opens with a list of major United States airports and their official abbreviations. Make a note of the abbreviation of the airport you want, and then click your browser's Back button.

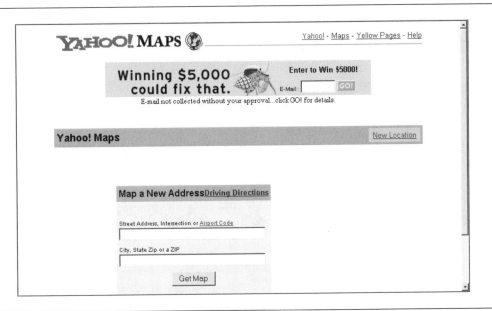

FIGURE 10-1   Specifying a location to map

10

3. Enter the street address you want to map, the nearest intersection, or the airport code. If you don't know the exact address, you can enter the two closest cross streets. For example, you could enter Broad St. and Market St.

4. Enter the city and state, or just the zip code. (You do not have to enter any of this information if you are mapping the location to an airport code.)

5. Click Get Map. A map will appear, as shown in Figure 10-2.

If Yahoo! cannot locate the street, you may see a street with a similar name or a list of possible locations. If a list appears, select the location that matches the one you want to map, or else go back and enter another address. If you enter an intersection and a street is not found, you will see a city map.

Tips for Getting Accurate Maps

Here are a few steps you can take to help ensure that the maps you generate accurately reflect the locations you want to map:

- Use the proper abbreviations for street suffixes: Rd., St., Ave., Blvd., and so on. Moreover, use prefix abbreviations such as N (North), S (South), E (East), or W (West) where necessary.

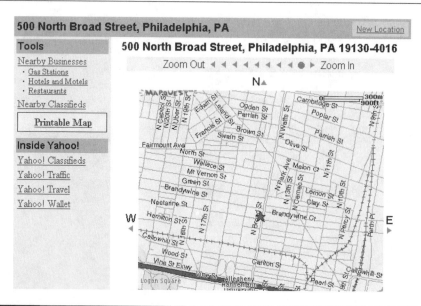

FIGURE 10-2   Typical Yahoo! map

- Enter a zip code whenever possible, rather than the city name and state, but make sure that the zip code is accurate.

- If you enter a city name, spell it correctly. Yahoo! can automatically correct some city names, but not all of them.

- If a map cannot locate a place or displays it in the incorrect location, go to www.mapquest.com and report the problem so that a map can be generated correctly in the future.

The position of the star that indicates the location you are looking for is placed by interpolation. MapQuest divides the street into equal segments based on the range of addresses. If a street contains numbers ranging from 1 to 100, for example, the location of the house at address 50 is placed in the middle. However, this placement may not be accurate where the addresses on a street are not equidistant from one another.

Zooming and Navigating Maps

There is a lot to a Yahoo! map page, so let's look at it in detail, starting with the map itself.

The location you entered is shown with a star in the center of the map. Yahoo! maps are interactive. You can start from a specific location and then use navigation controls to change the view.

How to ... **Locate an Intersection**

Instead of locating a specific street address, you can enter a nearby intersection. Locating an intersection is especially useful when mapping a new street or address that has not yet been added to the MapQuest maps. You can display a map of the closest intersection and thereby see the surrounding area.

Just enter the two street names, as in Broad and Chestnut, and then enter either the city and state or the zip code. To designate an interstate highway, use the designation IH, as in IH 95. Use the designation SR for a state route (a state highway), as in SR 40. The location IH 85 and SR 40 would represent the intersection of Interstate 95 and State Highway 40. When you click Get Map, Yahoo! displays a map of the area. You can then navigate around the map to find an exact location.

The Zoom Out and Zoom In bar above the map lets you determine how much detail is displayed. The round dot indicates the current zoom level. The closer the dot is to the right (Zoom In), the more detail is displayed. The closer the dot is to the left, the less detail is displayed, although you can see a wider geographic area. Click an arrow to the left or right of the dot to zoom in or out.

Less detail, larger area   More detail, smaller area

Zoom in, for example, if you have trouble reading street names. If you zoom in all the way, however, you may no longer see the names of landmarks such as hospitals, schools, and parks. Zoom out if you want to see what roads lead to the area or what communities surround it. Figure 10-3, for example shows the same location as Figure 10-2, but now the map has been zoomed out by two levels. Notice as you zoom that the scale in the upper-right corner changes. The scale shows the approximate distances represented on the map.

Note *Zooming out all of the way shows the entire North American continent.*

If you want to see a surrounding area in the same detail, you can't use the Zoom In and Zoom Out bar. Instead, click one of the compass points: N (north), S (south), E (east), or W (West). To see what is just to the east of the displayed area, for example, click E. The map is redrawn, and the star that indicates the original location you searched for moves accordingly.

10

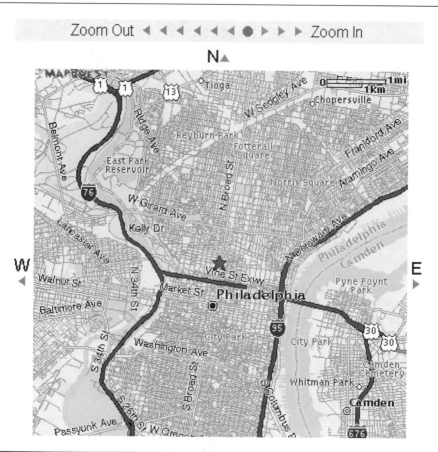

FIGURE 10-3   Map zoomed out two levels (compare this to Figure 10-2)

You can also change the center position of the map to another location. To do so, click the location on the map that you want to be the center. To return from the center to the original location, click the star that marks the location you specified.

If you want to create a map for another address, click New Location or scroll down the page to see the Map A New Address box. Enter the new location and click Get Map.

Printing and Annotating a Map

To print a copy of the map, click Printable Map. Yahoo! removes the other page elements, as well as the navigation and zoom controls, and you get a map like the one shown in Figure 10-4. You can now print the map using your browser's Print button or the Print command from its File menu.

500 North Broad Street, Philadelphia, PA 19130-4016

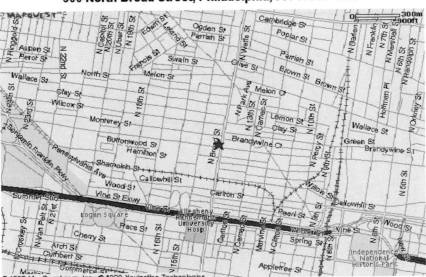

FIGURE 10-4   A printable map

Because the map is a separate object in the browser window, you can also save the map and annotate to it in the Windows Paint program. Here's how:

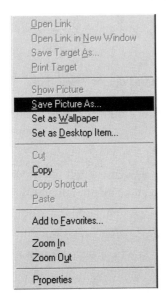

1. Right-click the map to see a shortcut menu, such as the menu at left if you're using Microsoft Internet Explorer.

2. Choose Save Picture As from the shortcut menu to open the Save Picture box. Note the location of the files displayed.

3. Enter a name for the map.

4. Pull down the Save As Type list and choose Bitmap (*.bmp)

5. Click Save.

6. Click the Start button on the Windows taskbar and choose Programs, Accessories, and Paint.

7. Choose Open from the File menu.

8. Locate and open the file you saved.

9. Add any text to the map as desired, as shown in Figure 10-5.

10. Save and print the annotated map.

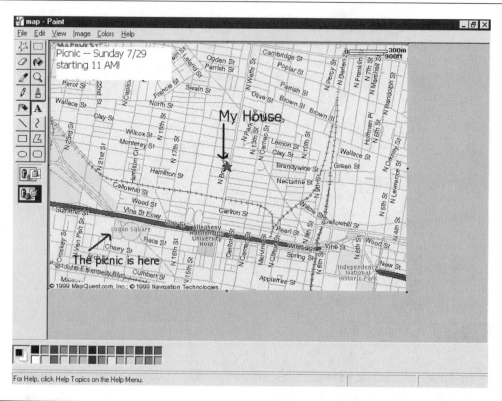

FIGURE 10-5   An annotated map in Paint

Locating Businesses

The Tools section of the map pages lets you locate businesses in the area being mapped. This is a great way to locate a hotel, restaurant, or other business in the area. The links take you to the Yellow Pages search feature discussed in Chapter 8. When you arrive in the Yellow Pages, the location is set already to the location being mapped.

Click Nearby Business (or Find Nearby Businesses under the map) to select from the Yellow Page categories, or click one of the other links to go directly to a list of service stations, hotels or motels, or restaurants.

For example, suppose you want to locate a hotel in an area that you've mapped. Follow these steps:

1.   Click Hotels And Motels to see a listing such as the one shown in Figure 10-6. The listing shows the name, address, and phone number of hotels, as well as their distance

500 North Broad Street, Philadelphia, PA   Change Location

Top > Travel and Transportation > Hotels and Lodging > **Hotels and Motels**

Featured Businesses   Make your listing a Featured Business

Business Name	Address	City	Phone	Miles**	
Holiday Inn	4100 Presidential Blvd	Philadelphia, PA	(215) 477-0200	4.0	Website

1 to 20 of 43

Business Name	Address	City	Phone	Miles**	
Divine Lorraine Hotel	699 N Broad St	Philadelphia, PA	(215) 765-0521	0.3	
Hawthorn Suites Philadelphia	1100 Vine St	Philadelphia, PA	(215) 829-8300	0.5	
Wyndham Franklin Plaza Hotel	17th & Race	Philadelphia, PA	(215) 448-2000	0.5	Website Reviews
Mary Jane Home Enrichment Ctr	1622 Ridge Ave	Philadelphia, PA	(215) 684-2847	0.5	
Korman Suites Hotel	2001 Hamilton St	Philadelphia, PA	(215) 569-7000	0.5	Reviews
Two Buttonwood Square	2001 Hamilton St # 501	Philadelphia, PA	(215) 569-7270	0.5	
Carlyle Hotel	1425 Poplar St	Philadelphia, PA	(215) 978-9934	0.5	

FIGURE 10-6   Listing of hotels in the mapped area

10

from the location being mapped. In some instances, there is also a link to the hotel's Web site or to a Web page with reviews.

2. Click the name of the hotel to see its detailed listing, including a map of its location.

As you learned earlier in this chapter, you can then click Interactive Map under the map to see the same zoom and navigation controls or get driving directions.

The Nearby Classifieds link opens the Yahoo! Classifieds page, as shown in Figure 10-7. From here, you can access classified and personal ads for the area. You'll learn more about classified ads in Chapter 21.

Getting Driving Directions

Once you know where you are going, you likely want to learn exactly how to get there. Yahoo! driving directions give you step-by-step, turn-by-turn directions from one location to another.

There are several ways to get driving directions:

■ From the initial Yahoo! Maps page, click Driving Directions to see the options shown in Figure 10-8.

FIGURE 10-7   Classifieds for the mapped area

- If you have already mapped the location, click Driving Directions under the map to
  see the same options shown in Figure 10-8. However, if you have already mapped the
  location, the destination is already filled in.

Enter the starting location and the destination location and then click Get Directions. Figure 10-9,
for example, shows directions for getting from San Francisco Airport to a location in Berkeley,
California. At the top of the page are the starting and destination addresses, the distance in miles
between the two, and the approximate driving time.

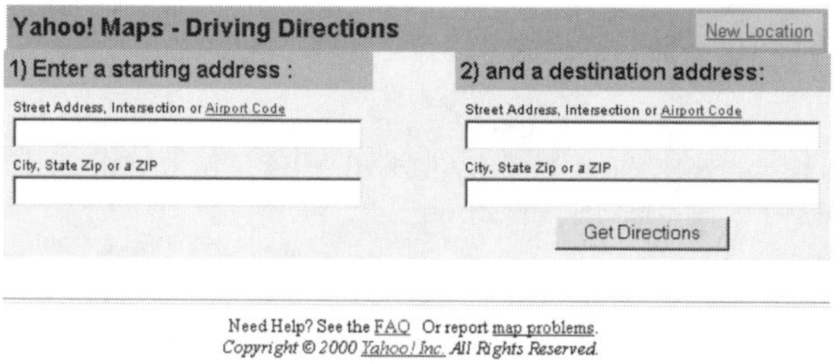

Yahoo! Maps - Driving Directions   New Location

1) Enter a starting address :	2) and a destination address:
Street Address, Intersection or Airport Code	Street Address, Intersection or Airport Code
City, State Zip or a ZIP	City, State Zip or a ZIP
	Get Directions

Need Help? See the FAQ Or report map problems.
Copyright © 2000 Yahoo! Inc. All Rights Reserved.

FIGURE 10-8   Getting driving directions

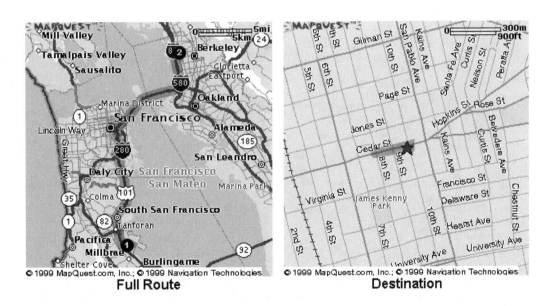

Yahoo! Maps - Driving Directions				New Location

Starting From:	Arriving At:	Distance	Approximate Travel Time:
SFO San Francisco, CA	1600 10th Street Berkeley, CA 94710-1816	24.1 miles	32 mins

	Directions	miles
1.	Start out going West on ARRIVING FLIGHTS ACC towards AIRPORT EXIT by turning left.	0.5
2.	Stay straight to go onto AIRPORT EXIT.	0.4
3.	Take the US-101 NORTH/I-380 WEST ramp towards SAN FRANCISCO(I-280)/SAN BRUNO.	0.1
4.	Keep LEFT at the fork in the ramp.	0.2

FIGURE 10-9   Driving directions

The actual driving directions are shown next along with the distance of each segment. Below the directions are two maps, one that shows the overall route and another that shows a closeup of the destination address.

Full Route

Destination

Note   *Below the maps are boxes for changing addresses and getting new directions.*

10

Let the Driver Beware

Depending on which vendor supplied the information to MapQuest, some driving directions are not totally accurate or up to date. Watch for new roads, changed traffic patterns, one-way streets, and other factors that might make driving directions more accurate. Pay particular attention to the location of on and off ramps on limited access highways and bridges, and give yourself extra time to reach your destination.

International Maps

The Maps and Driving Directions feature only works when you are seeking directions in the United States. If you want to map a location outside the United States, you need to look at the Yahoo! Travel service or access other sites that are linked to Yahoo!.

Yahoo! Travel offers information about hundreds of countries, including a country map and some maps of major cities and metropolitan areas. Go to the site at http://travel.yahoo.com/ to see the options shown in Figure 10-10.

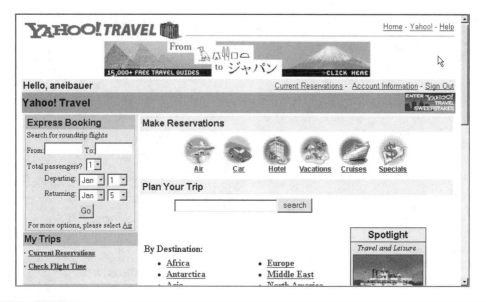

FIGURE 10-10   Starting a search for maps at Yahoo! Travel

Follow these steps to locate country or city maps:

1. Click the area in the Destination section to see a list of countries.

2. Click the country in which the destination is located. In the detail page about the country, you'll see a small map like this one:

3. Click Full-size Map to enlarge the map.

The detail page for the country may also list cities or regions within the country. If your destination is shown, click it to see additional details, including Travel Resources, as shown here:

· **Lodging**
Hotels,
Resorts...

· **Travel**
Resources
Guides, Tours,
Maps...

· **Getting**
Around
Car Rentals,
Taxis...

Click that link to see if maps of the area are available. Follow the links that appear to locate city maps and driving directions.

10

Part III

Personal Finance with Yahoo!— Taking Care of Business

Chapter 11

Build and Manage Your Portfolio

How to . . .

- Get stock quotes
- Research stocks, bonds, and funds
- Use the Stock Market toolbar
- Use the Yahoo! Companion
- Create an online portfolio
- Add investments to your portfolio
- Manage your portfolio
- Customize your portfolio
- Use the portfolio calendar
- Interact with the Java Portfolio Manager

Investing can be fun and profitable if you do it correctly, and the Internet has changed the basic nature of investing so that it can be fun and profitable for the average person. Information that was once privy to a select few insiders is now freely available to anyone with an Internet connection. Online research and investment tools make it easier to make sound decisions. Online trading with low commissions makes investing more efficient and profitable.

Yahoo! offers an amazingly significant range of tools for investors. On Yahoo!, you'll find information about thousands of companies, as well as the tools you need to make decisions and track your investments.

In this chapter, we'll look at the research information and tools that Yahoo! provides, as well as how to create and maintain your own portfolio.

Yahoo! provides three ways to access financial information:

- Yahoo! Companion
- Stock Market toolbar
- Yahoo! Finance page

Yahoo! Companion

If you installed the Yahoo! Companion toolbar on your browser, as described in Chapter 3, you have quick access to many investment tools no matter where you are on the Internet. Where are these tools? Click the down arrow beside the Finance button to see them on the pull-down list, shown at right.

Click the Finance button, for example, to go directly to the Yahoo! Finance page, or choose an option from the pull-down list to access specific features.

The first four options on the list let you display and manage your own personal investment portfolio. You'll learn about them in the next chapter.

The US Indices option displays the page shown in Figure 11-1. It contains information on the Dow Jones Averages, New York Stock Exchange, Nasdaq, Standard and Poor's, and 14 other indices from the AMEX Composite to the Wilshi 5000, United States Treasuries, and Commodities.

In addition to the information displayed, you will find links to sites that offer more details about each index. Clicking ^DJT, for example, displays detailed information about the Dow Jones Transportation average.

There are also links to more information, including Chart, News, and Components. Chart displays a graph of the indices, News offers current news stories about the indices, and Components lists the individual stocks or other items that make up each index. We'll look at these links in detail later on.

The Most Actives option on the Finance pull-down list displays information about the Nasdaq, AMEX, and NYSE volume leaders, as shown here:

Symbol	Name	Last Trade	Change		Volume	More Info
PAGE	PAGING NETWORK	11:13AM	$2\,^{29}/_{32}$	$+^{13}/_{16}$ +38.81%	22,575,200	Chart, News, SEC, Msgs Profile, Research, Insider
MCLL	METROCALL	11:13AM	$13\,^{1}/_{4}$	$+1\,^{5}/_{8}$ +13.98%	19,352,900	Chart, News, SEC, Msgs Profile, Research, Insider
TCSI	TCSI CORP	11:13AM	$7\,^{19}/_{32}$	$+4\,^{15}/_{32}$ +143.00%	15,904,700	Chart, News, SEC, Msgs Profile, Research, Insider

11

Major U.S. Indices

Mon Feb 7 11:21am ET - U.S. Markets close in 4 hours 40 minutes.

Name	Symbol	Last Trade		Change	More Info
Dow Jones Averages					
30 Industrials	^DJI	11:21AM	**10897.18**	-66.62 -0.61%	Chart, News, Components
20 Transportation	^DJT	11:21AM	**2610.50**	+1.54 +0.06%	Chart, News, Components
15 Utilities	^DJU	11:21AM	**309.66**	+0.36 +0.12%	Chart, News, Components
65 Composite	^DJA	11:21AM	**3076.73**	-11.31 -0.37%	Chart, Components
New York Stock Exchange					
Volume in 000's	^TV.N	11:20AM	**338605**	0 0.00%	N/A
Composite	^NYA	11:21AM	**623.35**	-3.55 -0.57%	Chart
Tick	^TIC.N	11:20AM	**-182**	-142 +355.00%	N/A
ARMS	^STI.N	11:20AM	**0.96**	-0.22 -18.82%	Chart

Nasdaq

FIGURE 11-1   Getting information about the major U.S. stock indices

Click a stock's symbol to get detailed information about a stock, or click any of the links in the More Info column. In addition to Chart and News, you can try out these links:

- **SEC**   Displays Securities and Exchange Commission filing information.

- **Msgs**   Accesses discussions about stocks on the Yahoo! message boards.

- **Profile**   Displays information about a company, including a business summary, the dates of upcoming events and earnings announcements, a financial summary, an address, officer and owner information, and a summary of the company's financial statistics.

- **Research**   Displays a summary of basic recommendations, such as buy and sell recommendations, and earnings estimates and recommendations. It also displays data about the company's earnings growth and history, as well as research abstracts.

- **Insider**   Displays a summary of trades by company directors and officers.

The World Indices option on the Finance pull-down menu displays a summary of major financial indices in other countries. The categories are Americas (8 countries), Asia/Pacific (15 countries), Europe (19 countries), and Africa/Middle East (3 countries). Click the links to get details or additional information about a stock index in a foreign country.

The Currency Exchange option on the Finance pull-down menu lets you convert one currency to another:

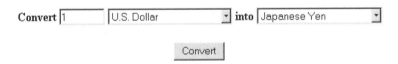

Here's how to use the currency converter:

1. Enter the amount of currency you want to convert.

2. Select which currency you want to convert—options range from the Afghanistan Afghani to the Zambian Kwacha.

3. Select the currency into which the conversion will be made.

4. Click the Convert button.

For example, the results of converting 50 Belgian francs into United States dollars is shown here:

Symbol	Belgian Franc	Exchange Rate		U.S. Dollar
BEFUSD=X	50	11:20AM	0.0242318	**1.21**

The Stock Market Toolbar

If you have downloaded Yahoo! Companion, you can also use the Stock Market toolbar to access investment information. To display the toolbar, click the Change Toolbar button on Companion and choose Switch to Stock Market Toolbar, as shown here on the right.

The Stock Market toolbar, which is shown here, offers the following buttons:

- ■ **Ticker**   Click the Folder icon next to the Ticker button if you want to get quotes for the stocks in your online portfolio or clear the contents of the symbol text box.

- ■ **Symbol Text Box**   Enter the stock symbol of a company for which you want a stock quote.

- ■ **Quotes**   Click Quotes to get the last trade amount, change, and volume of the stock in the symbol text box, as shown here:

Symbol	Last Trade	Change	Volume	More Info
PLSIA	11:42AM $1\,^{15}/_{32}$	$-^{1}/_{32}$ -2.08%	95,600	Chart, News, SEC, Msgs Profile, Research, Insider

- ■ **Charts**   Click Charts to see a graphic that presents stock prices in the past, as well as additional details about prices. Pull down the Charts menu and choose an option to track a stock over different time periods.

- ■ **News**   Click News to see recent news stories about a company, or pull down the list to choose a news source.

- ■ **Research**   Click Rsrch to get a research summary for the stock, or pull down the list to select the type of summary you want.

- ■ **Add To**   Click Add To to add a stock to your online portfolio.

- ■ **My Portfolios**   Click My Portfolios to choose which of your online portfolios to display.

- ■ **Markets**   Click the Markets button to go to the main Yahoo! Finance page, or pull down the list to select a specific section of Finance to be displayed.

11

 *You can also get stock information from the News Ticker, which is discussed in Chapter 18. Stock information is also available through Instant Stock Alerts and Instant Messenger, which are covered in Chapter 19. To get stock reports about your pager or personal digital assistant, see Chapter 7.*

Using a Stock Quote Report

From both the Companion and Stock Market toolbar, as well as many other locations including the Yahoo! Finance feature that you will soon learn about, you can get information about a stock or a market index.

Because investor information is available from so many locations, and because the information is essential for investment research, we'll take a detailed look at the information that you can get. For example, entering a stock symbol in the symbol text box and clicking Quotes on the Stock Market toolbar displays stock information such as that shown in Figure 11-2. The report shows the stock symbol, the trade price the last time it was updated (there is a delay of 15 or 20 minutes, depending on the market), the change in amount and percentage, and the volume. An increase change is shown in black; a decrease is shown in red. Below the statistics is a list of recent news stories about the company. Click a headline to read the complete story.

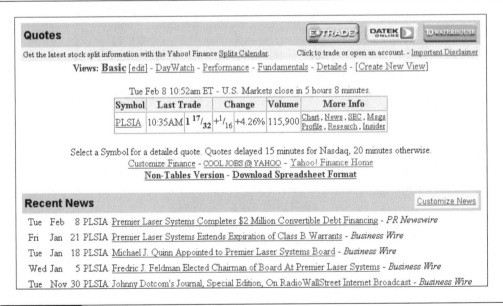

FIGURE 11-2   A stock price quote

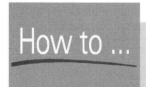

Download Stock Information for Charting

If you want to track or chart stock information in a spreadsheet program such as Microsoft Excel, click Download Spreadsheet Format. A box appears and asks if you want to open or save the file. Choose the Save This File To Disk option and then click OK to open the Save As dialog box. Note the location where the file will be stored and then click Save.

Yahoo! saves the information as a comma-separated values (CSV) file. You can now open the file in Excel or any other spreadsheet program that accepts files in the CSV format.

Viewing Reports in Different Ways

Yahoo! offers five different views of stock reports. Figure 11-3 shows the Basic view. The other views are DayWatch, Performance, Fundamentals, and Detailed.

■ **DayWatch**   Displays the symbol, last trade amount, change, column, average volume, opening price, and the day's range

11

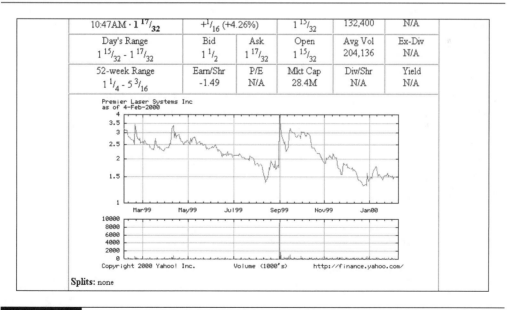

FIGURE 11-3   Detailed stock information and two charts

- **Performance** Displays the symbol, last trade amount, change, volume, shares owned, holdings value, day's value change, price paid, and the holdings gain and percentage

- **Fundamentals** Displays the symbol, name, last trade amount, market capitalization, earning per share ratio, P/E ratio, and the 52-week range

- **Detailed** Presents the most comprehensive data and even includes a chart, as shown here:

PREMIER LASER A (NasdaqNM:PLSIA) - More Info: News, SEC, Msgs, Profile, Research, Insider					
Last Trade	Change		Prev Cls	Volume	Div Date
10:47AM · $1\,^{17}/_{32}$	$+^{1}/_{16}$ (+4.26%)		$1\,^{15}/_{32}$	132,400	N/A
Day's Range	Bid	Ask	Open	Avg Vol	Ex-Div
$1\,^{15}/_{32}$ - $1\,^{17}/_{32}$	$1\,^{1}/_{2}$	$1\,^{17}/_{32}$	$1\,^{15}/_{32}$	204,136	N/A
52-week Range	Earn/Shr	P/E	Mkt Cap	Div/Shr	Yield
$1\,^{1}/_{4}$ - $5\,^{3}/_{16}$	-1.49	N/A	28.4M	N/A	N/A

Each of the views includes links so you can display additional information (shown in Figure 11-4).

Click Chart from any view, for example, to display detailed information about a stock as well as two charts. Below the chart are links that let you specify how you want to display the information. You can choose other charts and get historical quotes by the day, week or month. If appropriate, you can see charts that show how much in dividends was paid. Depending on the range of time you select, you may also be able to chart the stock against the S&P 500 or display a moving average chart.

Note *Later in this chapter, you will learn how to customize the views and create your own view in the section "Customizing Yahoo! Finance."*

Yahoo! Finance

The Yahoo! Finance page is your main portal to investment information. In a way, the Finance page opens an entire world of investment information, with thousands of links to market research; financial news; stock quotes; reference guides; and even taxes, insurance, and loan information.

To get to the main Finance page, which is shown in Figure 11-4, use one of these techniques:

- Click Finance on the Yahoo! Companion

- Click Markets on the Stock Market toolbar

- Click More on the Yahoo! home page and then click Finance & Stock Quotes in the Today's News section

The Yahoo! Finance home page is divided into several sections:

- Market Summary

- Stock Quotes And Symbol Lookup

- Links To Information And Tools

FIGURE 11-4   Yahoo! Finance home page

- Web Sites
- Latest Market News
- World Finance

Many of the sites lead to pages showing details on a particular market index or stock, and from these pages you can get additional details to help in your investment research.

> **Note** *The Java Mrg option in the list under the Welcome banner provide special ways to view your online portfolio.*

Market Summary

The market summary section at the top of the Finance page shows the current status of and links to these market indices:

- Dow
- NYSE Volume
- Nasdaq
- Nasdaq Volume
- S&P 500
- 30-Year Bonds

For example, next to Dow is the current Dow Jones level and the amount and percentage of change. Each index is also a link to more detailed information. Click Dow, for example, to see the page shown in Figure 11-5. It offers views, links to more information, and a small chart.

To customize the information that is displayed in the Market Summary, see "Customizing Yahoo! Finance," later in this chapter.

Below the chart are links to other chart formats. The Small option displays the chart in the same window. The Big option opens another window with a larger chart and links to recent news about the Dow.

Getting Stock Quotes

The Finance window also provides access to stock quotes:

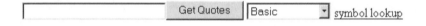

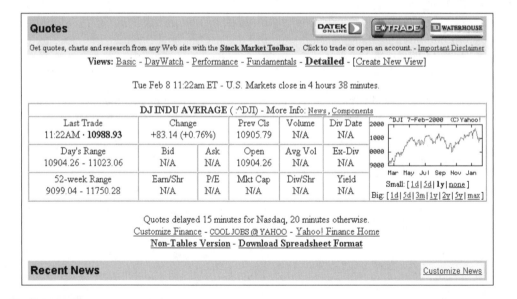

Enter the stock symbol, pull down the list to choose the type of view you want to display, and click Get Quotes to see the stock report.

If you do not know a stock's ticker symbol, click Symbol Lookup to see these options:

```
Enter any part of the company name, mutual fund, market index, or corporate bond:
                                            [ Lookup ]
              Or, try our alphabetical listing.
```

Enter the company's name and click the Lookup button, or click Alphabetical Listing and then choose a company name from the list that appears.

Yahoo! Finance Tools

The most powerful part of Yahoo! Finance are the numerous research tools that are available. They are listed under the Yahoo! Finance heading, as shown in Figure 11-6. Many of these tools are designed for knowledgeable investors who can interpret the information on their own. In this chapter, we'll briefly summarize each option.

Yahoo! Finance

- **U.S. Markets:** Major U.S. Indices, IPOs Most Actives, Mkt Digest, Mutual Funds

- **World Markets:** Major World Indices Currency Exchange Rates
  Canada: Markets, Most Actives, Mkt Digest

- **Research:** By Industry, Historical Quotes Stock Screener, Up/Downgrades, SEC Filings Financials, **Earnings:** Dates, Surprises, Calls

- **Loans:** Loan Center, Mortgage Quotes Credit Reports, Auto Loan Quotes

- **The Investment Challenge:** Enter Standings, Rules, Message Board

- **Reference:** What's New, Glossary Company & Fund Index
  Calendars: Economic, Splits

- **Yahoo! Bill Pay:** Sign-up, Tour

- **Editorial:** The Motley Fool, TheStreet.com Individual Investor, Worldlyinvestor, OLI

- **Financial News:** U.S. Markets, Business By Industry, IPOs, AP, S & P, ON24, Int'l Full Coverage, **Press Releases:** BusinessWire PRNewswire, PrimeZone, CCN

- **Taxes:** Tax Center, Refund Estimator Tips, Forms, Investor's Guide

- **Insurance:** Insurance Center
  Quotes: Auto, Life, Health, Home, Renters

- **Community:** Message Boards Stock Chat, Net Events, Finance Clubs

Related Resources: Instant Stock Alerts, Companion, News Ticker, Real Estate, Small Business

FIGURE 11-6   Resources and tools in the Yahoo! Finance home page

U.S. Markets

These options are for people who trade in United States stocks and mutual funds. The options are as follows:

- **Major U.S. Indices** Accesses the indices described earlier in this chapter in "Yahoo! Companion"—Dow Jones Averages, New York Stock Exchange, Nasdaq, Standard and Poor's, and 14 other indices, as well as United States Treasuries and Commodities.

- **IPOs** Offers timely information about initial public offerings (IPOs), including the latest IPOs, recent filings and withdraws for IPOs, and the latest IPO news. You can also list IPOs by company, industry, and underwriter.

- **Most Actives** Displays information on the Nasdaq, AMEX, and NYSE volume leaders.

- **Market Digest** Displays a summary of the NYSE, AMEX, Nasdaq, and Bulletin Board markets. It includes the number of advancing, declining, and unchanged issues; new highs and lows; and the up, down, and unchanged volume.

- **Mutual Funds** Displays a variety of links and tools for mutual fund investors. The Prospectus Finder, for example, provides access to prospectuses, applications, and other information about hundreds of mutual funds. Mutual Fund Screener lets you select a mutual fund based on criteria that you specify.

World Markets

The World Markets features are designed for traders in Canadian investments and markets in other countries. The features are as follows:

- **Major World Indices** Accesses indices on markets in other countries
- **Currency Exchange Rates** Provides tools for converting currencies and links to currency markets
- **Canadian Markets** Accesses information on major Canadian stock markets
- **Canadian Most Actives** Displays the most active Canadian stocks
- **Canadian Market Digest** Summarizes the status of Canadian markets

Research

The Research options provide links to research and historical information concerning individual stocks and industrial groups. The options are as follows:

- **By Industry** Displays basic information on a group of stocks in an industry of your choice
- **Historical Quotes** Lets you display stock prices—daily, weekly, monthly, or dividends—for a specific starting and ending period
- **Stock Screener** Lets you select stocks based on specific criteria

- **Up/Downgrades**   Lists stocks that have been upgraded (from a sell to buy recommendation, for example), downgraded, or just given recent coverage
- **SEC Filings**   Displays Securities and Exchange Commission (SEC) filing information
- **Financials**   Accesses financial reports on selected companies
- **Dates**   Lists when earnings reports will be issued by selected companies, as well as companies' estimated earnings per share
- **Surprises**   Lists companies whose earnings reports differed from the expected, both upside (higher than expected) and downside (lower than expected)
- **Calls**   Lists the dates of earnings conference calls, and provides access to past calls. Conference calls are live broadcasts in which a company announces it earnings

 While the past performance of a stock is no indication of its future performance, a historical look may show seasonal or cyclical trends in a stock price that can be useful to investors.

The Stock Screener is a useful tool for choosing potential investments. Clicking Stock Screen displays the options shown in Figure 11-7. Use the lists to set the criteria for the company and then click the Find Stocks button. The more criteria you specify, the more specific the search will be.

You could enter criteria, for example, to find a company in the computer hardware industry that has a strong buy recommendation with a maximum price of $50 per share.

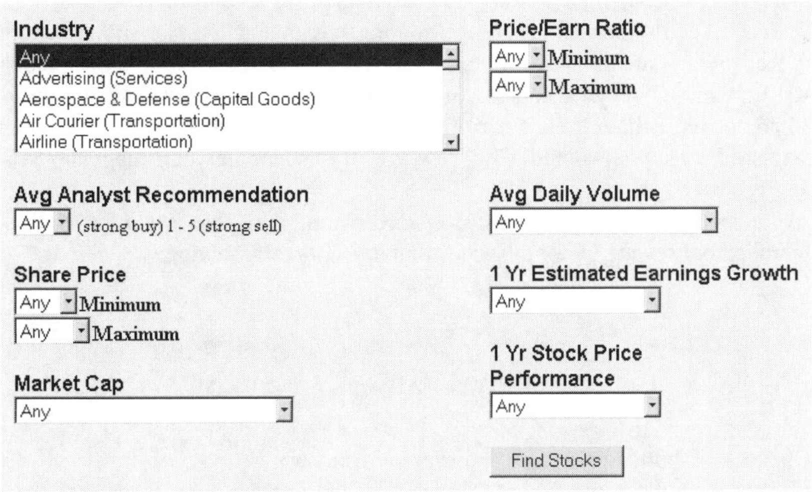

11

Industry

| Any |
| Advertising (Services) |
| Aerospace & Defense (Capital Goods) |
| Air Courier (Transportation) |
| Airline (Transportation) |

Avg Analyst Recommendation

Any (strong buy) 1 - 5 (strong sell)

Share Price

Any Minimum
Any Maximum

Market Cap

Any

Price/Earn Ratio

Any Minimum
Any Maximum

Avg Daily Volume

Any

1 Yr Estimated Earnings Growth

Any

1 Yr Stock Price Performance

Any

Find Stocks

FIGURE 11-7   Stock Screener

In addition to the industry, you can specify a buy-sell recommendation in a range from a strong buy (choosing 1 in the Avg Analyst Recommendation list) to a strong sell (number 5 in the list). You can select a minimum and maximum share price and whether the company is a large cap (over $1 billion), mid cap (between $500 million and $1 billion), or a small cap (under $500 million).

You can also select a minimum and maximum price to earnings (P/E) ratio. The P/E ratio is the ratio of the current share price by the company's earnings. A high ratio means that investors have faith that a company's future growth warrants higher stock prices.

The Average Daily Volume refers to the number of shares that sell per day. An active stock with a high volume is often considered a more desirable stock because investors feel it is worth trading.

The 1 Year Estimated Earnings Growth is a prediction by market analysts of the growth potential—or loss potential—of the corporate earnings over the next year. The options are shown at right.

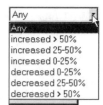

The 1 Year Stock Price Performance is a prediction of the change in value of the stock.

Loans

The tools in the Loans area help you make borrowing decisions. (For more information about these tools, check out the Web site auxiliary to this book.)

The Investment Challenge

Here is an opportunity to make money without any risk. The Investment Challenge is an online game in which you start with $100,000 fantasy dollars that you can invest as you please. You can make as many fantasy stock trades as you want. At the end of each month, the players' portfolios are compared, and cash prices up to $5,000 are awarded to the first, second, and third place finishers.

Click Enter in The Investment Challenge options to complete a registration form for entering the contest. Registering and playing is free. In the page that appears, complete the registration form by entering your name, your address, and a few general descriptions about your investment activity. When you have filled in the form, click Enter Investment Challenge. A screen reports that you have successfully registered. Click Trade to start spending your imaginary $100,000, as shown in Figure 11-8.

Choose whether you want to buy or sell, enter the number of shares and the symbol for the stock, and then click Preview Order to see a summary of the transaction:

Order to BUY

Shrs	Symbol	Name	Last Trade	Amount	Comm	Total
1000	KIDE	4 KIDS ENTRTN	9:34AM 29 $3/4$	$29750.00	$10.00	$29760.00

Click the Place Order button to receive an order confirmation.

You use the links on the Investment Challenge page to access other features of the game. Click Standings, for instance, to see the names of the 20 highest and lowest performers. The report shows players' names, holding amounts, and percentage returns, as well as links to players' holdings and a record of orders. At one point in time, the top-ranking player had a return of over 560 percent, having parlayed his $100,000 into $660,000.

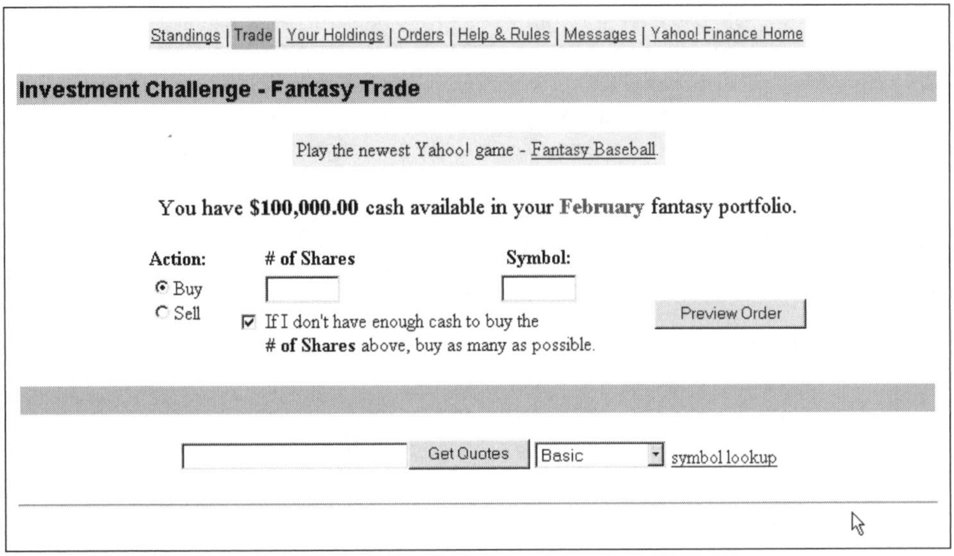

Standings | Trade | Your Holdings | Orders | Help & Rules | Messages | Yahoo! Finance Home

Investment Challenge - Fantasy Trade

Play the newest Yahoo! game - Fantasy Baseball.

You have **$100,000.00** cash available in your **February** fantasy portfolio.

Action:	# of Shares	Symbol:	
● Buy	[ ]	[ ]	
○ Sell	☑ If I don't have enough cash to buy the # of Shares above, buy as many as possible.		Preview Order

[   ] Get Quotes | Basic ▼ symbol lookup

FIGURE 11-8   Buying shares in The Investment Challenge

11

Reference

Use the Reference options on the Yahoo! Finance home page to learn more about investing and companies. The What's New option displays new Yahoo! Finance features with links to help information. The Glossary is a comprehensive dictionary of financial terms.

The Company & Fund option accesses information about over 9,000 public companies. Economic displays the dates when key economic and financial information will be released. Splits lists when stock splits will take effect.

Yahoo! Bill Pay

Yahoo! Bill Pay is a fee-based service from Yahoo! in which you can pay your bills online. When you sign up, you get three months of the service for free (as long as you make no more than 25 payments per month). After the free trial, you can choose between two payment options:

- ■ $2 per month plus $0.40 per payment
- ■ $7 per month for up to 25 payments, then $0.40 for each additional payment

You enter the names and addresses of the companies you want to pay, as well as the account number of the banking account from which you want to deduct the money. You can then go online to send a payment or schedule regular repeating payments.

To start using Bill Pay, click Sign-Up in the Yahoo! Bill Pay section, and then click Enroll Here!.

In addition to your Yahoo! ID and password, you'll get a security key. The key is an access number similar to the PIN you have for your bankcard. You need the key to access the protected area of the Bill Pay feature.

Click Sign Me Up!, and then enter your Yahoo! password and click Submit. In the screen that appears, enter and reenter to confirm a security key of at least six characters, and then complete the form shown here (the information will be used if you forget your key and need to retrieve it from Yahoo!). When you have finished, click Submit This Form.

Forgotten Key Question: [– select a question – ▼]

(note: we will ask you this question if you forget your Security Key)

Answer to Question: [ ]

Current Email Address: [alan@neibauer.net]

your Birthdate [December ▼] [1], [1960] (Month/Day/Year)

your Zip (or Postal) Code: [19111]

Country: [United States of America ▼]

You now select a payment plan, enter personal information, and designate the checking account from which money will be deducted to pay bills and your Bill Pay charges. Click Submit This Form when you have finished supplying the information.

It takes Yahoo! about a week to verify the registration information. While you are waiting, however, you can use the Bill Pay feature to specify who you intend to pay. When the verification is complete, Yahoo! sends you a Payment Activation Code that you use online to access the service, and you can start paying bills, as in the following illustration.

Schedule a payment or make multiple payments

Choose Payee: [Jane Doe ▼] Add New Payee

Amount: $[100.00]

Pay Date:
m/d/yy [4/1/00]
* Note: The earliest date a payment can be scheduled is 4 business days from today.

Payment Schedule: Make Payment [once ▼]
□ and remind me [monthly ▼]

[Make This Payment]

Editorial

The options in the Editorial section access the individual investment opinions of these services:

- The Motley Fool
- TheStreet.com
- Individual Investor
- WorldlyInvestor
- The Online Investor (OLI)

Each company offers its own brand of advice concerning individual investments and investing in general. The content on each site varies and represents the opinions of the company that provides the service.

Financial News

The Financial News options offer the latest financial news from a variety of sources. News stories are indexed by company name and stock symbol. The options in this section are as follows:

- **U.S. Markets**   Provides top financial news stories of the day.
- **Business**   Offers business headlines from a variety of sources, such as Reuters and AP.
- **By Industry**   Accesses news articles categorized by industry.
- **IPOs**   Offers a list of IPO filings and news.
- **AP**   Displays stories from the AP Financial news service.
- **S&P**   Displays stores from the Standard and Poor news service.
- **ON24**   Accesses multimedia audio and video clips, as shown in Figure 11-9. Click a headline preceded by [audio] to hear the clip; click a heading preceded by [video] to see a video clip.
- **Int'l**   Displays news from international markets.
- **Full Coverage**   Offers comprehensive coverage of investment and business news on all areas.
- **Press Releases**   Provides links to the full text of press releases on business news from Business Wire, PR Newswire, PrimeZone Media Network, and Canadian Corporate News (CCN).

Taxes

The Taxes options cover a range of tax tools. You can estimate your tax refund, get a checklist for tax preparation, get tax guides and calculators, and even file your taxes online through H&R Block.

11

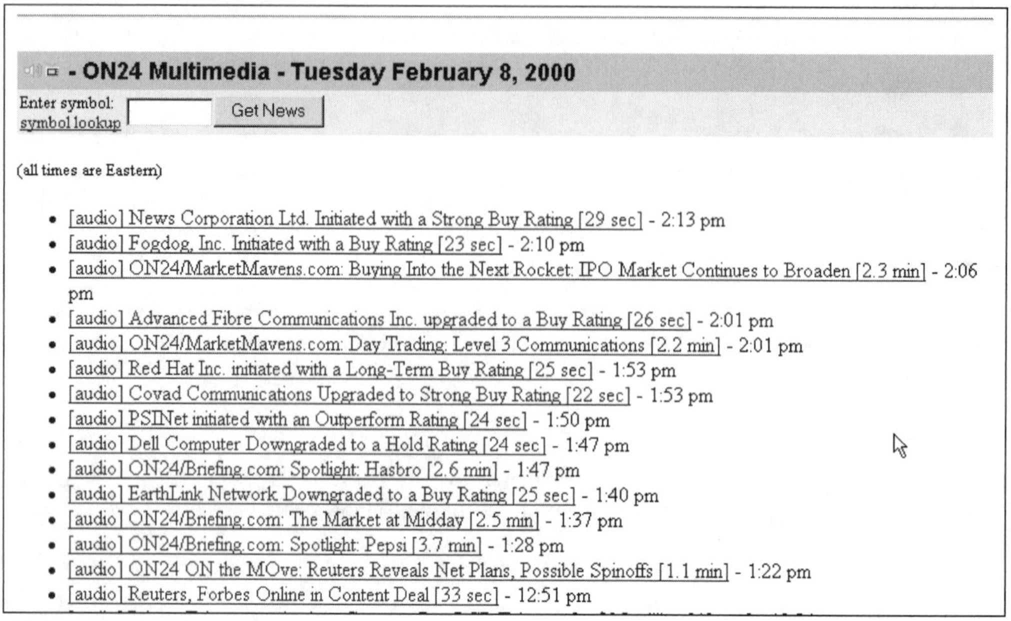

◄)) □ - ON24 Multimedia - Tuesday February 8, 2000

Enter symbol: [   ] [Get News]
symbol lookup

(all times are Eastern)

- [audio] News Corporation Ltd. Initiated with a Strong Buy Rating [29 sec] - 2:13 pm
- [audio] Fogdog, Inc. Initiated with a Buy Rating [23 sec] - 2:10 pm
- [audio] ON24/MarketMavens.com: Buying Into the Next Rocket: IPO Market Continues to Broaden [2.3 min] - 2:06 pm
- [audio] Advanced Fibre Communications Inc. upgraded to a Buy Rating [26 sec] - 2:01 pm
- [audio] ON24/MarketMavens.com: Day Trading: Level 3 Communications [2.2 min] - 2:01 pm
- [audio] Red Hat Inc. initiated with a Long-Term Buy Rating [25 sec] - 1:53 pm
- [audio] Covad Communications Upgraded to Strong Buy Rating [22 sec] - 1:53 pm
- [audio] PSINet initiated with an Outperform Rating [24 sec] - 1:50 pm
- [audio] Dell Computer Downgraded to a Hold Rating [24 sec] - 1:47 pm
- [audio] ON24/Briefing.com: Spotlight: Hasbro [2.6 min] - 1:47 pm
- [audio] EarthLink Network Downgraded to a Buy Rating [25 sec] - 1:40 pm
- [audio] ON24/Briefing.com: The Market at Midday [2.5 min] - 1:37 pm
- [audio] ON24/Briefing.com: Spotlight: Pepsi [3.7 min] - 1:28 pm
- [audio] ON24 ON the MOve: Reuters Reveals Net Plans, Possible Spinoffs [1.1 min] - 1:22 pm
- [audio] Reuters, Forbes Online in Content Deal [33 sec] - 12:51 pm

FIGURE 11-9 Multimedia financial news

Insurance

Use the Insurance options to learn about insurance, read insurance news, and get actual quotes from a variety of companies.

Community

The Community options put you in touch with other Yahoo! members who are interested in business and investment. The options are as follows:

- Messages Boards
- Stock Chat
- Net Events
- Finance Clubs

You'll find complete coverage of message boards, chats, and clubs in Chapters 20 and 21.

Web Sites and Categories

Even though the Yahoo! financial tools are comprehensive, you can get more investment information and guidance from other places on the Internet as well. The Web Sites section of the Yahoo! Finance page, which is shown here, provides links to thousands of other resources:

Clicking Finance and Investment, for example, displays over 40 subcategories from Banking to Youth Resources where you can get financial information. Use the links under Finance and Investment in the Web Sites list to go directly to a subcategory.

Web Sites

Finance and
Investment
· Quotes
· Financial News
· Internet Trading
· Mutual Funds
· Bonds
· Futures and Options
· Banking
· Insurance
· Loans and
Financing
· Taxes

World Finance

The links in the World Finance section of the Yahoo! Finance page access current market information from a variety of countries. The information is displayed in the country's language, so you'll need to know the language to take advantage of the site.

Getting Your Chance at IPOs

A growing number of new millionaires are making their mark by investing in Initial Public Offerings (IPOs), the first offering of stock in a private company. New, small companies that seek equity capital to expand usually offer IPOs. While IPOs present a degree of risk, some IPOs—especially IPOs from Internet and technology companies—have resulted in tremendous gains for investors as the stock price has risen sharply when it is traded on the market.

Unfortunately, company insiders and special customers of the stock's underwriter purchase most IPO stock before it becomes available to the public. Getting access to IPOs has become a major pastime of many investors as they try to take advantage of the possible high gains.

The Yahoo! IPO area offers a wide range of information about recent and new IPOs, as shown in Figure 11-10. To get there, either go to http://biz.yahoo.com/ipo/ or click IPOs in the Yahoo! Finance page.

The Filings section shows companies that have filed for permission to issue an IPO with the Securities and Exchange Commission (SEC). Click Profile under More Info to see details of an upcoming IPO. Armed with this information, you may be able to take part in the IPO through your broker or through the lead underwriter whose name is shown on the form.

You can get additional information about IPOs from the Business And Economy > Finance And Investment > Initial Public Offerings subcategory. One of the links in the subcategory provides access to companies that offer IPOs online, including IPO.com.

11

Initial Public Offerings

Features	Latest IPO Events					
Post-IPO Performance:	**Pricings**					More: Pricings
· 3 - mo: Best | Worst	Date	Symbol	Company	Price	Action	More Info
· 6 - mo: Best | Worst	Feb 9	DTEC	Delano Technology	$18.00	Priced	Profile, Chart, News, SEC
· 1 - yr: Best | Worst	Feb 9	VCNT	Vicinity Corp	$17.00	Priced	Profile, News, SEC
IPO Lists:	Feb 8	LCOR	Landacorp	$10.00	Priced	Profile, News, SEC
· By Company	Feb 8		Fastnet Corp	$12.00	Priced	
· By Industry	Feb 7	BUYC	Buy.com	$13.00	Priced	Profile, News, SEC
· By Underwriter						
In-Depth Profiles:	**Filings**					More: Filings
· World Wrestling ...	Date	Symbol	Company	Price	Action	More Info
· Webvan Group, Inc.	Feb 8	BDVU	Broadview Networks		Filed	Profile
· GDEN	Feb 8	RLMD	Real Media		Filed	Profile
	Feb 8	PRCS	Praecis Pharmaceutic		Filed	Profile
	Feb 8	ADOR	Adolor Corp	$12.00 - $14.00	Filed	Profile
Visit the IPO Center	Feb 7	ISKY	Isky		Filed	Profile
· Current Offerings	**Withdrawals**					More: Withdrawals
· Completed Offerings	Date	Symbol	Company	Price	Action	More Info
· Open an Account						

FIGURE 11-10   Yahoo! IPO information

Customizing Yahoo! Finance

Yahoo! offers a variety of means for personalizing the way financial information is displayed. You can customize the overall Yahoo! Finance page, as well as modify and create views of stocks and market indices.

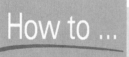

Trade Online

You cannot actually buy and sell stocks from within Yahoo!, but you can access online brokers. An *online broker* is a stockbroker that accepts buy and sell orders over the Internet. Online brokers can exercise the orders immediately.

There are hundreds of online brokers. Their fees and services vary widely. Most online brokers offer reduced commissions, sometimes as low as $4.95 per trade. Some brokers offer a certain number of free trades when you register for the first time. You have to register with the broker, and, unless you already have an account, you have to deposit an initial balance to cover your first trades.

Personalizing the Yahoo! Finance Page

To personalize the Yahoo! Finance page, click Customize on the page.

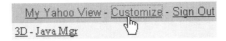

In addition to editing your general Yahoo! account information, you can choose sources for the news headlines, the number of headlines from each source that are displayed, and the time period in which news stories are gathered.

Use the Market Summary option to determine what market indices or individual stocks are shown in the market summary at the top of the Yahoo! Finance page. You can also choose to show the market summary on all quotes pages as well. You can specify up to six items to track on the summary in any combination of markets and stocks. If you are watching a particular stock, for example, replace one of the default markets with the stock's symbol so you can access a quote whenever you display the Yahoo! Finance page.

The Quote Display option lets you choose how quotes appear in your portfolio. The Charts option sets the default size and time period of charts.

Customizing Views

While the five view options for stock and market information are the most typical used by investors, you can edit each of the views and create your own new ones.

To edit a default view, follow these steps:

1. Display a quote page for a stock or market index.

2. Click the view that you want to change.

3. Click [edit] after the view's name (as shown in the illustration on the right) to display options for changing the view, as in Figure 11-11. Click the Delete This View button to remove the view from your Yahoo! Finance page.

Views: Basic [edit]

4. Choose whether you want this view to appear in the pull-down list of views from the Quotes menu.

5. Select up to 16 fields to display in the view. All of the possible fields are listed on the right. For each of the numbered items, pull down the list and choose the field to display.

6. Click Accept Changes.

11

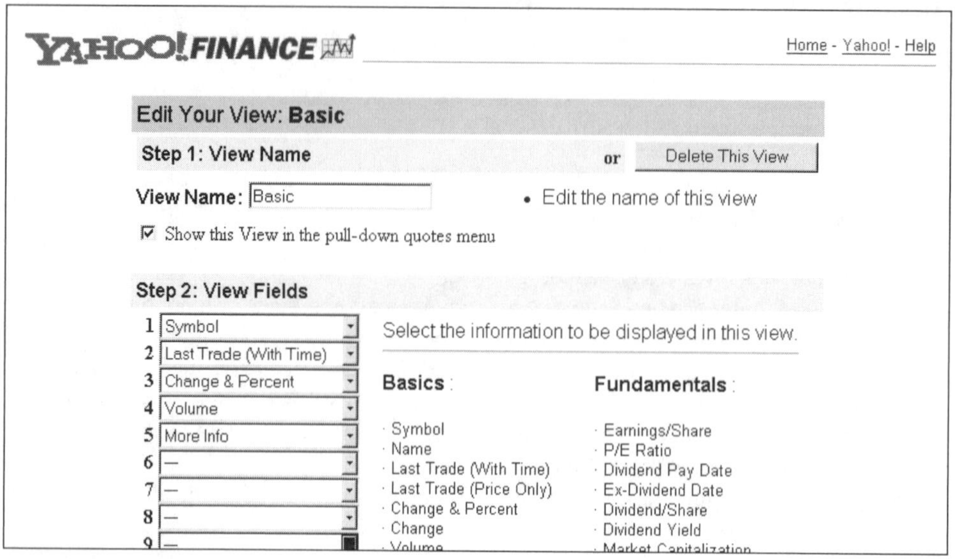

FIGURE 11-11   Editing a Yahoo! finance view

Creating a Portfolio

A *portfolio* is a record of your investments, as well as potential investments whose performance you want to track. It is easy to create a portfolio, but be prepared to provide Yahoo! with the proper information. Before you begin, make sure you know the ticker symbol of each stock you own, the number of shares you own, and the price you paid for the shares. You can add other data to a portfolio if you want, including the date you purchased securities and the commissions you paid. You can supply information about a security to Yahoo! at any time, but entering the information from the get-go saves time and provides information that Yahoo! can use to calculate gains and losses in your portfolio.

The options for working with portfolios are found under the Welcome banner of the Yahoo! Finance page, as shown here:

To create a portfolio, follow these steps:

1. Click Create to open the Edit Your Portfolio page.

2. Enter a descriptive name that will identify the portfolio.

3. Choose the portfolio currency.

4. Enter ticker symbols for the stocks that you want to track. As shown here, separate each symbol by a comma and a blank space:

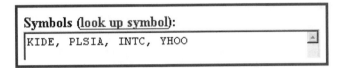

Symbols (look up symbol):

KIDE, PLSIA, INTC, YHOO

You can enter the same symbol more than once to track separate purchases of the same stock. If you want to keep track of cash accounts, such as money markets, enter a name for the account preceded by two dollar signs, like so: **$$cash**. If you are not sure what a stock's ticker symbol is, click Look Up Symbol. In the page that appears, type the name of a company and then click Lookup. You can also click a letter of the alphabet and search for symbols in the alphabetical list of company names.

5. Below the Ticker Symbols box is a list of several United States and International market indices, including the Dow Jones Industrials, the NYSE Composite, and the French CAC-40. Notice the check boxes next to each index name. Click a check box to add an index to your portfolio. You can also click More U.S. Indices or More International Indices to see additional indices, and then enter their symbols directly in the Ticker Symbols box.

> **Tip** *Index symbols start with a caret (^), as in ^DJI (Dow Jones) and ^IXIC (NASDAQ Composite).*

11

6. Scroll the page to see additional options, as shown in Figure 11-12.

7. Select the check box if you want the stocks to be listed in alphabetical order or in the order that you entered them.

8. Select the check box if you do not want the total value of your portfolio to appear on your My Yahoo! page. You may not want the total value to appear if you access Yahoo! where others can view your screen.

9. Select the check box if you want the portfolio to appear in a small font.

10. Choose the default view: Basic, DayWatch, Performance, Fundamentals, or Detailed.

11. In the series of check boxes that appears next, enable the check box next to each piece of information that you would like to enter in your portfolio. For example, if you choose Upper Limit, Lower Limit, or both, special icons appear next to the name of stocks in your portfolio to show when the share prices reach a limit that you specify. If you enter a purchase price, Yahoo! can calculate a stock's gain or loss.

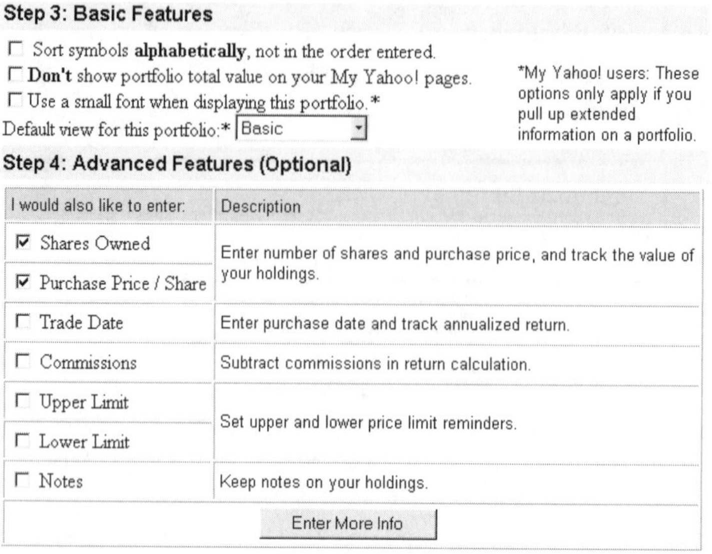

Step 3: Basic Features

☐ Sort symbols **alphabetically**, not in the order entered.
☐ **Don't** show portfolio total value on your My Yahoo! pages.
☐ Use a small font when displaying this portfolio.*
Default view for this portfolio:* | Basic ▾ |

*My Yahoo! users: These options only apply if you pull up extended information on a portfolio.

Step 4: Advanced Features (Optional)

I would also like to enter:	Description
☑ Shares Owned	Enter number of shares and purchase price, and track the value of your holdings.
☑ Purchase Price / Share	
☐ Trade Date	Enter purchase date and track annualized return.
☐ Commissions	Subtract commissions in return calculation.
☐ Upper Limit	Set upper and lower price limit reminders.
☐ Lower Limit	
☐ Notes	Keep notes on your holdings.
	Enter More Info

FIGURE 11-12   Additional portfolio options

12. Click Enter More Info. A page appears in which you enter the information that you specified, as shown here:

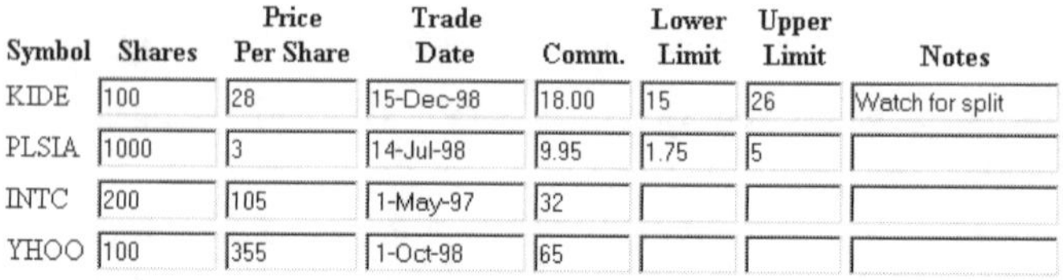

Symbol	Shares	Price Per Share	Trade Date	Comm.	Lower Limit	Upper Limit	Notes
KIDE	100	28	15-Dec-98	18.00	15	26	Watch for split
PLSIA	1000	3	14-Jul-98	9.95	1.75	5	
INTC	200	105	1-May-97	32			
YHOO	100	355	1-Oct-98	65			

Tip   *If you do not want to enter all the information at this time but would rather wait until later, click the Finished button.*

13. Enter the information. Depending on the items you added to your portfolio in step 11, you can enter this information:

   ■ The number of shares you own. Enter a negative number if you are in short position for a stock. For cash items, enter dollar amounts or the original purchase price.

   ■ The price you paid for the shares if you want Yahoo! to calculate your gain or loss.

   ■ The date you purchased the stock in either the M/D/YY or D-Mon-YY format.

- The commission you paid to purchase the stock.
- The high and low prices to which you want to be alerted.
- Any notes regarding the issue.

14. Click the Finished button. Your portfolio appears and looks something like the portfolio in Figure 11-13.

By clicking a stock's ticker symbol, you can open a page with detailed information about a stock. Click a link in the More Info column to get other information about a stock. When a stock reaches its lower limit, a small down-pointing character appears, as shown on the right. An up-pointing character tells you when a stock has reached its upper limit.

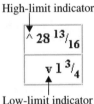

High-limit indicator

Low-limit indicator

You can click Download Spreadsheet Format to download stock information in spreadsheet format and thereby examine it in Microsoft Excel or another spreadsheet program. Click Non-Tables Version to see the listing in this format:

```
Symbol    Last Trade          Change           Volume    More Info
KIDE      11:56AM      29 1/8      +1/8    +0.43%     172,100   Chart, News, SEC, Msgs, Profile, Insider
PLSIA     11:33AM       1 5/8      -3/16   -10.34%     96,700   Chart, News, SEC, Msgs, Profile, Research, Ins
INTC      11:59AM   106 15/16     +2 5/16   +2.21%  10,723,700  Chart, News, SEC, Msgs, Profile, Research, Ins
YHOO      11:59AM     358 1/2      -3 13/16  -1.05%   2,228,500  Chart, News, SEC, Msgs, Profile, Research, Ins
```

11

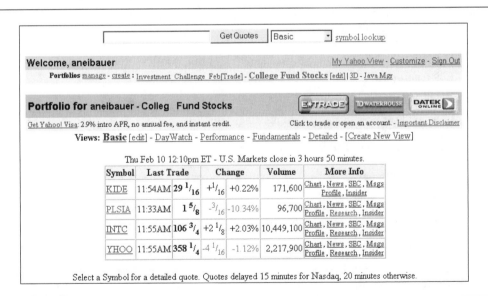

FIGURE 11-13   A Yahoo! portfolio

 *After you have viewed a non-tables version of your portfolio, click Tables Version to return to the original display.*

Below the stock information are headlines that you can click to get news stories about the stocks in the portfolio. Be sure to check the news periodically to see if buying more stock or selling the stock you own is necessary.

As with stock quote pages, you can display a portfolio in several different views. In Performance view, for example, you see the total value of your portfolio. If you entered the purchase price of the stock, you see how much your portfolio has gained or lost.

In the Yahoo! Finance home page, your portfolio is listed under the Welcome banner along with your Investment Challenge portfolio, if you have one.

Welcome, aneibauer   My Yahoo View - Customize - Sign Out

Portfolios manage - create : Investment_Challenge_Feb[Trade] - College Fund Stocks | 3D - Java Mgr

---

Click the portfolio to display the status of your stocks.

You can create more than one portfolio to better organize your holdings. To do so, create the second portfolio the same way you created the first one.

Managing Portfolios

When you want to make changes to a portfolio, click Manage in the line under the Yahoo! Finance Welcome banner. A list of your portfolios appears, as shown in Figure 11-14. From this page, you can perform these functions:

- Create a new portfolio
- Edit a portfolio
- Delete a portfolio
- Change the order in which portfolios are listed

To create a new portfolio from this page, follow these steps:

1. Select the currency from the Add New Portfolio pull-down list.
2. Click Create a New Portfolio.
3. Enter a portfolio name and complete the portfolio as you did previously.
4. Click Finish.

Shortcut *You can also create a new portfolio by clicking Create under the welcome banner in the Yahoo! Finance home page.*

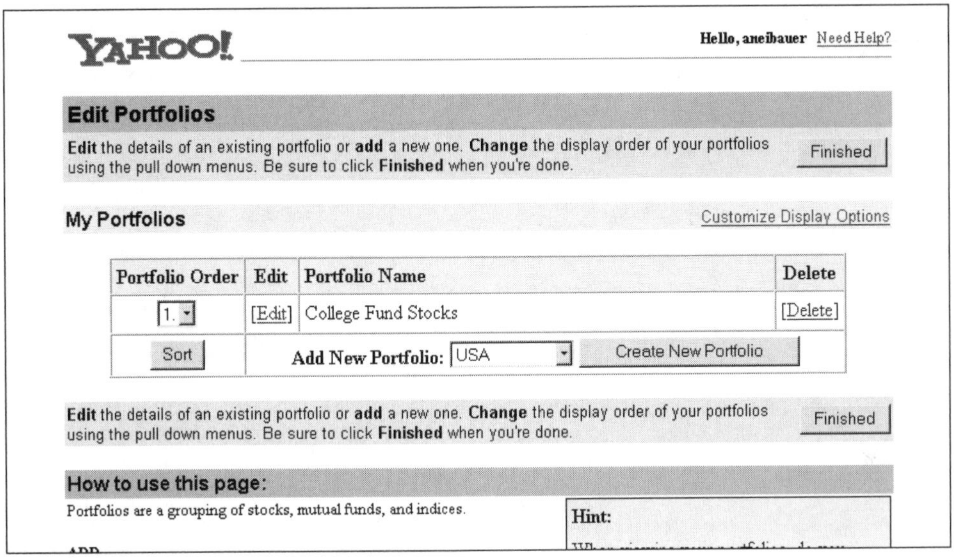

FIGURE 11-14   Managing Yahoo! portfolios

11

To delete a portfolio, click the Delete link on the right side of the portfolio's name.

To add stocks, delete stocks, or change the information you entered about a stock, click Edit in the column next to a portfolio's name. You can also click Edit following its name under the Welcome banner in the Yahoo! Finance home page or click Edit when the portfolio is being displayed. Doing so opens the Edit Your Portfolio page, as shown in Figure 11-15.

Delete a stock from the portfolio by deleting its symbol in the Ticker Symbols box. Just click in the box and then press the DELETE or BACKSPACE key as you would to delete a word in a word-processed document.

Add a stock to a portfolio by typing its ticker symbol in the box, separated from the others with a space. Click Enter More Info to add or edit the information about a stock. For example, you could change or edit the number of shares you purchased, the price, the purchase date, the upper and lower price limit, or whatever you entered in the Notes column.

Click Finished when you have finished to return to the portfolio.

Your Portfolios in My Yahoo!

Your portfolios can also appear on your My Yahoo! page (along with your Investment Challenge portfolio if you have one) as shown at right:

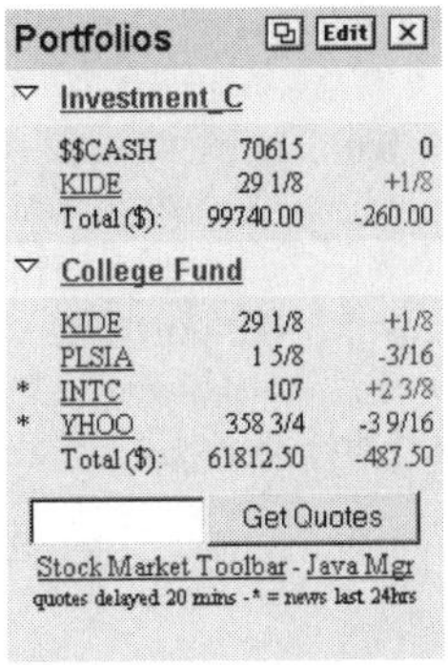

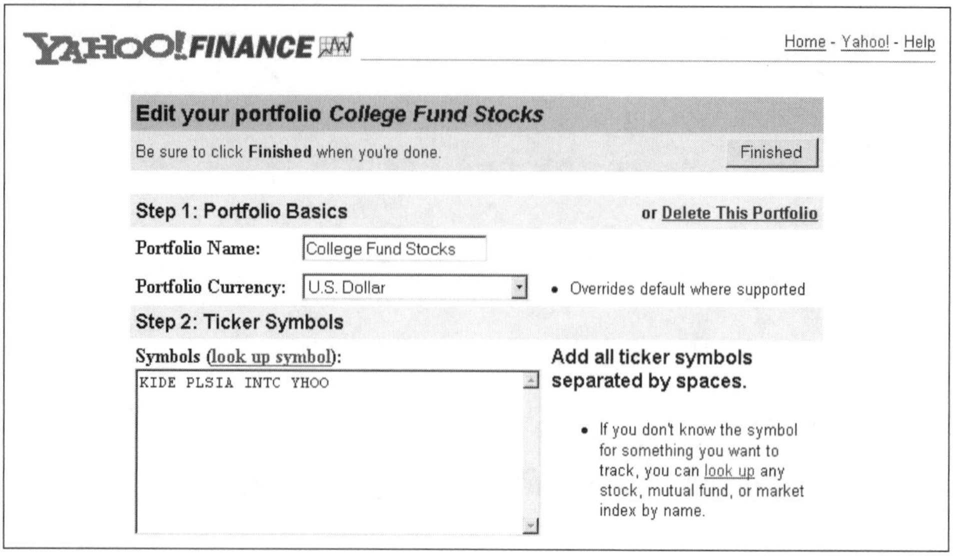

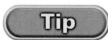

YAHOO! FINANCE
Home - Yahoo! - Help
Edit your portfolio College Fund Stocks
Be sure to click Finished when you're done.
Finished
Step 1: Portfolio Basics
or Delete This Portfolio
Portfolio Name:
College Fund Stocks
Portfolio Currency:
U.S. Dollar
• Overrides default where supported
Step 2: Ticker Symbols
Symbols (look up symbol):
KIDE PLSIA INTC YHOO
Add all ticker symbols separated by spaces.
• If you don't know the symbol for something you want to track, you can look up any stock, mutual fund, or market index by name.

FIGURE 11-15 Editing a portfolio

Tip *If your portfolios do not appear on the My Yahoo! page, click Content next to the Personalize icon, check the Stock Portfolios check box in the My Yahoo! Essentials section of the window that appears, and then click Finished.*

A down-pointing arrow next to a portfolio name indicates that the portfolio is expanded—that the items in the portfolio are displayed. A right-pointing arrow indicates that the portfolio is collapsed—that the items in the portfolio are not displayed. Click the arrow to collapse or expand a portfolio.

You can click a portfolio name to open it or click a stock name to view its quotes page.

Remove the portfolios from your My Yahoo! page by clicking the X icon, or click Edit to edit your portfolios.

To keep an eye on your portfolio as you surf the Web, click the Detach icon.

To display your portfolio appears in a separate window.

Close the window when you no longer want to see it onscreen.

You can navigate the Web and quickly redisplay the portfolio window at any time by clicking its icon in the Windows taskbar as shown at right.

My Yahoo! for aneibauer - Microsoft Internet Explorer

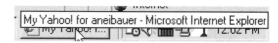

Customizing the Portfolio Display

You can adjust some of the ways that values appear in your portfolio by clicking Customize Display Options in the Edit Portfolios window. In the page that appears, choose from these options:

- Display Fractional Values As lets you display decimal amounts as fractions or decimals:
- Color to Indicate Price Change lets you display price increases in green and price decreases in black.
- Display Tripped Limits As lets you change the way that low and high limits are displayed.

Another way to customize portfolios is to change the order in which they are listed. To do so, you use the list in the Portfolio Order column:

Pull down the list in the Portfolio Order column next to each portfolio, and choose where in the list you want the portfolio to appear. After you assign a position to each portfolio, click the Sort button.

11

Portfolios and the Companion Toolbar

You can quickly access and manage your portfolios by using Yahoo! Companion.

When the main Companion toolbar is displayed, click the Finance button and make a choice to create, edit, or open portfolios, as well as display the portfolio calendar:

With the Stock Market toolbar, open the My Portfolios list to choose from the same options:

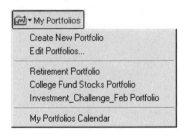

If you are viewing a stock's quote page, you can click the Add To button on the Stock Market toolbar to insert the stock into a specific portfolio or create a new portfolio with the stock inserted:

The Portfolio Calendar

A number of different events can be associated with a public company. For example, a company might announce its earnings on a certain day. Sometimes companies announce a stock split or an online broadcast of a financial report. Investors need to be aware of these dates so they can remain informed about the performance of a company and its stock.

In the Portfolio Calendar, Yahoo! automatically tracks events that are associated with your investments. To display the calendar, which is shown in Figure 11-16, take either of these steps:

- Pull down the Finance list in the Companion toolbar and choose My Portfolios Calendar.
- Click My Portfolios in the Stock Market toolbar and choose My Portfolios Calendar.

Each event in the calendar is also a link. Click the link to open the quotes page for the stock. To change the month that is displayed on the calendar, click the arrows next to the month:

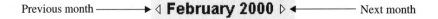

Previous month ——————▶ ◁ **February 2000** ▷ ◀———————— Next month

Using the Java Portfolio Manager (JPM)

The Yahoo! Finance and Edit Portfolio pages work well enough for managing your portfolios, but sometimes they can be unwieldy. For example, you cannot view the status of a portfolio and edit its information at the same time. You have to use a separate Yahoo! page for each function.

◁ **February 2000** ▷

My Portfolios Calendar -- Earnings Announcements, Stock Splits, Dividends, Conference Calls, etc...

Sun	Mon	Tue	Wed	Thu	Fri	Sat
30	31	1	2	3	4	5
				CL - Earnings		
6	7	8	9	10	11	12
13	14	15	16	17	18	19
	YHOO - Split					
20	21	22	23	24	25	26

FIGURE 11-16   Portfolio Calendar

To make working with portfolios easier, you can download and use the Java Portfolio Manager (JPM). Much like using a spreadsheet program such as Microsoft Excel, JPM provides an interactive view of your portfolio.

In Java Portfolio Manager, you can view the status of stocks and change the information about a stock at the same time. You can also sort stocks to change the order in which they are listed.

Here's how to start the Java Portfolio Manager:

1. Click Java Mgr, shown at right, under the Welcome banner.   Java Mgr

2. In the screen that appears, click Start The Java Portfolio Manager.

3. Click Start JPM. The Java Portfolio Manager appears, as shown in Figure 11-17.

Use the pull-down lists at the top of the window to select the portfolio you want to see and to view the portfolio in different ways. Click the Update button to get the most recent price information. Choose Restart on the File menu to reload and restart the Java application if your portfolio does not appear to be working correctly.

As with other portfolio displays, click a stock name to see its detailed quotes page, or click the letters in the More Info column for these features:

N   News

C   Charts

S   Securities and Exchange Commission Filings

P   Profile

R   Research

M   Yahoo! Message Boards

I   Insider Trades

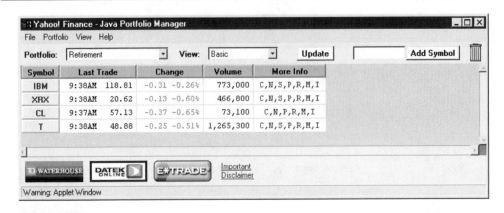

FIGURE 11-17   Java Portfolio Manager

Use the View menu to create, delete, or rename views. You can also select Fit Window To Portfolio in the View menu to adjust the size of the Java Portfolio Manager for the current view.

Sorting Stock Information

Stocks in the Java Portfolio Manager appear either in alphabetical order or in the order in which you entered them, depending on which options you selected when you created your portfolio. However, you can change the order of stocks in the table to make your portfolio easier to read and understand.

For example, if you're interested in seeing which stocks have gained the most in value, you can sort them in descending order in the Change column. Or, if you are considering selling unprofitable securities, you can sort stocks in the Change column in descending order to place the least profitable stocks at the top of the table.

To sort the table, click the column heading you want to sort by. Click once to sort the column in descending order or twice to sort in ascending order. You can sort the rows using any column.

Moving Rows and Columns

You can also change the order of rows and columns by dragging them with the mouse. To move a row to another position, for example, follow these steps:

1. Click and hold down the mouse on the stock symbol at the start of the row.

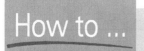 **Add and Remove Stocks**

- To add a stock to your portfolio, enter the symbol in the Add Symbol box and then press ENTER or click the Add Symbol button. The stock appears in a new row at the bottom of the table.

- To delete a stock from your portfolio, drag its stock symbol to the trash icon in the upper-right corner of the Java Portfolio Manager window. If you delete a security by mistake, you'll need to enter it again.

2. Drag the mouse to its new location. As you drag, the insertion point appears as a four-directional arrow.

3. Position the pointer in between the two rows where you want the stock to appear. To move the row to the top of the chart, point between the first row and the row labeled "Symbol."

4. Release the mouse.

Use similar techniques to drag a column to a new location.

Adding Columns

Adding a column of information to the Java Portfolio Manager is easy. Follow these steps to do so:

1. Select Edit Columns from the View menu. You see a window with the names of columns you can insert.

2. Select the check boxes of the columns you want to add. A column is added immediately to the start of the table when you select a check box.

3. Deselect the check boxes of the columns you want to remove. The column is immediately deleted.

4. Click the Done button.

You can now drag the columns into any position.

 *From the Edit Portfolio Columns box, you can drag the blue box containing a field name to the location in the table where you want to insert it.*

11

Saving Portfolios

You do not have to take any special action to save your portfolios from within the Java Portfolio Manager. When you select a new portfolio, change the view, or edit the Java Portfolio Manager, Yahoo! saves the information automatically.

If you changed the order of the stocks, however, choose the Save With Stock Order command on the File menu.

Use the Save command from the File menu to save your portfolio at any time.

Changing User Information

Columns that contain information you entered, such as the number of shares and the purchase price, are displayed in yellow. You can change the information in these columns directly in Java Portfolio Manager. To do so, click in a yellow cell, add or edit the information there, and press ENTER or click in another cell. Data in the columns that are not yellow is obtained by Yahoo! and cannot be changed manually.

Use the Portfolio menu of the Java Portfolio Manager to create a new portfolio, delete a portfolio, or rename a portfolio.

For example, Performance view includes two yellow columns, Shares (Shrs) and Paid, as shown in Figure 11-18. You can change the information in these columns, and Yahoo! will automatically adjust the other data as appropriate when you press ENTER. Changing the number of shares, for example, affects the figures in the Value, Value Change, and Gain columns all across the row, and the totals are changed as well.

Changing the amount paid will affect the information in the Gain column.

The Totals row, by the way, reflects the portfolio's total value and overall change and gain.

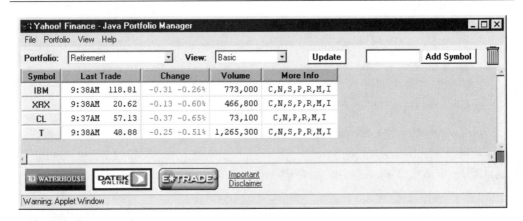

FIGURE 11-18   Performance view contains editable columns.

Chapter 12

Buying and Selling Real Estate

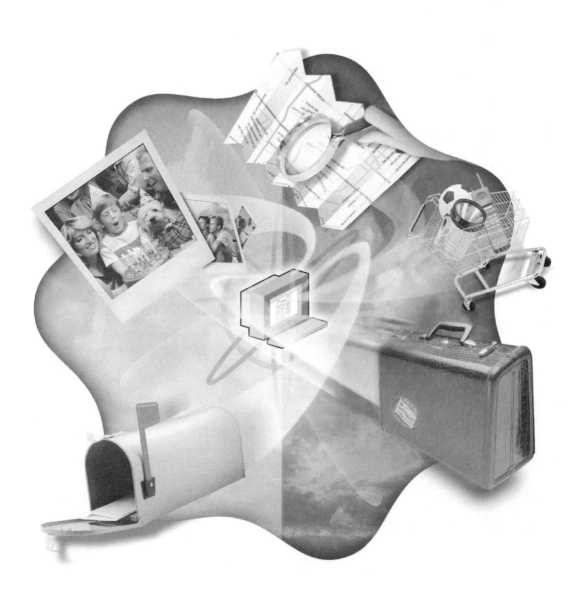

How to . . .

- Find a home on Yahoo!
- Rent a home
- Sell a home
- Compare the standard of living in different cities
- Research school districts
- Find child care

Buying or renting a home is usually the largest part of anyone's budget. Buying or renting a home can be an exciting decision but also one that is fraught with pitfalls of all types. Location, the type of home, the amenities that the home and community offer, and whether the home needs improvements are all factors that have to be considered carefully if you want to make sure that the living space you inhabit is indeed a home.

Yahoo! Real Estate

Yahoo!, working in conjunction with a number of online companies, can help make finding a home an easier and more pleasant experience. If you are interested in selling, buying, renting, or leasing a home, go to the Yahoo! Real Estate page, which is shown in Fgure 12-1.

FIGURE 12-1   Yahoo! Real Estate

There are two quick ways to get to the Real Estate page:

- Point your browser directly to http://realestate.yahoo.com.
- Click More on the Yahoo! home page, and then click Real Estate in the Other Guides section of the page that appears.

Yahoo! Real Estate offers sections devoted to buying, selling, renting, and financing homes. It also offers research tools, real estate news, links, Yellow Pages links, mortgage rates, and a featured area. All are described in this chapter.

Buying a Home

If you are interested in purchasing a home, click Buying to open the Yahoo! Real Estate—Buying a Home page, which is shown in Figure 12-2.

The Finance Calculators and Yahoo! Loan Center options on the Yahoo! Real Estate—Buying a Home page access calculators and tools about loans and mortgages. For information about using the Relocation Tools, see "Taking Advantage of the Research Tools," later in this chapter.

Buyer's Tools

Buyers Tools is the first place to start searching for a home. The Search For A Home option accesses the Yahoo! Classifieds, where you can start looking. You'll find advertisements for

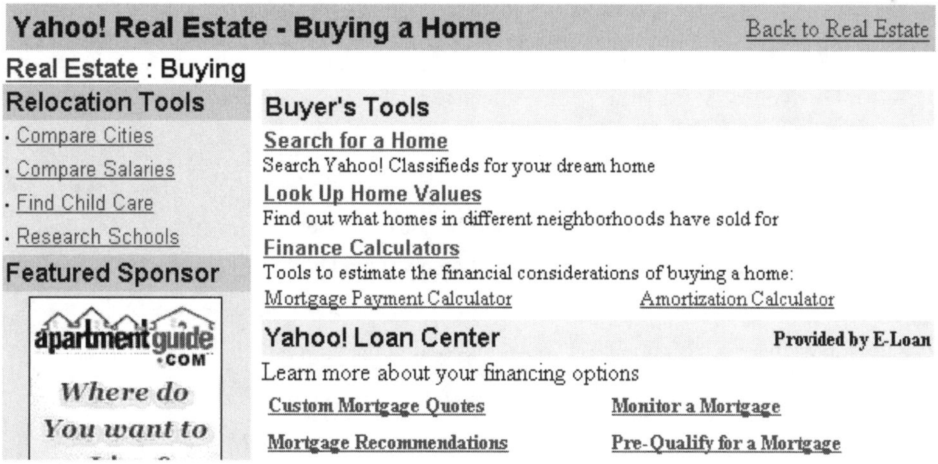

Yahoo! Real Estate - Buying a Home   Back to Real Estate

Real Estate : Buying

Relocation Tools
- Compare Cities
- Compare Salaries
- Find Child Care
- Research Schools

Featured Sponsor

apartmentguide
.COM
Where do You want to

Buyer's Tools

Search for a Home
Search Yahoo! Classifieds for your dream home

Look Up Home Values
Find out what homes in different neighborhoods have sold for

Finance Calculators
Tools to estimate the financial considerations of buying a home:
Mortgage Payment Calculator   Amortization Calculator

Yahoo! Loan Center   Provided by E-Loan
Learn more about your financing options
Custom Mortgage Quotes   Monitor a Mortgage
Mortgage Recommendations   Pre-Qualify for a Mortgage

FIGURE 12-2   Yahoo! Real Estate—Buying a Home page

homes around the country and beyond. We'll look at using the classifieds to buy and sell items of all types in Chapter 21.

The Look Up Home Values option is for investigating the recent sales prices of homes in a specific area. You can search by location or price range. If you search by location, you can look for homes on a specific street or get the sales history of a specific address. Searching by price range lets you locate properties in a specific city.

Note *The Look Up Home Values feature only covers these states: AZ, CA, CO, CT, FL, GA, IL, KY, MD, MA, MI, MN, MO, NC, NV, NJ, NY, OH, OR, PA, RI, SC, TX, VA, VT, WA, DC, and WI.*

The Search By Location option displays the form shown here:

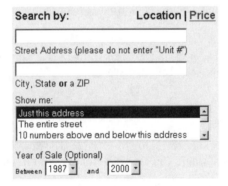

Here's how to use the form to examine the sales prices of homes in a certain area:

1. Enter the address of the property.

2. Select how you want the results to be displayed:

■ Just the address you entered

■ The entire street

■ Homes that are 10 numbers above and below the address

■ Homes that are 50 numbers above and below the address

■ Homes that are 100 numbers above and below the address

■ Homes that are 200 numbers above and below the address

■ Homes that are 1000 numbers above and below the address

3. You can also select a time period between 1987 and the current year.

4. Click the Find Home button to see a list of home sales, as shown in Figure 12-3.

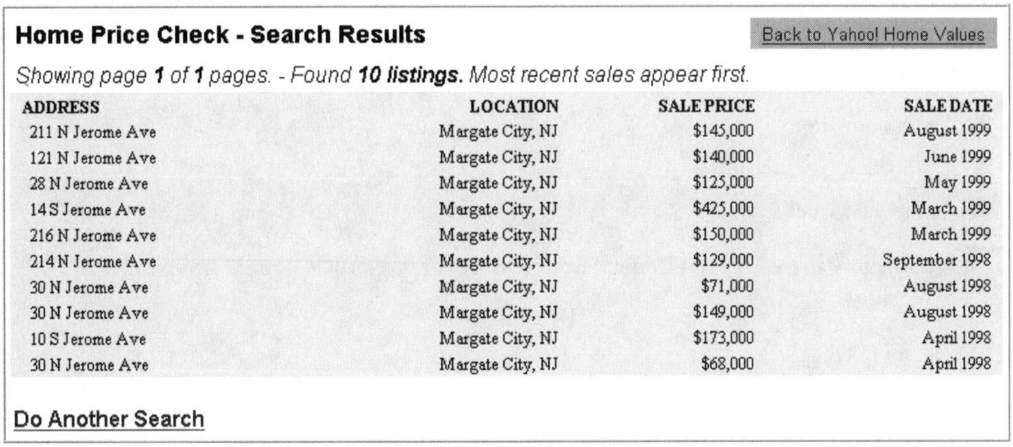

Home Price Check - Search Results Back to Yahoo! Home Values

*Showing page **1** of **1** pages. - Found **10 listings.** Most recent sales appear first.*

ADDRESS	LOCATION	SALE PRICE	SALE DATE
211 N Jerome Ave	Margate City, NJ	$145,000	August 1999
121 N Jerome Ave	Margate City, NJ	$140,000	June 1999
28 N Jerome Ave	Margate City, NJ	$125,000	May 1999
14 S Jerome Ave	Margate City, NJ	$425,000	March 1999
216 N Jerome Ave	Margate City, NJ	$150,000	March 1999
214 N Jerome Ave	Margate City, NJ	$129,000	September 1998
30 N Jerome Ave	Margate City, NJ	$71,000	August 1998
30 N Jerome Ave	Margate City, NJ	$149,000	August 1998
10 S Jerome Ave	Margate City, NJ	$173,000	April 1998
30 N Jerome Ave	Margate City, NJ	$68,000	April 1998

Do Another Search

FIGURE 12-3 Recent home sales in a selected location

You can now perform another search or ask to be notified when homes sell in the neighborhood by using these options:

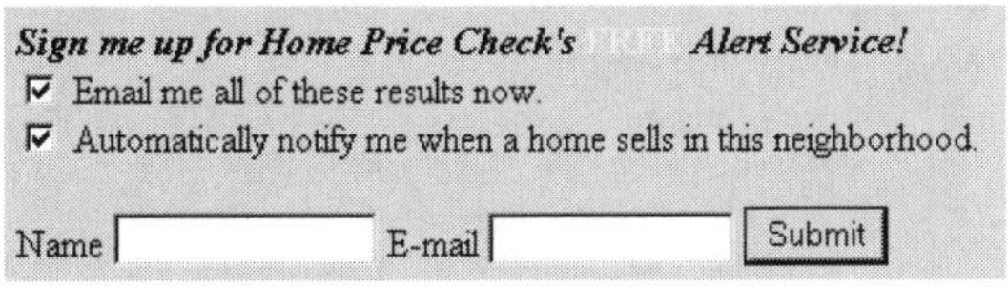

Sign me up for Home Price Check's Alert Service!
☑ Email me all of these results now.
☑ Automatically notify me when a home sells in this neighborhood.

Name   E-mail   Submit

If you selected to search by price range, you'll see this form:

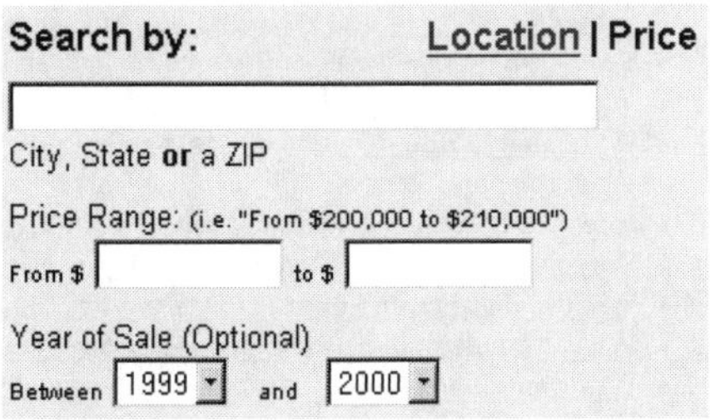

Search by: **Location | Price**

City, State **or** a ZIP

Price Range: (i.e. "From $200,000 to $210,000")
From $ to $

Year of Sale (Optional)
Between 1999 ▾ and 2000 ▾

Enter the location, a price range, and the year of the sale, and then click the Find Homes In This Price Range button.

12

Buyer's Library

The Buyer's Library offers insightful articles on a wide range of topics. The topics are organized into these categories:

- Finding a Home
- Offers and Negotiations
- Financial Issues

Click a category in the Buyer's Library section to see a list of articles, as shown in Figure 12-4.

Renting a Home

Yahoo! also offers resources for people who are looking for a home to rent—an apartment, condo, or house.

From the Yahoo! Real Estate page, click Renting to access tools and resources for renters, as shown in Figure 12-5. In addition to the Rent Vs. Own Calculator, the Renting A Home page offers the Search For Rentals link. Click it to access the Yahoo! classifieds.

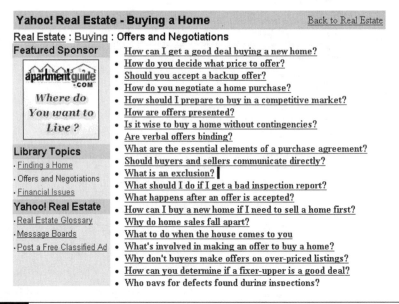

Yahoo! Real Estate - Buying a Home   Back to Real Estate

Real Estate : Buying : Offers and Negotiations

Featured Sponsor

apartmentguide.com
Where do You want to Live ?

Library Topics
- Finding a Home
- Offers and Negotiations
- Financial Issues

Yahoo! Real Estate
- Real Estate Glossary
- Message Boards
- Post a Free Classified Ad

- How can I get a good deal buying a new home?
- How do you decide what price to offer?
- Should you accept a backup offer?
- How do you negotiate a home purchase?
- How should I prepare to buy in a competitive market?
- How are offers presented?
- Is it wise to buy a home without contingencies?
- Are verbal offers binding?
- What are the essential elements of a purchase agreement?
- Should buyers and sellers communicate directly?
- What is an exclusion?
- What should I do if I get a bad inspection report?
- What happens after an offer is accepted?
- How can I buy a new home if I need to sell a home first?
- Why do home sales fall apart?
- What to do when the house comes to you
- What's involved in making an offer to buy a home?
- Why don't buyers make offers on over-priced listings?
- How can you determine if a fixer-upper is a good deal?
- Who pays for defects found during inspections?

FIGURE 12-4   Articles in the Buyer's Library

Yahoo! Real Estate - Renting A Home   Back to Real Estate

Real Estate : Renting

Relocation Tools   **Renter's Tools**
· Compare Cities   **Search for Rentals**
· Compare Salaries   Apartments, houses, rooms and more
· Find Child Care   **Rent vs. Own**
· Research Schools   Find out which makes more financial sense for you

Featured Sponsor   **Renter's Library**

                                        Tenant and Landlord Issues
apartmentguide   Articles and common questions about rental applications, tenant's rights,
.COM   landlord responsibilities, roommates and more:
Where do
You want to   **Articles by Topic:**
                                        An Introduction
                                        Leases

| FIGURE 12-5 | Resources for renters |

You'll also find a series of articles of interest to renters:

- An Introduction
- Leases
- Housing Discrimination
- Rent and Deposits
- Repairs and Privacy
- Landlord Liability
- Evictions
- Statutes

Selling a Home

When your goal is to sell your current home, click Selling in the Yahoo! Real Estate page to open the Selling A Home page. The page includes the Look Up Home Values option as well as the calculators, shown at right.

Seller's Calculators
Tools to estimate the financial considerations of selling a home:

Net Proceeds Calculator   Move or Improve Calculator

Capital Gains Tax Calculator   Current Home vs. New Home Comaparison

The Net Proceeds Calculator, shown in Figure 12-6, helps determine how much cash will be left over after selling your home. Take advantage of this tool if you will depend on

12

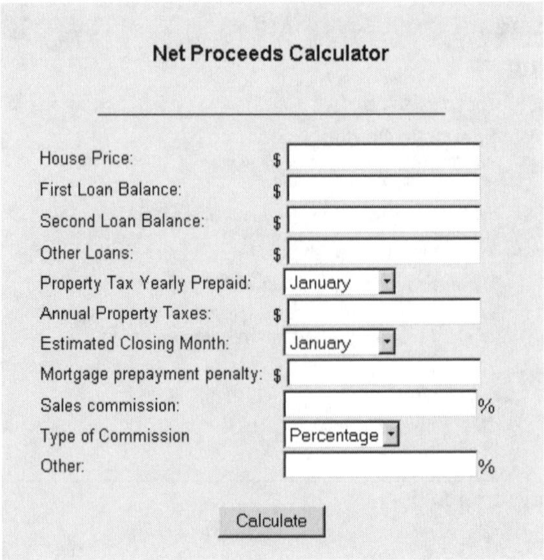

Net Proceeds Calculator

House Price:	$	
First Loan Balance:	$	
Second Loan Balance:	$	
Other Loans:	$	
Property Tax Yearly Prepaid:	January ▾	
Annual Property Taxes:	$	
Estimated Closing Month:	January ▾	
Mortgage prepayment penalty:	$	
Sales commission:		%
Type of Commission	Percentage ▾	
Other:		%

Calculate

FIGURE 12-6 Net Proceeds Calculator

the proceeds of your home to purchase another. Your outstanding home loans, property tax estimates, mortgage prepayments, and a sales commission are subtracted from the sales price of your home to obtain an estimate of how much you will profit when you sell it.

The Move Or Improve Calculator compares the cost of improving your home with the cost of buying a new home, even if you have to get a loan to finance the improvements. Here's how to use the Move Or Improve Calculator:

1. Click Move Or Improve Calculator on the Selling A Home page.

2. Enter the following information in the Current Mortgage column:

   ■ Current monthly mortgage
   ■ Annual property taxes
   ■ Current home selling price
   ■ Cost of improvement
   ■ Amount of loan for improvement
   ■ Interest rate on the improvement loan
   ■ Term of the improvement loan
   ■ Improvement loan fees

3. Enter this information in the New Mortgage column:

- Home price
- Down payment
- Loan term
- Interest rate
- Loan fees
- Annual property taxes
- Moving cost
- Transaction cost

4. Click the Calculate button to see a report like the one shown here on the right.

Improve		Move	
Current Monthly Property taxes	$ 416.67	New Monthly Property taxes	$ 375.00
Monthly Cost of Improvement	$ 1338.24	New Mortgage payment	$ 1236.86
Fixed Cost of Improvement	$ 10000.00	Fixed Cost Of Moving	$ 2501700.00
Total Monthly Obligation	$ 2954.91	Total New Monthly Obligation	$ 1611.86

The figures on the left side of the report show the monthly costs of staying in your current home but making major improvements. The figures show the monthly budget for property taxes and the monthly cost of paying for a home improvement loan, as well as your reported cash outlay for the improvements. The total monthly obligation also includes your regular mortgage payment.

The figures on the right side of the report show your costs if you decide to move, including real estate taxes and mortgage payments.

As shown in Figure 12-7, the Capital Gains tax calculator computes how much capital gains tax you might have to pay on the profits of a home.

Here's how to use the Capital Gains tax calculator:

1. Enter the purchase price.

2. Estimate the cost of capital improvement you made to the property.

3. Enter the sales price you expect.

4. Select your federal tax bracket. The options are 15%, 28%, 31%, 36%, and 39.6%.

5. Enter how many years and months you have owned the property.

6. Enter the total percentages of the state and local taxes.

7. Select Yes or No if this is your principal residence.

8. Specify whether you have lived in the house you want to sell for two of the last five years. If you have done so, you are entitled to certain tax breaks.

9. Select your martial status.

10. Click the Calculate button.

12

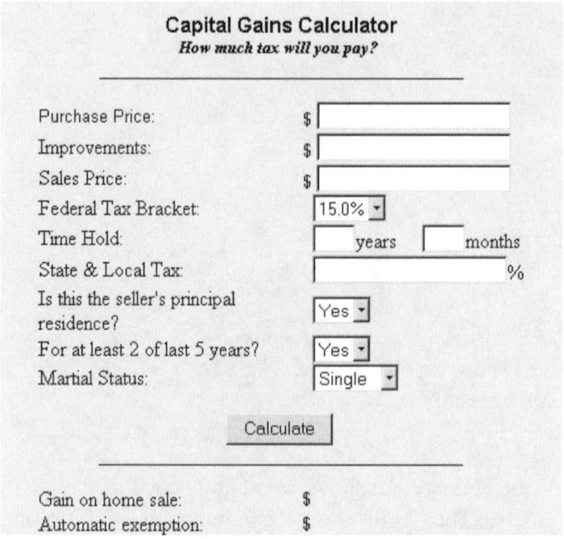

Capital Gains Calculator
How much tax will you pay?

Purchase Price:	$
Improvements:	$
Sales Price:	$
Federal Tax Bracket:	15.0% ▾
Time Hold:	☐ years ☐ months
State & Local Tax:	☐ %
Is this the seller's principal residence?	Yes ▾
For at least 2 of last 5 years?	Yes ▾
Martial Status:	Single ▾

Calculate

Gain on home sale:	$
Automatic exemption:	$

FIGURE 12-7   Capital Gains tax calculator

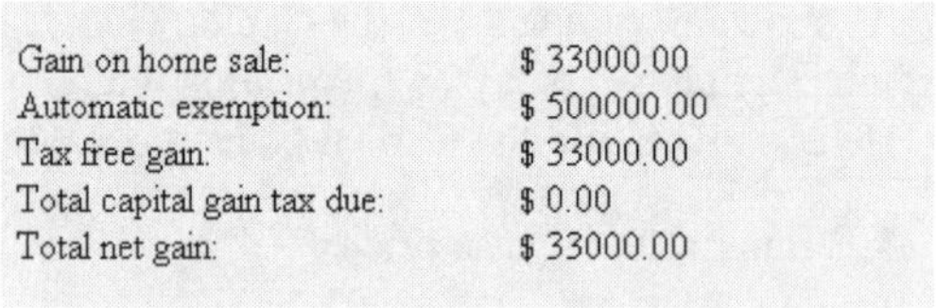

A sample capital gains calculation is shown here on the right.

Gain on home sale:	$ 33000.00
Automatic exemption:	$ 500000.00
Tax free gain:	$ 33000.00
Total capital gain tax due:	$ 0.00
Total net gain:	$ 33000.00

While the tax laws may change, there is currently an automatic exemption from capital gains taxes of $500,000 for married couples and $250,000 for singles. The exemption can be used on a principle residence, not a vacation property, if you've lived there for at least two of the past five years. The Capital Gains tax calculator computes the profit you would make on the sale of the home, and the amount of profit that is tax free and taxable based on your circumstances.

The Current Home Vs. New Home Comparisons (also called the Stay Put Or Buy Up Calculator) compares your current costs with those of purchasing a new home. It is similar to the Move Or Improve Calculator but does not take into account improvement costs. It contrasts your current real estate taxes and monthly mortgage payments to the new taxes and mortgage payments you would make if you purchased a home.

The Seller's Library section of the Selling A Home page is divided into two sections, Articles By Topic and Sellers Q&A By Topic.

In Articles By Topic, you'll find links to this information:

- Listing and Pricing
- Marketing a Home
- The Transaction

In Sellers Q&A By Topic, you'll find these links:

- Appraisals & Market Value
- Disclosure
- Escrow & Closing Costs
- Lease Options
- Negotiating
- Pricing the House to Sell
- Property Taxes
- Seller Financing
- Selling at a Loss
- Tax Considerations
- Whom to Contact
- Working with a Real Estate Agent
- Other Common Questions

Financing

The Financing option in the Yahoo! Real Estate page accesses these tools.

- Mortgage Recommendations
- Pre-Qualify for a Mortgage
- Mortgage Quotes
- Monitor a Mortgage
- Credit Reports

Taking Advantage of the Research Tools

The research tools in the Yahoo! Real Estate page offer help when making a decision whether to buy, sell, or rent a home. Before you finalize any offer or make a final commitment, take a look at these tools to gather information.

Comparing Cities

If you have some latitude in choosing where your new home will be, use the Compare Cities tool to help decide where to live. The tool compares the cost of living, real estate values, and the quality of life in two locations.

 *You can also use the Compare Cities tool if you are selling a home to find out if your community compares favorably to communities around you. Print out the comparison and distribute it to perspective buyers.*

Click Compare Cities to see the options in Figure 12-8. The two lists boxes contain cities for which comparisons can be made. Select a city in each box and then click the Compare! button.

 In the City Comparison page, you can also get profiles of different cities. Click City Profiles, and, in the page that appears, choose the city that you are interested in and then click View This Profile!.

Finance and Economy

The six indices in the Finance and Economy section compare the economic health of the two cities:

- Cost Of Living is based on a national average of 100. A high number indicates a high overall cost of living.

- Job Growth indicates the percent of new jobs that were made available in the year shown on the report. While this is not an indication of future job growth, it offers a general way to compare opportunities in different cities.

- State Income Taxes and Local Income Taxes compare the amount of tax that a family of four whose annual income is $50,000 must pay. You can use the tax figures as a general guide, as some states have a progressive tax that increases as salaries increase. Moreover, the rates for single taxpayers may vary.

- Sales Tax Rate compares the general sales tax in the two cities. If you are comparing cities in different states, however, keep in mind that taxable items may vary. Some states tax clothing and food, for example, whiles others do not.

- Unemployment Rate is the percentage of unemployment for the year shown on the report.

- Median Family Income is the average income for all families in the city. People in some cities, however, earn a wide range of salaries. Professional and executive salaries may actually be higher in one city than another where the median income is smaller due to a large proportion of low-paying jobs. Such is often the case in cities with many seasonal jobs.

Real Estate

The indices in the Real Estate area concern the cost of purchasing and maintaining a home. The costs represent the average cost of a two-thousand–square-foot home. Property tax rate is the percentage of the average annual property tax, while the property tax shows the actual tax on a two-thousand–square-foot home.

The electricity cost shows the approximate monthly electricity charges for a two-thousand–square-foot home, although the actual costs vary widely depending on how well the home was constructed.

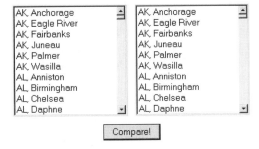

Yahoo! Real Estate - City Comparison   Real Estate Home

Top: City Comparison

Compare Two Cities:

Compare: Cities | Salaries

- Select two cities and compare them by cost of living, real estate, and quality of life.
- If you want to look at information on just one city, go to City Profiles.
- Click on Salaries to see what your income is equivalent to in another location.

AK, Anchorage	AK, Anchorage
AK, Eagle River	AK, Eagle River
AK, Fairbanks	AK, Fairbanks
AK, Juneau	AK, Juneau
AK, Palmer	AK, Palmer
AK, Wasilla	AK, Wasilla
AL, Anniston	AL, Anniston
AL, Birmingham	AL, Birmingham
AL, Chelsea	AL, Chelsea
AL, Daphne	AL, Daphne

Compare!

| **FIGURE 12-8** | Comparing cities |

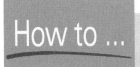

How to ...   **Compare Cities Nationwide**

12

If you want to rank all of the cities in a quality-of-life category, scroll to the bottom of the Compare Cities page to see these options:

Compare all Cities by Category:

- See how all our cities nationwide stack up according to any of our categories.

Cooling Index	Bachelor Degree Rate	Population Density	Annual Precipitation
Electricity Costs	Job Growth	Property Tax	Air Quality
Heating Index	Crime Index	Property Tax Rate	Average Jan Low
Home Purchase Costs	Auto Insurance Rates	Local Income Tax	Average July High
Median Family Inc.	Average Commute Time	State Income Tax	Unemployment Rate
High School Grad. Rate	Population	Sunny days per year	

Click the category that you are interested in to see ratings of all cities with links to their detailed profiles.

Education

The two items in the Education section reflect the general education of the population. The High School Grad. Rate is the percentage of the population that graduated from high school, while the Bachelors Degree Rate is the percentage that holds a Bachelors degree.

Use the Research Schools tool to learn about the educational system in a city.

Quality of Life

The four items in the Quality Of Life category are general indicators of the quality of life. The air pollution index represents the amount of ozone in the air compared to a national average of 100.

Population reports the number of inhabitants in the last reported census, while the population density shows the number of persons per square mile. Population density is often considered a more accurate reflection of the quality of life than total population.

Crime Index reports the number of crimes committed per 100,000 people, a very good indication of the quality of life.

Travel and Transportation

The Travel And Transportation items reflect the cost of transportation in dollars and time. Auto insurance reports the average annual cost of car insurance, while commute time is the average one-way commute time in minutes.

Weather

The six indices in the Weather section reflect the overall climate, including the average low temperature in January, and the average high temperature in July.

- **Heating Degree Days**   The accumulated number of degrees for days below 65 degrees. For example, if the temperature one day was 55 degrees, ten heating degree days are added to the accumulated total. A high number means that more energy is required to heat a home.

- **Cooling Degree Days**   The accumulated number of degrees for days above 65 degrees. A high number indicates higher air-conditioning costs.

- **Sunny Days**   The average number of sunny days per year. Annual precipitation is the average inches of rain per year.

Comparing Salaries

The Compare Salaries tool compares the buying power of a salary in two cities. If you are relocating, use the tool to determine whether you can maintain your standard of living with your current salary. You can also use the tool to determine if you should ask for a cost-of-living increase before making a move.

Click Compare Salaries in the Research Tools section of the Yahoo! Real Estate page. In the page that appears, choose two cities, the one where you currently live and the one where you contemplate living; enter a salary amount; and click the Compare Salaries! button.

You can also access this tool at the bottom of the Compare Cities report, as shown at right. Since the two cities are already selected, just enter the salary and click the Compare Salaries! button.

Compare Two Cities

The report shows the salary you need to maintain the same quality of life in each city. For example, the report illustrated here shows that $75,000 in Malibu, California, purchases what $38,304 purchases in Haddonfield, New Jersey. So if you are considering a move from Haddonfield to Malibu, you would need almost double the salary to maintain the same standard of living.

> A salary of **$75000** in Malibu, CA is equivalent to a salary of **$38304.72** in Haddonfield, NJ.
> (In other words, what you can afford with $75000 in Malibu, CA requires $38304.72 in Haddonfield, NJ.)
>
> Also, a salary of **$75000** in Haddonfield, NJ is equivalent to a salary of **$146848.74** in Malibu, CA.
> (In other words, what you can afford with $75000 in Haddonfield, NJ requires $146848.74 in Malibu, CA.)

On the other hand, a salary of $75,000 in Haddonfield offers the same buying power as almost $150,000 in Malibu. So if you are living comfortably in Malibu on $150,000 a year, you would experience twice the buying power by moving to Haddonfield with the same salary.

Research Schools

Research Schools is an important tool if you are relocating with school-age children or you plan to have children in your new home. The tool provides information about the quality of school districts in every state.

Clicking Research Schools offers two main options: Browse By Metros and Browse By State. Each is followed by a series of locations. Start by clicking a location in the metropolitan area or state of your choice. Then click a county for a side-by-side comparison of local school districts, as shown in Figure 12-9.

For detailed information about a school district, click its name in the list. Click a specific school district for a more detailed report in four categories.

General Information

In the General Information section of the report, you'll find some overall information about the district, including

- Total number of students
- The student-to-teacher ratio
- Average number of students in an elementary school
- Total number of high school students
- Average number of students in a first grade class
- Average number of students in a high school math class

12

Yahoo! Real Estate - School Reports   Yahoo! Real Estate

Top: School Reports: New Jersey: Atlantic

- Click on the school district name for more detailed information

School District	Total Students	Students : Teacher	Grade 1 Class Size	SAT Avg.	ACT Avg.	% to 4-yr college	% to 2-yr college
Absecon	908	13	23	819	N/A	25 %	28 %
Atlantic	7063	15	25	921	N/A	53 %	26 %
Brigantine	1119	13	25	921	N/A	53 %	26 %
Buena	2455	15	24	932	N/A	30 %	27 %
Egg Harbor City	593	9	22	1024	0	50 %	29 %
Egg Harbor Township	4860	14	25	1002	N/A	42 %	44 %
Estell Manor	310	10	19	932	N/A	30 %	27 %
Folsom	235	6	17	998	N/A	47 %	30 %
Galloway	3521	10	23	1024	0	50 %	29 %
Hamilton-Atlantic Co.	2316	13	25	990	N/A	37 %	33 %
Hammonton	2115	14	23	998	N/A	47 %	30 %
Linwood	900	10	19	1037	N/A	58 %	21 %

FIGURE 12-9   Comparing school districts

Test Scores

The Test Scores items reflect the level of college-bound students and their test scores. They include these factors:

- The percentage of high school graduates who plan to attend a four-year college or university
- The percentage of high school graduates who plan to attend a two-year junior college
- The average combined Scholastic Aptitude Test (SAT) scores
- The average composite American College Testing Program (ACT) scores

Secondary Education

The Secondary Education items reflect the diversity of classes in the district's secondary schools. These items are

- The number of foreign languages offered
- The number of advanced placement classes offered
- The number of fine arts classes offered
- The existence of a science club
- The existence of a drama program
- The existence of a chapter in Students Against Drunk Driving
- The number of girls, boys, and co-educational interscholastic sports programs

Additional Items

The final section of the report summarizes several other key indicators, including

- The number of formal foreign languages studied
- The grade where computers are introduced
- The number of band instrument lessons
- The number of gifted student pull-out programs
- The availability of after-school daycare programs

For further information about a school district, you can order a free comparison report of three districts. The service is sponsored by advertisers; and to qualify for the free report, you have to allow one of the sponsors to send you information. Here's how to get the report:

1. At the bottom of the Yahoo! school report, click the link shown at right.

> **Go to theschoolreport.com**

2. In the page that appears, select a state from the list box and then click Go.

3. Select the city or the county, and then click Go.

4. In the sample report that appears, click the link shown on the right to display the application form.

> To Create Your Free School Report
> Click Here.

5. Enter your name and address.

6. Select up to three school districts from the lists.

7. Answer the short questionnaire about your relocation.

8. Select at least one of the corporate sponsors.

9. Click Submit.

The report, and information from the selected sponsor, will be mailed to you.

Finding Child Care

Use the Find Child Care tool from the Yahoo! Real Estate page to locate child care providers by zip code, or city and state. Here's how to use this feature:

1. Click Find Child Care.

2. In the page that appears, enter the zip code, or the city and state, and then click Search.

Search by Zip Code	OR Search By City and State	
Enter Zip Code:	Enter City:	
[ ]	[ ]	
Search	Enter State:	
	Select state ▾ Search	

12

3. In the page that appears, specify the age of the child by selecting one of these options: Less Than 1 Year Old, From 1 Year To 12 Years, or Older Than 12.

4. Select the program type: Any, Child Care Center, Preschool, Home/Family Care, Montessori, or School-Age Program.

5. Click the Search button and Yahoo! searches the Yellow Pages for listings in your area.

Other Real Estate Page Features

In addition to the features already discussed, the Real Estate page offers a variety of links to interesting news stories, sites, and online information.

For links to a variety of interesting and useful sites, for example, use the items in the Cool And Helpful section. Through these links, you can access the Yahoo! classified section, look up real estate terms in the glossary, order a credit report, or go to the Yahoo! Insurance Center. You can also go to the Yahoo! message board to find discussions about real estate, as well as connect to the United States Postal Service's relocation services site. Use the Get Local link in the section to get information about a state or local community, including special events, weather reports, entertainment ideas, maps, and even coupons. The Web Sites link takes you to the Yahoo! real estate categories. From the categories, work your way through subcategories to find information of interest.

The address of the Postal Service relocation service is http://www.usps.gov/moversnet/.

The Yellow Pages section of the Yahoo! Real Estate page includes links to real estate resources.

The Real Estate News section displays headlines about real estate. There are two links under the Real Estate News banner: Click InmanNews or Real Times to review the headlines from each service. The current source being displayed does not appear as a link.

This Week's Poll presents a question about real estate. You can take part in the poll by clicking the option that pertains to you and then clicking Submit My Vote to see the current results. You can also click View Results Without Voting to go directly to the results.

Advertiser Links

As you work with the Yahoo! real estate pages, you'll see advertisements for mortgage and finance companies, realtors, and other companies that offer real estate services. Some of the ads, for example, include links to these sites:

- **http://www.homebid.com/**   For online home auctions and links to realtors
- **http://www.apartmentguide.com/**   To locate apartments for rent
- **https://www.ditech.com/**   For a credit reporting service
- **http://www.mortgageexpo.com/** and **http://www.mortgagequotes.com/**   For two mortgage companies

Click advertisements that you feel will offer a helpful service, but remember that these companies are not part of Yahoo! and usually charge for their services.

Chapter 13

Buying, Selling, and Maintaining Automobiles

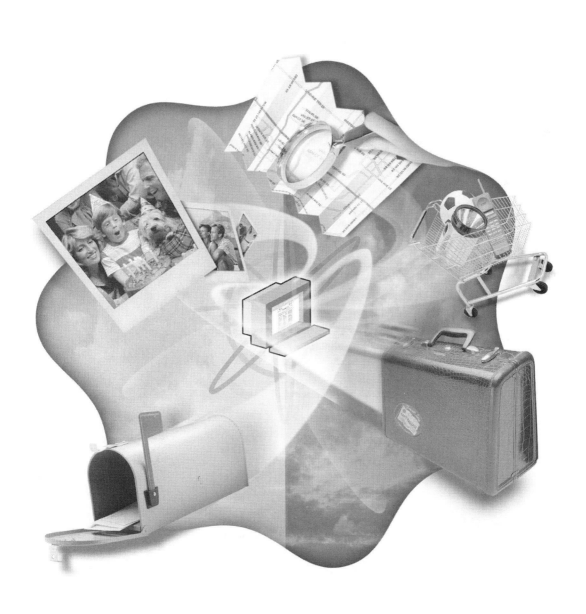

How to . . .

- Get new car prices
- Compare models side by side
- Get used car prices
- Check for a lemon
- Maintain service records online
- Troubleshoot automotive problems

Chances are your automobile is, after your home, the most expensive thing you have purchased. In fact, if you rent, you may spend more money on your car than on your home. Monthly car payments, insurance, fuel, and maintenance can take a big chunk out of your budget. Sometimes, you even have to spend money for car repairs before you make repairs to your home.

Decisions about buying, selling, and maintaining cars should not be taken lightly. Luckily, you have Yahoo!.

Yahoo! Autos

Yahoo!, in conjunction with a number of online companies, can help you make decisions when it comes to a car, truck, or SUV. If you are interested in selling a car, buying a car, or just keeping a vehicle running, go to Yahoo! Autos, which is shown in Figure 13-1.

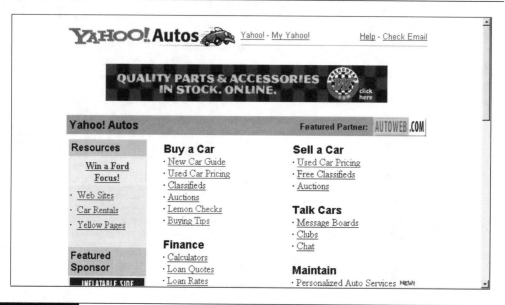

FIGURE 13-1   Yahoo! Autos

There are two ways to get to the page:

- ■ Point your browser directly to http://autos.yahoo.com/.
- ■ Click More on the Yahoo! home page, and then click Autos in the Other Guides section of the page that appears.

Yahoo! Autos has sections devoted to buying, selling, financing, and maintaining autos. You will also find helpful links to other resources, news stories, a weekly poll, and personalized services. We'll take a look at all of these features in this chapter.

Much of the information in Yahoo! Autos is provided by Edmunds.com, one of the first sites to offer free automobile price information online. You can go directly to their site at http://www.edmunds.com to read reviews, get consumer information, or visit a messages area called the Town Hall where you can share your automotive experiences with others.

Buying an Automobile

If you are interested in purchasing a new or used automobile, check out the links under Buying in the Yahoo! Autos page. The Auctions and Classifieds links take you to Yahoo! features where you can actually purchase a car online. You'll learn more about these features in later chapters. Use the other links to get the information you need to purchase a new or used car.

New Car Guide

As shown in Figure 13-2, the New Car Guide provides access to detailed information about hundreds of models, as well as the ability to compare cars side by side, feature by feature.

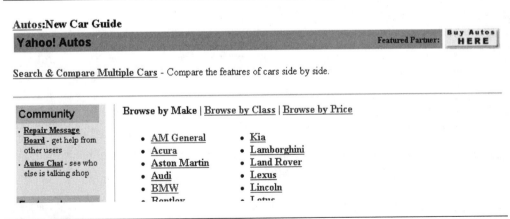

Autos:New Car Guide

Yahoo! Autos   Featured Partner: **Buy Autos HERE**

Search & Compare Multiple Cars - Compare the features of cars side by side.

Community
- Repair Message Board - get help from other users
- Autos Chat - see who else is talking shop

Browse by Make | Browse by Class | Browse by Price

- AM General
- Acura
- Aston Martin
- Audi
- BMW
- Bentley

- Kia
- Lamborghini
- Land Rover
- Lexus
- Lincoln
- Lotus

FIGURE 13-2   Yahoo! New Car Guide

13

To get information about a specific model, use one of the Browse options: Browse By Make, Browse By Class, or Browse By Price. With Browse By Make, you start by selecting the car's manufacturer. Browsing by class, you start with these choices:

Browse by Class	
• Compact Pickup	• Luxury Wagon
• Convertible	• Minivan
• Family Coupe	• Sport Utility
• Family Sedan	• Sports Car
• Fullsize Pickup	• Sports Car/Convertible
• Fullsize Van	• Sports Car/Luxury Coupe
• Luxury Coupe	• Sports Coupe
• Luxury Sedan	• Sports Coupe/Luxury Coupe
• Luxury Sedan/Sports Sedan	• Sports Sedan
• Luxury Sport-Utility	• Station Wagon

Browsing by prices lets you select the price range you are comfortable with:

Browse by Price	
• $0 - $15,000	• $30,000 - $35,000
• $15,000 - $20,000	• $35,000 - $50,000
• $20,000 - $25,000	• $50,000 - $75,000
• $25,000 - $30,000	• More than $75,000

As an example, let's locate a car by maker:

1. In the New Car Guide, click Browse by Make if it is not already selected.

2. Choose the manufacturer to see a list of models to choose from. The page is labeled "Autos: Toyota Guide," as shown here, or whatever manufacturer you selected.

   Autos:Toyota Guide

3. Choose the model you are interested in to see a summary of models in the Vehicle Matches page, as shown in Figure 13-3.

Click Price above the list to sort the cars in ascending order by price, or click Price below the list to sort in descending order.

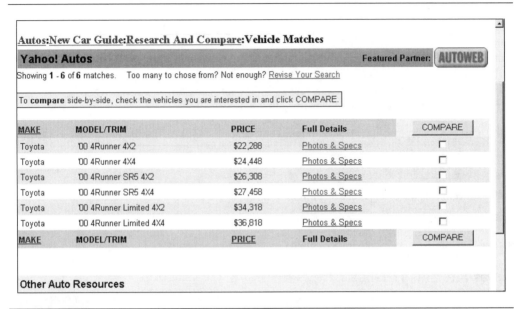

Autos:New Car Guide:Research And Compare:Vehicle Matches

Yahoo! Autos   Featured Partner: AUTOWEB

Showing **1 - 6** of **6** matches.   Too many to chose from? Not enough? _Revise Your Search_

To **compare** side-by-side, check the vehicles you are interested in and click COMPARE.

MAKE	MODEL/TRIM	PRICE	Full Details	COMPARE
Toyota	'00 4Runner 4X2	$22,288	Photos & Specs	☐
Toyota	'00 4Runner 4X4	$24,448	Photos & Specs	☐
Toyota	'00 4Runner SR5 4X2	$26,308	Photos & Specs	☐
Toyota	'00 4Runner SR5 4X4	$27,458	Photos & Specs	☐
Toyota	'00 4Runner Limited 4X2	$34,318	Photos & Specs	☐
Toyota	'00 4Runner Limited 4X4	$36,818	Photos & Specs	☐
MAKE	MODEL/TRIM	PRICE	Full Details	COMPARE

Other Auto Resources

FIGURE 13-3   Comparing prices for various car models

How to ... **Get More Information**

From the carmaker's guide page, you can also access information about a manufacturer by clicking these links:

- **Yellow Pages: Dealers**   Lists dealers in your area
- **Official Site**   Takes you to the manufacturer's official Web site
- **Other Web Sites**   Displays Yahoo! categories that relate to carmakers
- **Acura Books**   Offers links to books in the Yahoo! Shopping area
- **Acura Parts**   Displays Yahoo! categories that relate to automobile parts
- **Used Prices**   Lets you find the retail and trade-in value of used vehicles

For details about a specific model, click Photos and Specs next to the model's name to see a photograph, description of the vehicle, and lists of the major standard and optional features. You also get a summary that includes the base price, dealer invoice, required packages, standard engine, and standard transmission. Not taking into account optional equipment, the price you should expect to pay is somewhere between the base price and the dealer invoice amount.

Following the summary are details arranged by category, as shown in Table 13-1.

The specifications page also includes links to this information:

- Optional equipment prices—both retail and dealer invoice prices
- Performance information
- Available colors and trim options
- Current rebates and special incentives
- Other available information

You can also choose to display similar cars by class or price if you want to compare models.

Side-by-Site Comparisons

While you're viewing models in the Vehicle Matches page, you can compare several models at once. To do so, select the check boxes in the Compare column next to each model you are interested in, and then click Compare. You'll see photographs of each model and a side-by-side comparison of features, as shown in Figure 13-4.

You can also go directly to the comparison feature from the New Car Guide home page. Here's how:

1. In the New Car Guide, click Search & Compare Multiple Cars.

Category	Items Included
Price and Standard Engine	Base price, engine type, displacement, number of valves, horsepower and torque, type of fuel system and transmission, city and highway fuel economy
Interior Dimensions	Front and rear headroom, leg room, shoulder room, and hip room
Exterior Dimensions and Weight	Curb weight, weight distribution as a percentage front and rear, wheelbase, track, length, width, and height
Capacity and Volume	Cargo volume, fuel capacity, tow capacity, standard and optional seating, EPA class, passenger volume
Steering, Suspension, and Brakes	Steering diameter, engine location and drive, brake type front and rear, suspension front and rear, and tire size
Warranty	Length in months and miles, power train, and rust coverage

TABLE 13-1   Details Shown in a Vehicle Listing

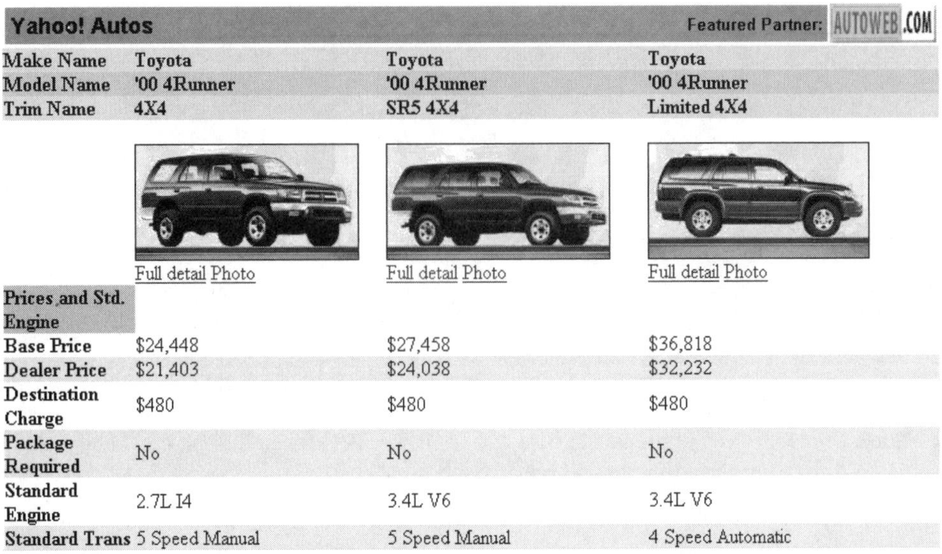

Yahoo! Autos			Featured Partner: AUTOWEB.COM
Make Name	Toyota	Toyota	Toyota
Model Name	'00 4Runner	'00 4Runner	'00 4Runner
Trim Name	4X4	SR5 4X4	Limited 4X4
	Full detail Photo	Full detail Photo	Full detail Photo
Prices and Std. Engine			
Base Price	$24,448	$27,458	$36,818
Dealer Price	$21,403	$24,038	$32,232
Destination Charge	$480	$480	$480
Package Required	No	No	No
Standard Engine	2.7L I4	3.4L V6	3.4L V6
Standard Trans	5 Speed Manual	5 Speed Manual	4 Speed Automatic

FIGURE 13-4   Comparing models side by side

Note   *You can also select Compare This Car when you are viewing a car's details page.*

2.   In the page that appears, select a class of cars.

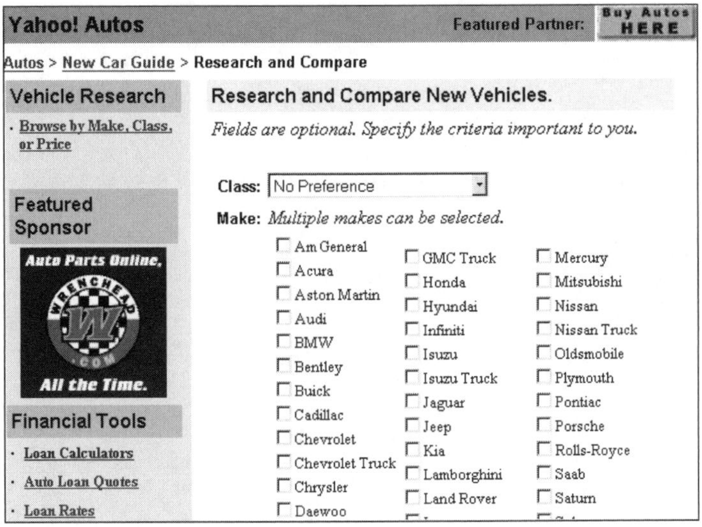

Yahoo! Autos   Featured Partner: Buy Autos HERE

Autos > New Car Guide > Research and Compare

Vehicle Research

· Browse by Make, Class, or Price

Featured Sponsor

Auto Parts Online.
WRENCHEAD
.COM
All the Time.

Financial Tools

· Loan Calculators
· Auto Loan Quotes
· Loan Rates

Research and Compare New Vehicles.

Fields are optional. Specify the criteria important to you.

Class: No Preference ▾

Make: *Multiple makes can be selected.*

☐ Am General
☐ Acura
☐ Aston Martin
☐ Audi
☐ BMW
☐ Bentley
☐ Buick
☐ Cadillac
☐ Chevrolet
☐ Chevrolet Truck
☐ Chrysler
☐ Daewoo

☐ GMC Truck
☐ Honda
☐ Hyundai
☐ Infiniti
☐ Isuzu
☐ Isuzu Truck
☐ Jaguar
☐ Jeep
☐ Kia
☐ Lamborghini
☐ Land Rover

☐ Mercury
☐ Mitsubishi
☐ Nissan
☐ Nissan Truck
☐ Oldsmobile
☐ Plymouth
☐ Pontiac
☐ Porsche
☐ Rolls-Royce
☐ Saab
☐ Saturn

3. Select the makers you are interested in.

4. Select a starting and ending price, if desired. Click Search & Compare to list all makes and models.

5. Select the check boxes next to the names of the models you want to compare.

6. Click Compare.

Pricing Used Cars

Yahoo! Auto has not overlooked those of us who want to buy or sell a used vehicle. You can quickly find the retail and trade-in value of many old cars, as well as see if the vehicle you are considering has been resold to the manufacturer as a lemon.

To find out how much a used car is worth, whether you are buying or selling, follow these steps:

1. Click Used Car Pricing under the Buy A Car Or Sell A Car heading on the Yahoo! Autos page. A list of car manufacturers appears.

2. Click the make of car you are interested in buying or selling to see a list of years for which price information is available. Click the year that the vehicle was made to see a list of models. Click the model of the vehicle to see a report, shown in the following illustration. The report lists the base trade-in and market (retail) value of the vehicle.

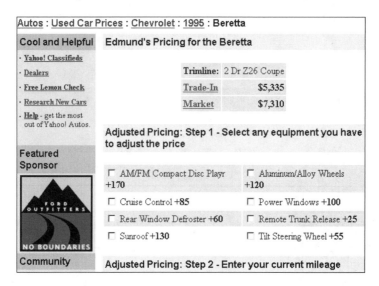

 Click Trade-In or Market to see a definition of the term.

3. Under Step 1, choose the adjustment options that are relevant to the vehicle. Each option describes a feature that adds value to the vehicle.

4. Under Step 2, enter the current mileage. Then, click the link shown at right.

> Click Here to Price Your Vehicle

You will see a summary of the options, as well as the total of the adjustment options, the adjustment for high or low mileage, and the total vehicle value. You'll also see the Edmund's rating for the car and a list of new features that were available with the model in later years:

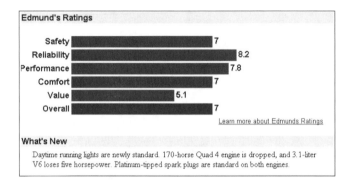

At the bottom of the page are links to sites for more information, including

- The Edmund's home page
- A tutorial about negotiating the purchase of a car
- Road test reports
- Automobile safety information
- Sources for Chilton repair manuals

There is also a link labeled Discount Financing for applying for a used car loan.

Checking for a Lemon

Under the Lemon Law, a manufacturer must repurchase a vehicle that has had repeated problems. The manufacturer, however, is allowed to repair the vehicle and resell it as a used vehicle. Before purchasing a used car, you should see if it was repurchased as a lemon. If it was, you might consider not purchasing the car or using its history to negotiate better terms with the seller.

To check if a car was a lemon, you need the car's vehicle identification number (VIN). The VIN is a 17-character number assigned to all cars manufactured after 1981. The VIN is usually found on a plate on the front corner of the dashboard. To find it, stand outside the car and look at the driver's side of the dashboard. If you cannot find the VIN there, look under the hood of the car.

13

When you have the VIN, go to Yahoo! Autos and click Lemon Checks under Buy A Car to see a page with this box:

VIN #: [   ]

Enter the VIN exactly how it appeared on the car and then click this link:

[Click Here for your FREE Vehicle Lemon Check!]

Carfax, the company that provides this service, checks its database of over one billion vehicles and reports if yours is a lemon.

Buying Tips

The Buying Tips option of Yahoo! Autos offers informative articles on all phases of buying a car. Click Buying Tips for access to these reports:

- First Steps
- Researching a Used Car
- Researching a New Car
- Negotiating a Price
- Closing the Deal

Selling a Car

Under Yahoo! Autos, you will find information about selling a car, including used car prices, auctions, and classified ads. Before selling your car or trading it in, find out how much it is worth through the Used Car Pricing feature described previously in the section "Pricing Used Cars." The guide shows both the market and trade-in value, so you'll be prepared whether you want to sell your car or trade it in. You can also sell your car by placing it in Yahoo! Auctions or posting a classified ad in the Yahoo! Classifieds.

Financing a Car Purchase

The Finance section of Yahoo! Autos provides access to financial tools for auto buyers.

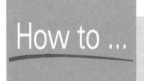

How to ... Get a Used Car's History

Even if the dealer tells you that the used car you're interested in was owned by a "little old lady who only drives it to church," it still pays to know the car's history. At Carfax.com, you get reports on used cars. The cost of the service is $19.95 for a 60-day period. During the 60 days, you can get as many reports as you want, as long as you know the vehicles' VIN numbers.

The Calculators option in the Finance section, however, offers a few tools that are unique to Yahoo! Autos.

The Lease Payment Calculator, for example, estimates the monthly lease payments based on these items:

- Negotiated price
- Sales tax rate
- Term of the lease
- Residual price for which you may purchase the car after the lease
- Down payment
- Value of a trade-in
- Rebates

Enter the information that you have and then click Calculate Lease Payment to get a report like the one shown here:

	LEASE
ESTIMATED MONTHLY PAYMENT:	$ 396
TOTAL COST OF ALL MONTHLY PAYMENTS:	$ 9498
DOWN PAYMENT:	$ 0
VALUE OF CURRENT TRADE-IN:	$ 0
COST TO PURCHASE LEASED VEHICLE:	$ 14,000
TOTAL COST TO PURCHASE:	$ 23,498

The Loan Payment Calculator is similar to the Lease Payment Calculator, except it does not require a residual value. It reports the estimated monthly payment on an automobile loan.

The Lease Vs. Loan Calculator compares the virtues of leasing and buying. This tool combines the Lease Payment Calculator and the Loan Payment Calculator and shows you the total cost to purchase by both means.

13

 Use the Talk Cars section of Yahoo! Autos to connect with other members in the message boards, clubs, and chat rooms.

Maintain Your Car

Once you have your dream car—or whatever car you can afford—you have to keep it running. For help in keeping your car on the road, use the options in the Maintain section of Yahoo! Autos to store your car's maintenance records online, stay updated about recalls, and learn how to repair and troubleshoot problems.

Personalized Auto Services

Yahoo! Personalized Service offers a central place for maintaining service records and being informed when a manufacturer recalls a car. You can use the records to track expenses and to make sure your car is properly maintained.

You can also use the feature to track repairs and parts warranties. For example, suppose you purchase a new battery with a 48-month warranty and you record the purchase in your online file. The next time the battery has to be replaced, you can check your service records to determine if it is still under warranty.

You start your online maintenance file by describing the vehicle. You can then add maintenance records as they pile up. You can store information for as many vehicles as you want.

As an example, let's go through the process of describing a car and entering a repair record:

1. Click Personalized Auto Service in the Yahoo! Autos page.

Note *After you describe a vehicle, selecting Personalized Auto Service on the Yahoo! Autos page takes you to the last viewed vehicle screen.*

2. In the screen that appears, click New User or Get Started Now to see a list of automotive manufacturers.

3. Select the make of your vehicle to open the form, shown in the following illustration.

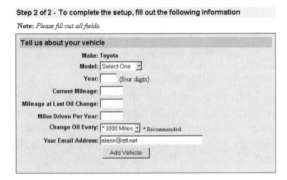

4. Choose a model from the drop-down list.

5. Enter the year of your car.

6. Enter your car's current mileage.

7. Enter the mileage as of the last time you changed the oil.

8. Estimate the number of miles you drive each year.

9. Select the period for changing the oil.

10. Enter your e-mail address if it is not already shown.

11. Click Add Vehicle. You will see the vehicle's maintenance page, as shown next.

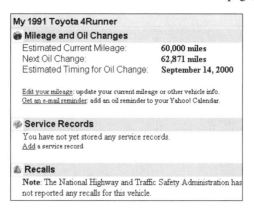

In the Mileage And Oil Changes section, you can change the current mileage to keep it up to date, or you can click Get An E-Mail Reminder to place the reminder on your Yahoo! calendar. The Service Records section summarizes the maintenance records you have entered. The Recalls section automatically lists recalls reported by the National Highway and Traffic Safety Administration.

> **Note**   *The Get An E-Mail Reminder option changes names and becomes Remove E-Mail Reminder if you want to delete a reminder from your calendar.*

Adding Service Records

To maintain an online record of services done to your car, click Add in the Service Records section of the vehicle's page to see the form shown in Figure 13-5. Enter information about the repair or maintenance, and then click the Add This Record button.

The Service Records page appears and summarizes each of the records. The heading of the page looks something like the on shown here on the right. Each of the items in the heading is a link:

Yahoo! Autos

Home > All Vehicles > My 1991 Toyota 4Runner > Service Records

- Click Home to return to the Yahoo! Autos home page.
- Click All Vehicles to see a list of the vehicles you have entered into the system.
- Click the name of the vehicle to see its maintenance page.

My Autos
- 1991 4Runner
- **1994 Corolla**

- View all autos
- Add a vehicle

Maintenance and service records pages offer links to each automobile you have entered in the system, as well as the means to see a list of all vehicles or describe a new vehicle, as shown here.

13

Add a Service Record

Date of Service: [Select One ▾] [ ] , [ ] (Month/Day/Year)

Mileage: [ ]

Type of Service Performed: [Select One ▾]

Service Station: [ ]

Description: [ ]

[Add This Record] [Cancel]

FIGURE 13-5 Describing repairs or services done to a car

Repair and Troubleshooting

Selecting the Repair And Troubleshooting option in the Maintain section of the Yahoo! Autos page displays a page with two options: Troubleshooting and Repair Index.

Choosing Repair Index displays an alphabetical list of common automobile repairs, from ABS: Antilock to Windshield Washers And Wipers. Click the name of a repair to see links that you can click to obtain detailed articles that explain how to make repairs.

Choosing Troubleshooting lists symptoms that your car might be experiencing:

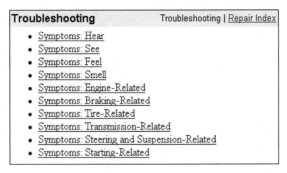

Troubleshooting   Troubleshooting | Repair Index

- Symptoms: Hear
- Symptoms: See
- Symptoms: Feel
- Symptoms: Smell
- Symptoms: Engine-Related
- Symptoms: Braking-Related
- Symptoms: Tire-Related
- Symptoms: Transmission-Related
- Symptoms: Steering and Suspension-Related
- Symptoms: Starting-Related

Click a symptom to further define a problem and perhaps learn how to remedy it. For example, suppose you smell a rotten egg odor from the back of your car:

1. Click Symptoms: Smell to see a list of odor-related symptoms.

2. Click There Is A Rotten Egg Smell Coming From The Exhaust to see a list of possible causes.

3. Click a cause to obtain how-to articles in the repair index.

Maintenance Tips

Click the Maintenance Tips option in the Maintain section to access car maintenance tips from Ren Volpe, author of "The Lady Mechanic's Total Car Care for the Clueless." The tips are organized in these categories:

- General service mechanics
- Oil and filters
- Tires and brakes
- Fluids
- Winterizing

Click an option to display and read the related article.

Auto Stores

The Auto Stores option in the Maintain section of Yahoo! Autos leads you to an extensive collection of links to online automobile parts and equipment dealers. You'll get access to stores carrying these items:

- Parts and accessories
- Clothing and collectables
- Tires and wheels
- Car care products
- Tools
- Lubricants
- Audio equipment
- Scooters and motorcycles
- Bumper stickers
- Police, fire, and emergency vehicle equipment

All of the stores are part of Yahoo!'s secure shopping service.

News Stories

The News Stories section of the Yahoo! Autos page offers links to news stories that pertain to automobiles. Click a link to read an article or click Full Coverage below the list of stories to open the Automotive News page of the Yahoo! Business Full Coverage feature.

The Automotive News page includes links to additional stories, as well as specific news sources, including these magazines: *Car and Driver, Motor Trend,* and *Road & Track.*

There is also a section that offers links to Web sites where information about automobile shows, government and safety agencies, and automobile associations can be obtained.

13

Other Yahoo! Autos Page Features

In addition to the features already discussed, the Autos page offers a variety of other information and links. In the Cool And Helpful section, for example, you will find information about local traffic, automobile racing, personal testimonials about cars by Yahoo! members, and help information. By clicking the Traffic link, for example, you can specify your location and get road and traffic reports.

This Week's Poll is a weekly question about automobiles. "Which of these SUV models would you most like to buy?" is an example question. You can take part in the poll by clicking the option that pertains to you, and then clicking Submit My Vote to see the current results. You can also click View Results Without Voting under the option buttons to go directly to the results.

The Resources section has links to Yahoo!'s automobile Web sites, car rental information from the Yahoo! Travel department, and the Yellow Pages so you can locate companies in your area.

There is also a Featured Sponsor link to one of Yahoo!'s automotive partners.

Part IV

Auctions and Shopping— Buy and Sell Anything

Chapter 14

Buy and Sell at Yahoo! Auctions

How to . . .

- ◼ Register for Yahoo! auctions
- ◼ Place items up for sale
- ◼ Find items to buy
- ◼ Bid on items
- ◼ Track auctions
- ◼ Ask the seller questions
- ◼ Get auction alerts
- ◼ Protect yourself in auctions

Yahoo! Auction is a great place to buy and sell items. If you're cleaning out the attic or garage, or disbursing a childhood collection, the auction gives you access to thousands of buyers. When you're looking for a new addition to a collection or an unusual gift, the auction is a terrific source to obtain bargains and hard-to-find items.

Best of all, the auction is free—except for what you purchase, that is. Yahoo! doesn't charge a thing to put an item up for sale. Unlike other auction sites, Yahoo! charges no listing fee or final sale fee.

Registering for Yahoo! Auctions

In order to participate in Yahoo! auctions, you have to be signed in with your Yahoo! ID and password. If you have not yet signed in when you go to the Auction page, enter your ID and password and then click the Sign In button.

The first time you put up an item for sale or place a bid on an item, you are asked to register for Yahoo! Auctions. As shown in Figure 14-1, the page that appears asks you to confirm your first name, last name, and e-mail address. So that you can complete transactions, your e-mail address will be given to persons who buy items from you and persons from whom you buy items.

The registration page also contains an About Me box. Use this box to enter information about yourself that you want bidders and sellers to know. Most of the registration page, however, is an agreement that describes your commitments and Yahoo!'s policies and liabilities as regards auctions. Read the agreement and then click I Agree at the bottom of the page.

Understanding the Feedback System

The feedback system is a way in which the Yahoo! community polices itself. When a transaction has been completed, the buyer and seller can rate each other with what is known as a *feedback rating*. Both the buyer and the seller receive an e-mail with a link that they can click to enter feedback.

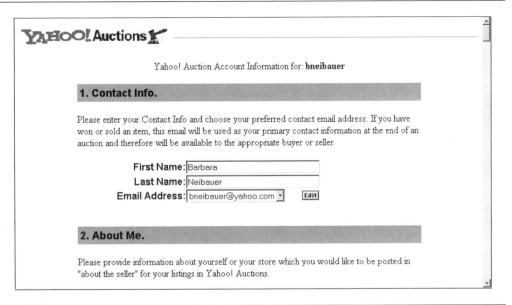

Each positive feedback is counted as 1 point and each negative feedback is counted as negative 1 point. A neutral feedback counts as zero. The total feedback rating appears after the name of each seller and bidder name on an auction page, as shown here.

Seller (rating):	jazzie100 (65)

Of course, you can't please everyone; but, generally speaking, a negative rating indicates that one or more persons have had a bad experience dealing with the seller or buyer. Bidders should think twice about purchasing from a seller with a negative rating or at least ask to use an escrow service as a means of protecting their interests.

If you are a seller, ask a buyer with a negative rating to pay by money order, or wait until the check clears before shipping the item. You can also require bidders with negative ratings to provide credit card verification, or you can block certain bidders so that they cannot participate in your auction.

Note   *Refer to "Checking a Seller's Feedback Rating," later in this chapter, for more information about screening sellers.*

Selling at an Auction

Selling an item at Yahoo! auctions is very easy, but it pays to be prepared before you start.

14

If you have access to a scanner, scan a picture of the item you want to auction. That way, you can include a picture of the item in the listing and make it more attractive to buyers. You can include up to three pictures with each item, but the combined size of the pictures cannot exceed 1.5 MB. To save time, make sure you know the names of the pictures and where they are located on your computer before you upload them.

Tip   *The larger the picture file, the longer it takes potential bidders to download and display it. Try to keep picture files small so you do not discourage bidders.*

You'll need to enter a title and description of the item. Because the title and description help sell an item, choose a title and write the description before you go online. Be sure to thoroughly describe the item so that bidders understand its condition and value.

Note   *Type the title and description offline in a word-processing program or Windows Notepad. You can fine-tune the description without the pressure of being online, and then copy and paste it when you are actually posting the item on Yahoo!.*

You'll also need to enter a starting bid amount, and an optional reserve and buy price. The *starting bid* is the amount of money you want to accept for the first bid. If you make the starting bid too high, potential bidders may be scared off. A *reserve price* is the lowest price for which you are willing to sell the item. If bidding does not reach the reserve price, you are not obligated to sell the item, but you can sell it if you feel that the highest bid is adequate. A *buy price* is a bid amount that will automatically stop the auction and award the item to the person who bid that amount.

Placing an Item Up for Auction

After you've prepared your ad and perhaps scanned a photo or two of the item you want to offer at auction, you can go online and place the item up for bid. If you typed the title and description in your word processor, open the file so you can switch to it and copy the text into the Windows Clipboard.

Connect to Yahoo! and follow these steps to post your item:

1. Click Auctions on the Yahoo! home page to open the page shown here.

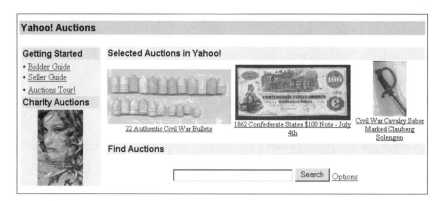

2. Click Submit Item to see a list of categories, as shown next.

Welcome, aneibauer		Submit Item - View Alerts - My Auctions - Options - Sign Out

Yahoo! Auctions

Top > Submissions

Choose a category:

Antiques & Collectibles	Computers	Toys & Games
Advertising	Domain Names	Action Figures
Art	Hardware	Beanbag Collectibles
Autographs	Software	Beanie Babies
Books	Networking	Bears
Clocks & Timepieces		Building Sets
Cultures & Groups	**Electronics & Cameras**	Cards
Disneyana	Amateur Radio	Decorative
Holiday & Seasonal	Audio	Diecast
Home & Garden	Calculators	Dolls
Memorabilia	Cameras & Equipment	Fast Food Toys
Militaria	GPS	Fisher Price
Miscellaneous	Hobbyist	Furby
Numismatics	Laser Pointers	Games
Science & Nature	Phones	Hobbies
Science Fiction	Video	Models
Stamps	Other	Pokemon
Transportation		Science Fiction

Categories are divided into these areas:

■ Antiques & Collectibles
■ Arts & Entertainment
■ Business & Office
■ Clothing & Accessories
■ Computers
■ Electronics & Cameras
■ Home & Garden
■ Sports & Recreation
■ Toys & Games
■ Trading Cards
■ Travel & Transportation
■ Other Goods & Services

3. Under each category are several subcategories, each one a link. Click the name of the subcategory in which the item belongs. You can always go back and choose a different category before submitting the bid. A list of additional subcategories appears. For example, if you are selling a computer book, notice that books are listed under Arts & Entertainment. Clicking Books displays 39 additional categories, some with subcategories by themselves, as shown here on the right.

> Sports
> Baseball, Basketball, Football.

14

4. Work your way through the system, choosing categories that relate to your item, until you see the Submitting An Item form shown in the following illustration.

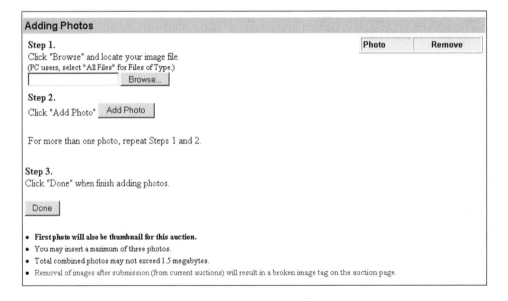

5. If you do not have a photograph to upload, skip to Step 10. Otherwise, to post a photo along with a description of the item you want to offer, click Upload Photos. You see the window shown in the following illustration.

Adding Photos

Step 1.
Click "Browse" and locate your image file.
(PC users, select "All Files" for Files of Type.)
[   ] Browse...

	Photo	Remove

Step 2.
Click "Add Photo" [Add Photo]

For more than one photo, repeat Steps 1 and 2.

Step 3.
Click "Done" when finish adding photos.

[Done]

- **First photo will also be thumbnail for this auction.**
- You may insert a maximum of three photos.
- Total combined photos may not exceed 1.5 megabytes.
- Removal of images after submission (from current auctions) will result in a broken image tag on the auction page.

6. Click the Browse button to open the Windows Choose File dialog box, locate the photo on your computer, and click the Open button.

7. Click Add Photo. Yahoo! copies the photograph from your computer to its system.

8. Repeat Steps 6 and 7 to post another photo, if you want to. You can post three photos at most.

9. Click the Done button.

10. Enter a title for the item. If you typed the title in a word-processing program, switch to the document, and select and copy the text. Switch back to your browser, right-click in the title text box, and select Paste from the shortcut menu.

11. Type a description. You can copy and paste it from a word-processing document.

12. Choose from the Sales Policies options shown here:

Sales Policies:	☑ Accepts Personal Checks	⦿ Buyer Pays Shipping
	☐ Accepts Cashiers Checks and Money Orders	○ Seller Pays Shipping
	☐ Accepts Credit Cards (MC, VISA)	⦿ Ships upon Receipt of Payment
	☐ Prefers to use escrow service	○ Ships on Auction Close

13. Enter the quantity of the item. The quantity refers to the number of bidders who can purchase the item from you. If you have a set of five, for example, and you are selling all five together as a set, enter **1**. Enter more than 1 if you want to sell each of the items to separate bidders.

14. Enter the starting bid.

15. Select the number of days for the auction. The default is 5, but you can also select from 2 to 10 days.

14

You can click Continue now to submit the item, or you can choose from the optional items on the page. Keep reading to learn about them.

Optional Seller Settings

The information you entered so far, except for a photograph, is required to put up an item for auction. The Submitting An Item form, however, includes optional items that you may take advantage of. After selecting any optional item, click Continue to confirm and finalize the submission.

Minimum Bidder Rating

The minimum bidder rating determines if bidders must submit a credit card number to place a bid on an item. The options are 0, None, and All Bidders:

- **0**   Bidders who have a negative rating must submit a credit card number to place a bid. Nothing is placed on their charge, and the charge is not used to complete the transaction. The charge number just helps to eliminate crank bidders and those who have received more negative than positive feedback from sellers and buyers.
- **None**   No bidders must submit a credit card.
- **All Bidders**   Bids are only accepted from bidders who have credit card authorization.

Auto Extension

Frequently, most bids occur in the closing minutes of an auction. Bidders wait until the end to place or raise their bids in the hope that they will bet a better price. Choose the Auto Extension option if you want bidding to be extended automatically for five more minutes when a bid is placed near the end of the auction. This way, last-minute bidders get a chance to win the item.

Allow Early Close

Choose the Allow Early Close option if you want to be able to end the auction before closing time. You may want to close an auction, for example, if you change your mind about selling the item.

Reserve Price

If you want to establish a minimum price for your item, enter it in the Reserve Price text box. If the bidding does not meet the reserve, you are not obliged to sell the item to the highest bidder.

Buy Price

Enter the maximum price you want for the item in the Buy Price box. When a person enters a bid for the buy price, the auction ends and the bidder who entered the buy price is declared the winner. Use this option only if you are in a hurry to sell an item and you are willing to stop the bidding as soon as a certain price is reached.

Closing Time

Choose the time that you want the auction to end in the Closing Time box. Normally, an auction ends a set number of days after you begin it. However, you may want to end your auction during high-traffic hours or evening hours when there is more action. Times are set in Pacific Time.

Auto Resubmit

If no one bids on your item or no bid meets the reserve price, you can automatically resubmit the item. In the Auto Resubmit list, choose the number of times you want to resubmit. The options are from 0 to 5.

Confirming the Submission

When you click the Continue button on the Submitting An Item form, the Item Page appears, as shown in Figure 14-2. The page summarizes the auction information.

The Item Page looks much like the auction page that bidders see. The page has three tabs:

- Item Information
- Bid History
- Question & Answer

Scroll the page and confirm that all the information is correct. At the bottom of the form are two buttons: Back and Submit Auction. Click Back if you need to change something about the item; click Submit Auction to begin the auction online.

The Thank You screen appears and shows the title, quantity, starting bid, and ending time of the auction. There are also links for submitting another item in the same category and viewing the item as it appears in the auction. The link to an auction item looks like this:

http://auctions.yahoo.com/auction/18743141

The number at the end of the link is the unique ID number that is assigned to each item. Make a note of the number in case you need to refer to it later on.

14

FIGURE 14-2   The Item page

The Feature This Auction link on the Thank You page lets you bid for a featured spot on the list of items. Featured items appear at the top of the categories listing page. The featured items are placed in order by the amount sellers pay to be featured. The more you pay, the higher your item appears on the list.

You actually bid for a position on the list, starting at 25 cents per day. You can later increase your bid in 25-cent increments to obtain a better position. Payments for placing an item on the Featured List are made through the Yahoo! Wallet and are billed to your credit card.

Click Feature This Auction for these options shown on the right.

Click the Yes check box, enter the amount you want to bid for a featured position, and click Continue.

> Check My Current Balance
>
> ☐ Yes, I have read the Billing Terms of Service and
> I want to spend $ [   ] per day(for 5.00 days) Continue

Bidding on an Item

Thousands of interesting items are auctioned on Yahoo!. No matter what you collect or what your interests are, you'll probably find at least one item that you want to add to your collection.

There are two steps to finding and winning an item:

1. Locate the item.

2. Place your bid.

Locating Items

To bid on an item, click Auctions on the Yahoo! home page. Then sign in using your Yahoo! ID and password.

Next, you have to find an item worth bidding on. To find an item, you can browse through the categories or perform a search.

You browse through auction categories in much the same way that you look for sites on the Web (Chapter 8 explains how to search the Internet). Select a category on the auction home page and then choose subcategories until you locate a page with the type of article you are looking for, as shown in Figure 14-3.

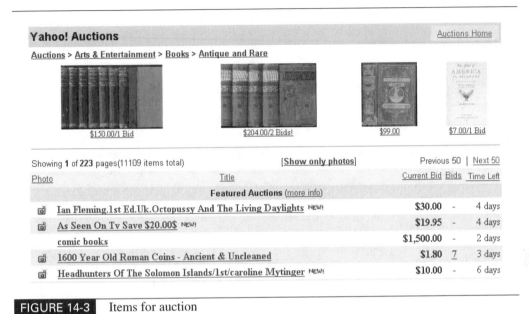

FIGURE 14-3   Items for auction

At the top of a page are photographs from auctions selected at random. Below each photograph is the current bid and the number of bids on the item. Under the photographs are a page number, the total number of pages of items, and the total number of items, as shown here:

Showing 1 of 223 pages (11109 items total)

That notation means that the category contains a total of 11,109 items that are divided into 223 pages, the first of which is being displayed. Scroll the page to see all of the items on it, and click the Previous 50 or Next 50 button to move backward or forward from page to page.

Next on the page are the featured items, and then comes the complete list of items for the category. The items are listed in five columns:

- Photo
- Title
- Current Bid
- Bids (number of bids)
- Time Left

14

Tip *Click Show Only Photos to display thumbnail sketches of all items that have photographs.*

A camera icon appears in the Photo column when a photograph has been uploaded. You can sort the list on any column by clicking the column head. For example, to list items by the amount of time left in the auction, click Time Left.

You can also locate an item by searching for it. To do so, use the search box on any auction page, as shown here:

Enter a word or phrase that describes the item and then choose what you want to search in the pull-down list. The options are All Auctions and Just This Category. After you have made your choice, click Search. One or more pages of items that contain the word or phrase in the title or description will appear.

By clicking the Options link next to the Search box, you can conduct an advanced search or locate an item by its seller or unique ID number.

When you find an item you are interested in, click it to see its complete description. The description page offers an Item Information tab, Bid History tab, and Question & Answer tab, as well as photographs if any were uploaded and other details, as shown in Figure 14-4.

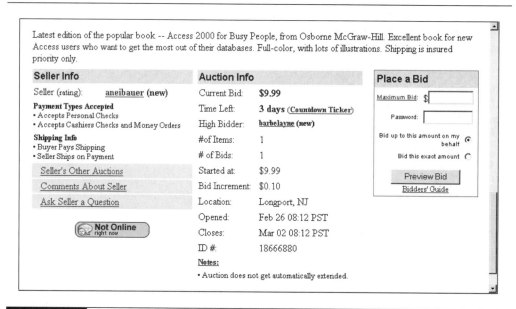

FIGURE 14-4   An item's detail page

On this page, you can click the seller's or high bidder's name if there is one to get information about a seller or bidder. You can also click Countdown Counter to watch the time remaining count down, as shown here:

If you find an item that you think a friend may be interested in, you can send your fiend an e-mail about it. Click E-Mail To A Friend at the top of the page to open the form shown in Figure 14-5. Enter your friend's e-mail address, enter a note about the auction, and click Send E-Mail.

> **Note** *The Add To My Calendar and Add To Watchlist options are discussed in "Tracking Auctions as a Bidder," later in this chapter.*

There are three other links to use that may help you decide if you want to place a bid on an item:

■ **Seller's Other Auctions**   Lists all the items that the seller has up for bid.

14

Email a Friend
New Star Wars / Episode I Neon Poster

To:	_____
	(Separate multiple email addresses with commas ",")
From:	Barbara Neibauer alann@att.net
Subject:	Interesting Yahoo! Auction: New Star Wars / Episode I Neon Poster
Message: (optional)	I saw this item for sale on Yahoo! Auctions, and thought that you might be interested.

Send Email | Clear

FIGURE 14-5   E-mailing a friend about an item being auctioned

■ **Ask Seller A Question** Lets you communicate with the seller to get additional information about the item or the seller's policies. See "Questions and Answers" later in this chapter for more information.

■ **Comments About Seller** Lets you check the seller's feedback rating before you decide to bid.

Checking a Seller's Feedback Rating

Click Comments About Seller to see the Auctions Profile page, as shown in Figure 14-6. The page has three tabs: Rating, Auctions, and About Me.

Go to the Auctions tab to see a list of all the items that the seller has up for bid. The About Me tab shows the seller's About Me text.

The Rating tab is important because it gives an indication of the seller's dependability. It shows the number of positive and negative comments and the seller's total score. By looking at the Auctions With Comments Over Time table, you can review comments made in the past week, past month, and the last six months, as well as the totals.

The summary is followed by the details of each comment, as shown here:

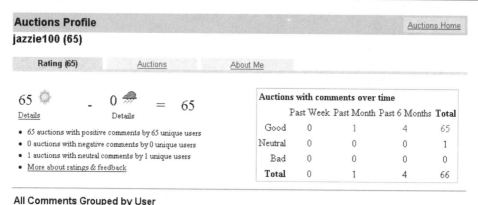

Rated a Excellent ☼ Seller by bktanner13x2 (2)
Cast Iron Dipper (Jan 22 18:48 PST) $10.75
Buyer gives a Excellent Seller rating.
*Comment:*Dipper as advertised; well packed and prompt. (Feb 11 12:07 PST) **(most recent)**

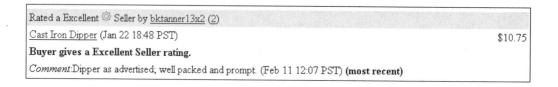

Auctions Profile   Auctions Home
jazzie100 (65)

| Rating (65) | Auctions | About Me |

65 ☼ - 0 🌂 = 65

Details   Details

- 65 auctions with positive comments by 65 unique users
- 0 auctions with negative comments by 0 unique users
- 1 auctions with neutral comments by 1 unique users
- More about ratings & feedback

Auctions with comments over time			
	Past Week	Past Month	Past 6 Months	**Total**
Good	0	1	4	65
Neutral	0	0	0	1
Bad	0	0	0	0
Total	0	1	4	66

All Comments Grouped by User

FIGURE 14-6   Auctions Profile about the seller

The feedback shows the name of the buyer and his or her rating. You also see the title of the item that was purchased and the price that was paid for the item, as well as a comment about the seller. You can click the buyer's ID to see details about a buyer, or click the item title to see details about it.

> **Tip** *Click the Details link under the number of positive or negative comments to list just those comments.*

Placing Your Bid

After you locate an item that you want to bid on, you can make your bid in two ways, with a straight bid or an automatic bid.

A *straight bid* is a fixed amount that you offer for the item. If someone outbids you, you will be notified by e-mail, at which time you'll have to return to the page where the item is found and place a higher bid if you still want the item.

With Automatic Bidding, you enter the highest amount you are willing to pay for the item. Yahoo! places the bid for you at the next highest increment over the current high bid. The seller and other bidders are not made aware of your maximum bid. For example, suppose $10 has been bid for an item and the increment is 25 cents. If you enter an automatic bid of $15, your offer is posted at $10.25. If another bidder offers $10.50, your bid is increased to $10.75.

> **Caution** *The high bid for any item can quickly increase to the maximum amount if other bidders are using automatic bidding as well.*

You place your bid in the Place A Bid section of the item's page. Follow these steps:

1. Enter the amount of a fixed or maximum bid in the Maximum Bid box.

2. Choose whether you want Yahoo! to bid up to the amount or enter it as a fixed bid.

3. Click Preview Bid. You are asked to confirm the bid, as in the following illustration. If you did not bid at least the required increment, you'll be told as much and be given the chance to increase your bid.

14

You Must Confirm Your Bid to Continue

Auction: Access 2000 for Busy People - GREAT BOOK!
Auction ID: 18666880
Last Bid: $9.99 (Automatic)
Your Bid: $9.99 how bidding works
Quantity: 1
Comment: (Optional) This will be displayed to the other bidders.

[Place This Bid] [Cancel]

4. Click the Place This Bid button.

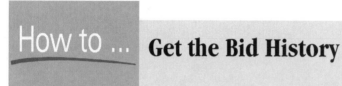

Get the Bid History

Click Bid History to see the ID of each bidder, the amount of the bid, and the time of the bid, as shown here:

Bidder	Comment	Bid Amount	Quantity	Initial Bid
azakuto_2000 (new) HIGHEST	-	$10.09	1	Feb 28 06:52 PST
barbelayne (new)	-	$9.99	1	Feb 27 06:51 PST

You can then click Advanced Bid History to see a detailed log of the entire auction history, as shown here:

[Feb 28 06:52 PST] azakuto_2000 places proxy bid at 10.09

[Feb 28 06:52 PST] azakuto_2000 places bid for 1 at 9.99

[Feb 27 06:51 PST] places bid for barbelayne 1 at 9.99

[Feb 26 08:12 PST] Auction created with quantity 1 at 9.99

A message appears confirming the bid and telling you whether you are the high bidder. Yahoo! will also send you an e-mail to confirm your bid. It will also send you an e-mail if you are later outbid.

Questions and Answers

Before placing a bid, you may need more information than is presented in the title and description of an item, not to mention its photograph. The Question & Answer tab lets you communicate with the seller to get additional information about an item and learn about the seller's policies.

To ask the seller a question, click the Question & Answer tab, as shown in Figure 14-7. Type your question about the item and click the Submit Question button.

Yahoo! e-mails the question to the seller and posts the question on the Question & Answer tab for everyone to read.

The seller receives the question in an e-mail message. The message includes a link to a site, as shown here. The seller can click the link and respond to the question (see Figure 14-8):

To respond to this question you will need to be logged in to Yahoo! Auctions. Then go to this URL:

http://auctions.yahoo.com/show/qanda?aID=18666880

If you are a seller and are sent a question, first sign in to Yahoo! and then click the link to see the page shown in Figure 14-8. Each question is numbered. Select the number of the question

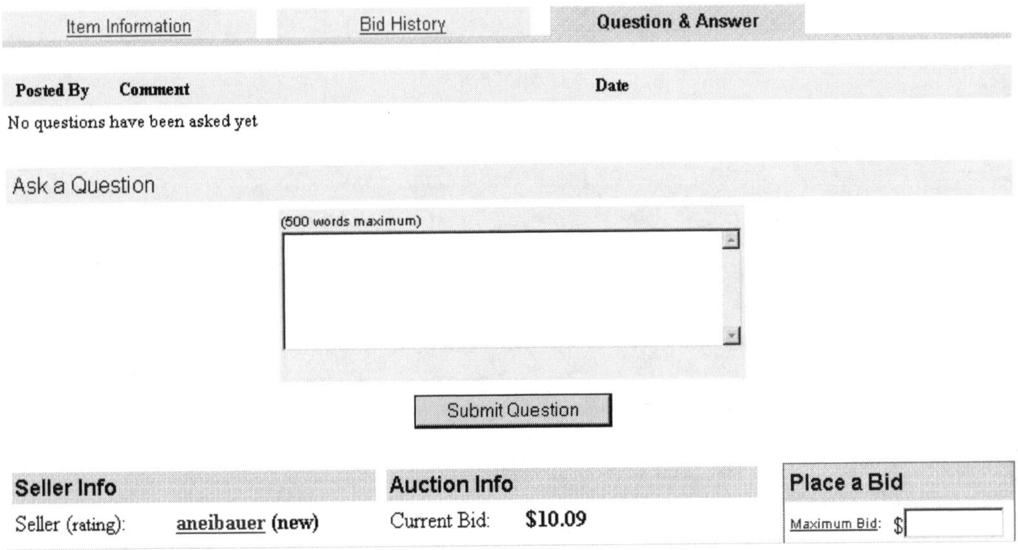

Item Information	Bid History	**Question & Answer**

Posted By Comment		Date

No questions have been asked yet

Ask a Question

(500 words maximum)

[Submit Question]

Seller Info	Auction Info	Place a Bid
Seller (rating): **aneibauer (new)**	Current Bid: **$10.09**	Maximum Bid: $

FIGURE 14-7   Asking the seller a question

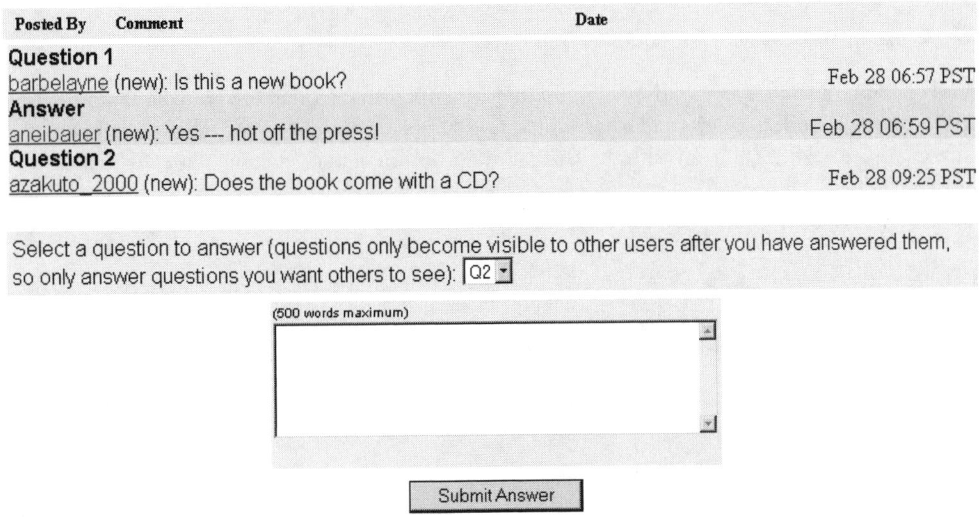

Posted By Comment	Date
Question 1	
barbelayne (new): Is this a new book?	Feb 28 06:57 PST
Answer	
aneibauer (new): Yes --- hot off the press!	Feb 28 06:59 PST
Question 2	
azakuto_2000 (new): Does the book come with a CD?	Feb 28 09:25 PST

Select a question to answer (questions only become visible to other users after you have answered them, so only answer questions you want others to see): Q2 ▾

(500 words maximum)

[Submit Answer]

FIGURE 14-8   Responding to a bidder's question

14

you want to answer from the pull-down list (Q1, Q2, and so on), enter your response, and click the Submit Answer button.

Yahoo! posts the answer on the Questions & Answers tab and e-mails the answer to the bidder.

Tracking Auctions as a Bidder

Once you find an auction that you are interested in, you may want to keep track of it. Perhaps you have considered bidding on the item being auctioned. Or you merely want to see how the bidding is going.

One way to track an auction is to add it to your *watchlist*. A watchlist is a list of auctions that you can quickly access.

From an item's page, click Add To Watchlist to see a page similar to the one in Figure 14-9. The page shows all the items that you added to your watchlist, ID numbers, titles, current bids, the IDs of high bidders, and how much time is left in each aution. Click the title to go directly to the item. To remove an item from the list, select its check box and click the Remove button.

Whenever you want to view your watchlist, click My Auctions at the top of any auction page and then click Watchlist.

Use the links at the top of the watchlist to access other ways to look at items:

- **Info**   Displays the My Auctions menu
- **Bidding**   Lists items on which you have placed bids
- **Selling**   Lists items that you are selling
- **Won**   Lists auctions that you have won
- **Closed/Sold**   Lists your auctions that have been completed

You can access these same options by clicking My Auctions to open the page shown in Figure 14-10. The Bulk Loader and Order Manager options are for sellers who have established a business account with Yahoo!. With the Bulk Loader option, a person can enter information

My Auctions				Auctions Home

Info - **Watchlist** - Bidding - Selling - Won - Closed/Sold

Remove | checked items.

	ID#	Title	Current Bid	High Bidder	Time Left
☐	17920698	New Star Wars / Episode I Neon Poster	$139.99	-	30 min
☐	18666880	Access 2000 for Busy People - GREAT BOOK!	$11.09	barbelayne	2 days

Remove | checked items.

FIGURE 14-9   A watchlist

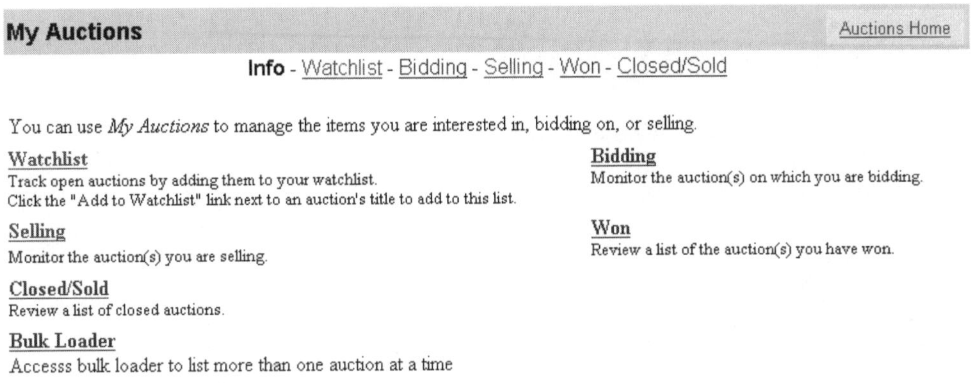

My Auctions   Auctions Home

Info - Watchlist - Bidding - Selling - Won - Closed/Sold

You can use *My Auctions* to manage the items you are interested in, bidding on, or selling.

Watchlist   **Bidding**
Track open auctions by adding them to your watchlist.   Monitor the auction(s) on which you are bidding.
Click the "Add to Watchlist" link next to an auction's title to add to this list.

Selling   **Won**
Monitor the auction(s) you are selling.   Review a list of the auction(s) you have won.

Closed/Sold
Review a list of closed auctions.

Bulk Loader
Accesss bulk loader to list more than one auction at a time

FIGURE 14-10   My Auctions page

about many items and then post them all onto the auction pages in one step. The Order Manager option, which only appears on the My Auctions page if you are seller, is used to track orders and credit card invoices.

Auction Alerts

As you learned in Chapter 7, you can create an alert and have Yahoo! remind you of some activity by e-mail, by Yahoo! Messenger, or by pager. You can also create alerts to stay informed about auctions that you are interested in.

From any Yahoo! Auction page, click View Alerts to see the page shown in Figure 14-11. If you have already created alerts, they appear on the page.

You can create these types of alerts:

- **Category Alert**   Informs you when an item is added to the category of your choice.
- **Seller Alert**   Informs you when a specific seller offers an item.
- **Keyword Alert**   Informs you when an item is up for auction and its description includes keywords that you specify in the title.

Click the type of alert you want, and then complete the prompts that appear onscreen.

If you choose a category alert, for example, a list of Yahoo! auction categories appears. Click a category to display its subcategories, continue selecting subcategories until you find the one that you want, and then click this link:

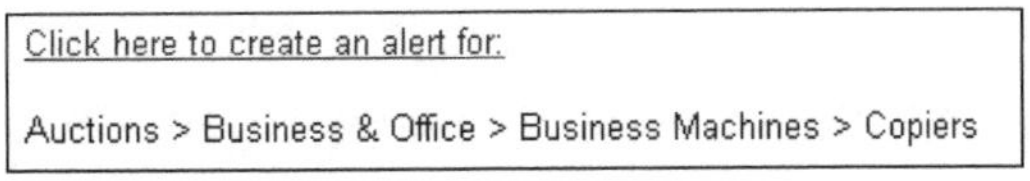

Click here to create an alert for:

Auctions > Business & Office > Business Machines > Copiers

14

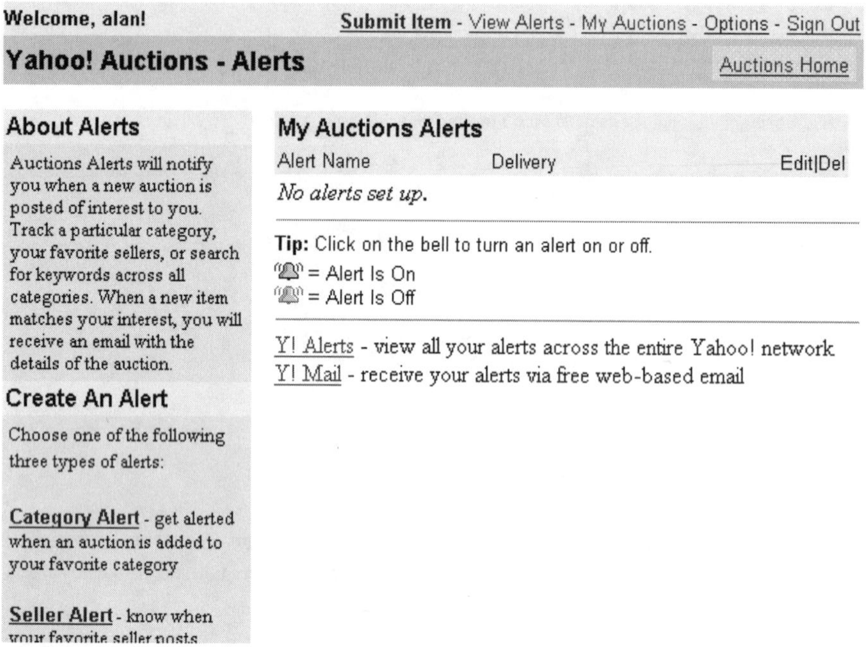

Welcome, alan! Submit Item - View Alerts - My Auctions - Options - Sign Out

Yahoo! Auctions - Alerts Auctions Home

About Alerts

Auctions Alerts will notify you when a new auction is posted of interest to you. Track a particular category, your favorite sellers, or search for keywords across all categories. When a new item matches your interest, you will receive an email with the details of the auction.

Create An Alert

Choose one of the following three types of alerts:

Category Alert - get alerted when an auction is added to your favorite category

Seller Alert - know when your favorite seller posts

My Auctions Alerts

Alert Name   Delivery   Edit|Del
No alerts set up.

Tip: Click on the bell to turn an alert on or off.
🔔 = Alert Is On
🔔 = Alert Is Off

Y! Alerts - view all your alerts across the entire Yahoo! network
Y! Mail - receive your alerts via free web-based email

FIGURE 14-11 Creating auction alerts

The Yahoo! Auctions—Alerts page opens, as shown in Figure 14-12.
Create an alert by following these steps:

1. Enter a name to identify the alert.
2. Select whether you want to be alerted to any item in the category or just those that contain certain keywords that you specify.
3. Enter the e-mail address where the alert is to be sent.
4. Choose when the alert should be sent to you.
5. Click the Finished button.

If you select a Seller Alert, enter the ID of the seller in the page that appears and then click Create Alert to display the Yahoo! Auctions—Alerts page.

If you select a Keyword Alert, the Yahoo! Auctions Alerts page appears. There, you can enter the keywords to watch for.

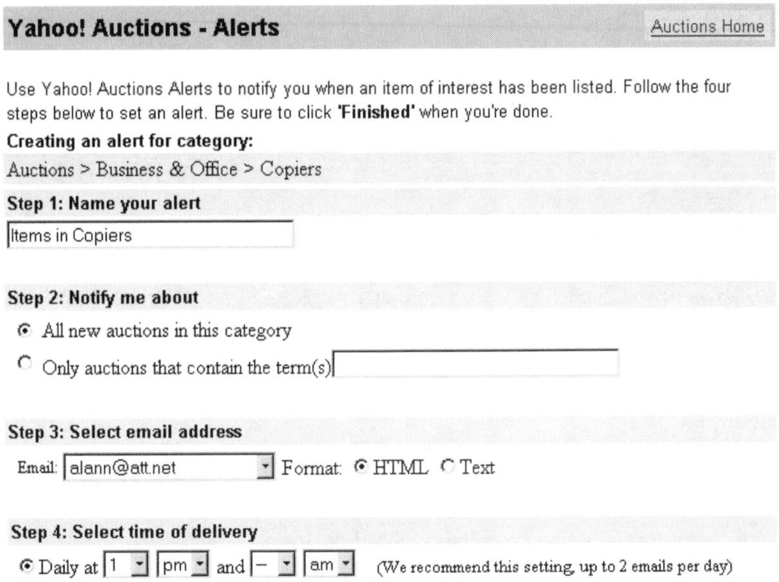

Yahoo! Auctions - Alerts   Auctions Home

Use Yahoo! Auctions Alerts to notify you when an item of interest has been listed. Follow the four steps below to set an alert. Be sure to click **'Finished'** when you're done.

Creating an alert for category:

Auctions > Business & Office > Copiers

Step 1: Name your alert

Items in Copiers

Step 2: Notify me about

(•) All new auctions in this category

(○) Only auctions that contain the term(s)

Step 3: Select email address

Email: alann@att.net   ▾ Format: (•) HTML (○) Text

Step 4: Select time of delivery

(•) Daily at 1 ▾ pm ▾ and - ▾ am ▾   (We recommend this setting, up to 2 emails per day)

FIGURE 14-12   The Yahoo! Auctions – Alerts page

Managing Auctions as a Seller

As a seller, you can use the My Auctions and Alerts pages to keep informed about your auctions and other auctions as well. You can also make changes to your auction and take other steps through the Manage option.

When sellers view one of their auction items, they see a report on the item page similar to the one shown here at right.

The report shows the number of times the page has been opened, how many times it has been e-mailed to a friend, and how many times it has been added to a watchlist. There are also links to feature the item and perform management options.

You can also access the Manage options in the My Auctions page by following these steps:

You are the Seller:

Total Pageviews: **18**

Total Emails to a Friend Sent: **0**

Total Times added to a Watchlist: **1**

Click here to manage this auction.

1. Click My Auctions.

2. Click Selling to see the list of items that you are auctioning.

ID#	Title	Current Bid	High Bidder	Time Left To Do
18666880	Access 2000 for Busy People - GREAT BOOK!	$11.09	barbelayne	2 days [Manage]

3. Click Manage at the end of the list in the To Do column to see the option, as in the following illustration.

Access 2000 for Busy People GREAT BOOK   <u>Auctions Home</u>

Number of pageviews for this auction: -   <u>Back to My Auctions</u>

<u>Get Featured</u>
Bid on featured spots to promote your auction.

<u>Cancel Auction</u>
If your auction has no bids you may cancel it.

<u>Close Auction</u>
If your auction has bids and you chose the "Close Auction Early" option at the time of submission, you may cancel your auction by clicking here.

<u>Cancel Bid</u>
You may cancel an individual's bid.

<u>Edit Auction Description</u>
You may edit the item description.

<u>Edit Your Personal Blacklist</u>
Block bogus bidders permanently from participating in your auctions. Click here to update or edit your personal blacklist.

The Get Featured option lets you bid on a featured position.

Use the Cancel Auction item to withdraw an item from an auction. You can withdraw an item as long as no bids were placed on it. Click Cancel Auction, and then click Confirm Cancel.

To stop an auction before its ending time, choose Close Auction and then click Confirm Close. You can only close an auction early, however, if you selected the Allow Early Close option when you put your item up for bid.

Use the Cancel Bid option to remove a person's bid from an auction. You might want to cancel a person's bid if you feel that the bidder is not serious or you want to close an auction that already has bids. Choose Cancel Bid to open the item's bid history. Click Cancel after the person's name, and then click Confirm Bid Cancel. From this screen, you can also add the person's name to your blacklist so that he or she cannot bid on any item you put up for auction.

The Edit Auction Description option opens the Update Item page. From there, you can upload an item, write more descriptions, change your sales policy, and take advantage of other options as well. Click Continue to confirm the changes.

The Edit Your Personal Blacklist option is for adding people to and removing persons from your blacklist. The vast majority of bidders are serious buyers, but some Yahoo! members bid frivolously and don't actually make purchases. If you identify such people, you can add their names to a blacklist, and thereby prevent them from bidding on your items. Select Edit Your Personal Blacklist, and, in the page that appears, type the person's Yahoo! ID and click Add To Blacklist. To remove a person, select the check box next to his or her name and then click Delete.

Note   *If you encounter a frivolous bidder who wins your item but does not pay, be sure to leave a negative feedback as well as add the person to your blacklist.*

Auction Options

As with most parts of Yahoo!, you can customize certain features that pertain to auctions. Click Options on any Auction page to see the options shown in Figure 14-13. The options are divided into three areas: Personal Information, Notification, and Seller Options.

Under Personal Information, click the Edit Contact Information option if you want to change the name and e-mail address that you maintain for auctions. Click Edit "About Me" Profile to change the information that appears on your About Me page.

Notification Options

Use the Notification options to determine when and how Yahoo! sends you information about auctions. Click Set Event Notification to display the page shown in Figure 14-14.

Use the Email Address box to specify where e-mail notifications should be sent, then use the options under Step 2: Notification Preferences to determine when and where e-mails are sent. E-mail messages can be sent to your e-mail address, as instant messages when you are logged on to Yahoo! Messenger, or to your pager.

The Notification Preferences section is divided into three categories:

- As both a buyer and seller
- As a bidder
- As a seller

Options   Auctions Home

Personal Information	Notification	Seller Options
Edit Contact Information	**Set Event Notification**	**Customize My Auctions Booth**
Update or verify your email address.	Receive email when an auction you are bidding on or selling has changed status.	Seller, customize the look of your personal Yahoo! Auctions Booth.
Edit "About Me" Profile	**Set Auction Alerts**	**Edit Blacklist**
Personalize your "About Me" section of your Auction Profile.	Receive email for a particular listing and/or when a selected seller has posted a new auction.	Seller, block selected bidders from participating in your auctions.
		Customize Winning Emails
		Seller, customize the email sent to the winning bidder.
		Billing Summary
		Check my billing summary.

FIGURE 14-13   Yahoo! auction options

14

Options - Notification Options   Auctions Home

Step 1. Contact Information

Email Address: | alann@att.net | ▼ | Edit Email Addresses

If you have won or sold an item, this email will be used as your primary contact information at the end of an auction and therefore will be available to the appropriate buyer or seller.

Have auctions notifications sent to your cell phone or pager. Click here to **configure your device**.

Step 2. Notification Preferences

Select whether you want to be notified via email, Yahoo! Messenger or an alpha-numeric pager (or any combination of those) regarding auctions you are involved in. You will need the latest version of Yahoo! Messenger.

As both a Buyer and a Seller:

Email	Messenger	My Pager	Instance
☑	☐	☐	**Auction Closed** - Sent when an auction you're involved with closes.
☑	☐	☐	**Rating Notification** - Sent whenever anyone leaves feedback on you

As a Bidder:

Email	Messenger	My Pager	Instance
☑	☐	☐	**Outbid** - Sent when you have been outbid by another user on an auction

FIGURE 14-14   Event Notification options

As both a buyer and seller, you can be notified that an auction has closed and when someone has left feedback about you.

As a bidder, you can be notified when you are outbid, when your bid has been declared a winner if the previous high bid is disqualified, when a seller has canceled your bid, when an auction has been canceled, and when a seller has responded to your question.

As a seller, you can be notified when your auction has been created, when a bidder leaves a question, and when your auction has been resubmitted.

Select the check boxes for the notifications you want, deselect the check boxes to turn off notifications, and then click Submit at the bottom of the page.

Note   *The Set Auction Alerts link on the Options page lets you create or remove auction alerts. How to do that is described in "Auction Alerts," earlier in this chapter.*

Seller Options

The Seller Options let you customize how your auctions operate and appear onscreen. You can create a customize page with your own logo to display your items, called an Auction Booth; customize the notification sent to winners; and edit your bidder blacklist.

Your Auction Booth

Each seller has a special page called the Auction Booth in which his or her auction items appear. People can access the booth by going to this address, where *your-ID* is the Yahoo! user ID:

http://auctions.yahoo.com/booth/*your-ID*

You can place a custom logo and title on the Auction Booth page. You can also designate a Web site such that clicking your logo opens your Web site. Follow these steps to customize your Auction Booth:

 The logo must be in the .gif or .jpg format, be no higher than 35 pixels, and be no wider than 300 pixels.

1. Click Customize My Auctions Booth to open the page shown next.

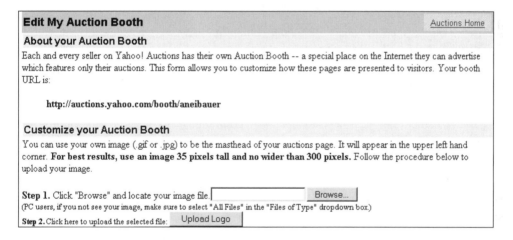

Edit My Auction Booth   Auctions Home

About your Auction Booth

Each and every seller on Yahoo! Auctions has their own Auction Booth -- a special place on the Internet they can advertise which features only their auctions. This form allows you to customize how these pages are presented to visitors. Your booth URL is:

http://auctions.yahoo.com/booth/aneibauer

Customize your Auction Booth

You can use your own image (.gif or .jpg) to be the masthead of your auctions page. It will appear in the upper left hand corner. **For best results, use an image 35 pixels tall and no wider than 300 pixels.** Follow the procedure below to upload your image.

Step 1. Click "Browse" and locate your image file. [   ] Browse...

(PC users, if you not see your image, make sure to select "All Files" in the "Files of Type" dropdown box.)

Step 2. Click here to upload the selected file: Upload Logo

2. Under Step 1, click Browse, locate and select the .gif or .jpg logo file, and click Open.

3. Click Upload Logo.

4. Enter a heading in the Your Booth Title box.

5. Enter a URL in the Your Website URL box. When a person clicks your logo, the site specified in this URL will be displayed.

6. Click Update My Booth to display the booth. Clicking the custom logo opens the URL you entered in the Your Website URL box.

 When you view your own Auction Booth, you can click the Edit My Seller's Page link to make changes to your booth.

14

The Edit My Auctions Booth page also offers a Promote Your Auction Booth section in which you will find sample add banners and HTML code that you can use to place the banner on your Web site. Clicking a banner takes visitors to your Auction Booth.

Editing Your Blacklist

Use the Edit Your Blacklist option to add bidders' names to or remove bidders' names from your blacklist. Remember, persons on your blacklist will be prevented from bidding on the items that you auction.

Customize Winning E-Mails

When a bidder wins one of your auction items, he or she is sent a form e-mail from Yahoo!. You can customize the e-mail to include information such as a personal thank you, a note about your billing policies, or a link to your Web site.

Choose Customize Winning E-Mails on the Options page. In the page that appears, enter your personal message and then click the Finish button.

 The Billing Summary and Bulk Loader Options are advanced features used by persons who maintain a Yahoo! store.

Finalizing the Sale

When the auction is over, the seller and high bidder are notified by e-mail and told to contact each other to complete the sale. They should then make arrangements to exchange the payment and ship the merchandize.

Besides informing the buyer and seller that the sale is complete, the e-mail message contains a link to the closed auction page, as shown here:

> 2. LOOK UP WINNER(S)
>
> Winner(s) email addresses are provided on the closed auction page. We encourage you to contact your winner(s) promptly. Prompt responses and transactions will ensure a happy customer.
>
> http://auctions.yahoo.com/auction/18666880

The actual page to which the link goes depends on whether you are the seller or buyer, but it contains instructions for completing the transaction and a link that you can click to leave a comment.

The seller's closed auction page presents information about the high bidder and a list of other bidders. The other bidders, called Reserved Bidders, can be contacted if the high bidder fails to complete the transaction.

When the transaction is complete, the buyer and seller should leave feedback on each other. From the buyer's closed auction page, click the link to comment on your experience. From the seller's closed auction page, click the Leave Feedback link after the high bidder's name.

Choose a rating for the individual: Excellent, Good, Average, Poor, or Bad. Then type a comment up to 255 characters long. Click Rate Seller or Rate Buyer to display a buyer or seller's feedback page, as shown earlier in Figure 14-6.

Chapter 15

Shopping on Yahoo!

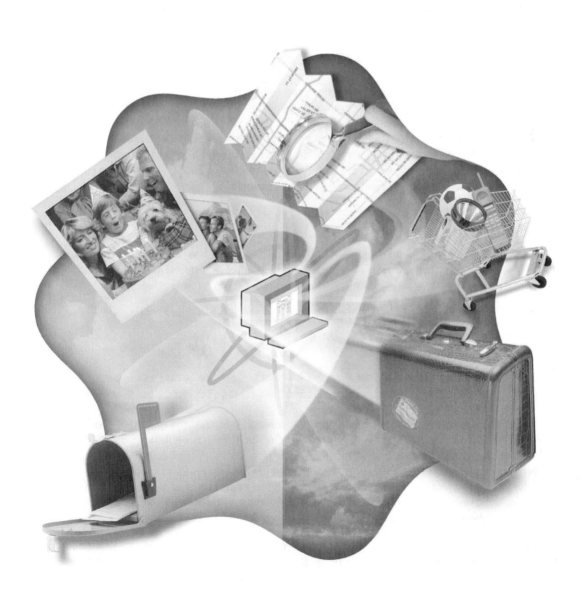

How to . . .

- ■ Shop for items
- ■ Compare prices
- ■ Check the status of orders
- ■ Create a Yahoo! wallet
- ■ Create a gift registry
- ■ Earn Yahoo! points
- ■ Redeem Yahoo! points

Forget about standing in department store lines and fighting for parking spots in crowded parking lots. The Internet has marshaled in the era of e-commerce so that you can shop from the comfort of your home or office. With Yahoo! Shopping, you can locate products of all types, compare merchants to get the best price, and have merchandise delivered directly to your door.

Yahoo! lets you create a gift registry, a wish list of items you'd like to have that friends and relatives can purchase for you with a click of a mouse. And with Yahoo!, you can even earn free merchandise by shopping online and earning Yahoo! points.

Yahoo! Shopping

Start your shopping trip from the Yahoo! Shopping area of the Yahoo! home page. From there, you can access several departments or categories of items, featured stores, and products that are listed that day.

Yahoo! Shopping - Thousands of stores. Millions of products.		
Departments	**Stores**	**Products**
· Apparel · Flowers	· Sports Authority	· Digital cameras
· Bath/Beauty · Food/Drink	· Gap	· Pokemon
· Computers · Music	· Eddie Bauer	· MP3 players
· Electronics · Video/DVD	· Macy's	· DVD players

Selecting a category is like visiting a large department store. You get access to items in the department and can choose subcategories until you find the item you want. Items come from a variety of merchants that have arrangements with Yahoo!. By shopping through departments, you can compare prices from different merchants and get the best prices for items.

By choosing a featured store from the Yahoo! Shopping section, you can access all of the items sold by a specific merchant. You can then browse through the merchant's online catalog and place orders.

Note   *Some online merchants also have retail stores or printed catalogs. Not all of the same merchandise may be available from all of the sources. You may be able to purchase a product online that is not available in person, or visa versa.*

The Yahoo! Shopping section also features several specific types of items. Choose one of these items to see specific brands and models that are being sold by Yahoo! merchants.

To access all of Yahoo!'s shopping features, however, click Yahoo! Shopping. You go to the main shopping page shown in Figure 15-1. This is the best place to start an online shopping trip because it gives you access to a variety of items and specials.

Shopping Carts and Wallets

As you select items to purchase on Yahoo!, items are grouped into shopping carts, with one cart for each merchant. You can view each cart individually to place items in it or remove items from it, as well as finalize a purchase at checkout time.

Each cart is independent of the other, so finalizing one order does not commit you to finalizing another. Your credit card information is not copied from one merchant to the other, but securely transmitted directly to each individual merchant.

If you shop regularly with Yahoo!, you might find it bothersome to enter your credit card and shipping information with each order. In that case, you can create a Yahoo! *wallet,* a secure site that stores a copy of your credit card information and provides it automatically to a merchant when you check out. The information is stored online in a secure site at Yahoo! so you can access your wallet from any computer.

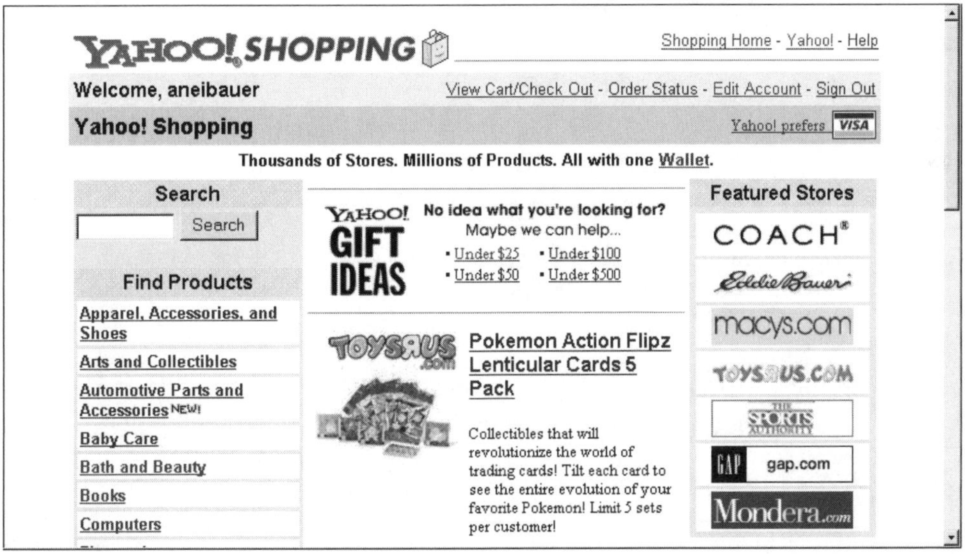

FIGURE 15-1   The Yahoo! Shopping home page

Finding a Product

If you simply want to browse, you can search through Yahoo! by department. Searching by department is much like searching through categories to locate information or auction items. You can start the search in two ways:

■ Click the department in the Yahoo! Shopping section of the Yahoo! home page.

■ Select a department from the categories in the Find Products section of the Yahoo! Shopping home page.

A page that shows subcategories of items in the department will appear. Continue selecting subcategories until you locate the specific type of item you are interested in purchasing.

For example, suppose you're looking for a small gift for a friend with a sweet tooth who likes to cook and bake. You would follow these steps to choose a gift:

1. Select the Food and Beverages category to display categories and featured items, as shown in the following illustration. The subcategories are listed in the Find Products section, with featured products and stores in the current category to its right.

2. Click Baked Goods in the Find Products list to display a list of items in that category. The path you took to get to each shopping page, by the way, is shown at the top.

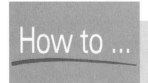 **Search by Keyword**

You can also locate products by entering a keyword in the Search box. Enter the keyword and click the Search button. A page with a list of all items that match the keyword appears. You can then select an item to display additional information and complete the purchase.

3. Click Cakes in the Find Products section to open a page that lists cake items.

4. Click Cake Mix in the Find Products section to see the individual items in the subcategory of your selections, as shown next.

The top of the page shows the total number of items in the subcategory and the number of merchants who are represented.

By default, the items are listed by relevance to the subcategory. In this example search, therefore, all cake mixes are listed first, and then related items are listed. You can choose to display the items in a specific price range or sort the entire list by price. Use this line, for example, to choose the range of prices you are interested in:

(Or, Show Me Products in this Price Range: **$0-$1** [23], **$1-$2** [61], **$2-$5** [28], **$5-$13** [27], **$14-$50** [17], **$50-$350** [5])

Each link for a price range is followed by the number of items in that range. In our example search, there are 23 items in the $0 to $1 range, and 61 items in the $1 to $2 range, and so on. Use a price range listing to display only items in the price range of your choice.

The price ranges that are listed for a category of items are based on the overall range of prices and the number of products. Price ranges do not take into account sales taxes or the costs of shipping. Those costs, if they apply, are added to the total when you check out.

As an alternative to listing items by price range, you can sort the entire list in ascending or descending order by price. To do so, use these options:

sort listing by: relevance | increasing price | decreasing price

15

Each item in a category appears like this:

The name of the item is followed by its price, a photograph or drawing, and the name of the merchant who is offering the item. If the merchant in question offers similar products, a link similar to the one shown on the right appears above the merchant's name so you can click the link and display all of the items.

See all **5 matches** at

To read more about a product or to purchase it, click its name. You are taken to the merchant's Web site within the Yahoo! shopping area. From this point forward, the Web sites that appear and the options you are offered vary from merchant to merchant. Usually, however, clicking the name of an item takes you to a Web page where the item is described, its price is listed, and links to the merchant's other Web pages appear. Of course, the Web page invariably includes a button that you can click to purchase the item. On merchants' Web pages, the Order button is sometimes labeled Add To Cart, Submit Order, or something similar.

Click the Order button, Add To Cart button, or a button with a similar name to display the merchant's shopping cart, as shown in the following illustration. Again, the arrangement of the cart depends on the merchant you are dealing with. Typically, the cart shows all of the items that you are purchasing from the merchant and the total purchase price.

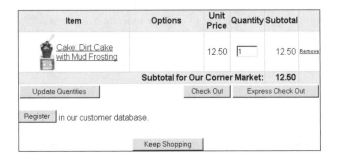

Note *Displaying the shopping cart does not yet place the order. You can still change your mind by removing items from the cart or discontinuing the process.*

Usually, you find a Quantity column that shows how many items you ordered. You can change the quantity and recalculate the totals by editing the number and then clicking the Update Quantities button, Update Cart button, or a similarly named button.

There will also be a button labeled Continue Shopping, Keep Shopping, or something similar. Click this button if you want to select other items before finalizing the purchase. After you click it, you go back to the merchant's site or another Yahoo! shopping page where you can continue looking for items.

Caution *Check the quantity for each item every time you view the shopping cart.*

When you are ready to finalize and make your purchases, click Check Out or Express Checkout from the shopping cart. Use the Express Checkout button if you have already created a Yahoo! wallet in which your credit card and shipping information has been saved.

After you click the Check Out button, pages appear in which you enter your mailing address, enter credit card information, and choose shipping information. You can then click Continue to display the final invoice and print it for your records.

Note *You will receive an e-mail confirmation of the order.*

Checking the Status of Orders and Shopping Carts

When you are looking at a merchant's invoice, you may see the options shown here:

> Welcome, aneibauer   Order Status - Privacy Policy - Edit Acct - Sign Out
> Shopping Carts: Our Corner Market - The Renovated Home - View All Carts

Use the Order Status option to list orders you placed recently through Yahoo! Shopping, shown next. Click a merchant's name to see all of the orders you placed with the merchant. Click Order ID to see the details of a particular order.

Welcome, aneibauer		Order Status - Edit Acct - Shopping Carts - Sign Out
Order Status		Yahoo! prefers **VISA**

Sign up for Yahoo! Wallet
Save time shopping - store your billing and shipping information for future purchases.

Shopping Carts		Order Status	
Store	**Date**	**Order ID**	
Our Corner Market	1-Mar-2000	ourcornermarket2-514	
Calyx & Corolla	5-Feb-2000	cc1725-1043	

Use the Edit Acct option to change your Yahoo! account information. Use the Sign Out option to cancel all of your current items.

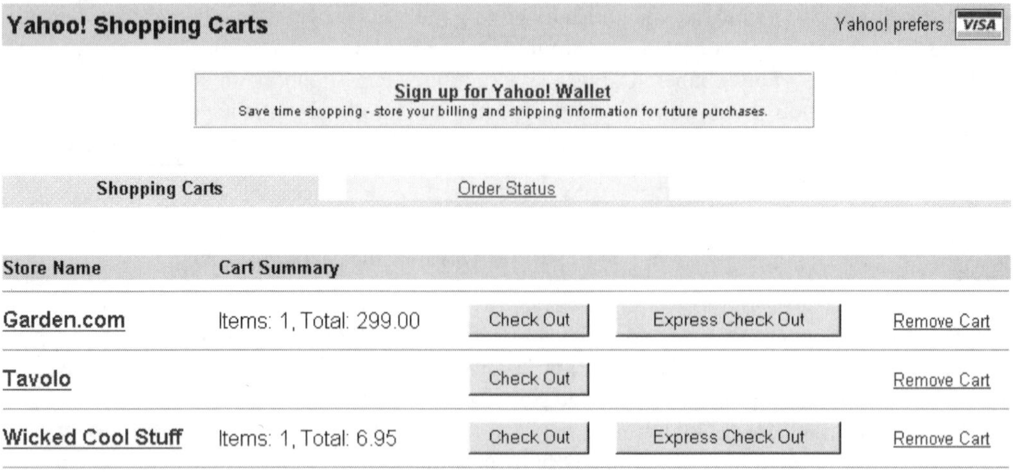

Yahoo! Shopping Carts   Yahoo! prefers `VISA`

<u>**Sign up for Yahoo! Wallet**</u>
Save time shopping - store your billing and shipping information for future purchases.

Shopping Carts	Order Status

Store Name	Cart Summary			
Garden.com	Items: 1, Total: 299.00	Check Out	Express Check Out	Remove Cart
Tavolo		Check Out		Remove Cart
Wicked Cool Stuff	Items: 1, Total: 6.95	Check Out	Express Check Out	Remove Cart

FIGURE 15-2   Shopping carts that contain items

There is also a list of all open shopping carts and an option called View All Carts. Select a shopping cart to view its contents or change the checkout order. Click View All Carts for a list of all carts, as shown in Figure 15-2.

The Yahoo! Shopping Carts page shows each merchant's name and the number and total price of the items in each cart, as well as links for checking out. Click Remove Cart to delete the cart and all of its items.

There are links to shopping carts and order status information on most Yahoo! shopping pages.

Yahoo! Wallet

If you do not want to enter your credit card number and shipping address with each order, you can sign up for a free Yahoo! wallet. The wallet stores your credit card and shipping information in a secure site. When you check out, the information is transferred to a merchant using the standard Secure Sockets Layer (SSL) technology. You can use the wallet with the standard or express checkout options.

You can also use the wallet to pay for other Yahoo! charges, such as purchasing additional online storage, or paying for auction fees for featuring an item, or maintaining an auction merchant account.

When you buy items with the Express Checkout service, the amount is automatically charged to your account. For safety, however, the item you purchase can only be shipped to the address that is stored in the wallet. So use Express Checkout only if you do not have special shipping instructions or unusual requirements for the order.

When you sign up for the wallet, you're asked to enter a special security code word. To access your wallet, you submit the security code word. The security code is saved in a "secure cookie" that is transferred to Yahoo! over SSL but automatically expires after one hour for security purposes.

To sign up for the Yahoo! wallet, click a Wallet link such as this one on the Yahoo! Shopping home page:

> **Thousands of Stores. Millions of Products. All with one Wallet.**

In the page that appears, click Get Started Now to display the sign-up form shown in Figure 15-3, and then follow these steps:

1. Enter your Yahoo! password and ID if you have not yet logged on to Yahoo!.

2. Enter and retype a security keyword.

3. Enter the requested credit card information, including the card's type, number, and expiration date.

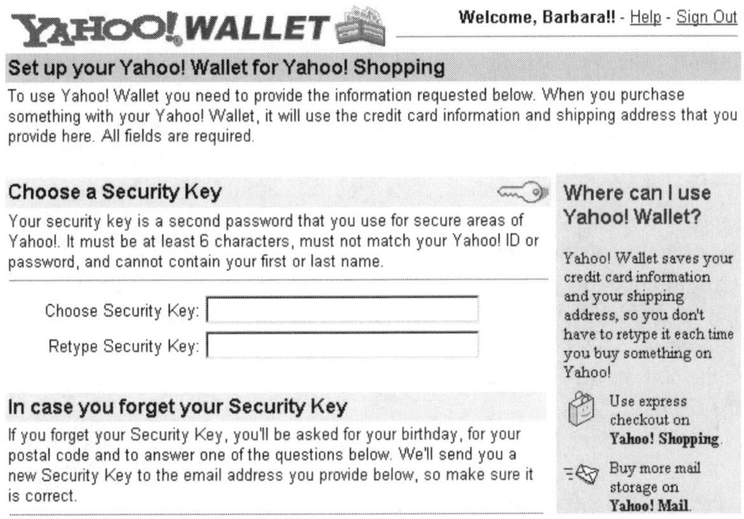

YAHOO! WALLET   Welcome, Barbara!! - Help - Sign Out

Set up your Yahoo! Wallet for Yahoo! Shopping

To use Yahoo! Wallet you need to provide the information requested below. When you purchase something with your Yahoo! Wallet, it will use the credit card information and shipping address that you provide here. All fields are required.

Choose a Security Key

Your security key is a second password that you use for secure areas of Yahoo!. It must be at least 6 characters, must not match your Yahoo! ID or password, and cannot contain your first or last name.

Choose Security Key: [＿＿＿＿＿＿]

Retype Security Key: [＿＿＿＿＿＿]

In case you forget your Security Key

If you forget your Security Key, you'll be asked for your birthday, for your postal code and to answer one of the questions below. We'll send you a new Security Key to the email address you provide below, so make sure it is correct.

Where can I use Yahoo! Wallet?

Yahoo! Wallet saves your credit card information and your shipping address, so you don't have to retype it each time you buy something on Yahoo!

Use express checkout on **Yahoo! Shopping**.

Buy more mail storage on **Yahoo! Mail**.

15

FIGURE 15-3   Signing up for a Yahoo! wallet

4. Enter your billing and shipping addresses.

5. Click Submit This Form to display a summary of the sign-up information you entered.

6. Click Continue To Yahoo! Shopping.

If you ever need to change the information in your wallet, click a Wallet link and select Already Enrolled. Then enter your security keyword and click Continue to display the Edit Wallet Information page. Make any necessary changes to the information that appears and click Finished.

Next time you check out from a shopping cart, your credit card and shipping information will be available automatically to the merchant from whom you are making a purchase.

Other Yahoo! Shopping Features

Searching for items or browsing categories are just two ways to locate an item you want to purchase. You can also go directly to a featured merchant's Web site, choose a featured item, or click the other links that appear on the Yahoo! Shopping home page from time to time.

Earlier in Figure 15-1, for example, there are links to gift ideas in four price ranges. Click one of the links to display selected items from Yahoo! Gift Ideas. You might also see sections that offer holiday gifts and special offers.

Most Yahoo! Shopping pages contain featured items and stores as well. Selecting a featured item shows the details of that item from a specific merchant. The Featured Stores section of a Yahoo! Shopping page shows the names of merchants who are being highlighted at the time. Click a merchant's name to go directly to its online catalog.

The Editor's Picks section of the Yahoo! Shopping home page includes links to special gift selections and product reviews chosen by editors of magazines such as *New York Magazine* and *Consumer Review*. The items are selected from a variety of merchants and include links to the merchants' Web pages, where you can get additional information and perhaps purchase items.

The Hot Products section features best-selling items. Click a product to display a page of various models or versions. You can then select a specific item to see a comparison of prices from various merchants, as shown in Figure 15-4, or see detailed specifications about the item and a link to a page where you can compare prices.

The Yahoo! Shopping home page also offers a link labeled Look At What Other Shoppers Are Buying. Click the link to see a random sample of the products that others purchased over Yahoo! in the last hour.

There is also the Yahoo! Resources section, as shown here on the right.

Most of the links listed here take you to other Yahoo! features that are not necessarily related to shopping, but the Gift Registry and the Gift Recommender are useful shopping tools.

Yahoo! Resources

- Create or view a Gift Registry
- Try our Gift Recommender
- Send a Yahoo! Greeting
- Search offline with Yellow Pages
- Build a Yahoo! Store
- Browse store listings
- Safe online shopping tips
- Buy Yahoo! Gear

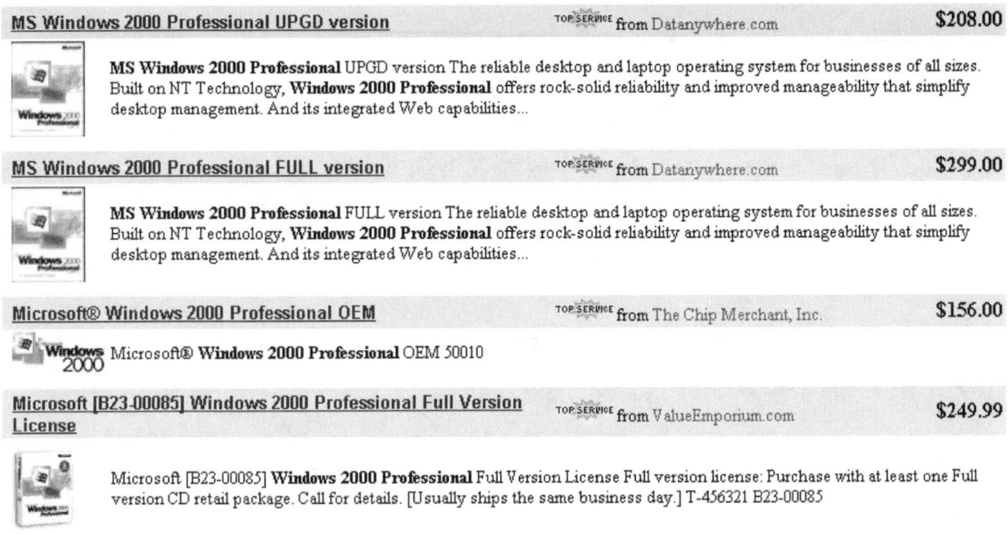

MS Windows 2000 Professional UPGD version   TOP SERVICE from Datanywhere.com   **$208.00**

MS **Windows 2000 Professional** UPGD version The reliable desktop and laptop operating system for businesses of all sizes. Built on NT Technology, **Windows 2000 Professional** offers rock-solid reliability and improved manageability that simplify desktop management. And its integrated Web capabilities...

MS Windows 2000 Professional FULL version   TOP SERVICE from Datanywhere.com   **$299.00**

MS **Windows 2000 Professional** FULL version The reliable desktop and laptop operating system for businesses of all sizes. Built on NT Technology, **Windows 2000 Professional** offers rock-solid reliability and improved manageability that simplify desktop management. And its integrated Web capabilities...

Microsoft® Windows 2000 Professional OEM   TOP SERVICE from The Chip Merchant, Inc.   **$156.00**

Windows 2000 Microsoft® **Windows 2000 Professional** OEM 50010

Microsoft [B23-00085] Windows 2000 Professional Full Version License   TOP SERVICE from ValueEmporium.com   **$249.99**

Microsoft [B23-00085] **Windows 2000 Professional** Full Version License Full version license: Purchase with at least one Full version CD retail package. Call for details. [Usually ships the same business day.] T-456321 B23-00085

FIGURE 15-4   Comparison shop by selecting a hot product.

Creating a Gift Registry

A *gift registry* is a wish list of items that you can store online. Friends and relatives who want to buy you a gift can visit the registry and can get you the gift you really want simply by clicking an item. Your shipping information is already on file. All others have to do is pay for the items!

You can create as many registries as you want, each with different items, for different occasions, or for different groups of friends. For example, you may have a registry of inexpensive items that you make available to one group of friends and a registry of expensive items for another group.

You can also create two types of registries, public and private:

- ■ A public registry is listed in the Yahoo! Gift Registry directory. Anyone can search the directory for your name and access your wish list of items.

- ■ A private registry can only be viewed by the Yahoo! members whom you designate and invite to use your registry.

As the owner of a registry, you can change the items in the wish list and the names of persons who can access it. You can also designate other Yahoo! members as owners, however, to share the registry with a spouse or other individual.

15

Creating a Gift Registry

When you create a registry, you give it a name and specify who can access it. You then add the items to the registry that others may purchase for you. Follow these steps to create a registry:

1. Go to the Yahoo! Shopping home page and sign in if you are not yet signed in.

2. Click Create Or View A Gift Registry in the Yahoo! Resources section. A page lists registries that you have already created, if you have created any, and friends' registries that you have access to, if you have access to any.

3. Click Create A Registry to see the form shown here.

> **Yahoo! Gift Registry: Create a Registry**
>
> **Step 1: Name Your Gift Registry**
> Keep the name short, but descriptive.
>   Name: [_____] (ex: My Christmas 99 Wish List)
>
> **Step 2: Select the Occasion**
> Are you creating your Gift Registry for a specific occasion? If so, please select from those listed below.
> (You can choose "Other" if nothing matches your occasion.)
> Occasion: [Select One ▾]
>
> **Step 3: Enter Date of Occasion** (optional)
> Month: [– ▾] Day: [– ▾] Year: [– ▾]
>
> **Step 4: Enter Shipping Address**

4. Enter a name for the registry.

5. Pull down the Occasion list and select an option: Baby, Bar Mitzvah, Birthday, Christmas, Confirmation, Hanukkah, Wedding, and Other.

6. Optionally, enter the date of the occasion.

7. Enter your shipping address. The address may already be filled in from your membership information. Buyers will only see the city and state, but the entire address will be sent to the merchant from whom the gift is purchased.

8. Choose a private or public registry.

9. Click Accept to see your gift registry page.

10. In the Gift Registry Tools section of the page, click Edit Settings.

11. In the page that appears, enter the owner's message and a brief description, and edit your shipping address if necessary.

12. Click Change Settings when you have finished. Your registry page now looks something like this.

Adding Items to Your Registry

You can now add items to the registry and invite friends to access it by following these steps from the registry page:

1. Click Shop For Items.

2. Click Begin Adding Items Now At Yahoo! Shopping.

3. Shop for an item you are interested in and add it to the merchant's shopping cart.

4. In the shopping cart, click the Add To Registry button. Not every merchant supports the registry feature, so the button does not appear in every shopping cart.

5. Your registry wish list appears with the item inserted.

6. Click Keep Shopping if you want to add more items in the same way.

The following illustration shows a typical gift registry with items.

15

The Big 55
My Big 55 Bash Wishlist

Hello, aneibauer , you are an **owner** of this registry   Sign Out

Registry Pages	Wish List			
Gift Registry Home	Showing items 1 - 2 of 2			
Create New Registry	**Item(s)**	**Merchant**	**Price**	**Buy**
Search	**Night at the Movies**	BravoGifts	$23.00	Requested: 1
				Bought: 0
Gift Registry Tools				Qty: 1
Shop for Items				[Delete this item]
Wish List	Add Comment			
Edit Items				
Send to Friends	**Blockbuster® GiftCard &**	BravoGifts	$21.00	Requested: 1
Edit Registry Access	**Gourmet Maltballs**			Bought: 0
Edit Settings				Qty: 1
				[Delete this item]

Inviting Friends to Visit Your Registry

You can now invite friends to access your private registry. From the registry page (Figure 15-5), follow these steps to invite others to visit your registry:

1. Click Send To Friends to see the Invite Someone To Join.

2. Enter the e-mail address or Yahoo! ID of the person.

3. Enter a personal message to include in the invitation.

4. Click the Send button.

Your friend will receive an e-mail with an invitation to join. The invitation will include a link to your registry. When your friend clicks the link and signs on to Yahoo!, your page appears, as shown in Figure 15-6. Your friend can choose an item and click Buy Now to purchase it and send it to your shipping address.

Note *A friend does not need to be a Yahoo! member to purchase items in your registry.*

To make changes to your registry, return to the Yahoo! Shopping home page and click Create Or View A Gift Registry to see the list of registries, as well as any friend's registries that you have access to, as shown here on the right. Click the registry you'd like to edit, or the friend's registry that you'd like to access.

Registries [Edit]

My Registries
  The Big 55

Friends' Registries

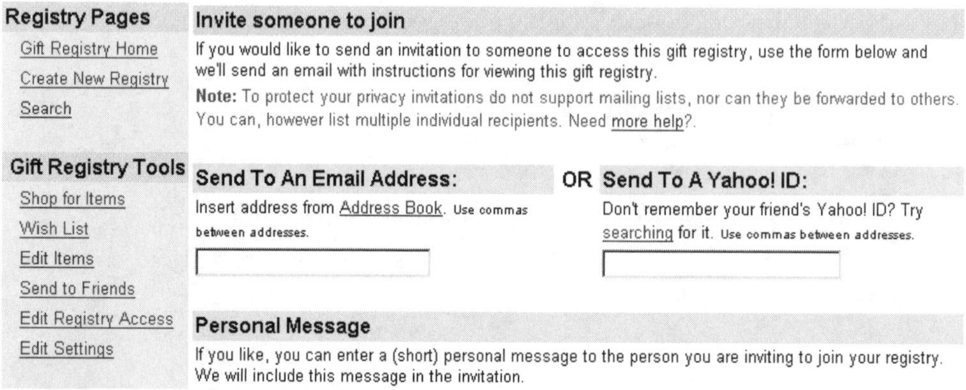

Registry Pages

Gift Registry Home
Create New Registry
Search

Gift Registry Tools

Shop for Items
Wish List
Edit Items
Send to Friends
Edit Registry Access
Edit Settings

Invite someone to join

If you would like to send an invitation to someone to access this gift registry, use the form below and we'll send an email with instructions for viewing this gift registry.

Note: To protect your privacy invitations do not support mailing lists, nor can they be forwarded to others. You can, however list multiple individual recipients. Need more help?.

Send To An Email Address: OR **Send To A Yahoo! ID:**

Insert address from Address Book. Use commas between addresses.

Don't remember your friend's Yahoo! ID? Try searching for it. Use commas between addresses.

Personal Message

If you like, you can enter a (short) personal message to the person you are inviting to join your registry. We will include this message in the invitation.

FIGURE 15-5   Inviting someone to join your registry

Registry Pages	**Owner's Message**		**Contact**
Gift Registry Home	Thanks for checking out my registry. I really don't		Send mail to the <u>owners</u> of this registry.
Create New Registry	expect anything, but if you are planning on getting		
Search	me something, here are some suggestions.		
	-- <u>aneibauer</u>		

Wish List

Showing items 1 - 2 of 2

Item(s)	Merchant	Price	Buy
Night at the Movies	BravoGifts	$23.00	Requested: 1 Bought: 0

Qty: 1

Buy Now!

FIGURE 15-6   A friend's view of your registry

Find a Registry

All the public registries are stored in Yahoo!'s registry database. To locate a public registry, select Create Or View A Registry on the Yahoo! Shopping home page, and then scroll the screen to see these options:

Search for a Registry

Find a friend's gift registry by entering their name and event information below. (None of the fields below are required.)

First Name	Last Name

Yahoo! ID	Event time
	month year

Search

Enter the name or Yahoo! ID of the person for whom you are looking, and, optionally, the date of the occasion. Then click Search.

15

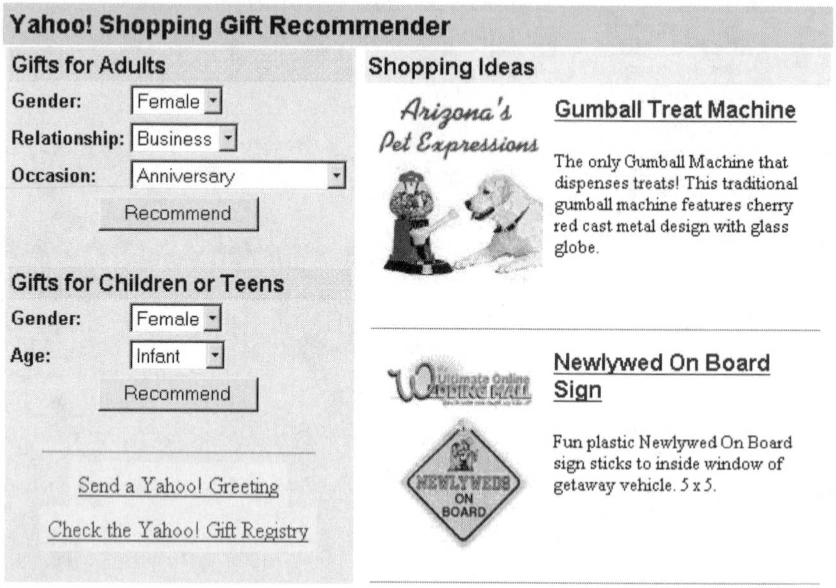

Yahoo! Shopping Gift Recommender

Gifts for Adults

Gender: [Female ▾]

Relationship: [Business ▾]

Occasion: [Anniversary ▾]

[Recommend]

Gifts for Children or Teens

Gender: [Female ▾]

Age: [Infant ▾]

[Recommend]

Send a Yahoo! Greeting

Check the Yahoo! Gift Registry

Shopping Ideas

Arizona's Pet Expressions

Gumball Treat Machine

The only Gumball Machine that dispenses treats! This traditional gumball machine features cherry red cast metal design with glass globe.

The Ultimate Online SPORE MALL

Newlywed On Board Sign

Fun plastic Newlywed On Board sign sticks to inside window of getaway vehicle. 5 x 5.

NEWLYWEDS ON BOARD

FIGURE 15-7   The Gift Recommender

The Gift Recommender

The Gift Recommender selects possible gifts based on the age and gender of the recipient, and the occasion. Click Try Our Gift Recommender on the Yahoo! Resources list to display the options shown in Figure 15-7.

Do the following to help the Recommender make a choice:

- If you are shopping for a gift for an adult, choose his or her gender, relationship to you, and an occasion from the list boxes. Then click the Recommend button.

- If you are shopping for a gift for a child or teenager, choose his or her gender and age, and then click Recommend.

A list of suggested gifts appears. You can select gifts from the list and add them to a shopping cart.

Earning Free Stuff with Yahoo! Points

The more you shop, the more Yahoo! points you'll accumulate. For each dollar you spend, you get one Yahoo! point, although Yahoo! sometimes offers two points for every dollar you spend. You can exchange Yahoo! points for gift certificates to Yahoo! merchants or use them to bid on items in special auctions.

The points are good for one year from the end of the calendar quarter in which you earn them. Points you earn in January, for example, will expire on March 31 of the next year. Points you earn in Yahoo! Shopping are held in reserve for 14 days, so you must wait at least 14 days to redeem them.

To sign up for the program, go to the site at http://points.yahoo.com or click the Join Or Enroll link that appears beside the star icon on many Yahoo! pages. In the page that appears, click Enroll Me Now to open your Yahoo! Points page, as shown in Figure 15-8. We'll look at this page in detail later on.

Earning Points

After you have registered to earn Yahoo! points, just shop as you would normally. When you check out, a message on the screen shows how many points you earned in the transaction.

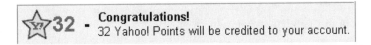

In addition to earning points when you shop, you can earn points by purchasing airline tickets. You earn 150 points for each airline ticket you purchase on Yahoo! Travel. There is a maximum, however, on the number of tickets you can purchase that earn points–up to four tickets in each of three transactions every other day. So you can only purchase four tickets at a time, in up to three purchases–twelve tickets in all every other day.

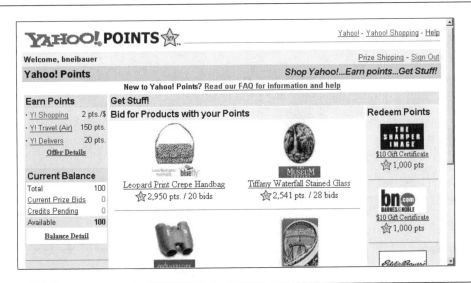

FIGURE 15-8   Yahoo! Points page

15

You can also earn points through a program called Yahoo! Delivers.

Yahoo! Delivers

The Yahoo! Delivers program gives you points for reading e-mail from Yahoo! merchants. You can earn 20 points just for reading a message, although in some cases you need to click a link and go to the merchant's Web site to earn the points.

 You must read the mail in the Yahoo! e-mail system.

Here's how to sign up for the Yahoo! Delivers program (see Figure 15-9):

1. Go to the Yahoo! Points page and click Y! Delivers in the Earn Points section. You see the Yahoo! Delivers form.
2. Select Yes in the Sign Up section.
3. Select the check boxes for areas of interest in the Select Your Interests section.
4. Scroll the page to display delivery options
5. Specify the e-mail address to send mailings.

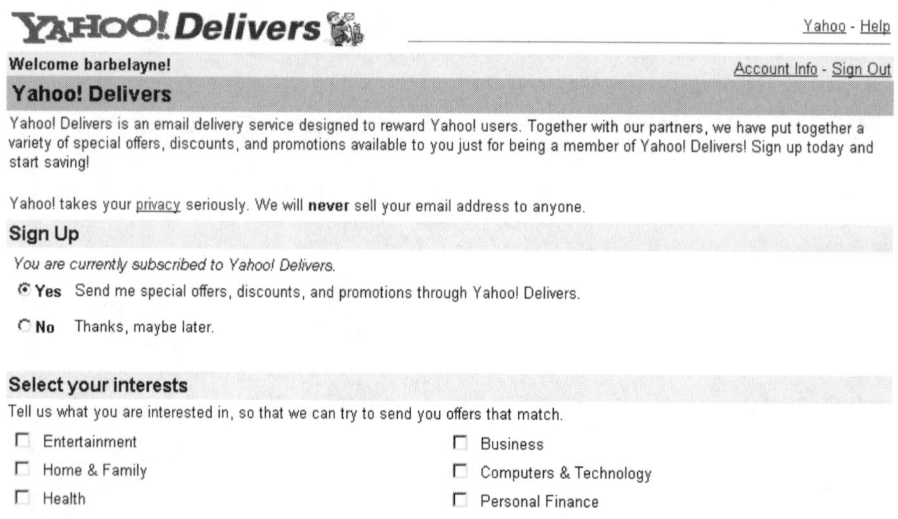

YAHOO! Delivers   Yahoo - Help

Welcome barbelayne!   Account Info - Sign Out
Yahoo! Delivers

Yahoo! Delivers is an email delivery service designed to reward Yahoo! users. Together with our partners, we have put together a variety of special offers, discounts, and promotions available to you just for being a member of Yahoo! Delivers! Sign up today and start saving!

Yahoo! takes your privacy seriously. We will **never** sell your email address to anyone.

Sign Up
You are currently subscribed to Yahoo! Delivers.

⊙ **Yes**   Send me special offers, discounts, and promotions through Yahoo! Delivers.

○ **No**   Thanks, maybe later.

Select your interests
Tell us what you are interested in, so that we can try to send you offers that match.

☐ Entertainment   ☐ Business
☐ Home & Family   ☐ Computers & Technology
☐ Health   ☐ Personal Finance

FIGURE 15-9   Signing up for Yahoo! Delivers

6. Choose the frequency of mailings. The options are one to three times a week or once a week.

7. Specify whether your e-mail program can read HTML-formatted mail or text-only mail. If you have AOL, choose text only.

8. Click the Finished button.

Now use your Yahoo! e-mail account to check for Yahoo! Delivers messages and read them online to earn points.

Redeeming Points

There are two ways to redeem your Yahoo! points for products:

■ Bid on items in special point auctions.

■ Redeem points for gift certificates with merchants on Yahoo! shopping.

Navigate to http://points.yahoo.com or click any Points link to go to the Yahoo! Points page. There, you will see the number of points you have earned and those that are being held in reserve, as shown in Figure 15-10.

The items up for auction are shown in the center of the page. To see more items, click More Points Auctions under the list. Clicking an item displays an auction page like the ones you learned about in Chapter 14. The only difference is that you bid with points rather than dollars.

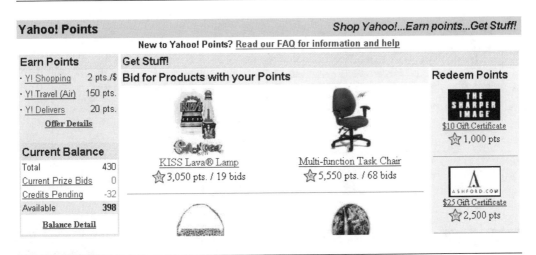

FIGURE 15-10   Your earned and pending points

15

The gift certificates are shown on the right side of the Yahoo! Points page. Click one of the options to display additional choices from the merchant in question, and then select the certificate you want to purchase. You'll see a page like the one shown in Figure 15-11.

Note *Some merchants also provide special discount offers to exchange for points.*

Select the e-mail address where you want your certificate sent and then click Send Me My Redemption Code. Yahoo! e-mails you a code with a link to the merchant's Web site. Make a note of the code and then click the link to visit the site. Select the items you want to purchase, and then, to get credit for the gift certificate amount, enter the code in the space for it in the shopping cart. The value of the certificate is subtracted from the total of the shopping cart.

Caution *After you click Send Me My Redemption Code, you cannot return the certificate to reclaim the points.*

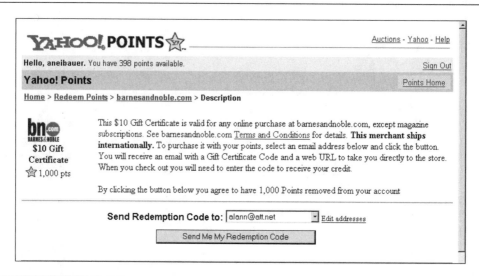

FIGURE 15-11   Redeeming your points for a gift certificate

Part V

Travel, Entertainment, and Current Events

Chapter 16

Planning and Booking Vacations

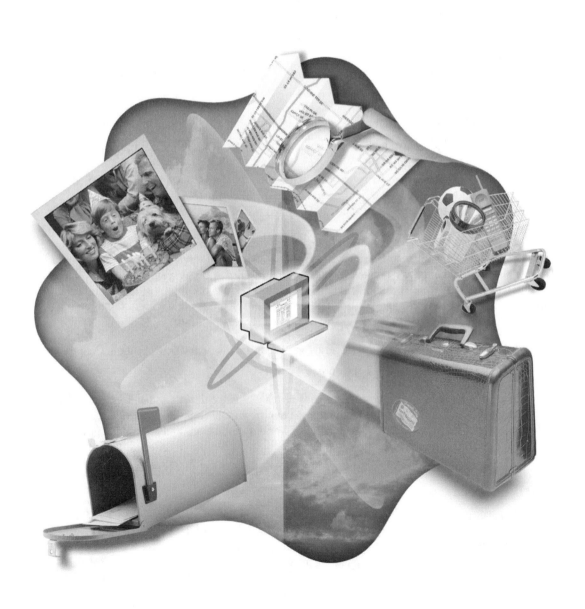

How to . . .

- Plan a trip by destination
- Plan a trip by activity
- Plan a trip by lifestyle
- View and download featured photographs
- Add travel photographs to your Yahoo! Web site
- Browse for travel information in the Yahoo! directories
- Make airline reservations
- Order airline tickets
- Make car rental reservations
- Reserve hotel rooms
- Book a cruise

Whether you are an actual or an armchair traveler, Yahoo! is a great place to plan a vacation or business trip. You can get detailed information about travel destinations the world over; find destinations that match your interests and hobbies; and actually make airline, hotel, and other kinds of reservations online.

Once you decide where you want to go, however, you have to make the arrangements to actually go and stay there. You'll need to make airline and hotel reservations or book a tour with a cruise line or tour company. You might need to reserve a rental car as well. And while you're at it, you might book arrangements for activities such as shows and sightseeing trips. You can do all of this from Yahoo!.

In general, there are two ways to get information about travel destinations:

- Use the search directories of categories and Web sites that you learned about in Chapter 8.
- Go directly to the Yahoo! Travel home page.

The great thing about researching travel plans on Yahoo! is the flexibility that Yahoo! provides. You can move about from site to site or country to country without committing to anything or being pressured by a travel agent. You can compare various destinations and itineraries in as much detail as you want before making a final decision.

Yahoo! Travel

For direct access to a wealth of travel information and resources, click Travel in the Yahoo! Home page. By choosing options at the top and down the left side of the page, you can make reservations for airline tickets, hotel rooms, rental cars, and cruises. We'll look at these options later in this chapter. The features for planning a trip are shown in Figure 16-1.

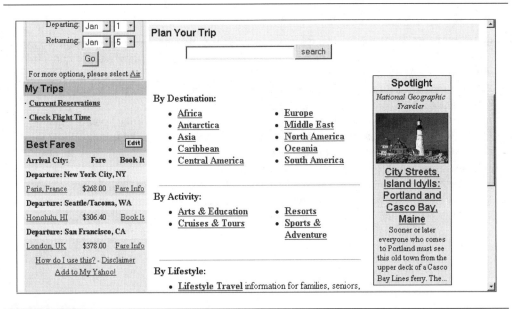

FIGURE 16-1   Yahoo! Travel planning features

You can get travel information in four ways:

- Searching by keyword
- Browsing by location
- Browsing by activity
- Browsing by lifestyle

Notice the "Spotlight" travel destination in the box on the right side of the page. It offers links to information about dining, lodging, nightlife, and points of interest in a specific place. Click the links for quick access to information about the destination, and then return to the Yahoo! Travel home page to look up more details about the location if it piques your interest.

Use the Search option to get travel information. Searching here is easier than browsing the categories for Web sites that cater to a specific hobby or interest. For example, suppose you are an avid bicycle rider and you want to plan a vacation around your hobby. Type **bicycle** in the Search box and click the Search button to see travel sites that feature bicycle tours.

Apart from the Search mechanism, the other options on the Yahoo! Travel home page let you browse categories, starting at one level and choosing subcategories until you locate a final destination.

16

Planning by Destination

Planning a trip by destination is a great way to get started if you have some idea of where you'd like to visit. Except for Antarctica, clicking a region displays a page that shows a map and a list of featured countries. (By selecting Antarctica, a Country Profile is displayed that we'll look at later.) By the way, Oceania refers to Australia and islands in the South Pacific, including Fiji, Guam, Micronesia, New Zealand, Papua New Guinea, and Tahiti.

On the left of most Yahoo! Travel pages is a small map of the area described on the page. Click the Full-Size Map link under the map to see a more detailed view in a separate window. There is also a Community section with links to chat rooms, message boards, and other Web sites where you can communicate with Yahoo! members whose travel interests are similar to yours.

Below the Featured Countries list is usually a section titled Web Sites For Other Countries. These links access categories and Web sites in the Yahoo! Web site directory that are not on the Featured list. The section for Oceania, for example, includes the smaller islands in the South Pacific.

Below the Web Sites For Other Countries section of the page is a Search box with which you can search all of Yahoo! Travel or just the current category:

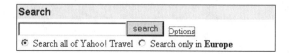

Featured Countries

The Featured Countries section of a travel page lists countries for which Yahoo! offers extensive travel information. Click the name of a county that you are interested in to open the country's travel page, as shown in Figure 16-2.

Each travel page is divided into several sections:

- Map
- Destination Pages
- Country Profile
- Weather
- Currency Converter
- Yahoo! Categories
- Vacation Search
- Featured Photo

Note *Choosing United States from the North America page displays a list of state links. Click the state that you plan to visit.*

Weather

The Weather section shows the current temperatures in selected cities or regions. Click a city or region to get a detailed weather report and forecast. You'll learn more about getting and using weather information in Yahoo! in Chapter 18.

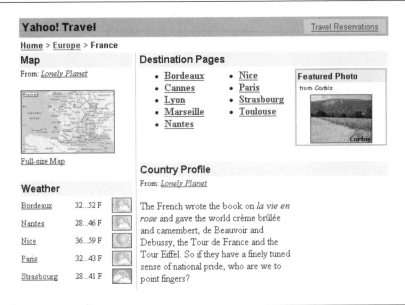

FIGURE 16-2   Country travel page

Currency Converter

The Currency Converter displays current exchange rates between the country's currency and the currency of several different countries. In the following illustration, for example, one United States dollar is equivalent to just over 6.8 French francs.

To convert another currency or a specific amount of money, follow these steps:

1.   Select the currency from the Currency list. The options are in alphabetical order by country, from the Algerian Dinar to the Zambian Kwacha.

2. Enter the amount you want to convert to the currency of the destination country.

3. Click Convert. Here, you see the results of converting 56 United States dollars into French francs.

Symbol	U.S. Dollar	Exchange Rate	French Franc
USDFRF=X	56	11:09AM 6.833600	**382.68**

Yahoo! Categories

The Yahoo! Categories section of the country page offers links to Yahoo! categories and Web sites. The options are

- **Country Travel Resources**   Offers links to information of all kinds.
- **Embassies And Consulates**   Presents links to the country's official diplomacy Web sites.
- **News And Media**   Offers links to popular publications, radio stations, and television stations.
- **Outdoors And Parks**   Provides information about outdoor activities, such as boating, camping, scouting, skiing, surfing, and hiking.
- **Tour Operators**   Provides links to general and specialized tour companies. In addition to bus- and boat-charter companies, you may also find links to auto racing, ballooning, culinary, cycling, paddling, and other specialized tours.

Note *In some Yahoo! Travel pages, you'll see the Vacation Search section that lets you locate tour packages meeting specific criteria.*

Featured Photo

The Featured Photo area of a Yahoo! Travel page is sponsored by Corbis, an online resource for images, digital photographs, and free electronic postcards. Corbis's Web site is located at www.corbis.com.

Click a featured photo to open a page like the one shown in Figure 16-3.

If you want to access the photograph at a later time or share it with others, click the Add To Briefcase option. Doing so places a link to the photograph in your Yahoo! Briefcase and opens the Briefcase page. As you learned in Chapter 7, the Briefcase is a convenient place to store files. By clicking the link to the photograph, you and others with whom you share your briefcase can display the photograph without taking the time to search for it or download it.

Note *You can also share the photograph by sending it as an electronic greeting card. You'll learn all about e-cards in Chapter 21.*

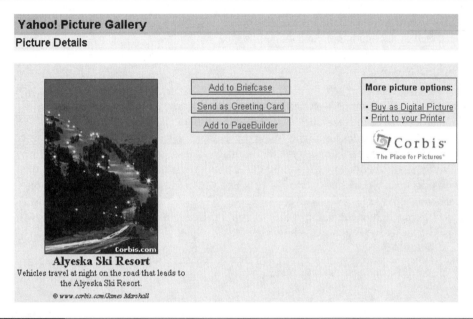

Yahoo! Picture Gallery
Picture Details

Alyeska Ski Resort
Vehicles travel at night on the road that leads to
the Alyeska Ski Resort.
© www.corbis.com/James Marshall

FIGURE 16-3   Featured Photo options

Click the Add To Page Builder option if you want to place the photograph on your Yahoo! Web site. Clicking Add To Page Builder launches the Page Builder application, in which you can choose which Web site page to place the picture on. After the page opens in Page Builder, position the photograph and make any other changes to the Web site that you desire.

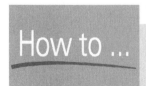 **Purchase a Photograph**

If you want to download a copy of the photograph to your computer, click the Buy As Digital Picture link to visit the Corbis Web site. From there, you can purchase the photograph for $3 and download it in JPEG format. From the Corbis Web site, you can also click My Corbis to access free Windows wallpaper files and search for additional photographs.

16

To print a copy of the photograph, click Print To Your Printer. The photograph appears in a separate browser window and the Print dialog box opens. Make sure your printer is ready and properly selected in the dialog box, and then click the Print button.

Country Profile

The Country Profile section of a Yahoo! Travel page offers social, geographic, economic, and other essential information about the country in question, as shown in Figure 16-4. If the introduction arouses your interest, click Continue to read more about the country.

The profile article includes highlights about the country, as well as some specific information for travelers. Most articles explain the type of visa that you need to enter the country and any health risks you might encounter by traveling there. Many countries, for example, do not require a visa if you plan to stay for a short period of time and you are from a wealthy European or North American country.

The profile may include the name of the country's currency and a section that explains the relative costs of meals and lodging, as shown here:

Currency: Franc
Relative costs:

- cheap meal: US$5-10
- restaurant meal: US$15-25
- cheap room: US$15-20
- hotel room: US$25-35

Time: GMT/UTC plus one hour
Electricity: 220V, 50Hz
Weights & measures: Metric
Tourism: 60.5 million visitors

According to this information on France, for example, the average meal in a restaurant costs the equivalent of $15 to $25; the average hotel room costs between $25 and $35. Travelers, however, should expect a wide range of prices depending on how they book their arrangements. Relative costs are strictly for comparing countries, not for planning a travel budget.

The profile page also lists the time zone or zones in which the country is located, the type of electricity used, the system of measurement in use, and the number of annual visitors.

The time zone is shown relative to Greenwich Mean Time (GMT), also known as Universal Time Coordinated (UTC). GMT is the time it is in Greenwich, England. It is used as a standard way to reference time regardless of location. The notation GMT/UTC plus one hour, for example, means that the country is one hour head of GMT. So when it is 2:30 P.M. GMT, it is 3:30 P.M. in the country. You can gauge a country's time in relation to your own by finding out your own area's time in relation to GMT. If you live in an area that is GMT/UTC minus one hour, for example, then you are two hours behind a country that is GMT/UTC plus one hour.

The type of electricity used is shown in volts. Knowing which type of electricity is in use is important if you plan to travel with electrical appliances such as a hair dryer or shaver. If the country uses a different electrical current than yours does, you need to purchase a special adapter and converter to use your appliances without damaging them.

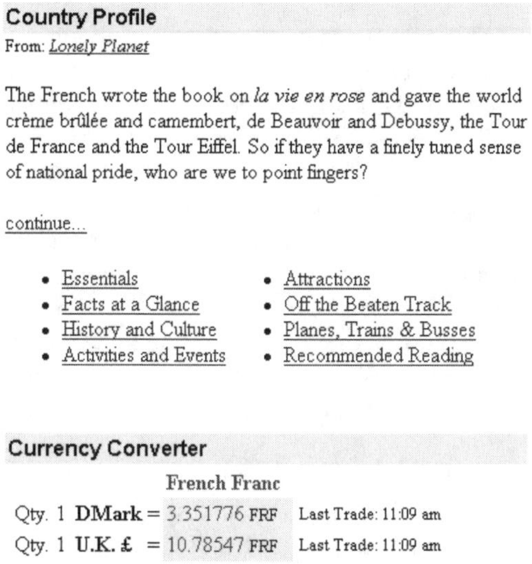

Country Profile

From: *Lonely Planet*

The French wrote the book on *la vie en rose* and gave the world
crème brûlée and camembert, de Beauvoir and Debussy, the Tour
de France and the Tour Eiffel. So if they have a finely tuned sense
of national pride, who are we to point fingers?

continue...

- Essentials
- Facts at a Glance
- History and Culture
- Activities and Events

- Attractions
- Off the Beaten Track
- Planes, Trains & Busses
- Recommended Reading

Currency Converter

French Franc

Qty. 1 **DMark** = 3.351776 FRF   Last Trade: 11:09 am

Qty. 1 **U.K. £** = 10.78547 FRF   Last Trade: 11:09 am

FIGURE 16-4   A country profile

In addition to the essentials discussed in the profile, the Country Profile section has links to
these categories:

- Essentials
- Facts at a Glance
- History and Culture
- Activities and Events

- Attractions
- Off the Beaten Track
- Planes, Trains & Busses
- Recommended Reading

Click the Facts At A Glance link for a summary of geographic and economic features,
including the country's area in square miles, its population, which languages are spoken, the type
of government, the titles of key officials, and the percentages of the population that belong to
different religious and ethnic groups.

Most of the profile pages also contain these three links:

Click here for more info from Lonely Planet | Check out these great travel snaps
Get a guidebook before you go

16

Lonely Planet provides Yahoo! with much of its information about travel. The links take you
to pages within the Lonely Planet Web site at http://www.lonelyplanet.com/, where you can get
additional travel information and purchase guidebooks.

Destination Pages

The Destination Pages section of the profile page provides links to information about different cities or regions within the country. Clicking a destination link leads to a page like the one shown in Figure 16-5. In addition to the familiar map, weather, and featured photo sections, you can get detailed traveler's information, read an article, and learn about any travelers' advisories that are in effect.

Click the Dining link to get a list of featured restaurants and an overview of dining in the city. You will also find links to restaurant Web sites, as well as a Rough Guide to the city. Rough Guide, like Lonely Planet, provides Yahoo! with dining information.

Click the Lodging link to see a list of featured hotels and an overview of dining in the city. There will also be links to Web sites where you will find hotel directories and information about vacation rentals. You can even book reservations. Room prices are shown in the country's currency, so you'll need to use the Currency Converter to get an idea of prices in your own currency.

Click the Nightlife link to see a list of featured clubs and an overview of nightlife in the city. There will also be links to Web sites where bars, pubs, clubs, cyber cafés, and operas are described.

The Points Of Interest link takes you to a list of featured sites and an overview of attractions in the city. There will also be links to Web sites where you can learn about museums, exhibits, and parks.

Click the Travel Resources links to find maps and photographs, newspapers, tour operators, travel agents, and travel guides.

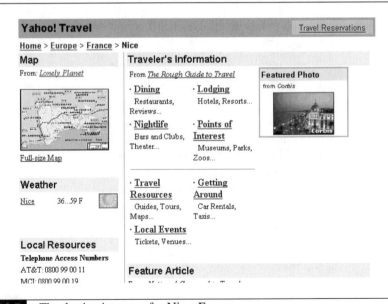

FIGURE 16-5   The destination page for Nice, France

The Getting Around link takes you to sites where you can learn about airports, limousines, and shuttle services.

Planning by Activity

If you are less interested in where you are going than what you'll do when you get there, plan your trip by activity. To do so, use these options in the Travel home page:

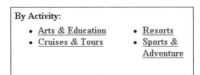

By Activity:
- Arts & Education
- Cruises & Tours
- Resorts
- Sports & Adventure

Click an option to open a page of featured activities, a spotlighted activity, or a featured article. Click an activity to read an Article that describes the activity and the locations where it can be enjoyed.

Select sites from the article that you'd like to visit, and then use the Search feature or return to the Yahoo! Travel home page and use the Destination options to learn more about the destination.

The Featured Article page also includes a Yahoo! Categories section with links to clubs and teams, regional information, tour operators, tours and events, and travelogues. If your particular interest is not listed under Featured Activities, choose an interest that is similar to yours and then use the Yahoo! Categories links to search further.

Planning by Lifestyle

If you want to plan your trip according to a particular lifestyle, then click the Lifestyle Travel link in the Yahoo! Travel home page. You'll see these options:

- Business Travel
- Family
- Lesbian, Gay And Bisexual
- Jewish
- Singles
- Naturist/Nudist
- Seniors
- Special Needs
- Women
- Vegetarian

16

Select an option to see a directory of categories and Web sites that feature information about the option you chose.

Travel Community

The Travel Community section of the Yahoo! Travel home page offers ways to communicate with other Yahoo! members who are interested in travel.

Click More Community Information to access online events such as special chats at locations outside of Yahoo! and audio/video channels that you can listen to and watch for travel-related entertainment.

Yahoo! Directories

As a supplement to using the Yahoo! Travel pages, you can also search for information through the Yahoo! directories.

The Regional options might be the first place to start if you know the location you would like to visit. Starting from the Regional selection, you can browse U.S. states, countries of the world, and regions of the world. Choosing a specific country, for example, may display the subcategories shown in Figure 16-6. By clicking a subcategory, you can access a wealth of local information.

Another place to start is the Society And Culture category. From there, you can access subcategories such as Events, Holidays and Observances, and Environment and Nature. In so doing, you can locate a particular interest and see how it is observed in other countries.

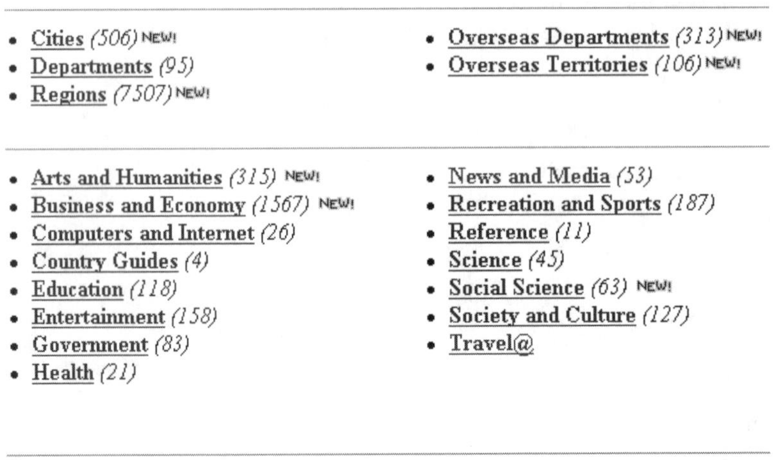

- Cities *(506)* NEW!
- Departments *(95)*
- Regions *(7507)* NEW!

- Overseas Departments *(313)* NEW!
- Overseas Territories *(106)* NEW!

- Arts and Humanities *(315)* NEW!
- Business and Economy *(1567)* NEW!
- Computers and Internet *(26)*
- Country Guides *(4)*
- Education *(118)*
- Entertainment *(158)*
- Government *(83)*
- Health *(21)*

- News and Media *(53)*
- Recreation and Sports *(187)*
- Reference *(11)*
- Science *(45)*
- Social Science *(63)* NEW!
- Society and Culture *(127)*
- Travel@

FIGURE 16-6 Subcategories for a region

The Recreation & Sports category is the place to start if you're looking for a trip that is centered around amusement and theme parks, hobbies, gardening, or gambling. The Travel subcategory of Recreation & Sports presents items by region, as well as the categories of travel.

These categories offer the richest collections of links to travel-related sites on the Internet. They include all of the activities and lifestyles that are available from the Yahoo! Travel home page, as well as many more.

The Virtual Fieldtrips link, for instance, takes you to sites that offer online multimedia tours. You can travel through the Holy Land, trek across deserts, or take an odyssey in Egypt and walk through an archeological excavation.

The Ongoing Travelogues link takes you to sites that follow travelers on their adventures. You can join a group driving a van across the United States, share the adventure of a 5000-mile kayak expedition from California to Columbia, or follow two young honeymooners in their three-year journey around the world in a small sailboat.

Travel Writing lets you learn about travel writers, as well as how to write and submit stories about your experiences for publication. There are also links to familiarization trips—special tours for travel agents and other professionals in the travel industry.

The Disabilities link offers recourses of all types for special travelers. For example, there is a searchable database of dialysis units, as well as links to organizations that offer travel opportunities for individuals with disabilities.

If you are really adventurous, use the Civilian Space Travel link to learn about plans for suborbital and orbital travel.

Signing In for Reservations

To access some of the reservation features of Yahoo! Travel, you must register for the service. Registering is free and must be done in addition to your Yahoo! membership. By registering, you can get detailed flight information and reserve tickets through the Sabre registration system. You can purchase tickets that are mailed to you. You can even follow up on your travel itinerary online.

When you access a service that requires membership, you see the screen shown in Figure 16-7. If you signed up already, enter your logon name and password. Otherwise, follow these steps to register for Yahoo! Travel:

1. Click the Become A Member button to open the New Member Information form.
2. Enter your name.
3. Enter your e-mail address
4. Enter your complete address.
5. Specify your home and business telephone numbers.
6. Enter the logon name that you will use to access the system.
7. Enter a password between four and eight characters long.

16

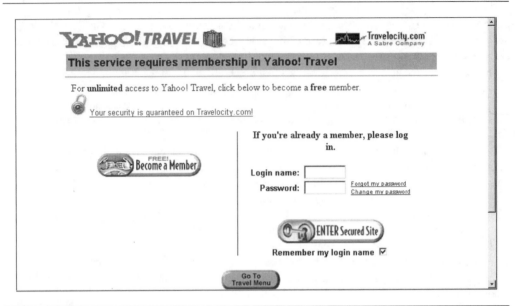

FIGURE 16-7   Registering for Yahoo! Travel

8. Retype the password to confirm it.

9. Enter your city of birth. The city's name will be used to confirm your request if you forget your password and need to obtain it.

10. Retype your city of birth to confirm it.

11. Select the check box if you want Yahoo! to remember your logon name so you only have to enter the password each time you access the system.

12. Read the terms and conditions, and click the I Agree button.

You will then see the Yahoo! Travel page that you selected.

Making Airline Reservations

There are several ways to make airline reservations from the Yahoo! Travel page. The techniques for making the reservations differ, however, only in the initial options that you choose to start the process. In all cases, you'll have the option—after you find the flight you want—of actually purchasing the tickets or placing them on hold for 24 hours. Either way, you are required to enter credit card information to complete the process. If you are not yet ready to purchase the tickets or use your credit card to hold them, you can go through the initial steps of locating and comparing flights as part of planning your trip.

Express Booking

One of the fastest ways to book a flight in Yahoo! Travel is to make use of the Express Booking options shown in Figure 16-8. Express Booking offers fewer options for booking a flight, but the process is quicker. Here's how to use Express Booking:

1. Enter the departure and destination locations.

2. Choose the number of passengers.

3. Select the departure month and date.

4. Select the return month and date.

5. Click Go.

The Select a Flight page appears, presenting one or more possible departure and return flights in ascending order by price. Scan the list to select the flight you are interested in, and then click the Buy button to purchase the tickets or the Hold button to reserve the tickets for 24 hours. In some cases, the Hold button indicates that holding tickets in reserve is not an option.

Placing Tickets on Hold

If you are not quite ready to purchase the tickets, you can reserve them for 24 hours. If you want the tickets, however, you'll have to purchase them within 24 hours so they are not released to other buyers.

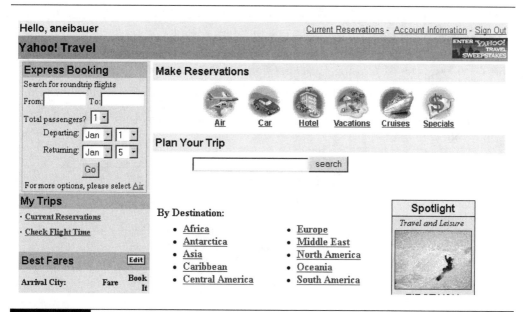

FIGURE 16-8   Express Booking

16

Note   *Putting a ticket on hold does not guarantee that it will be available when you are ready to purchase it.*

To hold airline tickets for 24 hours, follow these steps:

1. Click the Hold button to display a page that reviews the prices and flight information, and summarizes the rules and regulations that apply. Sometimes you can click a Rules button next to each flight listing to display the rules in detail. If the fare is non-refundable, you also see the check box shown here, in which case, you have to select the check box to continue with the process.

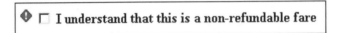

2. Read the information on the page and click I Agree to open the passenger information page.

3. Enter the names of your fellow travelers and specify whether they have any special meal or other service requests. You also need to enter your e-mail address, phone number, and frequent flyer number if you have one.

4. Click the Information Is Correct button to open the seat selection page for the departure flight. You need to select seats for each flight in the journey. As shown in Figure 16-9, you select a seat for each traveler. The Seat Map Legend explains the codes that appear in the seat layout on the right side of the page.

5. Enter which seats you want in the text boxes next to each passenger's name, and click Continue. A seat map appears for the next flight in the journey, either a return flight or a connecting flight.

6. Choose seats for the next flight and click Continue.

7. Repeat the process until you have made seat assignments for each flight in the itinerary.

Note   *Yahoo! makes no guarantees that you will get your reserved seat when you actually take the flight.*

8. When you click Continue after the last flight, you'll be prompted to enter your credit card information. Complete the form and then click Continue.

Buying Tickets

When you are ready to purchase the tickets for the flights you selected, click the Buy button on the Select A Flight page. A page appears so you can review your itinerary and read the rules and regulations that apply. Click the I Agree button at the bottom of the page to display the ticket delivery options.

FIGURE 16-9   Selecting seat assignments

How to ... **Bypass Seat Assignments**

If you don't want to bother selecting seats, you can bypass the seat assignment pages and have the airline select seats for you.

Rather than specifying seats, just select the type of seating you prefer from the options shown here, and then click Bypass Seat Maps:

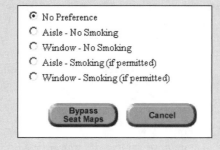

16

Tickets can be generated electronically, be mailed to you, or be delivered by Federal Express for an additional charge. When you select Ticket Electronically, you can access a copy of the passenger receipt online, but no tickets will actually be sent to you.

 The electronic ticketing option is not always available.

Make your choice and then complete the process by entering complete passenger and charge information.

Searching for the Best Airline Fares

If the price of tickets is your main concern, have Yahoo! search for the lowest fares starting from the Best Fares section of the Yahoo! Travel page, as shown in the following illustration at right. After you specify your departure and destination cities, Yahoo! automatically informs you what the best available fares are.

The feature works only for trips within the United States and trips to Canada, Puerto Rico, and the U.S. Virgin Islands, although European destinations sometimes appear as samples in the Best Fares section.

Best Fares		Edit
Arrival City:	Fare	Book It
Departure: New York City, NY		
Paris, France	$268.00	Fare Info
Departure: Seattle/Tacoma, WA		
Honolulu, HI	$472.30	Book It
Departure: San Francisco, CA		
London, UK	$378.00	Fare Info
How do I use this? - Disclaimer		
Add to My Yahoo!		

To add your itinerary, click the Edit button next to the Best Fares heading. You'll see the page shown in Figure 16-10. Select your departure and destination cities from the lists and then click the Add Selected Roundtrip button. The trip will be added to the section of the page labeled "You are already tracking these roundtrips." (To remove a trip from the list, click Delete in the column next to its name).

Click Finished to return to the Yahoo! Travel page, which now shows the trips you are tracking in the Best Fares section. That section has a number of links. Click the name of a destination city, for example, to open a Yahoo! Travel destination page about the city. Click Fare Info for detailed information about a fare.

You can also add the Best Fares module to your My Yahoo! page and be able to track the fares from that location. To do so, click Add To My Yahoo! to open the page shown in Figure 16-11. From there, click Add It to place the Best Fares module on your My Yahoo! page.

Booking a Best Fare

Click the Book It link next to a fare in the Best Fares section to actually make a reservation and either pay for the tickets or place them on hold for 24 hours. Clicking Book It opens a page on which you enter the number of travelers for whom you need tickets and whether they are between the ages of 2 and 11. Select the numbers in the appropriate lists and then click Show Me Airlines to open a page that shows the airlines with the lowest prices and a summary of the rules you must follow to purchase tickets. Typically, airlines have rules about advanced purchases, earliest and latest travel dates, and earliest and latest return dates. Click Rules to read a detailed description of the rules, read the rules, and then click Return To Previous Page.

Below the lowest rates is a list of other fares in ascending order by price. You might need to check out these fares if the rules that apply to the lowest fares are not acceptable to you.

FIGURE 16-10   Adding trips to the Best Fares list

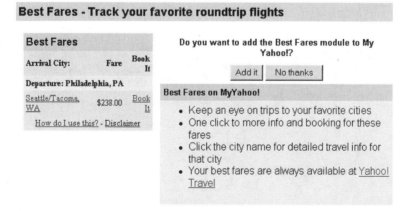

FIGURE 16-11   Adding the Best Fares module to your My Yahoo! page

16

Click Select next to a fare to display the calendar in which you select from the departure dates that are available for a certain rate, as shown in Figure 16-12. Days for which a fare is available are shown in yellow; days for which a fare is not available are shown in gray.

If your departure date is not available, you can use either of these links:

■ Try A Different Airline Or Another Low Fare

■ Get The Specific Date You Want, Even If The Fare Increases

If you choose to try a different airline or another fare, a page appears in which you make a selection. If you decide to get the specific date, you'll be able to search for a flight, as you'll learn to do in the next section of this chapter.

Tip   *A blue arrow appears on the edge of the calendar if there are other available days in other months. Click the arrow to scroll the calendar.*

If your date is available, click it in the calendar. Yahoo! displays a similar calendar that shows available return dates. If your return date is not available, you can choose one of these options:

■ Try A Different Departure Date

■ Try A Different Airline Or Another Low Fare

■ Get The Specific Date You Want, Even If The Fare Increases

Choose your return date to display a list of available departure flights. Click Select for the desired departure flight to display possible return flights. Select your return flight to display a page that summarizes the itinerary. You can then purchase the tickets or put them on hold.

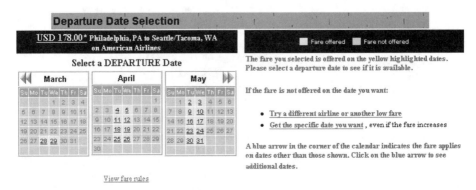

FIGURE 16-12   Selecting your departure date

Using the Air Option

You can also locate a flight by using the Air option in the Make Reservations section of a Yahoo! Travel page.

Make Reservations
Air
Car
Hotel
Vacations
Cruises
Specials

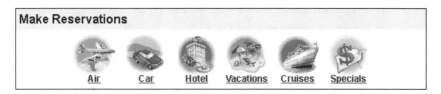

The Air options appear on the Yahoo! Travel home page, as well as the top or bottom of many other Yahoo! pages. When you locate a destination as you browse through Yahoo! Travel, for example, the Make Reservations section appears at the bottom of the page. You can use the options in that section to book reservations to the destination you are investigating.

Click Air in the Make Reservations section at the top of the Yahoo! Travel page to open the Roundtrip Flight Search page shown in Figure 16-13. Then complete the form by following these steps:

Tip *Click Check My Yahoo! Calendar if you need to select or clear a travel date.*

1. Specify the number of travelers.
2. Specify the number of travelers between the ages of 2 and 11.

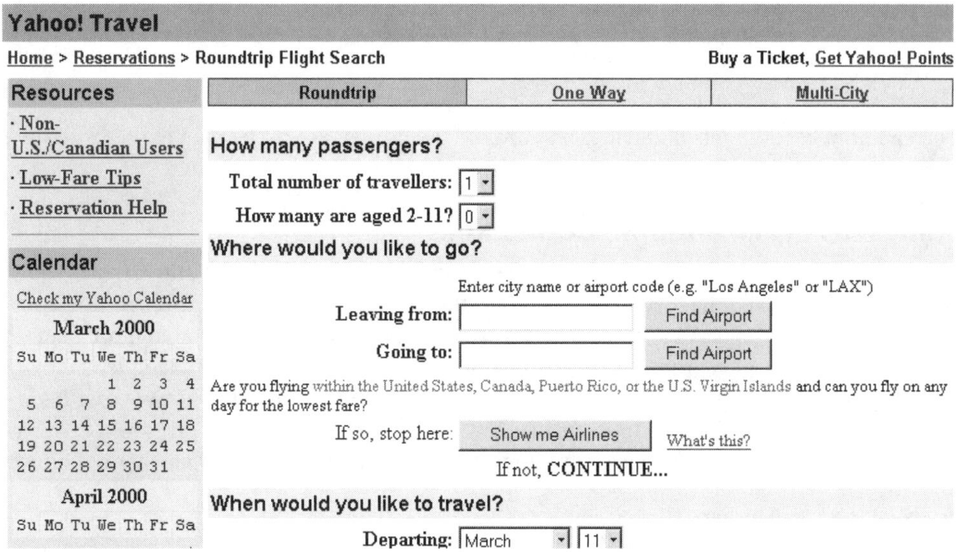

Yahoo! Travel
Home > Reservations > Roundtrip Flight Search
Buy a Ticket, Get Yahoo! Points
Resources
· Non-U.S./Canadian Users
· Low-Fare Tips
· Reservation Help
Calendar
Check my Yahoo Calendar
March 2000
Su Mo Tu We Th Fr Sa
1 2 3 4
5 6 7 8 9 10 11
12 13 14 15 16 17 18
19 20 21 22 23 24 25
26 27 28 29 30 31
April 2000
Su Mo Tu We Th Fr Sa
Roundtrip
One Way
Multi-City
How many passengers?
Total number of travellers: 1
How many are aged 2-11? 0
Where would you like to go?
Enter city name or airport code (e.g. "Los Angeles" or "LAX")
Leaving from:
Find Airport
Going to:
Find Airport
Are you flying within the United States, Canada, Puerto Rico, or the U.S. Virgin Islands and can you fly on any day for the lowest fare?
If so, stop here:
Show me Airlines
What's this?
If not, CONTINUE...
When would you like to travel?
Departing: March 11

FIGURE 16-13 Roundtrip Flight Search page

3. Enter the departure city or airport code. Click Find Airport to display a list of airport codes. Locate the airport from which you will depart and click the code to enter it in the Leaving From box and return to the Roundtrip Flight Search page.

4. Enter the destination city, or use the Find Airport button to locate the airport code. If you selected Air from a city's destination page in Yahoo! Travel, the destination is already entered in the Roundtrip Flight Search page.

5. If you are flying within the United States, Canada, Puerto Rico, or the U.S. Virgin Islands, and you can fly on any day for the lowest fare, click Show Me Airlines to see the lowest fares, as shown previously. Select your fare and continue as explained earlier in this chapter under "Searching for the Best Airline Fares." Otherwise, continue with the following steps.

6. Enter the departing date and time.

7. Specify the return date and time if yours is a round trip.

8. Choose the class of flight. The options are

   ■ Economy class with restrictions

   ■ Economy class without restrictions

   ■ Business class

   ■ First class

9. Select to see all flights or just list nonstop flights first.

10. Select to search all airlines or just one, two, or three airlines that you select.

11. Select to display the nine fares being offered for the best price on the dates you selected, or to search for all flights so you can make the decision.

12. Click Show Me Available Flights.

You can now select flights and either buy or hold the tickets, as you learned to do earlier in this chapter in the section "Express Booking."

One-Way Flights and Multiple Destinations

At the top of the Roundtrip Flight Search page, you can choose One Way or Multi-City. If you select One Way, you do not have to choose a return travel time.

Why the Multi-City option? Sometimes a business or pleasure trip takes you to more than one destination. You may fly from New York to Chicago to visit relatives, for example, and then take a flight to Las Vegas for a vacation. You may then return home to New York with a stopover in Atlanta to take care of some business.

A multiple destination itinerary is one that requires four flights, or more if any are not direct:

■ New York to Chicago

■ Chicago to Las Vegas

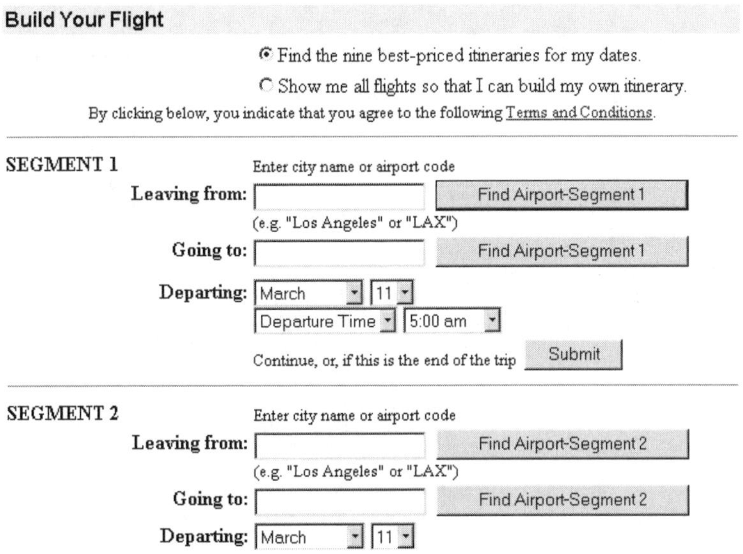

Build Your Flight

◉ Find the nine best-priced itineraries for my dates.

○ Show me all flights so that I can build my own itinerary.

By clicking below, you indicate that you agree to the following Terms and Conditions.

SEGMENT 1

Enter city name or airport code

Leaving from: [   ]   [Find Airport-Segment 1]

(e.g. "Los Angeles" or "LAX")

Going to: [   ]   [Find Airport-Segment 1]

Departing: [March ▾] [11 ▾]

[Departure Time ▾] [5:00 am ▾]

Continue, or, if this is the end of the trip   [Submit]

SEGMENT 2

Enter city name or airport code

Leaving from: [   ]   [Find Airport-Segment 2]

(e.g. "Los Angeles" or "LAX")

Going to: [   ]   [Find Airport-Segment 2]

Departing: [March ▾] [11 ▾]

FIGURE 16-14   Options for a multiple-city itinerary

- Las Vegas to Atlanta
- Atlanta to New York

When you choose the Multi-City option, you specify each leg of the journey as another segment, as shown in Figure 16-14. In each section, enter the departure and destination information for each leg of the journey. For the final section, enter your ultimate destination—a return to the starting point if you are booking a roundtrip itinerary

Making Car Reservations

Once you arrive at your destination, you likely need a way to get around on the ground. Through Yahoo! Travel, you can make reservations for car rentals and even arrange to rent a van, a sports car, or an SUV. See Figure 16-15. Follow these steps to make a car reservation:

16

1. Click Car in the Make Reservations section of a Yahoo! Travel page to open the Rental Car Search page.

2. Enter the city or airport where you want to pick up the car.

3. Enter the number of travelers.

4. Enter the date and time you want to pick up the car.

5. Enter the date and time you want to drop off the car.

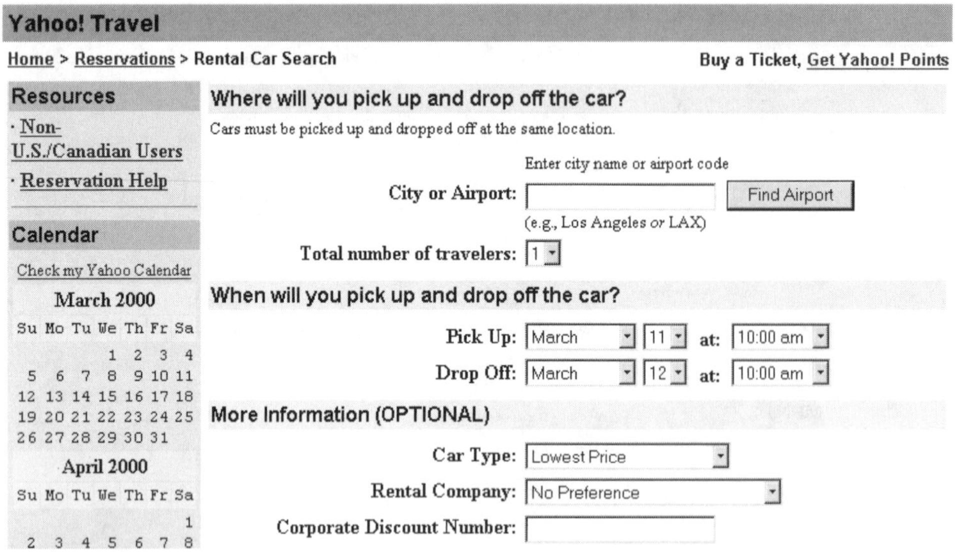

Yahoo! Travel

Home > Reservations > Rental Car Search   Buy a Ticket, Get Yahoo! Points

Resources
· Non-
U.S./Canadian Users
· Reservation Help

Calendar

Check my Yahoo Calendar

March 2000

Su Mo Tu We Th Fr Sa
          1 2 3 4
 5 6 7 8 9 10 11
12 13 14 15 16 17 18
19 20 21 22 23 24 25
26 27 28 29 30 31

April 2000

Su Mo Tu We Th Fr Sa
                   1
 2 3 4 5 6 7 8

Where will you pick up and drop off the car?

Cars must be picked up and dropped off at the same location.

Enter city name or airport code

City or Airport: [   ] [Find Airport]
(e.g., Los Angeles or LAX)

Total number of travelers: [1 ▼]

When will you pick up and drop off the car?

Pick Up: [March ▼] [11 ▼] at: [10:00 am ▼]
Drop Off: [March ▼] [12 ▼] at: [10:00 am ▼]

More Information (OPTIONAL)

Car Type: [Lowest Price ▼]
Rental Company: [No Preference ▼]
Corporate Discount Number: [   ]

FIGURE 16-15   Making a car rental reservation

6. Select the car type. There are 13 options, including size classifications options and options for renting specialty vehicles such as vans and sports cars.

7. Select a preference, if you have one, for a rental company.

8. Enter a corporate discount number if you have one.

9. Click Show Me Available Cars to see a list of rental companies, as shown next.

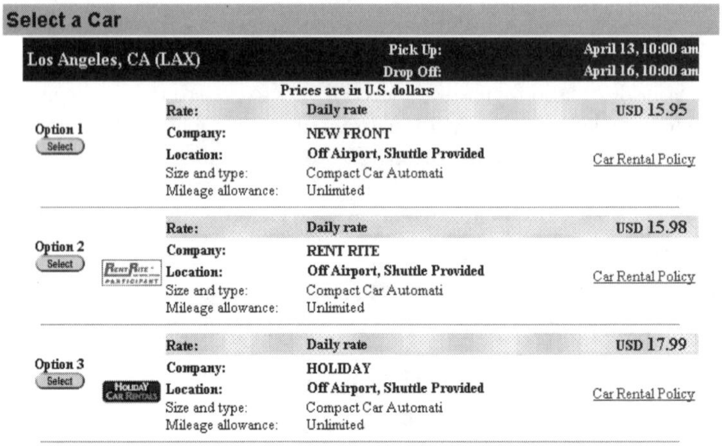

Select a Car

| Los Angeles, CA (LAX) | Pick Up: | April 13, 10:00 am |
| | Drop Off: | April 16, 10:00 am |

Prices are in U.S. dollars

Option 1 [Select]	Rate:	Daily rate	USD 15.95
	Company:	NEW FRONT	
	Location:	Off Airport, Shuttle Provided	Car Rental Policy
	Size and type:	Compact Car Automati	
	Mileage allowance:	Unlimited	
Option 2 [Select]	Rate:	Daily rate	USD 15.98
	Company:	RENT RITE	
	Location:	Off Airport, Shuttle Provided	Car Rental Policy
	Size and type:	Compact Car Automati	
	Mileage allowance:	Unlimited	
Option 3 [Select]	Rate:	Daily rate	USD 17.99
	Company:	HOLIDAY	
	Location:	Off Airport, Shuttle Provided	Car Rental Policy
	Size and type:	Compact Car Automati	
	Mileage allowance:	Unlimited	

Click Car Rental Policy to read the company's requirements and restrictions.

10. Click Select to display a summary of the rental details.

11. Click Continue.

Finally, in the page that appears, enter information about your fellow travelers and your credit card, and then complete the process to confirm the reservation.

Making Hotel Reservations

Getting a place to stay during a vacation or business trip is the next step in finalizing your itinerary. Yahoo! offers access to thousands of hotels and other lodging establishments around the world. You can see a picture of the establishment, select the type of room and rate that you want, and then actually make the reservation.

You can search for hotels from almost any Yahoo! Travel page. Most pages offer, in the Make Reservations section, the Hotel option. You can also browse destinations, and then book a hotel from the Lodging information on a site's Destination page.

To book a hotel from the Make Reservations section of a Yahoo! Travel page, follow these steps:

1. Click Hotel in the Make Reservations section of a Yahoo! Travel page to open the Hotel Search page shown in the following illustration.

Yahoo! Travel

Home > Reservations > Hotel Search   Buy a Ticket, Get Yahoo! Points

Resources

· Non-U.S./Canadian Users
· Reservation Help
·Yahoo! Lodging -
Browse descriptions and reviews of places to stay in the U.S.

Where do you need a hotel?

Enter city name or airport code

City or Airport: [_____] [Find Airport]
(e.g., Los Angeles *or* LAX)

Number of guests: [1 ▾]

Number of rooms: [1 ▾]

When would you like to stay?

Check In: [March ▾] [11 ▾]

Check Out: [March ▾] [12 ▾]

Calendar

Check my Yahoo Calendar

March 2000

Su Mo Tu We Th Fr Sa
            1 2 3 4
5 6 7 8 9 10 11
12 13 14 15 16 17 18
19 20 21 22 23 24 25
26 27 28 29 30 31

April 2000

Narrow Your Search (OPTIONAL)

If you would like a specific hotel, or a specific type of property, please select below. Select fewer options to get more results!

Hotel Company: [No Preference ▾]

Specific Hotel: [_____]

16

---

2. Enter the city or airport where you'll be staying.

3. Enter the number of guests.

4. Enter the number of rooms.

5. Enter the date you want to check in.

6. Enter the date you want to check out.

7. Select a preference, if you have one, for a hotel chain.

8. Enter a specific hotel if you want one.

9. Select the type of hotel from these options shown at right.

10. Choose an optional amenity, such as pets allowed or children's program.

11. Optionally, select a rate type. The options are standard, corporate, family plan, promotional, senior, and government/military.

Property Type:
- [ ] All Suites
- [ ] Apartments
- [ ] B&B
- [ ] Convention Facility
- [ ] Extended Stay
- [ ] First Class
- [ ] Historical
- [ ] Luxury
- [ ] Motel
- [ ] Ranch
- [ ] Resort

12. Enter a discount number if you have one.

13. Click Show Me Available Hotels. A numbered list of hotels appears, as shown in the next illustration. Hotels that are not available for the dates you specified have a red number and the Select button is not selectable. Hotels that are available have a black number.

● Available Hotels ● Not Available   **Prices are in U.S. dollars**   List View / Map View

Hotel Information	Distance from Search Point	Approximate Price Range
(Select) ❶ **WYNDHAM LOS ANGELES AIRPORT** Wyndham Hotels L.A. AIRPORT Los Angeles, CA 591 Rooms / 12 Floors Legend The Wyndham Hotel is the closest hotel to the Los Angeles International Airport. The hotel is convenient area attractions including ... Click for more info...	0.8 mi / 1.3 km	USD 154.00 -- USD 154.00*

Hotel Information	Distance from Search Point	Approximate Price Range
(Select) ❷ **CROWNE PLAZA LOS ANGELES APT** Holiday Inn CENTURY BLVD Los Angeles, CA 615 Rooms / 15 Floors Legend Click here to view the summary for this hotel...	1.1 mi / 1.8 km	USD 134.00 -- USD 189.00*

Note *If the city you enter cannot be found, a list of possible matches appears. Select the city and click Continue, or click Back and try again.*

14. Click Select to display the Select A Room page, which lists the types of rooms that are available and their prices. There may also be options for extras such as rollaway beds and cribs.

15. Click Select next to the room you want to see the hotel's reservation policy.

16. Click Select This Room to open the Traveler Information page.

17. Enter the names of each of your fellow guests and your credit card information.

18. Click Information Is Correct.

Then just follow the prompts that appear onscreen to complete the reservation process.

Another way to make a hotel reservation is from the lodging page. As you learned in Chapter 16, you can browse vacation destinations to find the country you want to visit, and then select a specific city or region to see its Destination page. Use the Lodging option on the Destination page to see a list of hotels in the location you are interested in.

The lodging page also contains the Book A Hotel section shown in Figure 16-16. The city's name will already appear in the City box, so all you have to do is enter the number of guests and rooms, and the check-in and check-out dates, and click Find Hotels. A numbered list of hotels appears from which you can select the one you want to book.

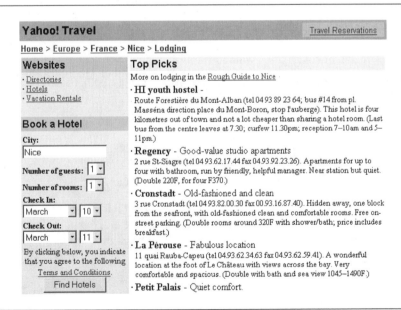

FIGURE 16-16   Booking a hotel from a city's lodging page

Signing Up for a Package Vacation

As an alternative to booking all of the components of a vacation yourself—the airline tickets, hotel rooms, and rental car—you sign up for a vacation package. A vacation package usually includes transportation and lodging, and sometimes meals and activities. There are even packages aimed at special interests and hobbies, such as bicycling through the French countryside or touring the town made famous by the classic "The Prisoner" television series.

Vacation packages can be great bargains because the tour operator negotiates with airlines and hotels to obtain low group rates. Tour operators also handle all of the arrangements for you—flying to the destination, going from the airport to the hotel, taking the local tours.

To access vacation packages in Yahoo!, you can start from a location's destination page or go to the Make Reservations section.

Destination Vacation Search

When you are browsing Yahoo! Travel and reach a location's destination page, you usually find the Vacation Search options shown in the illustration at right. The Region/Country and Keyword options are already filled in with the names of the region or the country of destination. However, you can change these options and look up vacations in other locations or search for specific activities by entering **Paris, ballooning**, or another term in the Keyword box.

Follow these steps to search for a vacation package:

1. Select the region or country you want to visit.

2. Select a Price Per Person. The options are Budget (Under $1,000), Standard (($1,000–$2,500), and Deluxe (Over $2,500).

3. Enter a range that describes the number of days you want to go on vacation, such as from 5 to 7.

4. Enter a keyword for the vacation. The keyword can be a specific country, city, or activity.

5. Click the Search button to display a list of vacation packages.

You can click any of the column headings, such as Duration and Price, to sort the list a different way. Click the name of a package you are interested in to read about it. On the details page, you can click More Information to go to the operator's Web site and get booking information.

To eliminate tours that you are not interested in, use the Narrow Your Search section. Pull down the Interest list to select from the options shown here, and then click the Search button.

If you do not want to search for a vacation starting from a destination page, click Vacations in the Make Reservations section of a Yahoo! Travel page. Doing so opens the Search For A Vacation page.

The options presented there are the same as the options in the Vacation Search section. Select options and then click Search to list vacation packages.

Booking a Cruise

Cruises are a very popular form of vacation because the vacation starts as soon as you board the vessel. You enjoy your vacation as you travel to a destination, or just float nowhere in particular on a sunny sea.

To locate and book a cruise in Yahoo!, follow these steps:

1. Click Cruises in the Make Reservations section of a Yahoo! Travel page to open the Search for a Cruise page.

2. Select the region or country you want to visit.

3. Choose the price per person.

4. Enter the minimum and maximum number of days.

5. Enter a keyword.

6. Click Search.

A list of cruise packages appears, as shown in Figure 16-17. Click the cruise you are interested in to read more information about it and perhaps visit the operator's Web site to book a reservation.

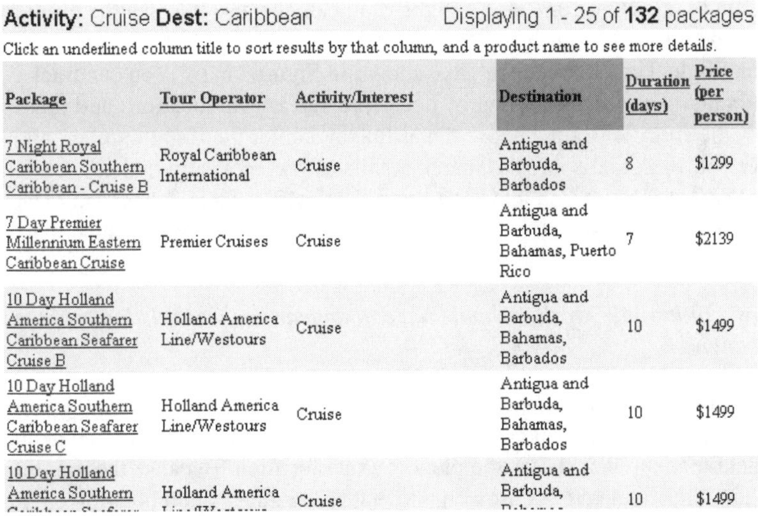

Activity: Cruise **Dest:** Caribbean   Displaying 1 - 25 of **132** packages

Click an underlined column title to sort results by that column, and a product name to see more details.

Package	Tour Operator	Activity/Interest	Destination	Duration (days)	Price (per person)
7 Night Royal Caribbean Southern Caribbean - Cruise B	Royal Caribbean International	Cruise	Antigua and Barbuda, Barbados	8	$1299
7 Day Premier Millennium Eastern Caribbean Cruise	Premier Cruises	Cruise	Antigua and Barbuda, Bahamas, Puerto Rico	7	$2139
10 Day Holland America Southern Caribbean Seafarer Cruise B	Holland America Line/Westours	Cruise	Antigua and Barbuda, Bahamas, Barbados	10	$1499
10 Day Holland America Southern Caribbean Seafarer Cruise C	Holland America Line/Westours	Cruise	Antigua and Barbuda, Bahamas, Barbados	10	$1499
10 Day Holland America Southern Caribbean Seafarer	Holland America Line/Westours	Cruise	Antigua and Barbuda, Bahamas	10	$1499

FIGURE 16-17   Booking a cruise

16

How to ... Find Vacation Specials

Airlines, tour operators, hotels, and others in the travel business frequently offer special deals and package plans. You can often save money by tailoring your travel plans and vacation plans to take advantage of one of these special offers.

To see what specials are currently available, click Specials int he Make Reservations section of a Yahoo! Travel page. Doing so takes you to the Search For A Vacation page. You can then choose from a list of airlines, rental car companies, hotels, tour operators, and cruise lines that are offering special deals. For example, use the link to ResortQuest to access a listing of over 17,000 privately owned vacation homes and condominiums.

My Trips

You can maintain a complete record of your reservations and itinerary, and check flight times, in the My Trips section of the Yahoo! Travel home page.

Click Current Reservations in that section to see a list of all the reservations you made through the Yahoo! Travel system. You can then click a reservation to see its details.

Use the Check Flight Time option to see if a flight is on time and exactly where the plane is located. Being able to track a flight is a great feature if you are expecting a visitor who is arriving by air or you want to track someone else's flight. You can also use it to see the exact route a flight takes in preparation for your own flight.

Click Check Flight Time to open the page shown in Figure 16-18. You can track a flight by entering its flight number or by searching by departure and arrival locations and times.

If you know the specific flight, choose the airline and enter the flight number, and then tell Yahoo! whether you want to display the search results as text or as a graphic. Click Find Flight. If you selected See Text Results, a table shows you the flight's status, its current location, its altitude, and its speed. If you selected See Graphic Results, a set of gauges and a map appears, as shown in Figure 16-19.

 *It takes a little while for the graphic page to appear because it is loaded as a Java application.*

The gauges show the flight's current speed, heading, and altitude. The country map (or world map depending on the flight) shows the overall flight path. Below the gauges, however, is a detailed map that shows the plane's exact location. Because the graphic is a Java application, you can leave it onscreen and watch the gauges and position change as the information is updated.

Check Flight Time

Home > Check Flight Time

This service searches real time FAA flight information on over 300 airlines. It shows flights
between major cities within the United States that are flying, have recently flown, or are about to
take off.

Locate a specific flight

Airline: | Aer Lingus   ▾ |

Show me more airlines

Flight Number: [   ]

⦿ See Text Results
○ See Graphic Results

[Find Flight]

OR, Search for a flight by city and time

NOTE: You **must** enter a departure and/or an arrival time.

Departure City: | Choose a City   ▾ |

Show me more cities

Checking the status of a flight

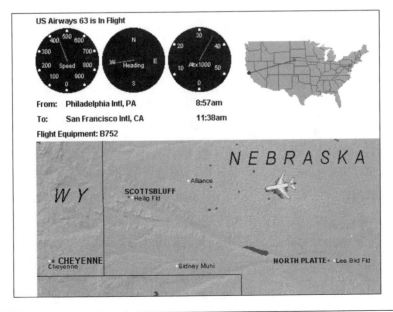

Graphic display of flight status

16

If you do not know the flight number, enter the departure and arrival cities and times. You'll see a list of flights with their status information. Click the icon of the United States to the right of a flight to display its status graphically.

Make Restaurant and Other Reservations

Extensive as they are, the travel and vacation planning you can do is not limited to the resources available in Yahoo! Travel. Many restaurants, hotels, travel companies, and tour operators have their own Web sites where they offer information and online reservations.

Use the online Yellow Pages of Yahoo! or the general search functions to locate these resources and complete your travel plans.

Chapter 17

Playing Yahoo! Games

How to . . .

- ■ Change your game ID
- ■ Enter a game room
- ■ Join a game
- ■ Host a game
- ■ Use voice chat
- ■ Play fantasy sports games

There's a lot of fun to be had on the Internet, and Yahoo! games should be the first place to start. Most Yahoo! games are multiple player. You can play chess, checkers, poker, mah-jongg, and other games against Yahoo! members in real-time. Each player can see and respond to the moves of other players, just as if they were sitting in the same room. As soon as you move a chess piece, for example, your opponent sees the move and can counter it. If you want to learn how to play a game, you can watch games in action but not participate. You can study the rules and watch how other players play before trying it yourself. Other games are single player and are played against a computer rather than a human opponent.

Rules of the Game

To play games on Yahoo!, all you need is your Yahoo! ID and password, and a browser that supports Java and JavaScript, such as version 4 or later of Microsoft Internet Explorer or Netscape Navigator. Java and JavaScript are computer languages that make it possible for Yahoo! games to be played in real-time across the Internet.

If games do not work on your computer, you may have an older version of a browser, or the Java and JavaScript features are not turned on.

To turn on Java and JavaScript with Microsoft Internet Explorer, follow these steps:

1. Click the Start button, choose Settings, and choose Control Panel to go to the Windows Control Panel.

2. Double-click on the Internet Options icon.

3. Click the Advanced tab.

4. Scroll the window to the Java VM section.

5. Select the check box labeled JIT Compiler For Virtual Machine Enabled (Requires Restart).

Games will not work with WebTV, if you have Windows 3.1, or with older versions of software from AOL, CompuServe, or Prodigy. They may also not work if you access the Internet through a proxy server or company firewall.

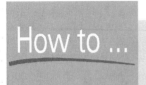 **Play Yahoo! Games on the Macintosh**

To play games on a Macintosh computer, you should be using the Macintosh OS Runtime for Java and Microsoft Internet Explorer 4.5.

To download the most recent version of Internet Explorer for the Macintosh computer, go to http://www.microsoft.com/mac/ie/default.asp.

To download the most recent version of Macintosh OS Runtime for Java, go to http://www.apple.com/java/.

Game Basics

After you select a game you want to play, you choose from different game rooms. If you choose to play chess, for example, you select from a number of rooms in which chess is being played. Within each room, one or more tables are set up. You can ask to join a table to play the game, watch the action as a nonparticipant, or create your own table. The person who starts a table is called the *host*. You can create three types of tables:

- A *public table* in which anyone can join or watch
- A *protected table* in which only invited players can join, but anyone can watch
- A *private table* in which only invited players can join or watch

In addition to playing the game, you can chat with other players by typing messages in a chat area. The Towers game even offers a voice chat so that you can speak with other players (if your computer is equipped with a microphone and speakers).

With some games you can also select a level of play. The available levels depend on the game, but you may be able to choose from these levels:

- Social
- Beginner
- Intermediate
- Advanced

The table host chooses whether he or she wants to play a rated game. When you play a rated game, statistics are saved about the winner and loser. Each player is given a rating that generally indicates his or her skill level. You can use the rating system to tell if you are playing an individual who is as skilled as you.

17

Some games offer special rooms called *ladders*. Every player that takes part in a ladders game is ranked in relation to other players. The more games you win, the higher you are on the game ladder.

When you play your first ladder game, you start from the bottom rung of the ladder. Winning games moves you up the ladder; losing games moves you down the ladder. If you do not participate in a ladder game for 30 days, Yahoo! automatically removes you from the ladder. However, to encourage competition, Yahoo! resets the ladder every three months. Every three months, all players are placed in the same position. Players' ratings in nonladder games, however, are not reset.

Playing a Game

Click Games in the Yahoo! home page to open the games home page shown in Figure 17-1. The Games page offers three tabs:

- Gameroom is where you start games and join games in progress.

- Reviews & News presents reviews of games and news for gamers.

- Communities takes you to chats, clubs, and other online gaming communities. You can also keep track of your playing schedule in your Yahoo! Calendar.

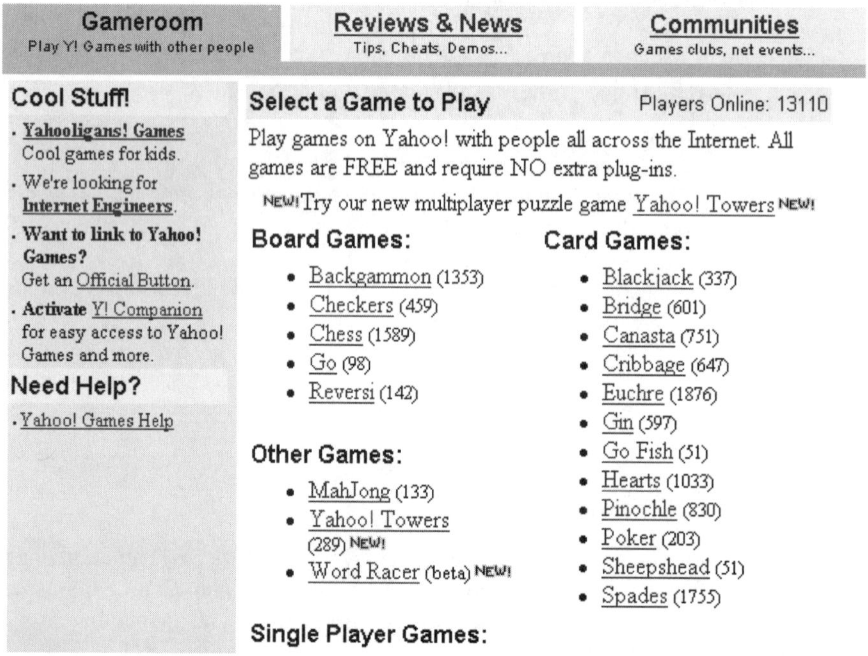

Gameroom Play Y! Games with other people	**Reviews & News** Tips, Cheats, Demos...	**Communities** Games clubs, net events...

Cool Stuff!

. **Yahooligans! Games**
Cool games for kids.

. We're looking for
Internet Engineers.

. **Want to link to Yahoo!
Games?**
Get an Official Button.

. **Activate** Y! Companion
for easy access to Yahoo!
Games and more.

Need Help?

. Yahoo! Games Help

Select a Game to Play   Players Online: 13110

Play games on Yahoo! with people all across the Internet. All games are FREE and require NO extra plug-ins.

NEW! Try our new multiplayer puzzle game Yahoo! Towers NEW!

Board Games:
- Backgammon (1353)
- Checkers (459)
- Chess (1589)
- Go (98)
- Reversi (142)

Other Games:
- MahJong (133)
- Yahoo! Towers (289) NEW!
- Word Racer (beta) NEW!

Single Player Games:

Card Games:
- Blackjack (337)
- Bridge (601)
- Canasta (751)
- Cribbage (647)
- Euchre (1876)
- Gin (597)
- Go Fish (51)
- Hearts (1033)
- Pinochle (830)
- Poker (203)
- Sheepshead (51)
- Spades (1755)

FIGURE 17-1   Yahoo! Games home page

The multiple player games are listed first in three categories: Board Games, Card Games, and Other Games. Glance at the numbers beside game names to see how many people are currently playing.

The single-player games are listed next. Anagram, Crossword, Cryptogram, Maze, and Wordsearch require only one player. You play Blackjack by yourself against a dealer. You play Hearts, Euchre, and Spades by yourself against computer-generated opponents.

Fantasy sports and contests are listed next. In fantasy games such as automobile racing, basketball, golf, and soccer, you pretend that you're the team owner. You create a team of real-life sports figures whose real-life performances determine your team's success and the success of other teams.

Last are links to games at Boxerjam, a Yahoo! partner site where you can win money and prizes by playing games online.

Choosing a Game ID

Each game participant and watcher can be identified by his or her Yahoo! ID. However, if you do not want players to see your Yahoo! ID, you can change the name under which you play by creating another profile. Follow these steps to do so:

1.   Click Edit on the right side of the game banner to open the Public Profile window.

2.   Click Create New Public Profile.

3.   Enter a profile name.

4.   Optionally, enter more information about yourself.

5.   Click the Click Here When Done button.

You can now select the identity you want to play under. Pull down the Playing As list and choose the name, as shown here.

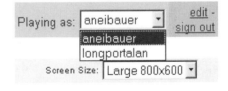

 You may also be able to select the room size from the Screen Size list. The options are Small 640 × 480 and Large 800 × 600.

Getting Started with a Game

While the rules and methods of play vary with each game, all games get started in the same way. You select the game you want to play, a room to enter, and a table to join or create.

 Click Yahooligans! Games to access games designed for children. For protection, children must select an anonymous player ID rather than use their Yahoo! ID or profile name.

From the Yahoo! Games home page, click the name of a game to open its room list, as shown in Figure 17-2.

17

FIGURE 17-2   Game room list

The names of rooms that are full and cannot accommodate any more tables or players are shown in black. The names of rooms that have empty tables or need players look and act like hyperlinks. If you like, you can read the rules of a game by clicking How To Play and studying the How To Play page. You can then display the rules of the game or get general help on Yahoo! games.

From the game room page, follow these steps to start playing a game:

1. If there are tabs showing levels of play, click the tab for the level of game you wish to join. Only rooms at that level will be displayed.

2. Click the room that you want to enter. A window opens that shows the tables in the room, as shown in the following illustration. The window may take a while to open.

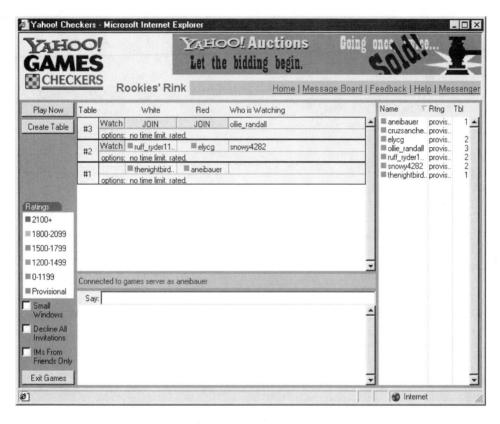

3. The first time you access a room devoted to the game you want to play, a message box appears. Click Yes to load the game.

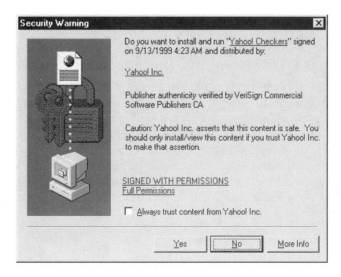

17

Tables are numbered and show the ID of each player and person who is watching. With chess and checkers, the color of each player is also indicated. Below the names of the players are any options that have been selected. Not all games have options. With board games, the options indicate whether the game has a time limit for moves and is rated. A rated game is one for which a player's rating is changed according to the outcome.

Along the right side of the window is a list that shows players' names, players' ratings, and the tables at which they are currently playing. The notation *provis* indicates a new player who has a provision rating. You can learn something about a player by double-clicking his or her ID and reading the player information window, shown at right.

The window contains the player's rating information, won and loss record, and other statistics. You can send players an instant message over Yahoo! Messenger, display a profile, or choose to ignore invitations from other players. To send a message, for example, type it in the Send Instant Message text box and click Send.

A color icon indicates each player's rating. The legend on the left side of the table page explains what the colors mean.

Below the rating legend are three options:

- ■ **Small Windows** Displays the game window in a smaller size. Use this option if banner ads or other distractions on the screen overlap and interfere with a larger window.

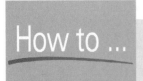 **Ping a Player**

The player information window includes a button labeled Ping. *Ping* means to send a signal someplace on the Internet that is bounced back to you. If the signal is not bounced back, the site you are pinging is not online. The time it takes for the ping signal to return tells you the speed of the overall connection between you and the site you pinged.

By clicking Ping on a player's information window, you can gauge the speed of the connection between you and the player. After you click Ping, a message tells you the number of seconds it took for the signal to reach the other player and return to you. Ping times over two seconds indicate a lag time in the play of the game. If you like a fast-paced game, avoid playing someone with a long ping time.

- **Decline All Invitations**   Automatically declines invitations to play games. Select this option if you are just observing and learning.

- **IMs From Friends**   Only rejects instant messages from persons not on your friends list.

If you see a Watch button, the table is public and everyone can view the action. To view the game, click the Watch button. The game's window opens so you can observe the game. However, you can't participate or select any options that affect the game's outcome.

Playing a Game

From within the table window, there are four ways to start playing:

- Click Join to join a specific game.

- Click Play Now to automatically join a table that has room for another player. Yahoo! selects the table for you.

- Click Create Table to start your own game and invite others to play.

- Wait until a table host invites you to play.

Where you see a Join button, the table has room for another player and is public. Click Join or Play Now to open the game table. Figure 17-3 shows a game table for Checkers. Click Sit to take your place at the table and then click Start Game. Yahoo! begins the game when all of the players have clicked Start Game.

While you are watching a game or just looking at the tables window, another Yahoo! member might invite you to join a game. When you are invited to a game, this box appears. It lists the name of the player who invited you, the options of the game, and where the game is located. Click Accept to be taken to the game table.

If you do not want to play, click Decline. However, good game protocol suggests entering a short message in the Reason box to explain why you don't care to play. Before you click Decline, enter something along these lines: "Thanks, but I'm just watching" or "Just don't have time now, maybe later."

Tip   *If you want to avoid getting invitations, select the Decline All Invitations check box.*

If you click Decline, this message shown at right appears on the other player's screen.

Yahoo! games are very realistic and follow the same rules as their counterparts in the real world. Figure 17-4, for example, shows a game of Blackjack in progress. The goal of Blackjack is to get a hand of 21 or a hand closer to 21 than the dealer's.

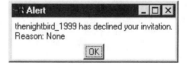

17

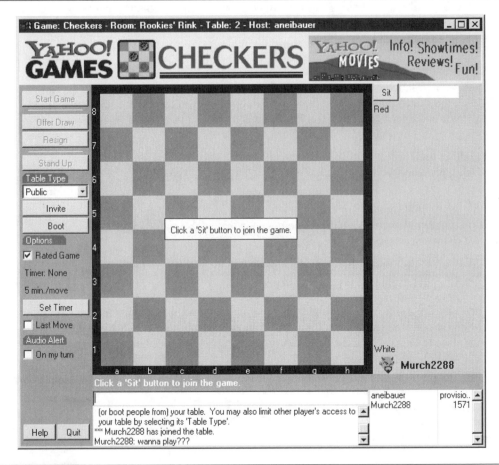

FIGURE 17-3   A typical game window

The host of Blackjack can select a slow, normal, or fast-paced game. The pace determines how long a player has to place a bid and make a decision on a hand. In a normal-paced game, for example, players have eight seconds to place their bets and thirty seconds in which to move. Fast-paced games provide only three seconds for betting and four for moves. Slow-paced games place no limit on bid times and a sixty-second limit on moves.

When your hand is dealt and it is not 21 or over, you can stay with the hand you have (stand) or draw another card (hit). When the dealer has an Ace face up, players may purchase insurance against the dealer having 21. Players can also double their bets and receive only one more card. If you are dealt a pair (two of the same value cards) or two cards with a total of 10, you can also choose to split and divide the cards into two separate hands.

Note   *Some casinos only allow players to split when dealt a pair.*

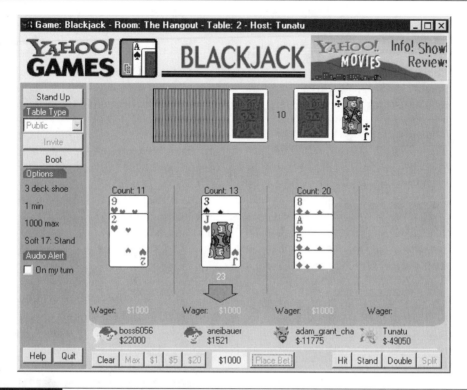

FIGURE 17-4   Playing Blackjack on Yahoo!

When each player either chooses to stand or draws cards totaling 21 or over, the dealer draws. Players are declared winners or losers and the winnings are increased or decreased.

In other games, a box reports who won the game, as shown at right.

Before you play a game, learn the rules and perhaps watch a few games to get comfortable playing. If the game has levels, start with a level that is appropriate for your skills. When you're learning a game, for example, start in a social or beginner room. Work your way up to the intermediate and advanced rooms as your rating increases.

Depending on the game, you may be able to select from one or more buttons along the left side of the table window. The Stand Up button, for example, gives you these options for ending the game before it is completed:

- Quit And Forfeit, which counts the game as a loss to you and a win to the opponent
- Quit And Cancel, which ends the game without changing any player's rating as long as the other players agree

17

- Quit And Save, which ends the game but saves it so you can continue playing at a later time, as long as the other players agree
- Never Mind, which continues the game

The Offer Draw button gives the other player the option of calling the game a draw—no winner or loser. The Resign button ends the game and declares the other player the winner. The Undo Turn button, which is available in a few board games, lets you retract your last move.

Hosting a Game

Hosting a game means to start your own table in a game room. Start a new table under these conditions:

- There are no games with open seats.
- You want to invite Yahoo! members to join you.
- You want to play a game with specific options that are not being used.

As the host of a game, you can choose the table type, choose the game options, and invite others to join. You can also boot—that is, remove—players from a game.

To host a game, follow these steps:

1. Select the game you want to host.

2. Choose a level tab, if level tabs are available for the game.

3. Go to the game room where you want to host the game.

4. Click Create Table.

5. In some cases, several options appear, as shown in the illustration at right, where a Yahoo! member is creating a Blackjack table.

6. Choose the table type: Public, Protected, or Private.

7. Choose from other options that are available, depending on the game. For example, sometimes you can sound an audio alert when it is your move, play a rated game, or set a time limit for moves. Choosing Set Timer for checkers, for example, opens the box at lower right.

If you created a public table, you can wait until other members click Join Or Play Now or you can invite others to play. To invite a player, click the Invite button to open the Invite box shown in

the illustration on the right. Type the ID of a person you want to
invite or select an ID from the list, and then click Invite.

As the host, you can also click the Boot button and eject a player
from the game. Click Boot to see a list of the current players. Then
either type the ID of the person you want to eject or select his or her
ID from the list and click Boot.

Playing Card Games Solo

Most card games require more than one player, or at least one player
and a dealer. Some multiple player card games, however, can be
played by yourself, which is a great way to learn a game without the
pressure of other Yahoo! members watching.

To play Blackjack by yourself, host a game and make it private.
The game will then pit you against the dealer. You can also play
Hearts, Euchre, and Spades by yourself against computer-generated opponents called *robots*.

Follow these steps to play a solo card game:

1.   Click Create Table to host a game.

2.   Select a private table.

3.   Click Sit to position yourself at the table.

4.   Click the Play Robot button.

Play Robot   Yahoo! will assign robot players to the other seats to fill out the table,
as shown in Figure 17-5.

Playing Single-Player Games

The single-player games are Anagram, Crossword, Cryptogram, Maze, and Wordsearch.
All except Maze are word games.

In Maze, which is shown in Figure 17-6, you have to find a path through the
computer-generated maze. You choose the level of difficulty, choose five options from easy to
hard, and click Start Clock if you want to time your progress. Then you drag the blue dot through
the maze and try to get to the flag on the right side of the maze.

Frustrated? Click Start Auto-Solve and Yahoo! will show you the path. Click Stop
Auto-Solve when you're ready to take over again. Click Path Verify and Yahoo! will tell you
when you took the wrong path so you don't get lost in the maze. Click New Maze to generate
another random maze, or click Clear Path to erase your path and start over.

Crossword is a typical crossword puzzle like the kind that you find in newspapers and
magazines, except you can click these buttons to help you along:

■   Reveal Letter shows the first letter of the current word.

■   Reveal Word shows the current word.

17

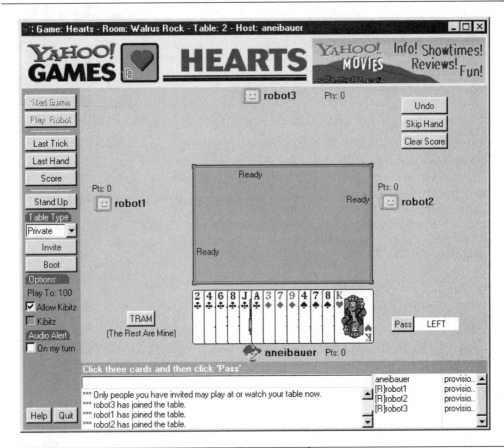

FIGURE 17-5 Playing against robot players

■ Reveal All solves the entire puzzle.

■ Letter Verify immediately indicates if the letter you entered is incorrect.

■ Save Puzzle lets you save the puzzle so you can continue later.

If you click the Save Puzzle button, a page appears with the Resume Puzzle button. Add the page to your browser's favorites or bookmarks list. When you want to resume playing, open the page you bookmarked and click the Resume Puzzle button.

In Anagram, the object is to unscramble characters to form words, and then use letters from each word to solve a puzzle, as shown in Figure 17-7.

The object of Cryptogram is to decipher a quotation, and the aim of Wordsearch is to locate words in a grid of letters.

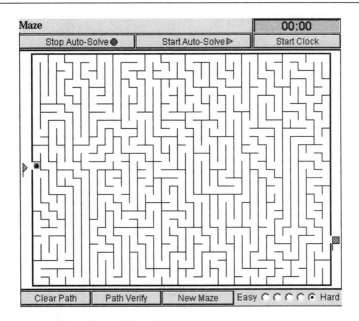

FIGURE 17-6   The Maze game

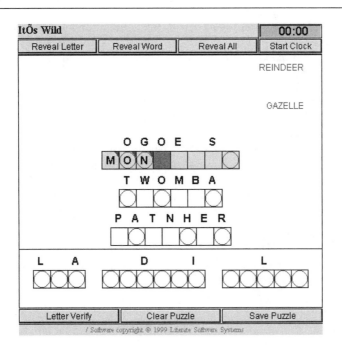

FIGURE 17-7   Anagram

17

Chatting with Other Players

All of the multiple-player games offer a chat area where you can send messages to and receive messages from other players. Just type your comment and click the Send button. All of the comments appear in the list box at the bottom of the window.

Some rooms in the Towers game, however, also offer voice chat. If your computer is equipped with a microphone and speakers, you can talk and listen to other participants and watchers. You can tell if a room is equipped for voice chat by looking for this link:

Tower of Babel * Voice Chat * social

When you enter the room, you'll see the Voice bar under the play area:

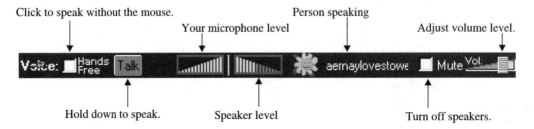

Click to speak without the mouse.   Your microphone level   Person speaking   Adjust volume level.

Hold down to speak.   Speaker level   Turn off speakers.

> **Note**   *If the Voice bar is not displayed or one of its features does not work, either the feature is not activated or your computer is not equipped or set up properly for voice. To use Voice, you need a sound card (either half or full duplex), speakers, and a microphone.*

As soon as you enter the room, you'll hear conversations taking place. The name of the person who is speaking appears in the Voice bar; the speaker's output level is shown on the right side of the level meter. To raise or lower the volume, slide the control on the right side of the bar. Click Mute to stop all voice output.

To speak to other players, click and hold down the Talk button, and then speak into your computer's microphone. Your output is shown on the left side of the level meter. Release the mouse when you have finished speaking. To speak without holding down the Talk button, click the Hands Free button. Just be sure to remember that the others in the room hear everything you say.

Fantasy Games and Contests

While most games are played onscreen in real-time, fantasy sports games and contests are played over a period of time. The sport games include

- Auto Racing
- Pro Basketball

- College Basketball
- Golf
- Hockey
- Soccer

In each of these games, you create your own dream team and add the names of real players to your team roster. The players' real-life performances determine your team's success and the success of other Yahoo! members' teams.

Each game is timed, with new contests starting each week or month or other interval. To participate in a contest, you create your team and select a team roster by a certain deadline.

The general procedure for creating a fantasy sports team is about the same. However, the initial setup options differ. As an example, however, follow these steps to create a Major League Soccer (MLS) dream team:

1. Click the sport you want to play from the Yahoo! Games home page, in this case, MLS Soccer.

2. Click Create Team in the page that appears.

3. Read the registration rules that appear and click Yes, I Accept to open the form shown next.

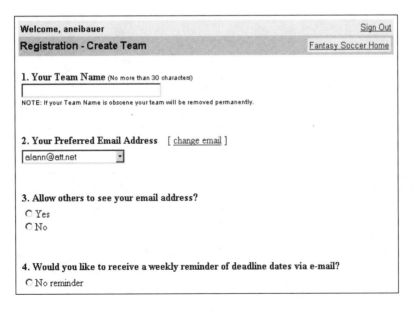

4. Enter a name for your team.

5. Select the e-mail address you want to use for the game, or click Change E-Mail to specify a new e-mail address.

6. Select Yes or No to say whether you want others to see your e-mail address.

7. Choose whether you want to get weekly reminders about deadlines and the number of days (1 or 2) to be notified before the deadline.

8. Select a starting formation from these options:

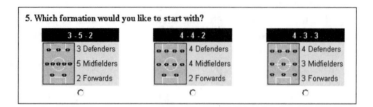

9. Specify whether you want to get e-mail updates from Major League Soccer.

10. If you are a Canadian resident, you must enter an answer to this question:

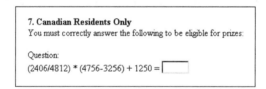

7. Canadian Residents Only
You must correctly answer the following to be eligible for prizes:

Question:
$(2406/4812) * (4756-3256) + 1250 =$ [   ]

11. Click Create Team. A message box reports that your team is registered.

12. Click Build Lineup. You'll see a list of the positions on the team. Next to each position is an Edit button. After you click Edit and assign a position to each player, the complete roster appears, as shown next.

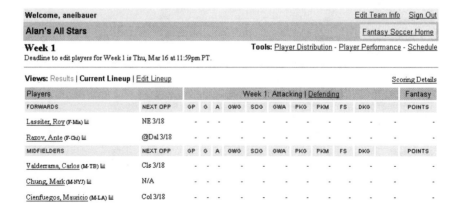

13. Click Edit next to each position to display a list of actual players and their statistics. Click a player's name to see a detailed profile.

14. Click the option button for the player you want to select for the position. Each player is assigned a number of points and a unit value. A maximum total unit value prevents you from selecting all the highest rated players.

15. Click Submit Changes.

16. Repeat steps 13 to 15 to complete the entire team roster.

17. Click Fantasy Soccer Home to open the page.

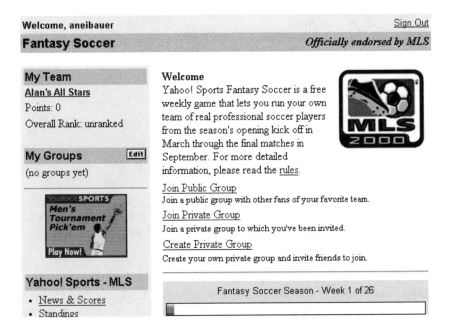

Henceforth, this same page appears whenever you select Soccer on the Yahoo! Games home page. Click the name of your team to view or change the roster and to see your performance statistics.

Note *Use the group options to share information with other sports fans.*

The Contests section in the Yahoo! Games home page offers these options:

■ College Tourney, in which you try to pick the winners of this year's tournament games.

■ Stock Market Challenge, in which you buy and sell shares to outperform other Yahoo! participants.

■ Oscar Pick'em, in which you try to guess this year's Oscar winners.

17

Welcome, aneibauer   Sign Out

Yahoo! Movies - Oscar Pick'em   Pick'em Home | Movies Home

My Groups - (none)

Alan's Theater's Picks

You can edit your picks as often as you like, up until a half hour before the live Academy Awards broadcast (7:30pm ET/4:30pm PT on Sunday, March 26, 2000).

Category	My Pick	Winner	Points Earned
BEST PICTURE	[edit] The Cider House Rules	--	--
BEST ACTOR	[edit] Kevin Spacey - American Beauty	--	--
BEST ACTRESS	[edit] Annette Bening - American Beauty	--	--
BEST SUPPORTING ACTOR	[edit] Michael Clarke Duncan - The Green Mile	--	--
BEST SUPPORTING ACTRESS	[edit] Catherine Keener - Being John Malkovich	--	--
BEST DIRECTOR	[edit] Lasse Hallstrom - The Cider House Rules	--	--
	[edit] East West - France		

Reviews and News

The Reviews & News tab of the Yahoo! Games home page is the place to go for up-to-date gaming information. The page features a review and lets you find game information by format or by keyword search.

There is also a list of current headlines that pertain to games, as well as links to new games and Yahoo! game resources.

A detailed review of a game shows its overall rating, the date it was released, the number of players, and the name of the publisher and developer. You'll see sample screens of the game and the recommended system requirements.

Chapter 18

Keep Up with News, Weather, and Sports

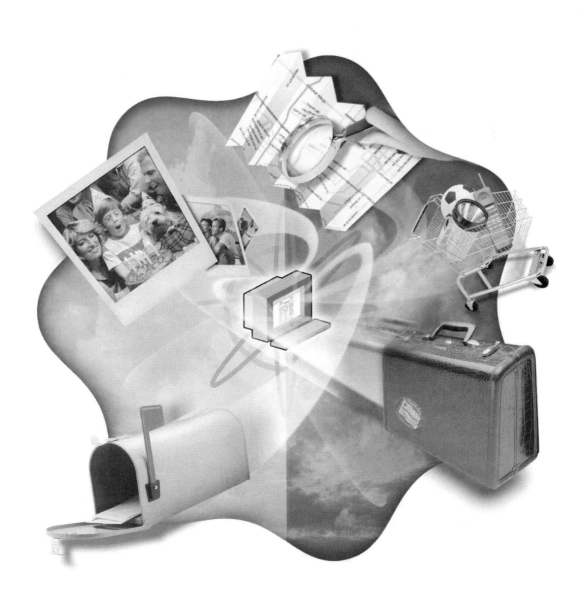

How to . . .

- ■ Get news online
- ■ Get local weather reports
- ■ Keep up with sports scores and news
- ■ Use the Yahoo! news ticker

You don't have to wait for the evening news to find out what's going on in the world. Headlines and in-depth news coverage, sports scores and analysis, stock reports, and up-to-the-minute weather reports are all available to you 24 × 7 from Yahoo!. You can even make news items scroll across your screen as you work or surf the Internet and instantly access details when you want them. All from Yahoo! and all for free.

Getting Today's Yahoo! News

Because Yahoo! wants to keep you informed, it offers top news stories in several easy-to-find locations. When you connect to the Yahoo! home page, look at the In The News section on the right side of the page for the top headlines. To read the details, click a headline. You also get news headlines and sports in your My Yahoo! page. As you learned in Chapter 3, you can customize My Yahoo! to get the information that you want.

For complete news coverage, however, go to the Yahoo! News home page, as shown in Figure 18-1. Or, you may use any of these techniques to get there:

- ■ Click News in the Yahoo! Home page.
- ■ Click More at the bottom of the In The News section of the Yahoo! home page.
- ■ Go directly to http://dailynews.yahoo.com/.

Down the center of the page are the top stories, each with a headline and a brief summary. First is the general news story and then come the top stories in categories such as these:

- ■ Business
- ■ World
- ■ Politics
- ■ Sports
- ■ Entertainment
- ■ Science
- ■ Internet Report
- ■ Technology
- ■ Public Opinion
- ■ Health

Click a headline to read the entire story. To see more headlines in the same category, click the link under the summary. Links are called More Top Stories or More Business Headlines.

FIGURE 18-1 Yahoo! News page

On the right side of the page are additional news sources. The Full Coverage section offers extensive coverage of a specific topic. Rather than show a single story, Full Coverage contains a collection of stories, photographs, and other material that covers the topic in detail. Figure 18-2, for example, shows the full coverage page for one story.

The Video Highlights section of the page contains a link to the Video Gallery, where, as shown in Figure 18-3, the Video Gallery offers many video stories. To play a video, either click the link that describes the speed of your modem in the Windows Media Player list or click RealPlayer.

The Photo Highlight section shows a selected photograph from the day's news. To see the entire photograph and access the stories that relate to it, click View Photo. Use the More International Photos list to access additional photographs and their related stories.

Sometimes the Yahoo! News page also offers a special section on the right side where a breaking story is featured. Other modules on the right side of the page include Audio Highlights and Today In History. Click Audio Highlights to hear sound clips that pertain to important news stories. Click Today In History for a perspective on news and events that took place on the same day in previous years.

Note *At the bottom of the Yahoo! News page are links that you can click to get the news in foreign languages.*

18

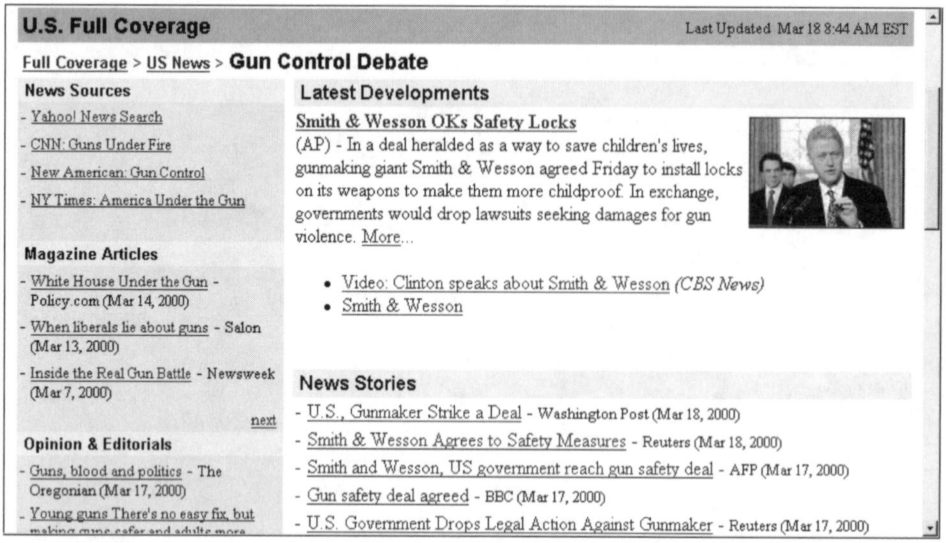

U.S. Full Coverage

Last Updated Mar 18 8:44 AM EST

Full Coverage > US News > **Gun Control Debate**

News Sources

- Yahoo! News Search
- CNN: Guns Under Fire
- New American: Gun Control
- NY Times: America Under the Gun

Magazine Articles

- White House Under the Gun - Policy.com (Mar 14, 2000)
- When liberals lie about guns - Salon (Mar 13, 2000)
- Inside the Real Gun Battle - Newsweek (Mar 7, 2000)

next

Opinion & Editorials

- Guns, blood and politics - The Oregonian (Mar 17, 2000)
- Young guns There's no easy fix, but making guns safer and adults more

Latest Developments

Smith & Wesson OKs Safety Locks

(AP) - In a deal heralded as a way to save children's lives, gunmaking giant Smith & Wesson agreed Friday to install locks on its weapons to make them more childproof. In exchange, governments would drop lawsuits seeking damages for gun violence. More...

- Video: Clinton speaks about Smith & Wesson (CBS News)
- Smith & Wesson

News Stories

- U.S., Gunmaker Strike a Deal - Washington Post (Mar 18, 2000)
- Smith & Wesson Agrees to Safety Measures - Reuters (Mar 18, 2000)
- Smith and Wesson, US government reach gun safety deal - AFP (Mar 17, 2000)
- Gun safety deal agreed - BBC (Mar 17, 2000)
- U.S. Government Drops Legal Action Against Gunmaker - Reuters (Mar 17, 2000)

FIGURE 18-2   A top news story in the Full Coverage section

Yahoo! News - Video Gallery

Last Updated Friday 17 March, 7:45 PM ET

To view the streaming video on this page, Download Players Here

Page 1 of 9   **Next Page**

President Clinton Attends Gala To Celebrate Irish-American Relations On The Eve Of St Patrick's Day
Windows Media - 28.8 | 56
Realplayer G2
Mar 17, 2000

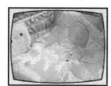

Consumer Report With Amanda Stultz For March 17
Windows Media - 28.8 | 56
Realplayer G2
Mar 17, 2000

Markets Report With Steve Dunlop For March 17
Windows Media - 28.8 | 56
Realplayer G2
Mar 17, 2000

Venezuelan President Hugo Chavez Launches A Re-Election Bid That He Says Will Crush His Opponents
Windows Media - 28.8 | 56
Realplayer G2
Mar 17, 2000

FIGURE 18-3   Video Gallery

Along the left side of the Yahoo! News page are additional resources, including the Search section, News Topics, News Alerts, and Yahoo! To Go.

Use the Search News option to search for news stories with a keyword or a name. Enter a keyword that describes what you want to look for and then select the type of coverage—news stories, photographs, or full coverage. Then click Go to locate the news.

Use the Advanced Search option to fine-tune your search and thereby get the information you want. When you click Advanced Search, you see the options shown in Figure 18-4. Use as many of the options as you need to define your search.

Follow these steps to search for the news topics you are interested in:

1. Choose how you want Yahoo! to sort the headlines (by relevance to the keyword you enter or by the date) and the number of stories per page.

2. Choose a normal keyword search, to search for all of the words that you enter, or to search for any of the words that you enter.

3. Select a date option to tell Yahoo! how far into the past to collect stories. You can choose options from one to 30 days old or enter a date range of your own. Enter a date in the format *mm/dd/yy*, or enter a range of dates in the format *mm/dd/yy-mm/dd/yy*.

4. Select the source of the news from the 16 sources shown. Each source is preceded by a check box. Click the check box next to each source that you want to search. To search all the sources, leave all of the check boxes empty,

5. Select a category from the options shown on the page. Again, click the check box beside each category that you want search. To search all categories, leave all of the check boxes empty.

6. Click the Search button.

News Topics

In the News Topics section, you will find major categories of news and a number of sources. Click a topic to see a list of stories compiled from all of the sources, as shown in Figure 18-5. To list stories from a particular source, select the source under the topic in the Yahoo! News home page.

The Top Stories Headlines page includes links to a number of stories, as well as Full Coverage pages, audio reports, Net Events, and Yahoo! categories.

Yahoo! Weather

It may be impossible to do anything about the weather, as Mark Twain noted a century ago, but today's technology at least makes predicting the weather possible. To get detailed weather reports, go directly to http://weather.yahoo.com/ or click Weather on the Yahoo! home page. In the Weather home page, enter your city or zip code and then click the Search button. You can also click the Browse To Locate A City links to find the location for which you need a weather report.

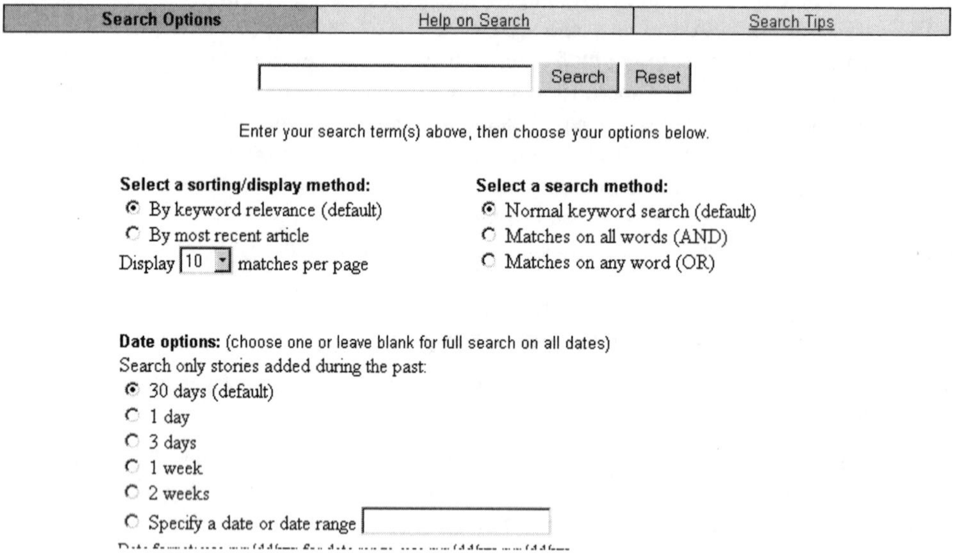

Search Options	Help on Search	Search Tips

[_____] [Search] [Reset]

Enter your search term(s) above, then choose your options below.

Select a sorting/display method:
⦿ By keyword relevance (default)
○ By most recent article
Display [10 ▾] matches per page

Select a search method:
⦿ Normal keyword search (default)
○ Matches on all words (AND)
○ Matches on any word (OR)

Date options: (choose one or leave blank for full search on all dates)
Search only stories added during the past:
⦿ 30 days (default)
○ 1 day
○ 3 days
○ 1 week
○ 2 weeks
○ Specify a date or date range [_____]

Date formats: mm/dd/yyyy for date ranges: mm/dd/yyyy-mm/dd/yyyy

FIGURE 18-4   Advanced Search options

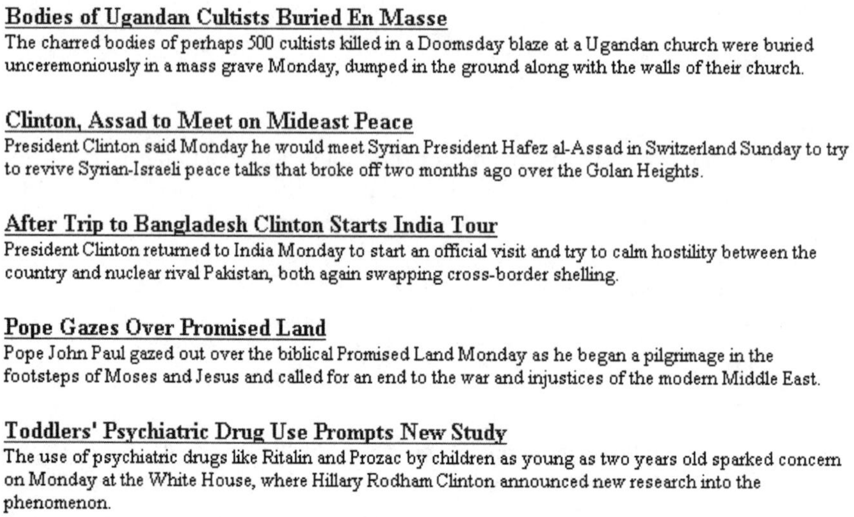

Bodies of Ugandan Cultists Buried En Masse
The charred bodies of perhaps 500 cultists killed in a Doomsday blaze at a Ugandan church were buried unceremoniously in a mass grave Monday, dumped in the ground along with the walls of their church.

Clinton, Assad to Meet on Mideast Peace
President Clinton said Monday he would meet Syrian President Hafez al-Assad in Switzerland Sunday to try to revive Syrian-Israeli peace talks that broke off two months ago over the Golan Heights.

After Trip to Bangladesh Clinton Starts India Tour
President Clinton returned to India Monday to start an official visit and try to calm hostility between the country and nuclear rival Pakistan, both again swapping cross-border shelling.

Pope Gazes Over Promised Land
Pope John Paul gazed out over the biblical Promised Land Monday as he began a pilgrimage in the footsteps of Moses and Jesus and called for an end to the war and injustices of the modern Middle East.

Toddlers' Psychiatric Drug Use Prompts New Study
The use of psychiatric drugs like Ritalin and Prozac by children as young as two years old sparked concern on Monday at the White House, where Hillary Rodham Clinton announced new research into the phenomenon.

FIGURE 18-5   The News Topics section

Figure 18-6 shows a Yahoo! Weather report. In the report is a four-day forecast, as well as a link to the marine forecast if one is appropriate. There is also a link to a page where you can get a comprehensive report with records and averages, including the average high and low temperatures, record high and low temperatures, the average participation, and the number of rainy and snowy days.

The Maps And Images section takes you to the same graphics that you are used to seeing on the evening weather report. A satellite map, for example, is shown in Figure 18-7. Satellite and radar maps are available in two forms: static images and animations. An animation shows the weather over a period of time, so you can see, for example, in which direction the clouds are moving.

By default, the static map appears when you click the Satellite or Radar option. On the page that appears, click Satellite Loop or Radar Loop to display the animated graphic. Click Current Radar Image or Current Sat Image to return to the static image.

The city weather page also includes a local forecast from the National Weather Service, links to Yahoo! resources, a Search box so you can get weather reports from other locations, and links to neighboring cities.

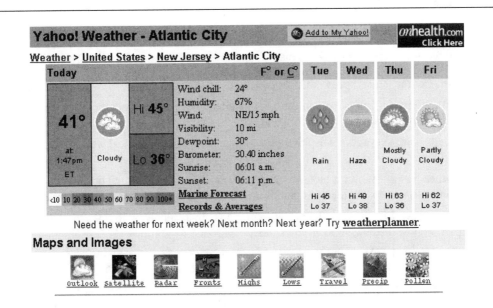

FIGURE 18-6   Yahoo! Weather report

East Usa Satellite Map

03/20/2000 12:45 PM EST   09:45 AM PST   17:45 GMT

FIGURE 18-7   Satellite map

Yahoo! Weather Resources

Most Yahoo! weather pages offer links to many weather resources:

- **Storm Center**   Lists severe weather alerts.
- **Weather Maps**   Offers a complete list of available weather maps in these categories: national, state, regional, local, and world.
- **Records And Averages**   Displays a list of cities for which historical weather data is available.
- **Weather News**   Shows weather-related news headlines and a Search box so you can obtain news stories, photographs, and full-coverage reports that pertain to the weather.
- **Ski Reports**   List the areas for which ski reports are available, with links to each report. Follow the links to locate a ski resort.
- **Yahoo! Travel**   Opens the Yahoo! Travel home page.

Yahoo! Weather Categories

The Yahoo! Categories section of a weather page offers links to these Web page categories in the Yahoo! directory:

- Meteorology
- Storm Chasing

- Weather Phenomena
- Maps And Observations
- National Weather Service

Keeping Informed with Yahoo! Sports

Whether you are interested in a specific player, team, league, or sport, Yahoo! is the place for sports fans. You'll find schedules, stats, analyses, and even a place to buy tickets to sporting events.

Go directly to http://sports.yahoo.com/ or click Sports in the Yahoo! home page to open the page shown in Figure 18-8. The Sports page contains a lot of information.

At the top of the page are three tabs:

- **Sports**   Covers major United States sports.
- **Worldwide**   Contains links to sports in other countries.
- **Fantasy**   Accesses the Fantasy Sport page of Yahoo! Games.

The Sports Page

From the Sports page, you can get sports information of all types. At the top of the page is a major sports story with links and photographs. The major story is followed by a list of headlines

FIGURE 18-8   Yahoo! Sports home page

with links, and Top Events. Under that is the Yahoo! Broadcast section with a schedule of the day's sports broadcasts and links to other media. Next come Expert Columns links that take you to sports publications such as The Sporting News and CNN Sports Illustrated.

At the bottom of the page are sections called Shopping & Auctions and Resources. From the Shopping links you can get items such as NFL jerseys, video games, and items from a specific team or player. The auction links offer items such as memorabilia and trading cards.

The Resources section of the Yahoo! Sports page is shown in Figure 18-9. On the page are Yahoo! categories, as well as links to popular sports-related Web sites.

Along the left side of the page is a list with the day's schedule and links to teams and scoreboards:

■ Click a team to see its detailed page.

■ Click the time to see a story about a game and its history.

■ Click Audio to access live sports broadcasts.

The stories and links on the Yahoo! Sports home page cover the gamut of sports. If you are interested in a specific sport, however, click the league hyperlinks along the top of the page:

| Top | NFL | NBA | NHL | MLB | NCAA Bball (M) | NCAA Bball (W) | NASCAR | Golf | Soccer | more... |

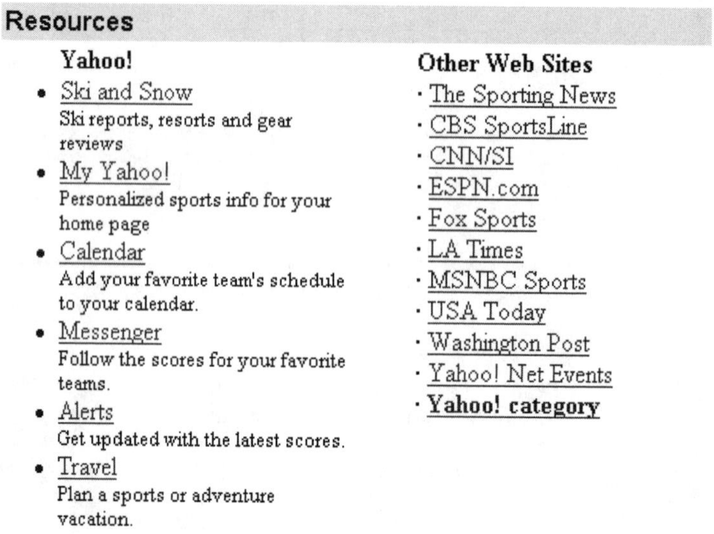

Resources

Yahoo!

- Ski and Snow
  Ski reports, resorts and gear reviews
- My Yahoo!
  Personalized sports info for your home page
- Calendar
  Add your favorite team's schedule to your calendar.
- Messenger
  Follow the scores for your favorite teams.
- Alerts
  Get updated with the latest scores.
- Travel
  Plan a sports or adventure vacation.

Other Web Sites

· The Sporting News
· CBS SportsLine
· CNN/SI
· ESPN.com
· Fox Sports
· LA Times
· MSNBC Sports
· USA Today
· Washington Post
· Yahoo! Net Events
· **Yahoo! category**

FIGURE 18-9   Sports Resources

Clicking NFL, for example, opens a page about the National Football League; while clicking Golf takes you to stories and links that pertain to golf. Clicking a league name also displays these options at the top of the league page:

Front - Standings - Scoreboard - Stats - Teams - Players

- Click Standings to see the current league and conference standings.

- Click Scoreboard to see the scores of today's games.

- Click Stats to get statistics, including team-by-team stats and stats about leading performers.

- Click Teams to list all of the teams in a league or conference and be able to click a link to visit a team's home page.

- Click Players for an alphabetical list of the players from which you can access Web pages about different players.

For a more complete list of leagues and sports, click More on the right side of the League hyperlinks. In the page that appears, as shown in Figure 18-10, you can access professional and collegiate sports pages, as well as pages devoted to sports not usually available in the Yahoo! Sports home page.

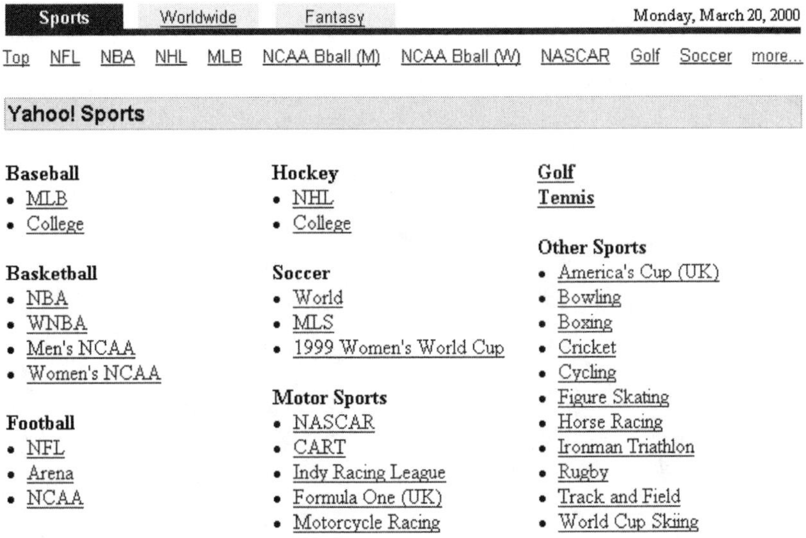

| Sports | Worldwide | Fantasy | | Monday, March 20, 2000 |

Top   NFL   NBA   NHL   MLB   NCAA Bball (M)   NCAA Bball (W)   NASCAR   Golf   Soccer   more...

Yahoo! Sports

Baseball
- MLB
- College

Basketball
- NBA
- WNBA
- Men's NCAA
- Women's NCAA

Football
- NFL
- Arena
- NCAA

Hockey
- NHL
- College

Soccer
- World
- MLS
- 1999 Women's World Cup

Motor Sports
- NASCAR
- CART
- Indy Racing League
- Formula One (UK)
- Motorcycle Racing

Golf
Tennis

Other Sports
- America's Cup (UK)
- Bowling
- Boxing
- Cricket
- Cycling
- Figure Skating
- Horse Racing
- Ironman Triathlon
- Rugby
- Track and Field
- World Cup Skiing

FIGURE 18-10   Accessing all sports

18

Worldwide Page

Click the Worldwide tab on the Yahoo! Sports page to investigate sports in other countries. You will find information about sports in Australia and New Zealand, Brazil, Canada, China, Denmark, France, Germany, Hong Kong, Italy, Japan, Korea, Mexico, Norway, Singapore, Spain, Sweden, Taiwan, and the United Kingdom and Ireland.

Some of the links on the page are to a country page; while others, as shown here, let you choose a specific sport or source of information.

Brazil
Esportes
Futebol

Team Pages

When the name of a college or professional team appears on a Yahoo! Sports page, it appears as a link that you can click to go to a detailed page. Clicking Utah Jazz, for example, opens the page shown in Figure 18-11.

On the page are links to information about the team's last and next games, analysis of its play, and the latest news about the team. There is a Team Report that discusses the team in detail

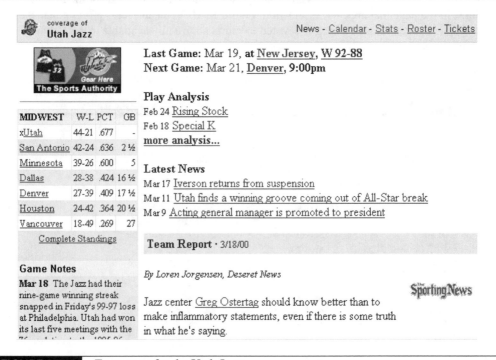

coverage of
Utah Jazz   News - Calendar - Stats - Roster - Tickets

Gear Here
The Sports Authority

Last Game: Mar 19, **at** New Jersey, W 92-88
Next Game: Mar 21, Denver, 9:00pm

MIDWEST	W-L	PCT	GB
xUtah	44-21	.677	-
San Antonio	42-24	.636	2 ½
Minnesota	39-26	.600	5
Dallas	28-38	.424	16 ½
Denver	27-39	.409	17 ½
Houston	24-42	.364	20 ½
Vancouver	18-49	.269	27

Complete Standings

Play Analysis
Feb 24 Rising Stock
Feb 18 Special K
more analysis...

Latest News
Mar 17 Iverson returns from suspension
Mar 11 Utah finds a winning groove coming out of All-Star break
Mar 9 Acting general manager is promoted to president

Team Report · 3/18/00

Game Notes

Mar 18 The Jazz had their nine-game winning streak snapped in Friday's 99-97 loss at Philadelphia. Utah had won its last five meetings with the

By Loren Jorgensen, Deseret News

Jazz center Greg Ostertag should know better than to make inflammatory statements, even if there is some truth in what he's saying.

SportingNews

FIGURE 18-11   Team page for the Utah Jazz

and an abbreviated two-week schedule at the bottom of the page. For a complete team schedule, click Calendar on the top of the page, or click Complete Schedule under the abbreviated schedule.

> **Note** *For college teams, the detailed page offers campus news and a seasonal schedule, but not the other links discussed here.*

The Stats link leads to detailed statistics concerning the team's players, including stats from to the most recent game. The Roster link shows each player; his or her position; personal statistics such as height, weight, number of years on the team; and, in the case of professional athletes, the college attended. The Tickets link lets you purchase game tickets through the Yahoo! Sports ticket purchasing program.

Keeping Informed with Yahoo! Ticker

One great way to keep up to date with news, weather, sports, and the stock market is to download and install the Yahoo! news ticker. The ticker is a scrolling bar that stays on the top of the screen whenever you are online.

You can read the information as it scrolls by or double-click a headline to display all the details in a browser window. The ticker will also notify you when mail has arrived in your Yahoo! account. You can decide for yourself what type of information appears. The ticker only displays the type of information that you selected for your My Yahoo! page.

To download the ticker, go to http://my.yahoo.com/ticker.html and click Download for Windows. If you have a Macintosh computer, use the OS/2 or UNIX operating systems, or connect to the Internet through AOL, and click Java Version instead.

When the File Download box appears, select Save This Program To Disk and then click OK. The Save As dialog box opens. Choose Desktop in the Save In list and then click Save. The program, about 300K in size, will download to your computer under the name ynt.exe. Soon you will see this icon appear on your desktop.

Close your browser and disconnect to go offline. Then double-click the icon and choose I Accept from the message box that appears. You are asked if you want to add a shortcut to the ticker to your Start menu and desktop. Click Yes to make the ticker easier to access. The ticker box appears, as shown in Figure 18-12. Enter your Yahoo! logon name and password, and click OK. Finally, click OK again in the message that appears, and then click Yes to restart your computer.

When you want to see the news ticker (shown next), either double-click this icon on the desktop, or right-click the taskbar, select Toolbars, and click Yahoo! News Ticker.

The ticker appears in the upper-right corner of the screen. If you are not already online when you double-click the ticker icon, your modem dials into the Internet. As I mentioned earlier, the ticker is synchronized to your My Yahoo! page; so the same information that appears on your My Yahoo! page—the headlines, portfolios, weather, and sports—also scrolls across the ticker. To change the information that appears on the ticker, you must change your My Yahoo! page, a subject explained in Chapter 3.

18

FIGURE 18-12   Enter your logon name and ID for the news ticker

Tip   *See "Changing Ticker Preferences," later in this chapter, if you do not want the ticker to connect to the Internet automatically.*

By default, the ticker remains on the top of the screen. So if you run a program such as Microsoft Word, the ticker appears in the foreground. With a full-screen program, the ticker sits on the program's title bar. When your screensaver turns on, however, the ticker grows in size and appears across the bottom of the screen, as shown in Figure 18-13.

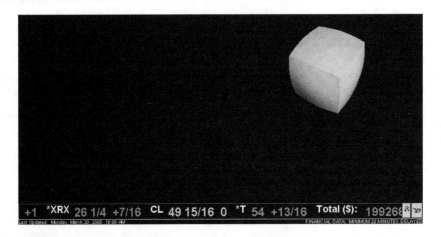

FIGURE 18-13   Enlarged News ticker with a screensaver in the background

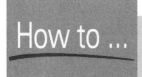

Start the Ticker Automatically

If you want the news ticker to automatically appear onscreen each time you start your computer, you have to add it to the Startup Folder. Follow these steps:

1. Close all open applications and make sure the Yahoo! News Ticker icon appears on the Windows desktop.

2. Right-click the Start button on the Windows taskbar and choose Open from the shortcut menu.

3. Double-click the Programs folder.

4. Double-click the Startup folder.

5. If necessary, drag the folder window out of the way so that the Yahoo! News Ticker icon is visible.

6. Point to the Yahoo! News Ticker icon, press and hold down the right mouse button, and drag the icon into the Startup Folder.

7. Release the right mouse button, and choose Copy Here from the shortcut menu.

8. Close all of the open windows.

Now the news ticker will appear each time you start your computer.

Using the Ticker

When you are online, information for the ticker is retrieved and downloaded to your computer at periodic intervals. As long as you remain online, the information is updated as new stories, scores, and stock prices are received. If you disconnect from the Internet, however, the ticker remains onscreen and continues to scroll. This way you can watch the headlines, weather, stock reports, and sports scores when you are offline.

On the far left side of the ticker is a double line that you can drag to change the ticker's width. Drag it to the left to make the ticker wider and be able to read more information at one time. Drag it to the right to make the ticker smaller and take up less space onscreen.

To move the ticker up or down the page, drag it with the left mouse button. When you click and hold the mouse on the ticker to drag it, by the way, the mouse pointer looks like this:

18

Drag the mouse to the left or right to change the direction of the scrolling headlines. Drag the mouse to the right, for example, to make the text scroll from left to right.

Use the second button on the left, the right-pointing triangle, to move between topics and stories. Because the ticker is synchronized with My Yahoo!, it cycles from module to module, like so:

- Portfolios
- Weather
- Sports Scores
- Top Stories
- Current Events

All of your portfolio information, for example, is displayed before weather reports come up. Next come sports scores, and so on. To go directly to a new module before its turn comes, click the triangle button. Each time you click, the ticker starts at the next module. Continue to click until you get the information you want. Once you are in a module, you can right-click the triangle button to jump between stories. When news headlines are being displayed, for example, right-click the button to jump from headline to headline, rather than wait for headlines to scroll by.

To read the details about a story that appears on the ticker, double-click it. If you are offline, the ticker dials into the Internet to retrieve the story.

The Yahoo! button on the far right of the ticker opens your My Yahoo! page.

The second button on the right converts the ticker into a search box that works just like the search box in Yahoo! Companion and the Yahoo! home page. Click the button to clear the contents of the scrolling ticker. Type a keyword or phrase that describes what you want to search for, and then press ENTER to begin the search.

Click the button again to return to the scrolling ticker.

Customizing the Ticker

While you can only change the content of the news ticker from your My Yahoo! page, you can customize the ticker to change its appearance and its operations by starting from the ticker itself. Right-click the ticker, for example, to see this shortcut menu:

The options are

- **Always On Top**   Keeps the ticker from remaining in the foreground when other applications are on the screen.

- **Glue To Desktop**   Converts the ticker into a resizable window. You can then drag a corner or border of the ticker to change its size. You can only resize the window, however, when the Always On Top option is turned off.

- **Fit To Caption**   Makes the ticker automatically adjust its height to the size of the contents.

- **Preferences**   Displays a dialog box with customization options. See "Changing Ticker Preferences," later in this chapter.

- **Update Now**   Retrieves new information from your My Yahoo! page to update the contents of the ticker.

- **Search Window**   Converts the ticker into a search box.

- **Help**   Accesses the Yahoo! help page on the news ticker.

- **Exit**   Closes the news ticker.

Changing Ticker Preferences

To further customize the ticker, choose Preferences on the shortcut menu. You see the Preferences dialog box, shown in Figure 18-14.

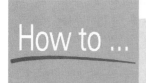

How to ...   Resize the News Ticker

Yahoo! offers many ticker options. Let's recap the ways that you can change the ticker's size and position.

You can always change the ticker's length by dragging the double line on the left and change its position by dragging with the left mouse button.

To change the height or shape of the ticker, both the Always On Top and Glue To Desktop options must be turned off. The ticker then appears like a window, as shown here:

You can then drag the top or bottom border to change the window's height, drag the left border to change its length, or drag a corner to change its proportions.

18

FIGURE 18-14   News ticker preferences

Deselect the Use 'My Yahoo!' option if you do not want to synchronize the ticker to your My Yahoo! page. When this option is turned off, the ticker displays news, stock, weather, and sports information without regard for your localized My Yahoo! settings. When the option is turned on, by contrast, stock prices are taken from your portfolio and weather reports are provided for the cities you designated. Turning off the Use 'My Yahoo!' option also displays additional tabs in the dialog box so you can choose content for the ticker.

Change the values in the Username and Password boxes if you want to use the settings from another Yahoo! ID. If you downloaded the ticker but are not a Yahoo! member, click the button under the boxes to register as a Yahoo! member.

The options in the lower half of the dialog box affect how the ticker appears onscreen:

■ Set the speed at which the information scrolls.

■ Determine if and how often the information is updated.

■ Hang up the modem and disconnect from the Internet after ticker information is updated.

■ Never automatically dial into the Internet to update the ticker.

■ Change the ticker's color scheme.

■ Adjust the scrolling to make it smoother and more constant.

■ Change the font of text from bold to regular.

■ Keep the ticker from appearing when your screensaver kicks in.

The Mail Alerts tab of the Preferences dialog box is for determining when and how the ticker alerts you to incoming e-mail in your Yahoo! Inbox. You can determine how often the mail icon appears and which sound is played when new mail arrives.

The Proxy tab of the Preferences dialog box lets you configure the ticker to run through a proxy server. You don't need to change any settings on this tab if you use Microsoft Internet Explorer. If you use Netscape Navigator 3.*x*, the ticker will automatically adjust these settings for you. You must manually set the options in this box, however, if you are using Netscape Communicator.

Unsynchronizing from My Yahoo!

The Use 'My Yahoo!' check box in the Preferences dialog box is for unlinking the ticker and your My Yahoo! page. When you deselect the option, News and Quotes tabs appear in the dialog box so you can determine what headlines and stock quotes appear on the ticker.

The News tab of the Preferences dialog box is shown in Figure 18-15. Select the check boxes next to each item that you want the ticker to display. Along with the weather option, you can see temperatures in Fahrenheit or Celsius, and you can enter the symbols of the airports for which you need weather information. You can also decide the maximum number of stories that can be reported for a given topic.

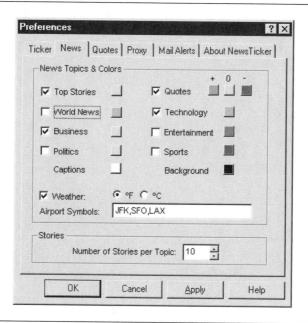

FIGURE 18-15   News tab of the Preferences dialog box

18

Click a color icon to the right side of each topic to choose which color the text appears in. After you click an icon, choose the color from the pallet that appears. For quotes, you can choose a color for issues that have increased, decreased, and not changed.

The Quotes tab of the Preference dialog box lets you choose which quotes appear in the ticker. The default settings are the Dow Jones, NASAQ, and Standard and Poor 500, as well as Intel, Microsoft, and Yahoo!. On the Quotes tab you can add and remove items from the ticker and look for stock symbols.

Part VI

Your Yahoo! Community

Chapter 19

Send and Receive Instant Messages— with Voice

How to . . .

■ Install Yahoo! Messenger

■ Add friends

■ Communicate with friends

■ Hold conference chats

■ Conduct voice chats

■ Change your online status

■ Send and receive files

■ Use Yahoo! Messenger Lite

Yahoo! Messenger is more than just a way to chat with friends. With Yahoo! Messenger, you can use voice chat to speak with friends; send and receive files over the Internet; and get stock quotes, news, weather, and sports. Best of all, Yahoo! Messenger is free. You just need to download and install it, and log on with your Yahoo! ID and password to get started.

Getting Yahoo! Messenger

The first step is to download and install the Yahoo! Messenger program. If you only have one computer, you can install the program while you are online without downloading and saving a copy on disk. You may want to download and save a copy, however, if you expect to reinstall it (after a system crash, for example) or install Messenger on more than one machine. You can download the program to a machine that is connected to a network, for example, and then copy it to other machines to install Yahoo! Messenger there as well (Figure 19-1).

 The older versions of Yahoo! Messenger are called Yahoo! Pager. Some help information on Yahoo! still refers to it by that name.

Follow these steps to Install Yahoo! Messenger:

1. Connect to the Internet and to the Yahoo! home page.

2. Click Messenger in the Yahoo! home page to display download information shown in Figure 19-1.

3. In the Quick Download section, click Windows or select another platform. As an alternative, you can click Get It Now and then select the platform from the page that appears.

YAHOO! *Messenger*   Yahoo! - Acct Info - Help

FIGURE 19-1   Preparing to download Yahoo! Messenger

4. Click Start Download. The File Download dialog box appears. It offers two options: Save This Program To Disk and Run This Program From Its Current Location.

- If you select Run This Program From Its Current Location and click OK, the program will be downloaded to a temporary folder on your computer and begin to install.

- If you select Save This Program To Disk, the Save As dialog box appears. Select the folder in which you want to store the file and then click OK. The file will be downloaded under the name Ymsgrie.exe. If you saved the file on the desktop, double-click the Ymsgrie.exe icon to start the installation. Otherwise, find where you saved the program and run it from there.

Installing Yahoo! Messenger

After the installation program starts, just follow the instructions that appear onscreen to complete the installation and setup of Yahoo! Messenger. Here are the steps to follow:

1. Click Yes if a message box asks if you want to install and run Yahoo! Messenger. The Yahoo! Messenger Welcome message box appears.

19

2. Click Next to see the license terms for using the program.

3. Click I Accept. The Select Destination Directory dialog box appears. You can change the location where the program will be installed, but Yahoo! recommends using the default location in the Program Files folder.

4. Click Next to accept the default location.

    The Ready to Install message appears with the option Run Automatically When I Start My Computer. If you leave this option selected and you have a dial-up ISP account, Yahoo! Messenger will run when you start your computer and automatically dial into the Internet. If you do not want to connect to the Internet automatically, deselect this option. If you have a cable or DSL Internet account, you are always connected to the Internet, and you can leave this option turned on to be logged on to Yahoo! Messenger whenever you are on your computer. You can always turn this option on or off later by using the Yahoo! Messenger Preferences option.

5. Click Next and wait until the program is installed.

6. Click the Finish button.

What happens next depends on whether you are online or offline. If you are already online and signed into Yahoo!, the box shown here tells you a little about using Messenger.

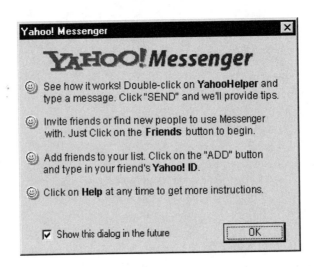

Unless you deselect the Show This Dialog In The Future check box, this box appears each time you start Yahoo! Messenger. Click OK to close the box and access the Messenger program. If you are not yet signed onto Yahoo!, the Login box appears, as shown here.

Enter your Yahoo! ID and password, and then click the Login button to sign onto Messenger.

Tip *Check the box labeled Remember My ID & Password so you do not have to enter your password and ID each time you start Yahoo! Messenger.*

If you are not online and Yahoo! cannot make the connection to the Internet through your ISP dial-in, this box appears:

Connect to the Internet as you normally do and then click the Try Again button. The LAN/Firewall options are for users who connect to the Internet through a local area network or company firewall.

If you set up any alerts to be received by Yahoo! Messenger, they will appear automatically when you log on. A stock alert, for example, appears as shown here. Close the box to display the Messenger window.

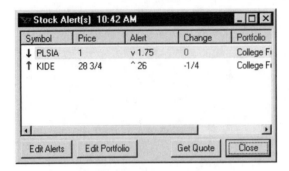

The Yahoo! Messenger window appears, as shown here.

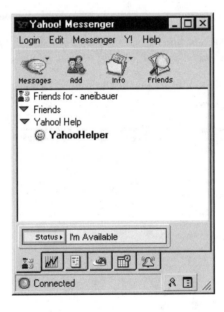

Sending a Message

You are now logged onto Yahoo! Messenger and ready to send a message to another Yahoo! user. If the person is online and running Messenger, your message will pop up on his or her screen. Otherwise, Yahoo! will save the message until the recipient next logs on to Messenger.

Follow these steps to send a message:

1. Click the Messages button and choose Send Instant Message. You see this dialog box.

2. In the To box, type the Yahoo! ID of the person to whom you are writing.

3. If you have more than one identity in Yahoo!, pull down the From list and select the ID from which you want to send the message.

4. Type a message and click the Send button. When the recipient receives the message, it looks something like this:

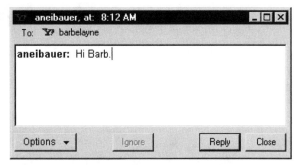

The recipient can click Reply to expand the message box, type a reply, and click Send. An ongoing dialog now appears in the box on both screens.

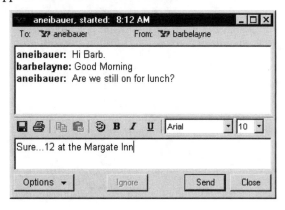

19

 *If the recipient is not logged on to Yahoo! Messenger when you send the message, it will arrive as an offline message when the receipient logs on. See "Getting Offline Messages," later in this chapter.*

While you are chatting on Yahoo! Messenger, you can use the toolbar buttons under the conversation window to save, print, and format messages. The buttons are shown here:

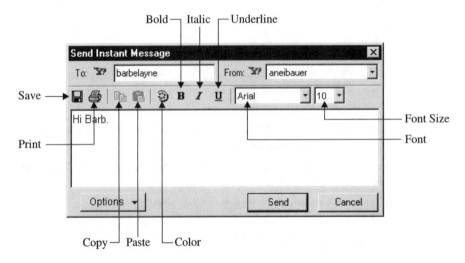

Click Save, for example, to save the entire conversation as a text file. Use the formatting buttons to format text just as you would in a word-processing program.

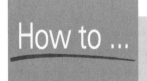 **Use the Messenger Tray Icon**

When you run Yahoo! Messenger, its icon appears in the system tray, the rightmost section of the Windows Taskbar. Right-click the icon to access these options:

Adding Names to Your Friends List

If you have friends or business associates who are Yahoo! members, you may want to communicate with them frequently using Yahoo! Messenger. By adding their Yahoo! IDs to your Friends list, you will be notified automatically when they are online. Likewise, a person can add your ID to his or her Friends list and see when you are online. To protect your privacy, however, you must grant permission before anyone can place your name on a Friends list.

Click the Add button in the top of Messenger to open the dialog box shown in the following illustration. Enter the person's Yahoo! ID, enter a message that describes why you want permission to put your friend's name on your Friends list, and click OK. Then click OK in the message box that tells you a message has been sent asking for permission.

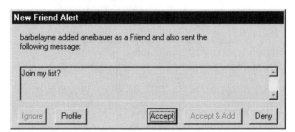

On the other end, the person gets this request:

The recipient can reply by clicking one of the buttons:

- Ignore sends no response.
- Profile display's the sender's profile.
- Accept gives permission to be added to the sender's Friends list.
- Accept & Add gives permission and also adds the sender's name to the recipient's Friends list.
- Deny does not grant permission.

19

Until a person accepts your invitation, the words "Waiting for Authorization" appear next to his or her name on the Friends list.

When a person is online and available, his or her ID appears in boldface on the Friends list and the smiling face icon appears to the left of the name. If the name is dimmed, then the person is not online, as shown on the right.

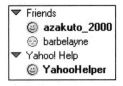

To send a message to a person on your Friends list, either double-click his or her ID, or click it and then select Send Instant Messages on the Messages list.

While you are chatting, you can use the Options menu at the bottom of the box to view a person's profile, add a person to your Friends list, create a conference chat, or start a voice chat.

Engaging in a Conference Chat

A *conference chat* is when you invite more than one person to join a Yahoo! Messenger conversation. You can start a conference whether or not you are already having a chat with someone.

If you are already chatting, select Conference on the Options list at the bottom of the conversation window. Otherwise, select Start A Conference on the Messenger menu. Both actions open the Invite Friends To A Conference dialog box shown in the following illustration. If you were already chatting with someone, his or her ID appears in the Chat Invitation List. However, you can remove a name from the Chat Invitation List by selecting it and clicking Remove.

Select the names of the persons you want to invite from the Friend List on the left and then click the Add button. To invite a person not shown on the list, enter his or her Yahoo! ID in the box under the Chat Invitation List box and click the Add button. Finally, click the Invite button to ask everyone to join the conference.

A message box on each person's screen invites participants to join the conference. The conference itself appears in the window shown next.

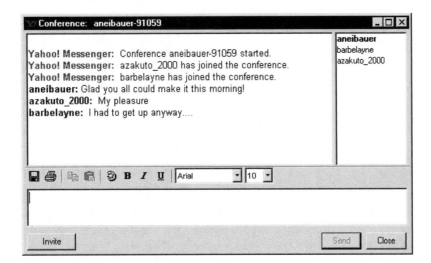

Engaging in a Voice Chat

If you have a microphone and speakers, you can talk and listen to friends who also have microphones and speakers on their computers. Talking and listening this way is called a *voice chat*. To start a voice chat, use either of these techniques:

- Pull down the Options menu at the bottom of a conversation window and select Voice Chat.
- Select Start A Voice Chat on the Messenger menu.

The Invite Friends To Voice Chat dialog box appears. Does it look familiar? It is almost identical to the Invite Friends To A Conference dialog box shown in the previous section. Specify the Yahoo! IDs of the persons with whom you want to speak, and then click Invite to open the Voice Chat window shown in the following illustration. You can still write and read messages as you can in a standard Messenger conversation, but you can also speak and hear other participants.

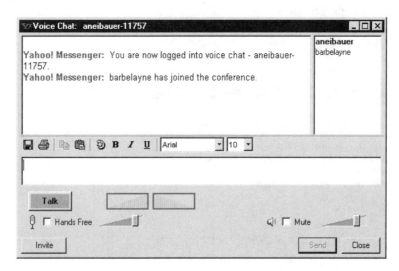

To speak, click and hold down the Talk button as you speak into the microphone. When you've finished, release the mouse button so another person can reply. When another person replies, his or her ID appears, as does the volume-level monitor:

If you do not want to hold down the Talk button while you are speaking, click the Hands Free button. Just remember that other people will hear everything you say near your microphone after the button is clicked. You can use the slide control next to the Hands Free button to control the volume of your microphone. Use the Mute button to turn off your speakers, and the slide control next to the Mute button to control the volume of your speakers.

Even in a voice chat, you can type messages if you are not pleased with the quality or response of the audio.

Getting Offline Messages

If someone sends you a message when you are not online or not logged on to Yahoo! Messenger, Yahoo! stores the message for you. When you do go online, the Offline Messages dialog box appears, as shown next. Select a message you want to respond to, and click the Reply button.

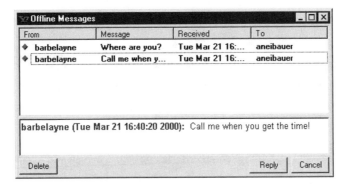

Working with Yahoo! Messenger

You now know the basics of using Yahoo! Messenger to chat with friends, hold an online conference, and conduct a voice chat. Yahoo! Messenger, however, offers a variety of other features to help you get the most out of this powerful communications program.

At the bottom of the Messenger window, below the tabs, is a bar that shows whether you are connected to the Yahoo! Messenger system. On the right side of the bar are buttons that you can click to convert the bar into a search box or hide the toolbar, tabs, and status indicator. Both buttons are toggles—click them to turn the feature on or off.

Searching for Friends

You must have the Yahoo! ID of a person to send him or her a message or invite him or her to a conference or voice chat. If you do not know a person's ID, you can look it up by using the Search For Friends feature. Here's how:

1. Click Add to open the Add dialog box.

2. Click Search For Friends to open the dialog box shown here.

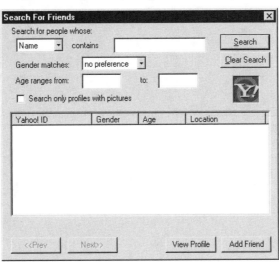

3. Select the item you want to use in your search: Name, Keyword, or Yahoo! ID.

4. Enter text to search for in the Contains box.

5. Select an option from the Gender matches list: Female, Male, or No Preference.

6. Enter an optional age range, with low and high values as desired.

7. Select whether you want to search only profiles with pictures.

8. Click the Search button.

A list of the people who match the search criteria appears. You can add any to your Friends list.

Creating Groups

By default, your Friends list includes a group called Friends. Rather than lump everyone with whom you want to communicate in a single category, you can organize your Yahoo! Messenger contacts into groups. You may want to have one group for friends and another for business associates, for example. To create a group, follow these steps:

1. Select Edit from the Messenger window and then select Group.

2. In the box that appears, type the new group name.

3. Click Create A New Group to open the box shown here.

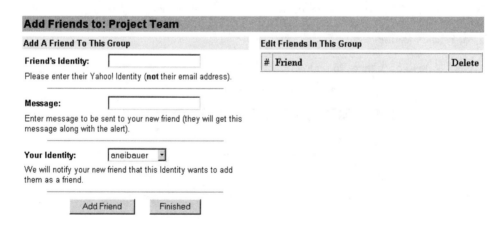

4. Enter the Yahoo! ID of the person you want to add to the group.

5. Type a message that invites the person to the group.

6. Select your identity from the pull-down list.

7. Click Add A Friend to invite the person to the list, and then either clear the boxes so you can invite another person or click Finished when you have finished inviting members at this time.

Changing Your Status

The Friends list shows whether a person is online or offline. Just because a person is online, however, doesn't mean that they are ready to join a Yahoo! Messenger chat. You may be busy writing an e-mail or surfing the Internet, for example, and not want to be disturbed by instant messages.

You can change your status to indicate your availability. To do so, pull down the Status list and select from these options:

The selected icon and message now appear next to your name on others' Friends lists:

aneibauer (Be Right Back)

Regardless of your status, you will be able to receive and send instant messages as long as you are online and logged onto Yahoo! Messenger.

The invisible status, by the way, makes it appear as if you are offline to other Yahoo! members. In addition, a special Idle message appears when you have not used your computer for a certain number of minutes. You can specify the idle time in the Preferences dialog box.

Using Yahoo! Messenger Tabs

In addition to chatting with friends, you can use the tabs at the bottom of the Yahoo! Messenger window to get information of all types. The information on the tabs is synchronized with your

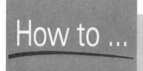

How to ... Create a Custom Status Message

If you don't think any of the status messages are appropriate, you can create your own. Select New Status Message from the Status list to open this dialog box:

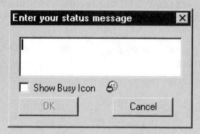

Enter the message you want to appear, choose whether you want to show the Busy icon, and then click OK.

My Yahoo! page, so you can personalize the information that appears. The default tabs on Yahoo! Messenger are shown here:

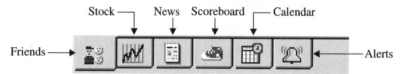

The Scoreboard tab of the dialog box, for example, is shown in the illustration at right. It shows the teams that you selected to appear in the scoreboard module of your My Yahoo! page.

Getting Help with Yahoo! Messenger

If you need answers to questions about using Yahoo! Messenger, pull down the Help menu and choose one of these options:

- Messenger Help
- Messenger Instructions
- About Yahoo! Messenger

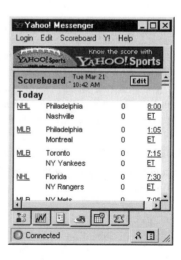

The first two options connect you to Yahoo! and access the Help system pages on Yahoo! Messenger.

Use Yahoo! Helper to get tips for using the program. Yahoo! Helper should be listed in the Messenger window (if it isn't listed, you can turn it on in the Preferences dialog box). Here's how to use Yahoo! Helper:

1. Double-click Yahoo! Helper to open a message window.

2. Type any message that you want and then click Send. You'll get an automated response from the Yahoo! help system.

3. Type another message and click Send. A tip or instruction for using Messenger appears.

4. Continue sending messages to receive tips.

Ignoring Instant Messages

If you start getting annoying invitations and messages, you can block them from reaching you in the future by adding the sender's Yahoo! ID to an ignore list or choosing to block messages from everyone not on your Friends list.

Select Ignore List from the Edit menu and then click Yahoo! Messenger Ignore List to open the dialog box shown here.

Select the option of your choice at the top of the box. If you choose to ignore specific persons, click Add. In the dialog box that appears, enter the Yahoo! IDs of the people you want to ignore and then click Ignore.

Inviting Friends to Sign Up

Yahoo! Messenger is a great way to keep in touch with friends. In fact, voice chat is a bit like making free long-distance telephone calls. If you want to chat with persons who are not Yahoo! members, you can send them an invitation to join Yahoo! (see Figure 19-2) and get them started with Yahoo! Messenger.

19

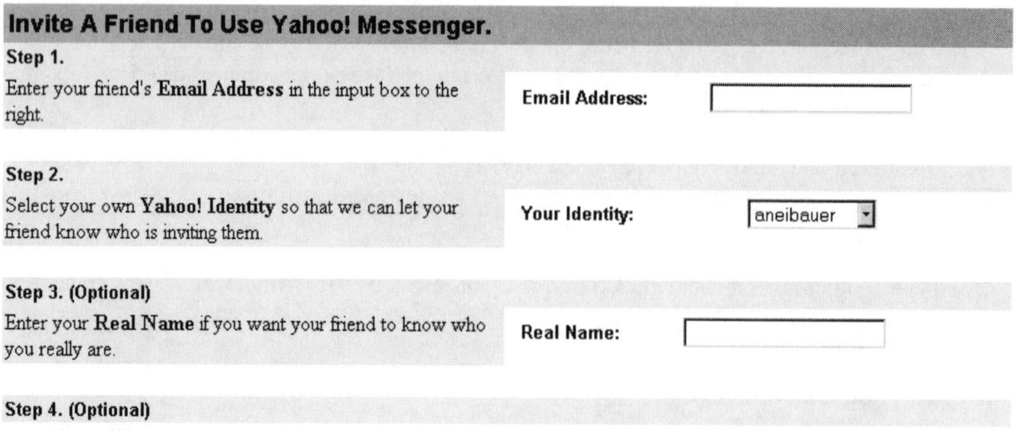

Invite A Friend To Use Yahoo! Messenger.

Step 1.

Enter your friend's **Email Address** in the input box to the right.

Email Address:

Step 2.

Select your own **Yahoo! Identity** so that we can let your friend know who is inviting them.

Your Identity: aneibauer

Step 3. (Optional)

Enter your **Real Name** if you want your friend to know who you really are.

Real Name:

Step 4. (Optional)

FIGURE 19-2   Inviting a friend to sign up for Yahoo! Messenger

Follow these steps:

1. Click the Messenger button in Yahoo! Messenger and select Invite A Friend To Sign Up to open the page shown in Figure 19-2.

2. Enter your friend's e-mail address.

3. Select the Yahoo! identity you want to use for the invitation.

4. Optionally, enter your real name.

5. Optionally, enter a message inviting your friend to join.

6. Click Invite Friend.

Yahoo! will send the person an e-mail with complete instructions for joining Yahoo! and signing on to Yahoo! Messenger.

Transferring Files

While you are online with Yahoo! Messenger, you can send files to and receive files from your friends. A file that you send is stored on a Yahoo! computer until the recipient downloads it to his or her computer.

Caution   *To keep from downloading a file that was infected with a computer virus, only open files that were sent to you by a trusted source.*

To send a file over Yahoo! Messenger, follow these steps:

1. If the person is listed in your Friends list, click his or her name.

2. Select Send A File/Attachment from the Messenger menu to open the dialog box shown here.

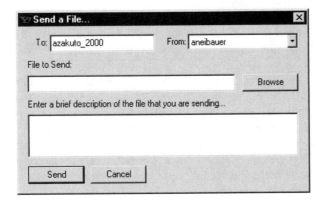

3. If you selected a name from the Friends list, his or her ID is already in the To box. Otherwise, enter the ID of the person to whom you will send the file.

4. Enter the path and name of the file in the File To Send box, or click Browse and locate the file on your disk.

5. Enter a brief message to accompany the file.

6. Click Send.

The Sending File box appears. It shows you the progress of the file transfer. After the file has been transferred successfully, you see a confirmation message. Click OK to close the message box. If the recipient is online, he or she receives a message such as the one shown in the following illustration. The recipient can either download the message right away or save the message and attachment as an offline message and retrieve it later.

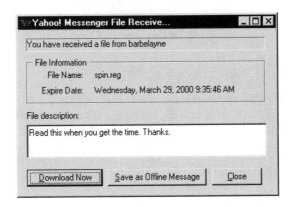

19

If the recipient is offline, the message appears when the recipient logs on to Yahoo! Messenger.

Toolbar and Menu Options

In addition to the features discussed already, you can use the toolbar buttons and menu bar options to perform Messenger functions.

The Messages toolbar button lets you send an instant message, add entries to your Yahoo! address book, start a conference or voice chat, and display offline messages. The Info button lets you view user profiles, edit your own profile, view a person's address book information, and open your address book.

The Login menu lets you log on, or log on under a different user name, disconnect, refresh the Friends list, and exit the program. The Edit menu lets you display and edit your profiles, create groups, work with the ignore list, change the tabs that are displayed, edit your Yahoo! account information, and display the Preferences dialog box.

The Messenger menu lets you send a message, view offline messages, start a conference or voice chat, send a file, add a friend or group, delete a friend or group, change your status, display only friends who are online in the Friends list, view profiles, search for friends, and invite a friend to sign up for Yahoo! Messenger.

The Y! menu offers access to the Yahoo! features shown here:

```
Yahoo! Home

Check Mail
Mark Calendar
Get Stock Quotes
Personalize Yahoo!

Shop Online
Bid On Auctions
Check Classifieds

Visit Clubs
Play Games
Chat with Friends
Read Personal Ads
Post a Message
```

Customizing Yahoo! Messenger

You can personalize the way Yahoo! Messenger works and looks by visiting the Preferences dialog box, as shown in Figure 19-3. Access the Preferences dialog box by selecting Preferences on the Messenger Edit menu.

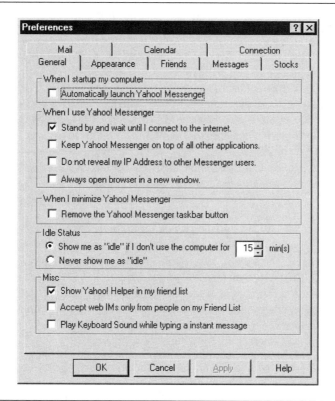

FIGURE 19-3   Yahoo! preferences

The dialog box offers eight different tabs. You can make a change and apply it immediately by clicking the Apply button. You can also make several changes and then click OK to close the dialog box and apply all of the changes. The following pages explain the different tabs.

General Preferences

Use the options on the General tab of the dialog box to make some basic changes to the way that Yahoo! Messenger works.

The Automatically Launch Yahoo! Messenger option determines whether the program runs each time you start your computer. Turn this option off if you have a dial-up ISP account and you do not want to make the connection automatically.

The options in the When I Use Yahoo! Messenger section determine how the program works. Selecting the Stand By and Wait Until I Connect To The Internet option, for example, leaves the Messenger window minimized when you are not connected. As soon as you connect, however, the Messenger window opens so you can see if friends are available for chatting.

19

Choose Keep Yahoo! Messenger On Top Of All Other Applications if you want the window to remain in the foreground. If you do not select this option, the window will go into the background and you may not see when friends are online.

Normally, all messages are channeled directly between you and your friends using your computer's and your friend's computer's IP address. In this way, however, someone else can learn your IP address. If you are connected to the Internet through a DSL or cable modem, you have the same IP address each time you are online, and a disreputable hacker could possibly access your disk drive. Select the Do Not Reveal My IP Address To Other Messenger Users option to channel all messages through the Yahoo! computers. This way, your IP address is not made available to others.

Selecting some features in Messenger, such as the features in the Help menu, opens a page in your Web browser. Select the Always Open Browser In A New Window option if you want to display Web pages in a new browser window. That way, the Web site you are currently viewing remains open.

When you minimize Yahoo! Messenger, an icon for it appears in the Windows Taskbar by default. The icon appears in addition to the red Y! icon in the system tray on the right side of the Taskbar. Select the Remove The Yahoo! Messenger Taskbar Button option if you do not want the Taskbar button to appear when you minimize Messenger.

The Idle Status section determines how long after you leave your computer an Idle message appears after your name on others' Friends lists. You can set the number of minutes you must be idle before that status is reported, or you can choose to turn this feature off.

The Misc section of the General tab offers these three options:

- **Show Yahoo! Helper In My Friend List**   Lets you access tips by sending a message to Yahoo! Helper from your Friends list

- **Accept Web IMs Only From People On My Friends List**   Automatically rejects messages from persons not on your Friends list

- **Play Keyboard Sound While Typing An Instant Message**   Plays the sound of an old-fashioned typewriter keyboard when you type

Appearance Preferences

The options on the Appearance tab of the Preferences dialog box determine how Yahoo! Messenger appears.

For example, you can specify which tabs are shown at the bottom of the Messenger window, choose the color of text, tile a background image so it is repeated over the entire window, or select a theme.

A Messenger theme, also called a *skin*, determines what the background area, toolbar buttons, and status icons look like. Several themes are provided, but you can also create your own and download themes that other Messenger users designed.

Choose the theme you want to use from the Current Theme list on the Appearance tab. The Games theme, for example, is shown in the following illustration. You can also click the Instructions For New Theme button to learn how to create and download themes.

Friends Preferences

Use the Friends tab of the Preferences dialog box to customize how you are notified when a person on your Friends list goes online or offline. For each event, you can specify one or more of these actions:

- Show a message at the bottom-right corner of the screen.
- Display a dialog box.
- Play a sound.

By default, the sound that is heard when a person comes online is a door knock. The sound when a person goes offline is a door closing. To choose a sound of your own, browse your computer for an alternate sound effect.

Messages Preferences

The options on the Messages tab, as shown in Figure 19-4, determine how you are notified when you get a message and what happens when you send one.

Your choices for receiving a message are to automatically show the message window or to minimize the window to the Taskbar.

19

Messages tab of the Preferences dialog box

When a message comes in, you can flash the message window or play a sound. Messages can appear in the font and color choices that the sender made or in your own default font and colors. Click the Fonts And Colors button in the dialog box to choose your font and color preferences.

Your options for sending a message include what happens when you press the ENTER key. You can press the ENTER key to send the message, or to insert a carriage return and thereby start a new paragraph in the message. You can also choose to keep the message window open after you have sent a message and disable the display of graphic smiley characters.

Stock Preferences

Options on the Stocks tab of the Preferences dialog box determine what occurs when you receive a stock alert.

You can choose, for example, to hide the Stock tab and not display stock alerts when they arrive. If you choose to display the tab and alerts, you can then choose between two categories of options: Send Me an Alert When options and When an Alert Arrives options.

In the Send Me An Alert When section of the tab, choose when alerts will be sent to you. The options are

- My Stocks Trip An Upper Or Lower Limit
- Volume For Any Stock Is __% Over Average Daily Volume
- Price Change For The Day Is Greater Than __%

The upper and lower limit amounts must be set in your My Yahoo! page, but you specify the two percentages in the Preferences dialog box.

The When An Alert Arrives section of the tab offers these options:

- Flash The Taskbar "Tray" Icon
- Display A Dialog Box
- Play A Sound

Mail Preferences

If you have a Yahoo! Mail or Yahoo! Personals account, you can be notified when new mail or personal messages are received.

You can choose to be alerted whenever a new message arrives, for example, or at an interval between 1 and 99 minutes. You can also choose to be alerted by a Taskbar icon, dialog box, or sound.

If you are not yet signed up for either feature, there are buttons to sign up for Yahoo! Mail or Yahoo! Personals.

Calendar Preferences

The Calendar tab of the Preferences dialog box lets you choose how to be alerted to an upcoming meeting on your Yahoo! calendar. You can choose to flash the Taskbar "tray" icon, display a dialog box, or play a sound.

Connection Preferences

The options on the Connection Preferences tab of the Preferences dialog box help you connect to Yahoo! Messenger if you connect through a proxy server or company firewall. The options are

- No Proxies
- Use Proxies
- Firewall With No Proxies
- No Network Detection

Leave this set to No Proxies if you use a standard dial-up connection on your computer. For all the other options, check with your network administrator or read the documentation that came with your proxy or firewall software.

Using Messenger Lite

If you are online but Messenger is not installed on your computer or you are not running Messenger, you can still send and receive messages by using the Lite version of Messenger. Messenger Lite is a Java-based version that runs from within Web browsers.

To start a Messenger chat with Messenger Lite, follow these steps:

1. Locate the Yahoo! profile of the person with whom you want to speak.

2. If the person is online, click the Send Me A Message button in his or her profile window. You see the screen shown here.

3. Type a message and click the Send button. When the recipient replies to the message, the Lite version of Messenger appears.

4. Click the person's name and then click Send.

A chat in the Lite version is shown here. It offers many of the same options as the full version of Yahoo! Messenger.

Chapter 20

Chat with Friends

How to . . .

- ■ Join a chat room
- ■ Send a private message
- ■ Participate in voice chats
- ■ Change chat rooms
- ■ Create a chat room
- ■ Join live chat events

Yahoo! Chat is another way to communicate over the Internet. With chats, you can send messages to and receive messages from any number of other Yahoo! members—friends as well as strangers—in real-time or take part in a voice chat in which you can speak to and hear other participants. You can even take part in a live event such as a chat with a celebrity who will respond to your questions.

Joining a Chat

The chats are organized by categories, such as Business & Finance, Entertainment & Arts, and Family & Home. Within each category are a number of chat rooms, each devoted to a specific interest. When you join a chat room, you only see messages from persons in that room.

Click Chat on the Yahoo! home page to go to the Chat page shown in Figure 20-1.

The first thing you need to do is determine which type of chat software you want to use. The Chat Software list offers three choices:

- ■ JAVA
- ■ Voice
- ■ HTML

HTML is the standard method for displaying Web pages in Web browsers. Because Chat is a real-time interactive process, however, it is better suited to the Java language than HTML. Java, an interactive computer language, provides better performance than HTML, but it may be incompatible with your Web browser or Internet service provider. The Voice option also uses Java. With the Voice option, you can participate in voice chats in which you speak to and hear other participants. In terms of computer resources, Voice requires the most, followed by Java, followed by HTML.

Tip *Click the Add/Change Profile link to access your profile and create an alias for use on chat rooms.*

If you want to take part in Voice chats, select Voice from the list; otherwise, choose Java. If your computer has difficulties or displays errors when you enter a chat room using Java, return to

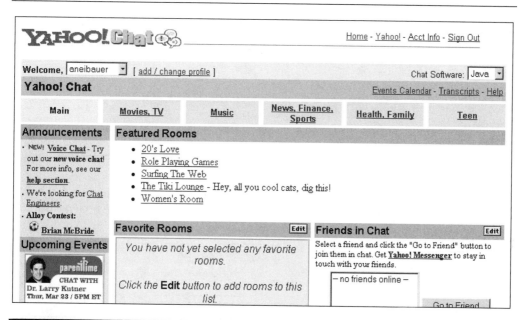

FIGURE 20-1   Yahoo! Chat home page

the Chat home page and choose the HTML option instead. To get the full benefit of the Voice and Java chat features, use the most recent version of your Web browser.

Across the top of the page are chat categories. Select a category to see chat rooms where similar topics are discussed. Then, to start chatting, use any of these techniques:

- ■ Click a featured room.
- ■ Select a category and choose a room from the list that appears.
- ■ Click Start Chatting to enter a randomly selected room.

You can also go directly to a chat room in which a friend is located. If you maintain a Friends list with Yahoo! Messenger, friends who are currently online and in a chat room are listed in the Friends In Chat box. To join a chat in which a friend is located, click his or her name and then click Go To Friend. You will enter the room in which the friend is chatting (as long as the chat room is not full).

Favorite Chat Rooms

If you find yourself returning periodically to the same chat rooms, you can add them to your Favorite Rooms list. This list appears in the Yahoo! Chat home page. Starting there, you can quickly enter a favorite room by clicking its name in the list.

To add a room to the Favorite Rooms list in the Yahoo! Chat home page, follow these steps:

1. In the Yahoo! Chat home page, click Edit next to Favorite Rooms. You see a page that lists all of the chat room categories.

2. Click a category for the room you want to add to see a list of rooms in that category, each room preceded by a check box.

3. Select the check box next to the rooms you want to add and then click Finished. (Remove the checkmarks beside the names of rooms you want to remove from the list.) The category list appears with the chat room next to the category.

4. Click Finished.

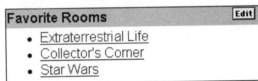

The room's name will appear in the Favorite Rooms list, as shown on the right. Click the room to enter it and participate in a chat.

Participating in a Chat

The first time you start a Java or Voice chat, a security warning message box appears. Click Yes in the message box to download the necessary software and open the chat room window shown in Figure 20-2. The figure, by the way, shows a room in which voice chat has been enabled. A Java chat room without voice capabilities looks the same but doesn't have the voice control bar.

The large conversation box on the left offers chat room instructions, notices, and messages. Along the right side of the window is the Chatters box. It lists the Yahoo! ID of all persons in the chat room.

To enter a message, type it in the Chat text box and then press ENTER or click the Send button. Your name and message appears in the conversation box. You can use the Bold, Italic, and Underline buttons, as well as the color list, to format your message before you send it.

While most persons in chat rooms are well behaved, you occasionally encounter someone who is downright annoying or vulgar. To prevent that person's messages from appearing on your screen, click his or her name in the Chatters box and then click the Ignore button.

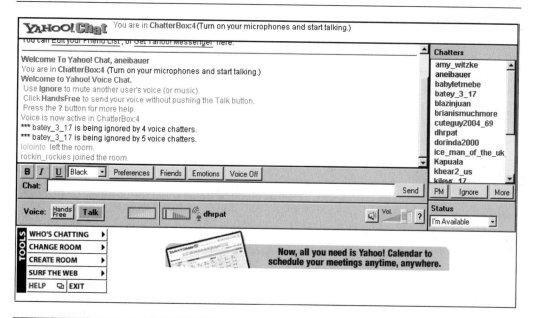

YAHOO! Chat You are in ChatterBox:4 (Turn on your microphones and start talking.)

You can Edit your Friend List, or Get Yahoo! Messenger here.

Welcome To Yahoo! Chat, aneibauer
You are in **ChatterBox:4** (Turn on your microphones and start talking.)
Welcome to Yahoo! Voice Chat.
Use **Ignore** to mute another user's voice (or music).
Click **HandsFree** to send your voice without pushing the Talk button.
Press the **?** button for more help.
Voice is now active in ChatterBox:4
*** batey_3_17 is being ignored by 4 voice chatters.
*** batey_3_17 is being ignored by 5 voice chatters.
lolointo left the room.
rockin_rockies joined the room.

Chatters
amy_witzke
aneibauer
babyletmebe
batey_3_17
blazinjuan
brianismuchmore
cuteguy2004_69
dhrpat
dorinda2000
ice_man_of_the_uk
Kapuala
kbear2_us
kilev_17

B *I* U Black ▾ Preferences | Friends | Emotions | Voice Off

Chat: [   ] Send | PM | Ignore | More

Voice: [Hands Free] [Talk] [   ] [||||] 🎙 dhrpat   🔊 Vol. ▮▮ ?

Status
I'm Available ▾

TOOLS
WHO'S CHATTING   ▶
CHANGE ROOM   ▶
CREATE ROOM   ▶
SURF THE WEB   ▶
HELP ⮑ EXIT

Now, all you need is Yahoo! Calendar to
schedule your meetings anytime, anywhere.

FIGURE 20-2   A voice-enabled chat room

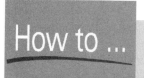 **How to ...**   # Send a Private Message

You can also send a friend a private message.
This is much like communicating with Yahoo!
Messenger, only the sender and the recipient
can read a private message. To send a private
message to a person whose name is listed
in the Chatters box, click the person's name
and then click the PM button. You see the
dialog box shown at right.

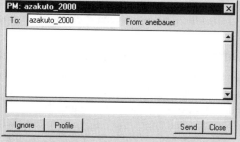

PM: azakuto_2000   ✕
To: [azakuto_2000]   From: aneibauer
[   ]
[   ]
Ignore | Profile   Send | Close

To send a private message to a person
whose name is not listed in the Chatters box but who is in another chat room, click PM and
enter the person's ID in the To box. Enter a message to the person and click the Send button.
You can then write back and forth as you would in Yahoo! Messenger.

See "Setting Your Chat Preferences," later in this chapter, if you do not want to be
bothered with requests for private messages.

Participating in a Voice Chat

When a chat room is voice enabled, you can speak and listen to other persons in the room just as you learned to do when you traded instant messages in Chapter 19. Hold down the mouse on the Talk button or click Hands Free to speak without holding down the button, and speak into your microphone. The name of the person who is speaking appears in the voice bar. You can use the volume slider on the right side of the voice bar to set the level of your speakers. To turn off the sound, use the speaker button.

Clicking Ignore also prevents you from hearing voice messages from a participant.

> **Note** *Voice and written messages are totally independent. You can both speak and type, listen and read.*

Setting Your Status

The conversation window reports when anyone enters or leaves the room. It also reports the status of members. For example, it reports who is being ignored. As with instant messages, you can change your status to tell others whether you are available to respond to messages. Pull down the Status list under the Chatters box and choose the option that pertains to you. Your status will appear next to your name in the conversation box.

> aneibauer is away. (Be Right Back)

You can also read a person's status by noting the color of his or her name in the Chatters box. The names of persons who are active appear in bold red, while participants who have not sent a message in more than one minute appear in light red. The names of persons you have chosen to ignore appear in gray. The names of users who have an Away status are in red.

In addition to designating yourself as away, Yahoo! will automatically show you as being away if you are idle for a specific number of minutes. The default time is 10 minutes, but you can change the time in the Chat Preferences dialog box.

Using Emotions to Make Chats Livelier

When you are in voice chat, you can let your voice get your emotions across. When you're writing back and forth, however, emotions are much harder to express. That's why Yahoo! gives you the Emotions list shown in Figure 20-3.

You can send an emotion message to the chat room in general or to a specific chatter.

To send an emotion to everyone in the room, click the Emotions button. Then, in the list that appears, double-click the emotion you want to express to insert it as a message, like so:

> aneibauer says, "Pardon me, do you have any Grey Poupon?"
> aneibauer hiccups and then searches for a glass of water

Emotions list

To send an emotion to a specific chatter, click the person's name in the Chatters box, select the emotion from the list, and click Emote User. The emotion will appear like this:

aneibauer chuckles at **azakuto_2000**

Changing Chat Rooms

If you are no longer interested in the discussion going on in a chat room, you can leave the room or switch to another room.

To leave a room, click Exit at the bottom of the Tools section. If you then reenter a new room, however, the Java chat applet will have to reload.

To change rooms without having to reload the Java Chat applet, click Change Room in the Tools section. You see a list of categories and rooms, as shown in the following illustration. Select the category on the left to list the rooms on the right. Click a room to enter it. You can list Yahoo! Rooms or User Rooms. *User rooms* are chat rooms that individual chat participants have created.

20

Finding Out Who's Chatting

The Chatters box shows only the names of persons who are in the chat room you are visiting, but you can chat with other persons as well.

If a person on your Friends list has entered the chat system, for example, you'll see a message such as the one shown here in the conversation window. You can click the person's name to send him or her a private message.

> *** barbelayne is now online.

You can also check at any time to see which friends are chatting by clicking the Friends button. A list of friends like the one shown here will be shown in the conversation:

> **Here are your Online Friends**: (Modify List)
> azakuto_2000

Click a friend's name to open the Select Action dialog box. From there, you can invite the person to come to the chat room, view his or her profile, or send a private message.

For a list of all the Yahoo! members who are chatting, click Who's Chatting in the Tools section at the bottom of the chat window. You'll see the letters of the alphabet and a search box. Click a letter to see a list of persons, as shown here. Click Goto to enter the chat room in which the person is located, or click Invite to invite your friend to your chat room.

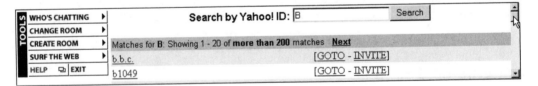

Creating a Chat Room

Sometimes you can't find a chat room where topics you are interested in are being discussed. Sometimes you don't care to chat with the people in a chat room. Fortunately, you can create your own room to discuss a certain topic or to invite members for a private chat.

Yahoo! offers three kinds of chat rooms:

■ A public room is shown in the User Rooms list. Anyone can enter it.

■ A private room is not listed in the User Rooms list. Anyone can enter the room by joining a person already there from either the Go To Friends feature or the Goto option from Who's Chatting.

■   A secure room is a private chat room. Only persons that you invite to attend can
      enter the room.

Follow these steps to create a chat room:

1.   Click Create Room to see the options shown here:

Room name:		Welcome Message:

```
Room name:                                    Welcome Message:
aneibauer's room                              Welcome to
                                              aneibauer's room.
Access:
 ⦿ Public  ○ Private  ·  ☐ Secured  ·  ☐ Voice Enable        Create my room
Private rooms will not show in the roomlist. Secure rooms cannot be entered           Cancel
```

2.   Enter a name for the room.

3.   Select the type of room: Public or Private.

4.   If you select a Private room, choose whether you want to secure it against
           uninvited chatters.

5.   Choose Voice Enable if you want to conduct a voice chat. Only users who have selected
           to load the Voice chat software, however, will be able to speak and listen.

6.   Click the Create My Room button.

You will be taken into the room. Only messages from persons in the room will be
seen or heard.

Next, follow these steps to invite persons to
come to your room:

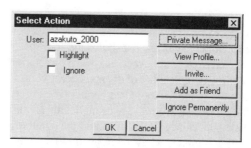

1.   Click More to open the Select Action
           dialog box shown at right.

2.   Enter the ID of the person you want
           to invite.

3.   Click the Invite button.

The other party receives a message like the one
shown at right and can click Yes to enter the room.
    To find out which chat rooms have been created
by users, click Change Room in the Tools section,
choose a room category, and then click User Rooms
on the right side of the window. User rooms are
temporary. The room is automatically deleted from the list of rooms when the last occupant exits
or changes rooms.

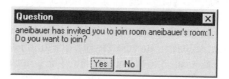

By the way, you can also use the Select Action dialog box to access other chat features. Either click a person's name in the Chatter box before clicking More to select an action relating to the person, or enter the person's ID in the User box and then take any of these actions:

- ■ Click Private Message to send a private message.

- ■ Click View Profile to read the person's profile.

- ■ Click Add As Friend to add the person to your Friends list.

- ■ Click Ignore Permanently to place the person on your ignore list.

- ■ Click Highlight to make the person's ID and message stand out in the conversation box.

- ■ Click Ignore to ignore the person.

Live Events

Live events are online chats with celebrities. The chats are moderated and they work like this:

1. You type a question to the celebrity.

2. The moderator reviews your question and forwards it to the celebrity if it is deemed legitimate.

3. The celebrity responds to the question in the chat window.

Live events that are currently taking place are shown on the top of the Yahoo! Chat home page, as shown at right. Click the link to enter the chat room.

```
Live Events
☆ Actress Lynn Redgrave · 6pm ET
```

To see a list of scheduled events in a chat category, scroll to the Upcoming Events section of the home page. The list shows the sponsor, title, and time of the event, as shown on the right.

For a complete list of events, click Events Calendar in the Yahoo! Chat banner (see Figure 20-4). Click an event to see more details about it. Click Add To My Calendar to add the event to your Yahoo! calendar.

```
COURT   Cruel and Unusual Punishment?
 TV     Thursday March 23, at 7pm ET/4pm PT.

TIME    doodie.com Creator Tom Winkler
        Thursday March 23, at 8pm ET/5pm PT.
```

If you missed an event and want to read the questions and answers, or want a record of an event that you joined, click Transcripts in the Yahoo! Chat banner. In the page that appears, select the category of the chat and then the chat itself to read the questions and answers.

In the Chat window, the celebrity's name appears in boldface. Responses by the celebrity are marked with a star. Enter your question in the Chat text box and click the Ask button to submit your question to the moderator. The conversation window also shows the status of other chatters and their messages, even those not submitted to the celebrity.

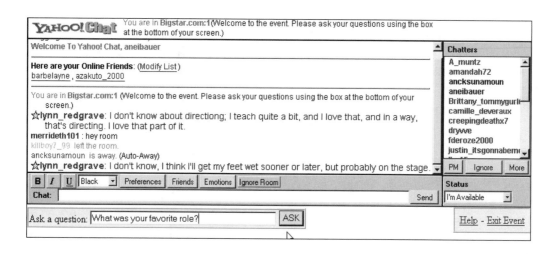

FIGURE 20-4 Events Calendar

Setting Your Chat Preferences

As with most Yahoo! features, you can customize Chat to some extent. To do so, click the Preferences button below the conversation list in a chat room to open the Preferences dialog box shown here.

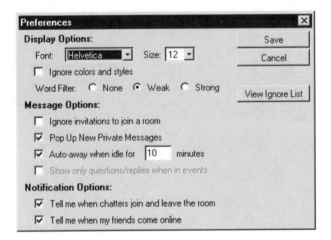

In the Display Options section, choose the default font and font size that you want for the text in the conversation list. Select the Ignore Styles And Colors check box if you do not want to see the sender's formats in messages.

The Word Filter options let you block out undesirable words. Choose Strong to block the largest number of offensive terms or Weak to block just a few words.

In the Message Options section, you can choose from these settings:

- **Ignore Invitations To Join A Room** This is a useful choice it you are receiving invitations to join chats about products or services and you only want to visit legitimate chat rooms.

- **Pop Up New Private Message** Deselect this check box if you are getting annoying messages from anonymous persons. You will still see invitations, but they will appear in the conversation list rather than a separate window.

- **Auto-Away When Idle For** Set the amount of idle time before an Auto-Away status is issued.

- **Show Only Questions/Replies When In Events** Display only questions and answers, not all chat messages, when viewing live events.

Use the Notification options to determine whether notices appear when chatters join rooms, when chatters leave rooms, and when friends come online.

Chapter 21

Communicating with Clubs, Message Boards, Personals, and More

How to . . .

- Share information on message boards
- Join a Yahoo! club
- Create your own club
- Share club photographs
- Voice-chat with club members
- Post a personal ad
- Respond to a personal ad
- Send an electronic greeting
- Buy and sell with Yahoo! classifieds

Yahoo! Messenger is just one way to communicate with people over the Internet. Besides trading messages, you can share information and photographs, keep in touch with friends, and meet people in a variety of ways for free with just your Yahoo! account.

You can use message boards to send and reply to messages, or join or create a club to share information about a specific theme. You can post and respond to personal advertisements to meet people online. You can send electronic greeting cards to celebrate birthdays, anniversaries, and other events. You can also post and reply to classified ads so you can buy and sell items and meet people who share a common interest.

Message Boards

A message board can be compared to a bulletin board on an office wall. It is a place to leave messages to others and to read their replies. Unlike a chat, which is conducted in real-time and in which all messages are temporary, conversations in messages boards are saved and can be read or replied to at any time.

Verifying Your Address

Before you can take part in a message board, Yahoo! must verify your e-mail address. The first time you try to add a message to a message board, you see a screen like the one in Figure 21-1. If the address on the screen is no longer valid, click the Change Address button and enter a new address. Otherwise, click the Send Verification Now button.

Yahoo! will send you an e-mail with a verification code and a link that you can click to return to the verification page, where you will find the box shown next.

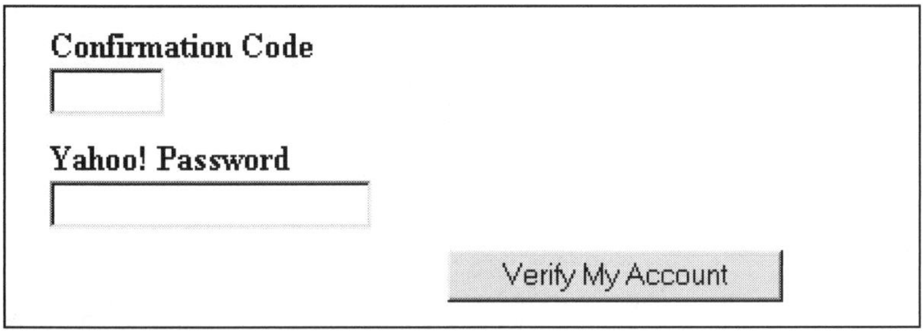

Confirmation Code

Yahoo! Password

Verify My Account

Enter the code you received, enter your Yahoo! password, and then click the Verify My Account button. When the congratulations message appears, click the Let Me Start! Button.

Accessing Message Boards

To access the message boards, click More in the Yahoo! home page and then click Message Boards or go directly to http://messages.yahoo.com/index.html. The Message Board home page is shown in Figure 21-2.

As with chat rooms, messages are organized into categories. Within each category are a number of boards where common subjects are discussed, and you will find one or more messages about each subject. The messages are organized by threads. A *thread* is a message and all of the responses to it. So if you see a topic that you are interested in, you can easily read the entire conversation.

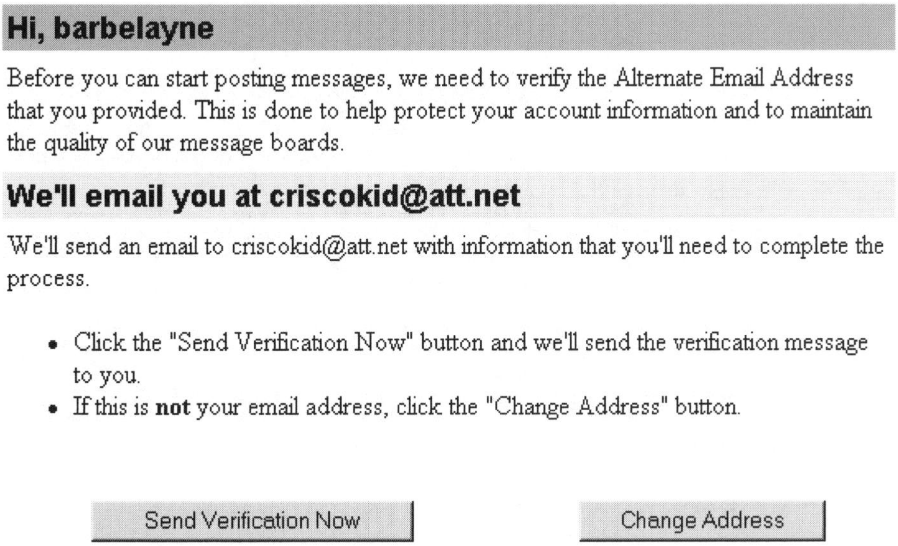

Hi, barbelayne

Before you can start posting messages, we need to verify the Alternate Email Address that you provided. This is done to help protect your account information and to maintain the quality of our message boards.

We'll email you at criscokid@att.net

We'll send an email to criscokid@att.net with information that you'll need to complete the process.

- Click the "Send Verification Now" button and we'll send the verification message to you.
- If this is **not** your email address, click the "Change Address" button.

Send Verification Now   Change Address

FIGURE 21-1   Verifying your address

21

FIGURE 21-2 Message Board home page

Navigate the categories until you get to a list of messages like the one shown in Figure 21-3. The topics are listed in the order in which they were started, beginning with the most recent. By clicking a heading, you can sort the list by the topic or number of messages in each topic.

Click a topic to read the first message in the thread, as shown in Figure 21-4. Click the Previous, Next, First, and Last buttons to move among messages in the thread, or click Msg List to see a listing of all of the messages in the thread, including each message's author and the date each message was submitted.

Below the message is a list of all of the messages in the thread. Click one of the messages to read it. To list just replies to the message, click View Replies To This Message.

To add your own comments to the thread, click the Reply button. Doing so opens the form shown in Figure 21-5. Complete the form by following these steps:

1. Select your identity.

2. Enter a subject.

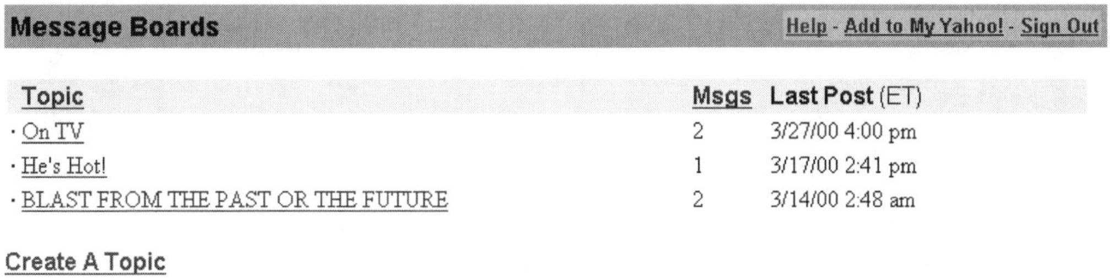

Message Boards		Help - **Add to My Yahoo!** - **Sign Out**
Topic	**Msgs**	**Last Post** (ET)
· On TV	2	3/27/00 4:00 pm
· He's Hot!	1	3/17/00 2:41 pm
· BLAST FROM THE PAST OR THE FUTURE	2	3/14/00 2:48 am

Create A Topic

FIGURE 21-3   List of messages

3. Type your message.

4. Click the Post Message button. You can also click Preview to see what your message will look like after you post it and edit the message as well.

If you clicked the Msg List option to display a list of all of the messages in the thread, the list looks like this. Click Post to add your comment to the thread.

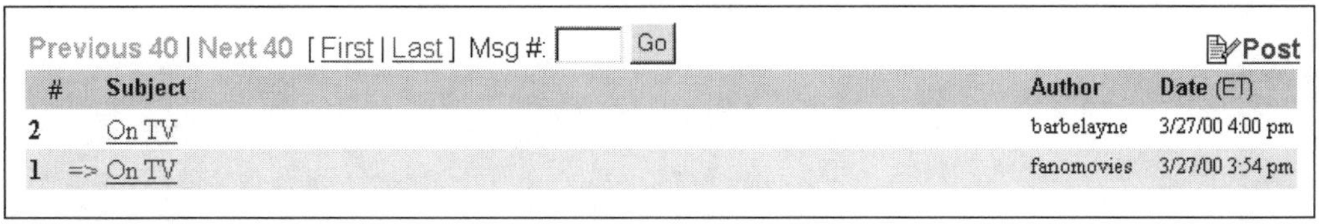

Previous 40 | Next 40 [First | Last] Msg #: [____] Go			Post
# **Subject**		**Author**	**Date** (ET)
2 On TV		barbelayne	3/27/00 4:00 pm
1 => On TV		fanomovies	3/27/00 3:54 pm

Starting a New Topic

When you want to start a new topic in the message board, click Create A Topic. You will find this option at the end of the topic list in the message board's home page (refer to Figure 21-3). Clicking Create A Topic brings up a form similar to the one that is used to post a reply.

Follow these steps to start a new topic on a message board:

1. Select your identity.

2. Enter the topic heading.

3. Type the text of the first message in the thread.

4. Click Create Topic.

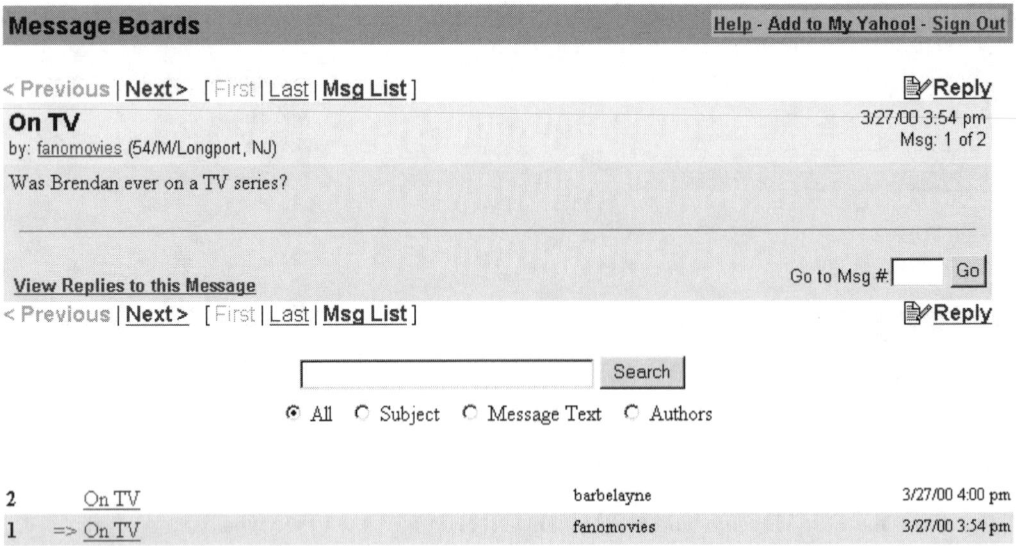

Message Boards   Help - **Add to My Yahoo!** - **Sign Out**

< Previous | **Next >**   [First | **Last** | **Msg List**]   **Reply**

On TV   3/27/00 3:54 pm
by: fanomovies (54/M/Longport, NJ)   Msg: 1 of 2

Was Brendan ever on a TV series?

_____

View Replies to this Message   Go to Msg #: [____] [Go]
< Previous | **Next >**   [First | **Last** | **Msg List**]   **Reply**

                        [_____] [Search]

                   ⦿ All   ○ Subject   ○ Message Text   ○ Authors

2   On TV   barbelayne   3/27/00 4:00 pm
1   => On TV   fanomovies   3/27/00 3:54 pm

FIGURE 21-4   Reading a message

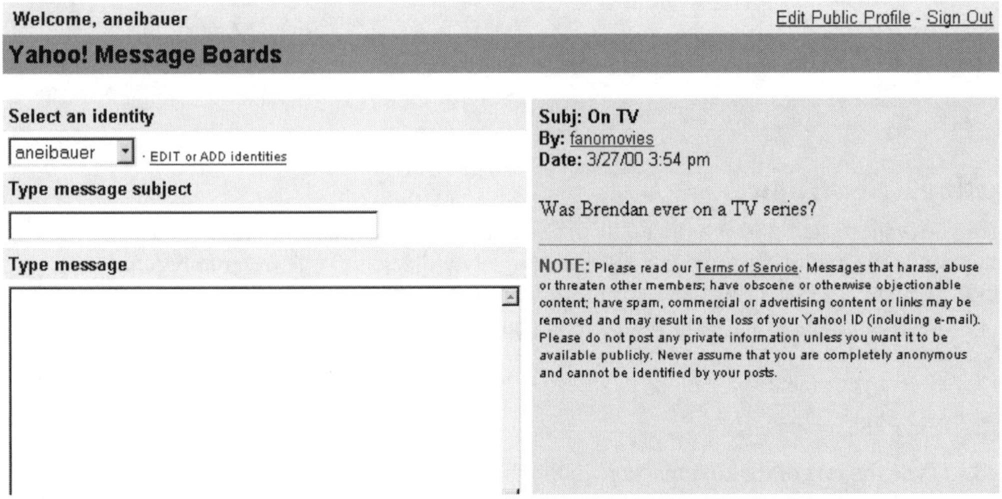

Welcome, aneibauer   Edit Public Profile - Sign Out
Yahoo! Message Boards

Select an identity   **Subj: On TV**
                                                By: fanomovies
[aneibauer ▾] · EDIT or ADD identities   **Date:** 3/27/00 3:54 pm

Type message subject
                                                Was Brendan ever on a TV series?
[_____]

Type message   NOTE: Please read our Terms of Service. Messages that harass, abuse
                                                or threaten other members; have obscene or otherwise objectionable
[   ]   content; have spam, commercial or advertising content or links may be
[   ]   removed and may result in the loss of your Yahoo! ID (including e-mail).
[   ]   Please do not post any private information unless you want it to be
[   ]   available publicly. Never assume that you are completely anonymous
[   ]   and cannot be identified by your posts.

FIGURE 21-5   Replying to a message

Exploring Yahoo! Clubs

A *club* is a group of Yahoo! members who share a common interest. Each club has its own message board and chat room, as well as places to share photographs, news, addresses, and links. You can create your own club and use it to share information about any topic that interests you or as a home page where friends and family can stay in touch.

There are three types of clubs:

- Official
- Listed
- Unlisted

An official club is one created by Yahoo! for and about a Yahoo! Partner, such as a company, celebrity, or sports team. These clubs are marked by an official logo in the list of clubs.

A listed club is one that is open to all Yahoo! members. To join the club, you simply fill out an online form. Don't worry, you cannot be rejected from a listed club.

An unlisted club is private. Only Yahoo! members who were invited to join may join the club and be able to access it. An unlisted club is ideal for sharing private information with family members or business associates.

Joining a Club

Access Yahoo! clubs by clicking Clubs on the Yahoo! home page or by going directly to http://clubs.yahoo.com/ to open the page shown in Figure 21-6. As you can see, clubs are also organized by categories, with several featured clubs at the top of the page. Any clubs to which you already belong are listed in the My Clubs section.

Use the categories to navigate to a club that interests you. As with message boards and chats, you may have to work your way through subcategories to find a list of specific clubs. Eventually, however, you'll get to an individual club listing like the one shown in Figure 21-7.

In this example, clubs about James Bond movies are displayed. There are 83 clubs in the group and they are shown in order of popularity. Beside the name of each club is a brief description and the number of members. You can also use the A–Z Index to list all of the clubs alphabetically or click New Clubs to see clubs that have recently been formed.

Click a club you are interested in to see its home page, as shown in Figure 21-8.

The page includes a message from the founder, a list of members who are currently online, and recent messages that have been posted to the club's message board. There are also links to the club's private chat room and statistics about active club members.

The Our Pages section of the page lists the pages and features that are available to members.

When you find a club that you'd like to join, click Join List Club in the upper-right corner of the page. In the page that appears, select the Yahoo! identity you want to use for the club and then indicate if you want to add the club to your profile. Then click the Receive Mail button.

Yahoo! Clubs

Get Started

Browse the Clubs Directory to join or create a club, or take the Clubs Tour.

My Clubs

You currently aren't a member of any Clubs. Once you join a Club, a link to each Club you are a member of will appear here.

Search Clubs

[   ] [Search Clubs]

Clubs Spotlight

- Jet Li and Aaliyah star in Romeo Must Die.
- MTV's Tom Green is battling cancer.
- Shaq and Kobe are leading the Lakers to the best record in the NBA.

🏠 **Visit the Clubhouse** - updated every Tuesday
Cool clubs, helpful hints, polls, top ten lists, and more.

Clubs Directory

Business & Finance
Investments, Industry

Computers & Internet
Internet, User Groups

Cultures & Community
Issues, Seniors, Teens, LGB

Hobbies & Crafts
Antiques, Collecting

Music
Rock & Pop, Rap, Country

Recreation & Sports
Travel, Cars, Wrestling

FIGURE 21-6   Yahoo! Club home page

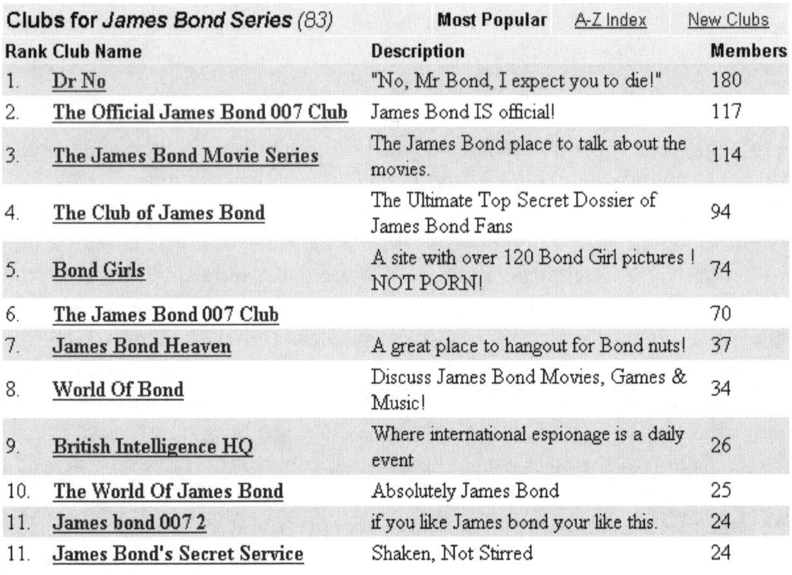

Clubs for *James Bond Series* (83)   **Most Popular** A-Z Index   New Clubs

Rank	Club Name	Description	Members
1.	Dr No	"No, Mr Bond, I expect you to die!"	180
2.	The Official James Bond 007 Club	James Bond IS official!	117
3.	The James Bond Movie Series	The James Bond place to talk about the movies.	114
4.	The Club of James Bond	The Ultimate Top Secret Dossier of James Bond Fans	94
5.	Bond Girls	A site with over 120 Bond Girl pictures ! NOT PORN!	74
6.	The James Bond 007 Club		70
7.	James Bond Heaven	A great place to hangout for Bond nuts!	37
8.	World Of Bond	Discuss James Bond Movies, Games & Music!	34
9.	British Intelligence HQ	Where international espionage is a daily event	26
10.	The World Of James Bond	Absolutely James Bond	25
11.	James bond 007 2	if you like James bond your like this.	24
11.	James Bond's Secret Service	Shaken, Not Stirred	24

FIGURE 21-7   Club listings

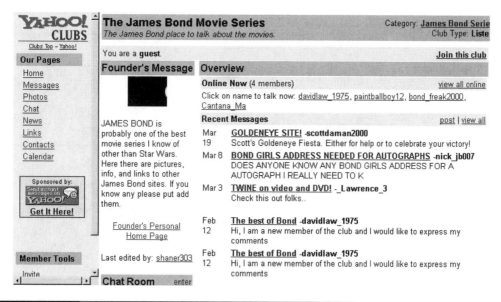

FIGURE 21-8   Club page

Note   *You must be invited to join an unlisted club.*

Yahoo! will send you an e-mail with a link to follow. Click the link to open a page similar to the one in Figure 21-9. Enter the comment that you want to appear next to your name in the list of members and then click Yes! I Accept.

The name of the club will now appear in the My Clubs section of the Yahoo! Clubs home page.

Now when you access the club, other members will see your name on the top of the page with the list of members who are online. Click a name to open Yahoo! Messenger Lite and send someone on the list an instant message.

After you are a member of a club, you can invite other people to join by following these steps:

1. Click Invite in the Member Tools section of the club page.

2. In the form that appears, enter the person's e-mail address or Yahoo! ID.

3. Type a short invitation to join the club.

4. Click Send Invitation.

The invitation includes instructions for joining Yahoo! and the club.

21

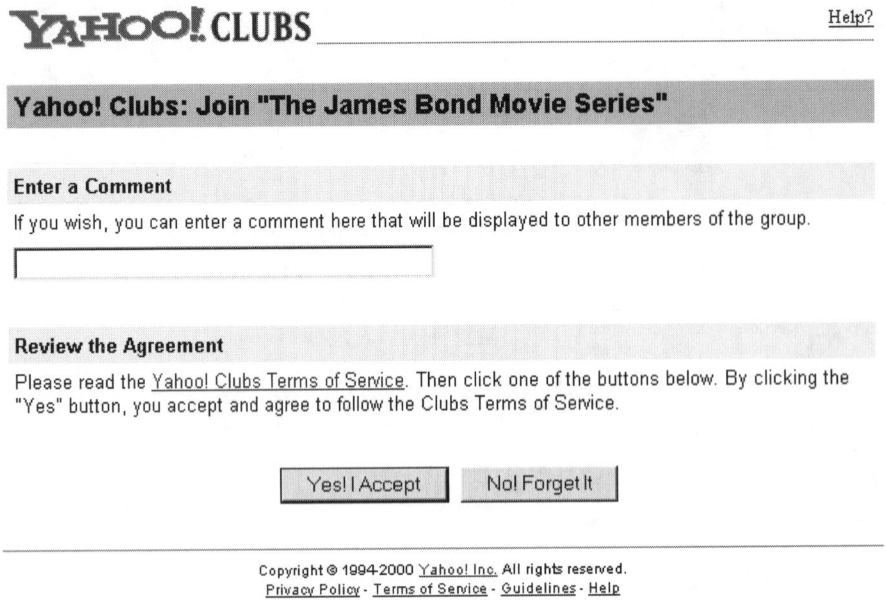
YAHOO! CLUBS
Help?
Yahoo! Clubs: Join "The James Bond Movie Series"
Enter a Comment
If you wish, you can enter a comment here that will be displayed to other members of the group.
Review the Agreement
Please read the Yahoo! Clubs Terms of Service. Then click one of the buttons below. By clicking the "Yes" button, you accept and agree to follow the Clubs Terms of Service.
Yes! I Accept
No! Forget It
Copyright © 1994-2000 Yahoo! Inc. All rights reserved.
Privacy Policy - Terms of Service - Guidelines - Help

FIGURE 21-9 Joining a club

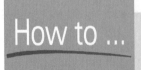

How to ... Use Club Member Options

Click the Options choice in the Member Tools section of a club page to access these four useful features:

- **Contact Founders** Lets you send an e-mail message to the founders of the club.
- **Edit My Clubs** Lets you quit a club.
- **Edit Public Profile** Lets you change the information in your Yahoo! profile.
- **Search Profiles** Lets you find other Yahoo! members.

Club Messages

Every club has its own private message board. Recent messages posted to the board are shown on the club's home page. Click Post in the Recent Messages banner to add your own comment to the board, or click View All or Messages in the Our Pages section to access the entire board.

Post a message on a club message board just as you learned to do on Yahoo! message boards earlier in this chapter in the section "Accessing Message Boards."

Sharing Photographs

The Photos option in the Our Pages section lets members share photographs and other graphics. Each club is given 5 MB of space to store photographs. The photos are organized into up to 30 albums, each with no more than 24 photos.

There are two types of albums: group and personal. Any member can place a photo in a group album and delete photos that he or she added as well. Only the creator of a personal album can add or delete photographs. Any club member can view photographs in both types of albums.

Click Photos to see a list of the albums that the club maintains. The listing, as you can see here, shows the name of the album, the number and total size of the pictures in it, and the creator of the album. It also tells you whether the album is a group or personal album. Notice as well the links with which to add, edit, and delete the album (which links appear depends on whether you created the album).

Photo Albums

Showing 1 - 2 of 2 albums (1024 KB total)   Add Album

Album Name	Pictures	Creator	Type	Add Photo	Edit	Delete
Blueraja's BOND GIRL Album	12 (278 KB)	blueraja3	Group	Add Photo		
James Bond	21 (287 KB)	shaner303	Group	Add Photo		

Click an album name to see a list of the photographs stored there, as shown in Figure 21-10. For each photo you will see the title, the contributor's name, the photo's size, and the date it was posted. Click a photo title to see the photo on your screen. Click View Thumbnails to see miniatures of all of the photographs.

Some photographs posted in clubs are not suitable for children.

Adding a Photograph to an Album   You can add a photo to an album starting from the list of albums or the list of photos in an album. Just follow these steps:

  1. If you are viewing the Photo Albums page, click Add Photo on the right side of the name of the album where you want to insert the photo. If you are looking at the list of photos already in an album, click the Add Photo button on the top of the page.

The James Bond Movie Series
The James Bond place to talk about the movies.

Category: James Bond Serie
Club Type: Liste

Blueraja's BOND GIRL Album

Back To: Album List

Created by blueraja3 on 22-Nov-1999

Add Photo

Showing 1 - 12 of 12 photos | View Thumbnails

Photo Name and Caption	Contributor	Size	Posted	Edit Delete
Denise Richards - Stunning Blue Bikini	blueraja3	21 KB	22-Nov-1999	
Denise Richards - Seductive Stare	blueraja3	22 KB	22-Nov-1999	
Denise Richards - Sexiest Denise Pic	blueraja3	48 KB	22-Nov-1999	
Denise Richards - Too Sexy! Too Sexy!	blueraja3	13 KB	22-Nov-1999	
Famke Janssen - Modeling Lingerie	blueraja3	53 KB	22-Nov-1999	
Famke Janssen - Sexiest Bond Girl Ever	blueraja3	13 KB	22-Nov-1999	
Famke Janssen - Sexy Black Leather	blueraja3	10 KB	22-Nov-1999	

FIGURE 21-10 Club photo album

2. In the page that appears, either enter the path and name of the photo on your disk or click Browse to locate the file. You can also click the On The Web link to designate a photograph located on a Web page.

3. Enter a name and description of the photo.

4. Select an option from the Resize Photo section. Resizing allows Yahoo! to adjust the size of the photograph to make better use of the club's Web space and to make photos easier to view. You can select Don't Resize, Large, Medium, or Small.

5. Click Preview to see how your photo will appear, or click Upload to move a copy of the photo into the club's Web space.

Note *The club's founder can delete any photograph or album from the club.*

Resizing does not affect the copy of the photograph on your disk, only the version in the album. None of the resizing options can enlarge a photograph—they just determine the largest size in which the photo will appear. Selecting Large, for example, reduces the photo so that its largest dimension is no more than 640 pixels. Medium reduces it to 480 pixels, and small to 300 pixels.

Adding an Album If you would like to make a number of photographs available to a club, you can create your own album by following these steps:

1. From the Photo Albums page, click Add Album.

2. In the page that appears, enter an album name.

3. Select the type of album: group or personal. After you create an album, you can only change its type by deleting it and starting over.

4. Click Create Album.

Club Chat

The Chat option in the Our Pages section opens a private chat area for club members. There is also a Chat section on the page that lists the members who are currently chatting. Click in the Chat section header to enter the Chat.

When you enter the chat area, a message box asks if you want to enable the voice-chat feature. Select Yes if you want to speak with other members, or Cancel for a text-only chat. Club chats use Java software, so you may experience problems if you usually use HTML software in a regular Yahoo! chat area.

Club News

The News section of Our Pages leads you to a page similar to My Yahoo!. It contains news headlines, portfolios, scores, and weather. The club founder can customize the page.

Club Links

Members can post Web site links that they want to share with other club members on the Links page. The page presents the address of the link, a short description, and the name of the member who contributed it.

Follow these steps to add a favorite link to the Links page:

1. Click Links in the Our Pages section of the club home page to open the Links page.

2. Click Add A Link.

3. In the page that appears, enter the Web address of the link.

4. Enter a brief description of the Web page.

5. Click Add Link.

If you contributed a link, you can edit or delete it from the Links page.

Club Contacts

The Contacts page lists the ID and other information about the club founder and every club member, as shown in Figure 21-11.

| The James Bond Movie Series | | | | Category: James Bond Serie |
| The James Bond place to talk about the movies. | | | | Club Type: **Liste** |

Contacts

Showing 1 - 20 of 115 members | next 20   Edit My Comments

Online Founders - Yahoo! ID	Age	Gender	Location	Comment
☺ shaner303 ☆	12	male	Illinois	no comment..

Online Members - Yahoo! ID	Age	Gender	Location	Comment
☺ Lawrence_3		neuter		no comment..
ace_jammer	15	male	Florida	no comment..
☺ agarber_28		male		Can't wait for The World is not enough
akaxlee		male		no comment..
☺ alain_desmier	16	male	London, England	Hey there, iam Alain
☺ aneibauer		male		Love the books -- even the new ones!
anjuliz2000	41	female	New York	no comment..
☺ asevilla_90023	35	male	Los Angeles Ca.	bring him on
☺ assassin_m9		male		no comment..
☺ BabyBlue_285	18	female	Wisconsin	no comment..

FIGURE 21-11   Contacts page

Click a member's name to open his or her profile. Click the Edit My Comments link to change the comment you made about yourself when you joined the club.

An icon next to each member's name indicates whether he or she is online. Click the icon to open Yahoo! Messenger Lite and send an instant message to a club member.

Club Calendar

The Calendar page is where members post events, such as special club chats or other activities, that are of interest to club members. You can view the calendar in day, week, month, or year format. Click Add Event to enter a new event on the calendar.

Use the same techniques to add an event or work with the calendar that you use to handle the Yahoo! Calendar. You learned about in the Yahoo! Calendar in Chapter 4.

Creating a Club

If you cannot find a club where your interests are discussed or you want to share information privately by means of a club, create your own club. As the club founder, you can invite others to join, delete members, control the contents of photo albums, and customize the photo and messages on the club's home page.

To create a club, follow these steps:

1. Navigate to the category in which you want the club to be listed.

2. Click Create Club.

3. In the form that appears, choose the identity you want to use as the club founder and then click Click Here To Continue. You see the form shown in Figure 21-12.

4. Enter a name for the club.

5. Optionally, enter your zip code. Choose the country if you are outside of the United States.

6. Choose to create a Listed or Unlisted club.

7. Click Yes! I Accept.

You'll see a page that tells you the club has been created. The page shows the club name and its Web address. You also get these options:

- ■ **Invite Friend**   Lets you invite others to join the club.
- ■ **Fix it Up**   Lets you add text and a photo to the club's home page.
- ■ **Let Me See It**   Opens the club's home page.

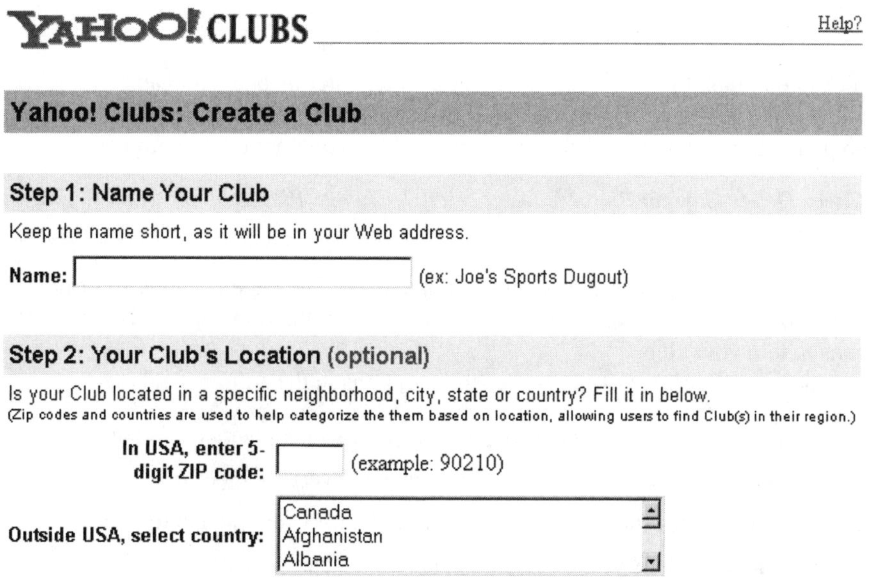

YAHOO! CLUBS _____ Help?

Yahoo! Clubs: Create a Club

Step 1: Name Your Club

Keep the name short, as it will be in your Web address.

Name: [   ] (ex: Joe's Sports Dugout)

Step 2: Your Club's Location (optional)

Is your Club located in a specific neighborhood, city, state or country? Fill it in below.
(Zip codes and countries are used to help categorize the them based on location, allowing users to find Club(s) in their region.)

In USA, enter 5-
digit ZIP code: [   ] (example: 90210)

Outside USA, select country: | Canada ▲
| Afghanistan
| Albania ▼

FIGURE 21-12   Creating a club

21

Click Fix It Up to see the Edit Club Settings options, and then follow these steps to personalize the club page:

1. Enter eight words or less to describe the club. These words will appear under the club name in the banner.

2. Enter a three- to four-sentence founder's message.

3. Enter the Web address of your home page if you have one.

4. Click Submit Changes.

If you want to add a photograph to the club page, click Change Picture in the Admin Tools section of the page that appears. You see these options:

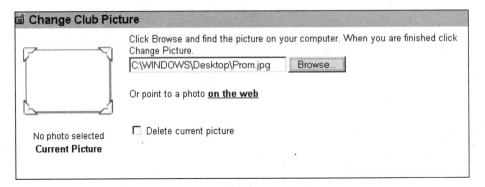

To load a photograph that is on your computer, either enter its path and name or click Browse to locate the photograph. Use the On The Web link to specify the location of a photograph on the Internet. Click Change Picture to add the photograph to your page.

 Check Delete Current Picture, and then click Change Picture if you want to remove the graphic from the page.

Figure 21-13 shows an example of a personal club page. The page contains all of the elements found on other club pages. Click the Invite option in the Member Tools section to ask other persons to join your club.

As the founder of the club, you'll also see these options in the Admin Tools section:

- **Edit Members** Lets you delete members or make a member a co-founder
- **Send Email** Lets you send an e-mail message to every member of the club at once
- **Edit Settings** Lets you change the founder's message and the photograph
- **Change Picture** Lets you delete or change the club photograph
- **Calendar Options** Determines the default setting of the club calendar

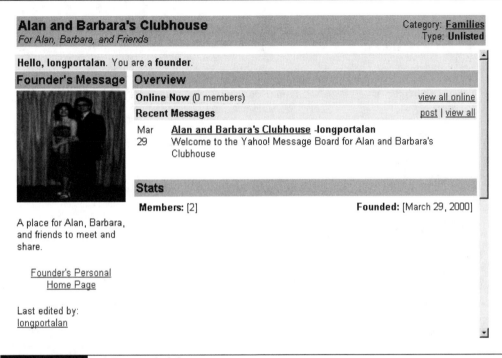

Alan and Barbara's Clubhouse
For Alan, Barbara, and Friends

Category: <u>Families</u>
Type: **Unlisted**

Hello, **longportalan**. You are a **founder**.

Founder's Message	Overview

Online Now (0 members)   <u>view all online</u>

Recent Messages   <u>post</u> | <u>view all</u>

Mar 29   <u>**Alan and Barbara's Clubhouse**</u> **-longportalan**
Welcome to the Yahoo! Message Board for Alan and Barbara's Clubhouse

Stats

Members: [2]   **Founded:** [March 29, 2000]

A place for Alan, Barbara, and friends to meet and share.

<u>Founder's Personal
Home Page</u>

Last edited by:
<u>longportalan</u>

FIGURE 21-13   A Personal club

Responding to and Posting Personal Ads

Another way to get in touch with other Yahoo! members is through the Yahoo! Personal ads. Yahoo! Personals are similar to the personal ads in newspapers and magazines wherein people seek companionship of some type. You can also use Yahoo! Personals to find pen pals and persons with whom to share activities.

Click Personals on the Yahoo! home page to see the Yahoo! Personals page shown in Figure 21-14.

The Browse section lists ad categories. The M4W category, for example, is for ads that were placed by men who are looking for women. Click the category you are interested in. In the page that appears, enter your city and state or zip code, and then click Continue to see a list of ads.

If you find an ad interesting, click More to read its full details. From the ad page, you can choose three options:

- Reply To Ad
- Forward Ad
- Clip This Ad

21

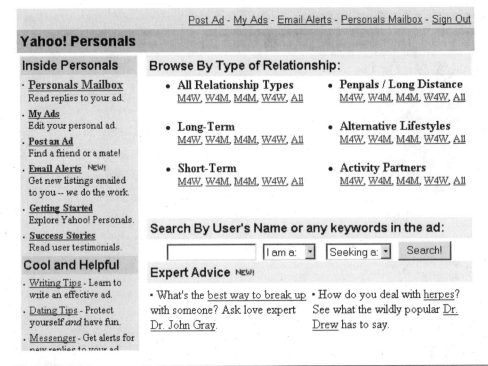

FIGURE 21-14   Yahoo! Personals home page

Click Reply to Ad to send the person a response. You see a form in which you enter your identity; a description of yourself; and, optionally, your e-mail address. Click Send Mail to send the reply.

Click Forward Ad to send a link to the ad to another person. Use the Clip This Ad option to save a link to the ad so you can return to it quickly. To see all of the ads that you've clipped, select Clipped Ad on the top of a personal page. You see a listing similar to the one in Figure 21-15. Click an ad to display its details.

Use the Narrow My Search section of the page, as shown at right, to refine your search.

Choose your ethnicity, religious, smoking, and age preferences, and enter a keyword. Then click Submit Search to see a list of ads that match the criteria you entered.

The Advanced Search option displays even more criteria that you can use in searches. The form is divided into four sections. In the first section, your specify your gender and the relationship type you desire.

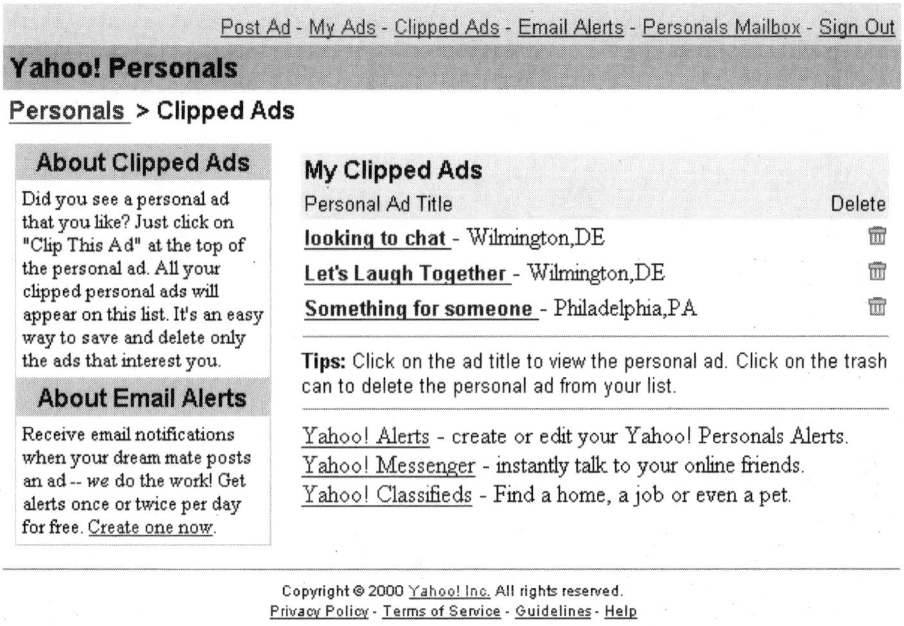
Post Ad - My Ads - Clipped Ads - Email Alerts - Personals Mailbox - Sign Out
Yahoo! Personals
Personals > Clipped Ads
About Clipped Ads
Did you see a personal ad that you like? Just click on "Clip This Ad" at the top of the personal ad. All your clipped personal ads will appear on this list. It's an easy way to save and delete only the ads that interest you.
About Email Alerts
Receive email notifications when your dream mate posts an ad -- we do the work! Get alerts once or twice per day for free. Create one now.
My Clipped Ads
Personal Ad Title
Delete
looking to chat - Wilmington,DE
Let's Laugh Together - Wilmington,DE
Something for someone - Philadelphia,PA
Tips: Click on the ad title to view the personal ad. Click on the trash can to delete the personal ad from your list.
Yahoo! Alerts - create or edit your Yahoo! Personals Alerts.
Yahoo! Messenger - instantly talk to your online friends.
Yahoo! Classifieds - Find a home, a job or even a pet.
Copyright © 2000 Yahoo! Inc. All rights reserved.
Privacy Policy - Terms of Service - Guidelines - Help

FIGURE 21-15 Clipped ads

The next section, called Tell Us About The Person You Are Seeking, includes these items:

- Location
- Ethnicity
- Gender
- Religion
- Age
- Drinker
- Body Type
- Smoker

This is followed by a box in which you enter any additional keywords to narrow the search. Finally, you can sort the ads by displaying all of them or only those posted in recent days. Click Find My Match to search the ads.

Posting an Ad

Click Post An Ad in the Personals page to open the form for writing ads, shown in Figure 21-16.

Note *All of the information on the form for posting personal ads is required except relationship preferences, hobbies, and interests.*

In the Personals page that appears, follow these steps:

1. Enter your zip code.
2. Select your identity.
3. Enter a title for the ad.
4. Choose your gender.
5. Select the gender preferred.
6. Select relationship preferences from these options:
   - Long-Term Relationship
   - Short-Term Relationship
   - Activity Partner

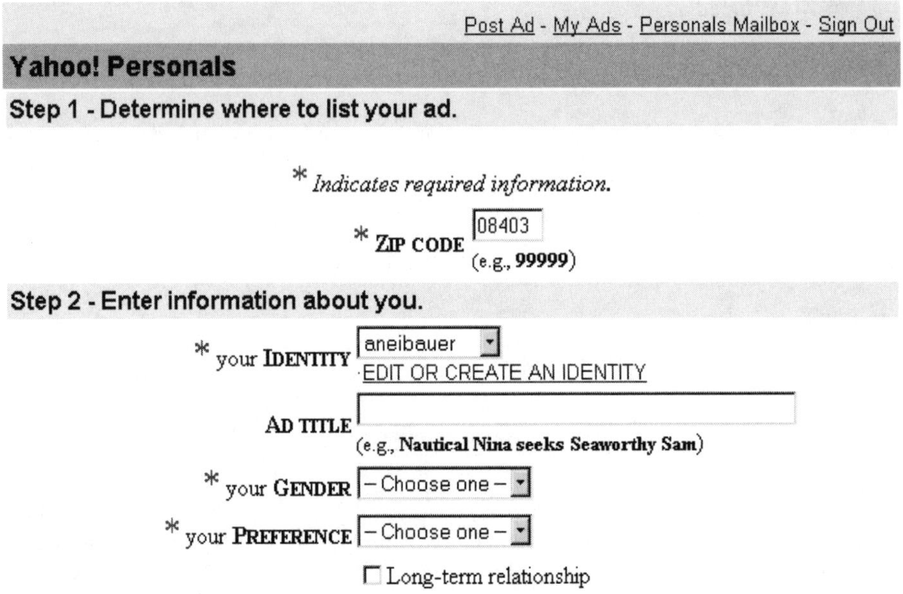

Post Ad - My Ads - Personals Mailbox - Sign Out

Yahoo! Personals

Step 1 - Determine where to list your ad.

* *Indicates required information.*

* ZIP CODE `08403`
(e.g., **99999**)

Step 2 - Enter information about you.

* your IDENTITY `aneibauer`
·EDIT OR CREATE AN IDENTITY

AD TITLE
(e.g., **Nautical Nina seeks Seaworthy Sam**)

* your GENDER – Choose one –

* your PREFERENCE – Choose one –

☐ Long-term relationship

FIGURE 21-16 Posting a personal ad

- Pen Pal / Long-Distance Relationship
- Alternative Lifestyles

7. Select your ethnicity.

8. Specify your educational level.

9. Choose your type of employment.

10. Select your religion.

11. Choose hobbies and interests.

12. Specify your body type.

13. Give your age.

14. Enter your height.

15. Specify whether you smoke.

16. Specify whether you drink.

17. Specify whether you have children.

18. Write a brief description of your interests and what you are looking for.

19. Click the Submit Entry button.

Yahoo! displays the details of the ad and reports that it will be posted within 24 hours. Click Edit Ad if you want to make any changes.

> **Note** *Yahoo!'s Email Alerts will send you an e-mail when new personals have been posted.*

To check for replies to your ad, click Personals Mailbox in the Inside Personals section of the Personals home page or at the top of any personals page. A list of your identities appears with the number of replies in each. Click an identity to see the list of messages, and then click Read in front of a message to read it. From the message, click Reply to send a response. Your personals mailbox can only store up to a hundred messages. Messages are retained for only one month.

Sending Online Greetings

Another way to stay in touch with a friend is to send an electronic greeting. A *greeting* is an online version of a holiday or other card that you mail on special occasions or just to say hello.

Electronic greetings include your own personal message, as well as graphics—sometimes animated graphics—and background music. The recipient gets an e-mail that includes a link where the greeting can be found. By clicking the link, the recipient opens his or her Web browser and sees and hears your greeting.

To send a Yahoo! greeting, click More in the Yahoo! home page and then click Greetings. You see the greetings categories, including anniversaries, birthdays, get well, and good luck.

Personalize your free greeting by filling out the form below!

Recipient's Name:
Insert from my Yahoo! Address Book

Recipient's Email:
Use commas between addresses

Your Name: Alan

Your Email: aneibauer@yahoo.com

Your Message:
(Max 4000 Characters)

Optional Message:
(Max 4000 Characters)

FIGURE 21-17   Personalizing a greeting

Select a category to see a list of greetings and then click the one that you want to send. In the page that appears, click Personalize and Send This Greeting to see a form like the one shown in Figure 21-17.

Complete the form and then click Preview Your Greeting to see what it will look and sound like to the recipient. Finally, click Send This Greeting. A confirmation message tells you that the greeting has been sent. The message includes a link that you can click to see the message on the Internet.

Sending Electronic Invitations

If you are planning an event, you can send online invitations to invitees who have e-mail addresses. Yahoo! will keep track of who has responded, as well as which guests have accepted or declined your invitation.

Click More in the Yahoo! home page and click Invites to see categories of invitations, such as birthday, dinner, wedding, and meeting. Click an occasion to see the Create Invite form shown in Figure 21-18.

Complete the information to describe the event. List the e-mail addresses of the persons you want to invite as well. Then click either Send Now or Preview And Customize.

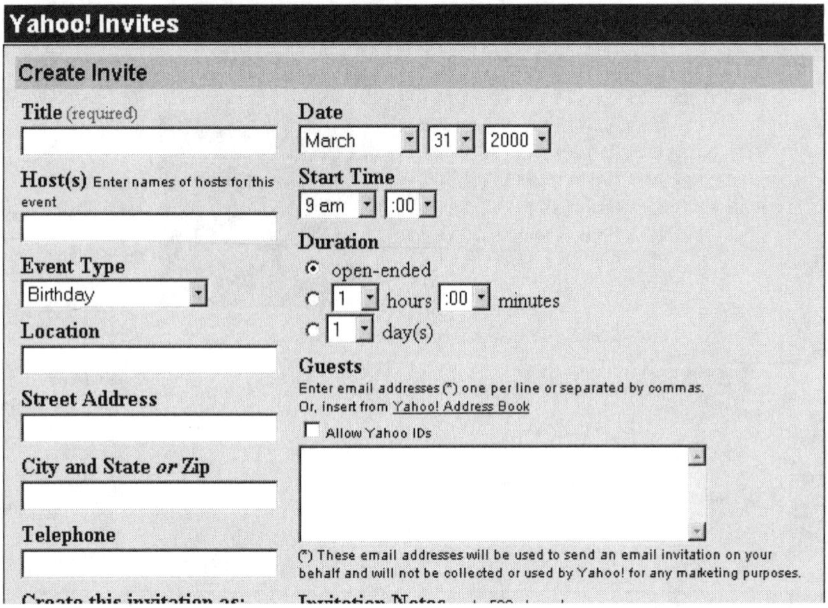

Yahoo! Invites

Create Invite

Title (required)

[   ]

Host(s) Enter names of hosts for this
event

[   ]

Event Type

[Birthday   ▼]

Location

[   ]

Street Address

[   ]

City and State *or* Zip

[   ]

Telephone

[   ]

Create this invitation as:

Date

[March   ▼][31 ▼][2000 ▼]

Start Time

[9 am ▼][:00 ▼]

Duration

⊙ open-ended

○ [1 ▼] hours [:00 ▼] minutes

○ [1 ▼] day(s)

Guests

Enter email addresses (*) one per line or separated by commas.
Or, insert from Yahoo! Address Book

☐ Allow Yahoo IDs

[   ]

(*) These email addresses will be used to send an email invitation on your
behalf and will not be collected or used by Yahoo! for any marketing purposes.

Invitation Notes

FIGURE 21-18   Creating an invitation

- **Send Now**   If you click Send Now, each invitee receives an e-mail message. In each message is a link that recipients can click to view the invitation.

- **Preview And Customize**   If you choose Preview And Customize, you see the page shown in Figure 21-19. Using the options on this page, you can change the guest list or the details of the event. Click Send Now if you have not yet sent the invitations.

When invitees click the link in their e-mail messages and go to the invitation on the Internet, they are asked to confirm their e-mail addresses and enter their names. Then they can click Submit to open a page similar to the one in Figure 21-19, where they can choose one of the options in the Will You Attend? section and click the Change Response button.

When you go to the Yahoo! Invites home page, a list of your invitations appears in the My Invites section, as shown at right.

Click the invitation to open the invitation page and review the responses in the Guest List section.

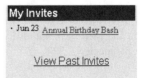

My Invites

· Jun 23 Annual Birthday Bash

View Past Invites

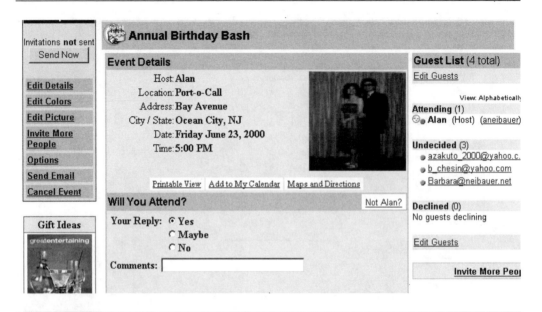

Invitations **not** sent
Send Now

Edit Details
Edit Colors
Edit Picture
Invite More People
Options
Send Email
Cancel Event

Gift Ideas
greatentertaining

🎂 **Annual Birthday Bash**

Event Details

Host: **Alan**
Location: **Port-o-Call**
Address: **Bay Avenue**
City / State: **Ocean City, NJ**
Date: **Friday June 23, 2000**
Time: **5:00 PM**

Printable View   Add to My Calendar   Maps and Directions

Will You Attend?   Not Alan?

Your Reply: ⦿ Yes
            ○ Maybe
            ○ No

Comments: [   ]

Guest List (4 total)
Edit Guests

View: Alphabetically

Attending (1)
☺ **Alan** (Host) (aneibauer)

Undecided (3)
● azakuto_2000@yahoo.c.
● b_chesin@yahoo.com
● Barbara@neibauer.net

Declined (0)
No guests declining

Edit Guests

Invite More Peo

FIGURE 21-19   Invitation page

Use the options on the left side of the invitation page to change a detail or two about the event, add a photo to the page, change photos, or invite more people. You can also choose Send Email to open a form in which you type a message and choose to whom to send it:

- Attending Guests
- Undecided Guests
- Declining Guests

The Options choice lets you select Yes or No for these features:

- Would You Like To Show The Guest List So That Others Can View It?
- Would You Like To Let Your Guests Invite Other People To This Event?

If you need to cancel the event, click Cancel Event on the left side of the invitation page. You can then have Yahoo! send a message to all of the guests to inform them that the event has been canceled.

Yahoo! Classifieds

Yahoo! personal ads are really just a part of a more comprehensive Yahoo! feature called Classifieds. Classifieds are ads that you post to sell a product or a service—from stuff you have sitting around the garage, to the house and the car themselves. Other Yahoo! members can reply to the ads. They can contact you by e-mail to ask questions or make an offer to purchase.

Click Classifieds in the Yahoo! home page. From there, you can post and respond to ads of all types, as well as access your Personals mailbox.

If you want to sell an item, click Post Ad on the top of the page to access a list of categories. Select a category and then drill-down through the subcategories until you see the form shown in Figure 21-20.

Complete the form by describing the item and your sales conditions, and then click Submit Entry. The process is much like submitting an item for auction except you can name the price you want, as well as choose from the options shown at right.

To purchase an item, use the Listings categories on the home page. After you select a category, enter your location on the page that appears and click Continue to see items for sale.

Click More Detail to read about an item and to reply to the seller. All communications about items are strictly between the buyer and seller. Unlike auctions, Yahoo! keeps no record of the offers or who is interested in making a purchase.

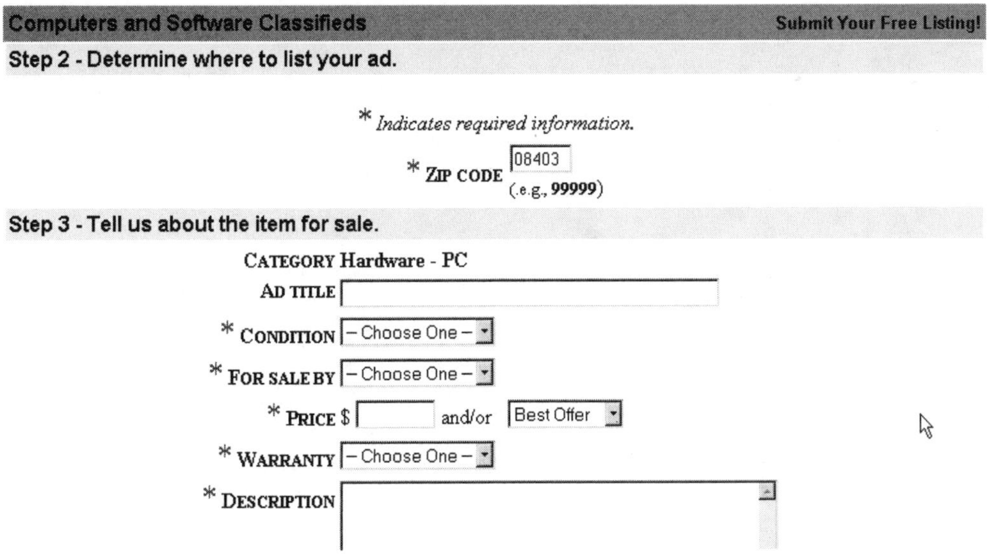

Best Offer ▾
Best Offer
Call
Firm
Negotiable
Free

Computers and Software Classifieds	Submit Your Free Listing!

Step 2 - Determine where to list your ad.

* *Indicates required information.*

* ZIP CODE `08403`
(.e.g, **99999**)

Step 3 - Tell us about the item for sale.

CATEGORY Hardware - PC

AD TITLE [   ]

* CONDITION [– Choose One – ▾]

* FOR SALE BY [– Choose One – ▾]

* PRICE $ [   ] and/or [Best Offer ▾]

* WARRANTY [– Choose One – ▾]

* DESCRIPTION [   ]

FIGURE 21-20   Posting a classified ad

Index